Sir Barton
and the Making of
the Triple Crown

SIR BARTON
AND THE MAKING OF THE
TRIPLE CROWN

JENNIFER S. KELLY

FOREWORD BY STEVE HASKIN

UNIVERSITY PRESS OF KENTUCKY

Paperback edition 2023
Copyright © 2019 by The University Press of Kentucky

Scholarly publisher for the Commonwealth,
serving Bellarmine University, Berea College, Centre
College of Kentucky, Eastern Kentucky University,
The Filson Historical Society, Georgetown College,
Kentucky Historical Society, Kentucky State University,
Morehead State University, Murray State University,
Northern Kentucky University, Spalding University,
Transylvania University, University of Kentucky,
University of Louisville, University of Pikeville,
and Western Kentucky University.

Unless otherwise noted, photographs are from the Keeneland Library Cook Collection.

Editorial and Sales Offices: The University Press of Kentucky
663 South Limestone Street, Lexington, Kentucky 40508-4008
www.kentuckypress.com

Library of Congress Cataloging-in-Publication Data
Names: Kelly, Jennifer S., 1977– author.
Title: Sir Barton and the making of the Triple Crown / Jennifer S. Kelly ;
   foreword by Steve Haskin.
Description: Lexington, Kentucky : The University Press of Kentucky, [2019] |
   Series: Horses in history | Includes bibliographical references and index.
Identifiers: LCCN 2018056722| ISBN 9780813177168 (hardcover : alk. paper) |
   ISBN 9780813177175 (pdf) | ISBN 9780813177182 (epub)
Subjects: LCSH: Sir Barton, 1916–1937. | Triple Crown (U.S. horse racing) |
   Race horses—United States—Biography. | Horse racing—United States.
Classification: LCC SF355.S57 K45 2019 | DDC 798.4/50929 [B] —dc23

ISBN 978-0-8131-9740-1 (pbk. : alk. paper)

This book is printed on acid-free paper meeting
the requirements of the American National Standard
for Permanence in Paper for Printed Library Materials.

Manufactured in the United States of America.

Member of the Association
of University Presses

For Jamie, my love, with whom all things are possible.
For Sammy, who finally has his story told.

But, you know, opinions die; it is only the records that stand.
—John E. Madden, in Kent Hollingsworth,
The Wizard of the Turf: John E. Madden of Hamburg Place

Contents

Illustrations follow page 124

Foreword

Right from the start of Jennifer Kelly's riveting jaunt through history and the birth of the American Triple Crown, the reader is thrust back in time and is right there at Kenilworth Park in Canada for the great match race between the legendary Man o' War and America's first Triple Crown winner, Sir Barton. Every scintillating moment of the events that led up to the race that captivated two countries is brought to life.

We are introduced one by one to some of the great iconic figures who helped shape Thoroughbred racing in America: John E. Madden, H. G. "Hard Guy" Bedwell, August Belmont Jr., Samuel Riddle, and J. K. L. Ross and his father, James Ross, who constructed the Canadian Pacific Railway, which would stretch across Canada from the Atlantic to the Pacific.

The younger Ross, one of the great yachtsmen of his time, would go on to command a naval vessel during World War I and eventually build up a prominent stable of racehorses, including future Hall of Famer Billy Kelly and his crowning achievement, Sir Barton, whom he purchased from John E. Madden for $10,000.

We relive the adventures of these great men—including Hard Guy Bedwell's journey from a cowpuncher in Oregon to the leading owner and trainer in America by age forty and John E. Madden's emergence from the coal mines of Bethlehem, Pennsylvania, to a larger-than-life figure and astute entrepreneur who founded historic Hamburg Place in Kentucky.

But these men are supporting players to the equine heroes of the era, as Kelly does a masterful job paralleling the careers of Sir Barton and Man o' War from their sale to their epic showdown at Kenilworth Park in 1920. While Sir Barton was being sold as a two-year-old to Ross at a paddock sale in Saratoga, twenty-one yearlings were being sold by August Belmont Jr., one of whom was Man o' War, named by Belmont's wife, Eleanor, and purchased by Samuel Riddle for $5,000, half the price of Sir Barton, who had finished far up the track in his four starts prior to the sale and then finished a dismal sixteenth in the Hopeful Stakes in his first start for Ross. After that, though, he suddenly turned into a champion racehorse, becoming the first horse to win the Kentucky Derby, the Preakness Stakes, and the Belmont Stakes in succession, which didn't become known as the Triple Crown until 1930.

But eventually it became obvious that Sir Barton was on a collision course with a horse who would become a legend, the idol of millions, a horse who on an October afternoon in 1920 turned Sir Barton into an afterthought, forgotten by racing fans until he was resurrected a decade later when he officially became racing's first Triple Crown winner. Not even Man o' War could take that title away from him.

What many don't realize is that Sir Barton's owner was reluctant to run against Man o' War, who had won nineteen of his twenty career starts and had broken a number of track records while carrying weights up to 138 pounds. Along the way, he had broken the hearts of many a racehorse. Sir Barton did not appear to be a match for the younger colt known as "Big Red" but had built up an impressive record of his own, going twenty-two consecutive races without finishing worse than fourth, racking up twelve wins, most of them in Maryland. But Ross was, as Kelly writes, a true "sportsman," and he knew what the publicity "could do for his native Canada."

Following the match race, Man o' War, now being called the "Horse of the Century," went on a victory tour before being retired to stud. Through his travels, every move was recorded by turf writers. But, as Kelly writes, "no such accolades were accorded his competitor." Sir Barton departed Kenilworth and returned to Maryland without a word in the newspapers. The great champion of 1919 and 1920 "was relegated to second-place status." With fourteen cameras positioned around Kenilworth, Man o' War's seven-length victory was recorded for posterity. That was all America would ever see of Sir Barton as he faded in the distance.

Following two third-place finishes and a second after this epic match race, Sir Barton was retired. Kelly describes the remainder of his life from Audley Farm near the Maryland–Virginia state line to his final years living the easy life on a ranch in Wyoming.

Kelly has taken a racehorse known only as racing's first Triple Crown winner who was crushed by the great Man o' War in a match race and given him life—a life that deserves to be chronicled with the great stories of the American turf.

Steve Haskin,
National Museum of Racing
and Hall of Fame Joe Hirsch
Media Roll of Honor

Prologue
October 12, 1920

The ground beneath his feet resonated like bricks, hard and fast, perfect for speed. Perfect for the big red chestnut colt who danced next to him, his head higher, his legs longer. Sir Barton skittered over the flat going, antipathy in his gait. His tender feet did not like this unyielding surface and longed for softer ground and familiar hands.

The rider on his back was new. The sights around him were unfamiliar; he had seen his share of crowds, yet the shouts and calls of the people packing the barebones track barraged him like none other. But this was race day, and his business was to run. He had conquered big moments with no hesitation: the coagulant mud of Churchill Downs, the vaunted oval at Saratoga, the Gotham crowd at Belmont, the familiar turns of Pimlico and Havre de Grace. He knew how to run and how to win, and the horses next to him often became the horses behind him. This big red horse next to him was just another horse to fly past on his way to the wire. He needed to run, wanted to run, and little detracted from that siren's call of instinct except the radiating discomfort each time his feet hit the packed earth.

He could feel the wear and tear of three seasons of racing on his delicate feet. He danced and shied, the nerves within him fraying. Sir Barton did not want to pound this compressed ground. He finally felt the tension of this moment, gave into it. The man on his back tried his best to calm him, but everything had an edge. This moment was sharp with noise, with stress, and with pain. The big red chestnut next to him strode calmly and confidently, throwing Sir Barton's fractious countenance into stark relief. Before them, finally, stretched the familiar white webbing, the only hurdle now to making or breaking reputations. He calmed at the sight of the business at hand.

Man o' War took his place on the rail, Sir Barton next to him. Two horses stood alone among a crowd of tens of thousands of men, women, and children, their cries reverberating across the empty track. Ringing the rail were men turning cameras, their job to record the two combatants battling across the Kenilworth oval. The flat prairie around the horses was bleak and colorless, but the Riddle black and gold and the Ross black and orange drew eyes toward the track. The spectacle was the gold standard of Thoroughbreds, yet their arena was dingy and clapboard, certainly not fitting the "Race of the Century." This disconnect between the talent at the barrier and the setting of their meeting bespoke the haphazard way the moment had come together.

Samuel Riddle, reluctant to run his Big Red against older company, had eschewed the numerous opportunities to do just that because of the intimidating numbers that accompanied any entry into a race. At two years old, Man o' War had already carried 130 pounds; at three, he had carried 138. The only reason why they were here in Windsor, Ontario, the only reason why they agreed to a match race at all, was not just the money, but the weight. Here, Man o' War carried 120 pounds, the standard weight for a three-year-old. Riddle had won before anyone even set foot on the track.

Commander J. K. L. Ross, reluctant to run his Sir Barton against the most dominant horse so far that century, knew what he was up against. He was a sportsman, though, a man who was as much a fan as he was the owner of the finest stable in the country. He had commanded a naval vessel during wartime. He had watched his father help connect Canada by train from sea to shining sea. John Kenneth Leveson Ross was no fool, but he was also no coward. He knew Sir Barton's chances, but he also knew what such a match race could do for his native Canada. Promoter A. M. Orpen had sold Commander Ross on Man o' War versus Sir Barton by appealing to his patriotism as well as to his sportsmanship.

Orpen had also talked faster than anyone else; no doubt Colonel Matt Winn still smarted from being late to the party with the exact same bid that Orpen had quoted to Ross and Riddle. Americans smarted with him, lamenting the fact that both colts were American bred and American born but now their clash would be outside their reach. Not Saratoga or Latonia or Havre de Grace or Churchill Downs, but antiseptic and foreign Kenilworth Park, hastily enlarged in anticipation of the spectacle, would have the race with the largest purse at that point in racing history.

Man o' War stood fresh on the outside, a good hand taller than his competitor, sleek and rippling with muscle. Every fiber of his body spoke of speed, his depths unknown since he had never been allowed to extend himself the way his body promised. On the rail, next to the tall red chestnut colt, Sir Barton, shorter and more compact, looked like any other horse. Sir Barton's speed came not with long strides but with the quickness of his tender feet, as if he wanted to outrun the discomfort. In any other company, the winner of America's first Triple Crown would have been the best horse on the track. Here, at the barrier, with the eyes of the racing world on them, Sir Barton faced yet another moment in which his shine went tarnished. Despite all that he had accomplished to this point, he had to share the spotlight again.

From this day on, he would never get it back.

1

Hello, Harry Hale?

Outside of Lexington, Kentucky, nestled among the bluegrasses and rolling hills that have nurtured horses from birth to death, lay John E. Madden's farm Hamburg Place. Named for the horse he sold for a then record $40,001, his two thousand acres of land encompassed paddocks, barns, and training areas where he bred, broke, and prepared horses for racing. In its time, Hamburg Place produced thousands of horses, including five Kentucky Derby winners and five members of horse racing's Hall of Fame.[1]

With his sale of Hamburg and the establishment of Hamburg Place, Madden laid the groundwork for racing history to be made many times over. The farm represented all of the things that racing could bring to one man, especially a man who had worked his way from hardscrabble beginnings to become a major player in the sport of kings in the early twentieth century.

Born to Irish immigrant parents in 1856, Madden grew up in the coal country of Bethlehem, Pennsylvania, fatherless and poor for the early part of his life. A large young man for his time, six feet tall, he was a good athlete, too, running foot races and eventually becoming an amateur boxer at county fairs.[2] His time spent at county fairs also exposed him to trotting horses. He started driving his own trotters, making enough money to buy horses and go from place to place, driving and trading, always with an entrepreneur's eye. As much as he learned about horses, he also learned how to parlay them into more money and more horses. He learned it was "better to sell and repent than keep and repent"—or, more succinctly, that it was simply "better to sell."[3] By the time Madden decided that the money lay more in the Thoroughbreds than in the trotters or pacers, he had made enough of a mark on harness racing that he was later inducted into its Hall of Fame in 1958.[4] His greatest impact, though, came through his breeding operation at Hamburg Place.

Madden may have made money on the buying and selling of horses, but once he laid down roots in Lexington, he turned his attention to their breeding and training. Hamburg Place might produce a hundred foals in a year and then sell a number of them before they reached the racetrack. Those that did not sell before age two would be sold before the end of their second year. Over time, Madden focused more on breeding and selling than on racing his horses. He also served as a consultant for a number of others seeking to get into racing, including B. B. Jones and Montfort Jones, the Whitney family, and more.[5]

Madden's greatest contribution to Thoroughbred racing in America would be made when he mated a British sire with an inconsistent sprinter and produced a history maker.

At the end of the nineteenth century, England had a decade with four Triple Crown winners, including Isinglass.[6] On the track, Isinglass was more of a lazy runner despite his talent, but his gentle disposition made him easy to shake up and motivate. After completing the English Triple Crown, Isinglass suffered the one defeat of his career in his next start, the Lancashire Plate, finishing second. When he retired at age five, he was England's all-time leading money winner, with £57,455 in purse money.[7]

In the breeding shed, Isinglass was as prolific as his own sire, Isonomy, getting a number of English stakes and classic winners, many of whom also became successful as breeders. But in America Isinglass's best-known progeny was Star Shoot, the country's leading sire in 1911, 1912, 1916, 1917, and 1919.

Star Shoot had been a promising two-year-old in England, winning or finishing in the money in all of his starts in 1900. At three, though, he was unplaced in two starts after developing breathing issues between his two- and three-year-old seasons.[8] In addition, Star Shoot's hooves had begun to bother him, both infirmities rendering him a less desirable sire in Britain.[9] The chestnut stallion was then sold to John Hanning, a Thoroughbred importer who shipped him to the United States. There,

Hanning sold Star Shoot to Runnymede Farm in Kentucky, where he stood stud until 1912, when John E. Madden purchased him for Hamburg Place.[10]

From the start, Star Shoot sired winners. By 1908, he was among the top-twenty sires in the country.[11] By 1911, he was leading the sire list, his book filled with up to ninety mares in a given year.[12] In England, he had been undesirable because of his infirmities, but in the United States he was one of the busiest and most prolific sires of stakes winners in the first part of the twentieth century, siring sixty-one of them in his career. His most accomplished progeny came when Madden mated him with another purple-pedigreed horse who had American classic winners in her lineage.

Sometimes horses make minimal impact on the racetrack but go on to influence their sport in a different way: in the breeding shed. For John E. Madden and Hamburg Place, that horse was Lady Sterling. A daughter of Hanover, Belmont Stakes winner and Horse of the Year in 1887,[13] Lady Sterling had been a decent if inconsistent sprinter on the racetrack, known for her fast workouts and uneven race performances. In her career, she ran fifty-four times, winning nine starts, mostly in claiming races.[14] During a workout in late 1902, Lady Sterling dumped her rider and ran three miles before grooms from a nearby barn tried to stop her. Frightened by their efforts, the filly ran into the track's outer rail, cutting her knee open and breaking her kneecap.[15] Her career over, Madden, who had owned her briefly during her two-year-old season, saw her potential as a broodmare and brought her to Hamburg Place, where she delivered a handful of foals for him before her death in 1920. Among her progeny were Sir Martin and Sir Barton.

Madden bred Lady Sterling to Ogden, a leading sire of the era, a mating that produced Sir Martin in 1906. He was chestnut, like Hanover, with a white blaze and a white sock. Madden raced Sir Martin in his cherry-red and white colors for the colt's two-year-old season in 1908, in which the colt won eight of his thirteen starts and $78,590.[16] After Sir Martin spent his juvenile year racing for Madden, a season in which he was the champion two-year-old of 1908, Louis Winans purchased the colt and then imported him to England.[17] There, Sir Martin was a favorite for the Epsom Derby, but he lost his rider when he became tangled up with other horses at Tattenham Corner, his chance at one of England's most prestigious races denied.[18] From there, Sir Martin won or placed in multiple races in both England and France before retiring to stud in England in 1913.[19] The Jersey Act, which mandated that all racing stock in England be descended from horses registered in the country's Stud Book, limited Sir Martin's appeal at stud, however. With diminishing interest in Sir Martin in England, Madden purchased the stallion from Winans in 1919 to replace Ogden, who by then was nearly twenty-five and ailing.[20] Sir Martin would stay at Hamburg Place until his death in 1930.

In the spring of 1916, Vivian Gooch, a noted horse expert who had purchased and trained Sir Martin for Louis Winans, was visiting Hamburg Place and his good friend John E. Madden. Gooch's visit happened to coincide with the birth of Lady Sterling's newest foal, a beautiful chestnut colt born April 26.[21] As a thank-you gift for his friend for his work with Sir Martin, Madden offered him a share of the foal, effectively making him the cobreeder, so when Lady Sterling's foal was registered with the Jockey Club, Madden and Gooch were listed as the colt's cobreeders.[22]

Now, though, John Madden had a problem.

Foal number 187-16, that chestnut colt with a white blaze, needed a name.[23] Fond of giving horses human names, Madden's original idea was to name the colt Harry Hale after the general who commanded the Eighty-Fourth Infantry Division, the army unit of Madden's son, Captain John E. Madden Jr. The name seemed like a good idea at first, but the elder Madden then decided against it, lest it look as if he were trying to brown-nose the general. So he instead gave Lady Sterling's newest foal a name similar to that of his half-brother. The chestnut colt number 187-16 became Sir Barton, named after the Scottish privateer Sir Andrew Barton.[24] Madden then purchased Gooch's share of the colt and prepared the son of Star Shoot for training.

Even as a yearling Sir Barton captured attention. In 1917, Frank Brosche, colt breaker at Hamburg Place, showed a visitor some of Madden's newest crop of yearlings in training. In one of the stables, he brought the visitor down to Sir Barton's stall and said, "And here's the king of them all."[25] The colt possessed "the look of eagles," that faraway gaze of confidence that defines great Thoroughbreds.[26]

Sir Barton's pedigree as a descendent of English Triple Crown winners and American classic winners portended greatness for the chestnut son of Star Shoot and Lady Sterling. No doubt that "look of eagles" came from the horses who preceded him, all passed down in the genes he inherited from the stallion and mare who came together to give him life—but he also inherited something else from his sire: a chronic physical issue that would plague him for the whole of his racing career.

Madden would keep a limited number of horses for himself at first, but he was never shy about selling a horse. As he grew older, he was less about racing his own horses and more about playing the role of breeder and elder statesman, supplying horses to the racing industry while also advising others and advocating for causes such as the United States Army Remount Service. Like many good horsemen, he had philosophies about breeding, training, and care that he was more than happy to share and, given his record of excellence, that the industry was more than happy to listen to.

Madden often would divide up his weanlings into groups of fifteen, running each group in its own field. He would use lightweight boys to catch the weanlings and slip halters onto each. The boys would attach snaffle bits and rope shanks to the horse's halter, thus improvising bridles, and then ride the horse saddleless for forty-five minutes each day. Madden would start this process with horses as young as five months and school them until they were about ten months old. As yearlings, horses would be saddled and galloped in the fields and then taken out to the training track in late spring, where each horse would remain in training until sold. The philosophy behind this type of education was that smaller, younger horses would be easier to break and thus had a reduced chance of injury than larger, older yearlings.[27]

Once horses were broken and in training for the track, Madden would sell them by the end of their two-year-old seasons at the latest, those who showed promise on the track going first. The unsold horses in his barn went to trainer William Walker, the former jockey who had won the Kentucky Derby on Baden Baden in 1877.[28] Walker and Madden would race these horses, and then Madden would sell them to new owners based on their inherent potential, arguing that their best efforts would come in time.[29] John E. Madden took his "king of them all," Sir Barton, in his two-year-old season, green but ready to race, to Saratoga to show him off and, as with his half-brother, to sell him to someone looking for a good horse.

On a summer's day, a consummate salesman sold that good horse on his unrealized potential to a man who had the potential to make him into something great.

2

The Major Players Emerge

Like many men of his generation, James Ross left his native land and emigrated westward, seeking opportunity in the New World. He went from the Highlands of Scotland to the excitement and adventure of America and Canada, working on the Canadian Pacific Railway and then successfully on the expansion of a number of industries within his adopted land. When James Ross died in 1913, his estate was worth $13 million, distributed among beneficiaries, including his wife, Annie, and their son, John Kenneth Leveson (J. K. L.) Ross.[1]

Jack, as J. K. L. was known to his family, stood six foot two, weighed 210 pounds, and carried himself like a swashbuckler. The only child of James and Annie Ross, Jack "was tall and vigorous and had a great splash of daring in his nature." After graduating from Bishop's College School and McGill University, the younger Ross worked for the streetcar company his father had a stake in and then later traveled to England, where he worked for the city railways of Birmingham and London. When he returned to Canada, he married Ethel Matthews in 1902 and moved to Nova Scotia to work on his business interests.[2]

For Jack Ross, though, his true passion was sporting pursuits of all types. He had set a record for the largest tuna caught with a rod and reel (680 pounds with no harness), had played squash and hockey in college, and had even won a national championship as part of the McGill University football team. A lifelong sailor like his father, Jack Ross weighed the same 210 pounds in his sixties as he did when he was playing football for McGill in his early twenties.[3] Though he had started a real estate company in Quebec and owned a controlling interest in Dominion Coal Company and Dominion Iron and Steel Company, the bulk of his fortune came from the inheritance he received upon his father's death. That money gave him the freedom to assume some of the same roles his father had late in his life—philanthropist and sportsman. Unlike his father, though, Jack Ross was a Thoroughbred enthusiast and harbored dreams of indulging that pursuit, even after his country called him to serve.

When Archduke Franz Ferdinand fell to an assassin's bullet in June 1914, his death started a chain of events that led to Britain declaring war on Germany, and because Britain's foreign policies determined Canada's as well, Canada went to war. With German U-boats threatening the shipping lanes between North America and Europe, the newly formed Royal Canadian Navy needed ships to help protect the home front, which gave Jack Ross a chance to play his part in the war effort.

Now in his late thirties and medically ineligible to sign up for military service, Ross donated two yachts and $500,000 to the war effort.[4] Then he parlayed those donations into a commission as a lieutenant with the Royal Canadian Naval Volunteer Reserve, keen to use his knowledge of sailing and the sea to defend his country.[5] Both of the yachts he purchased saw service in defense of his homeland. Ross purchased the *Tarantula* from W. K. Vanderbilt in 1914 and then sold it to the Canadian government; the Royal Canadian Navy then converted the high-speed yacht into a torpedo ship, retrofitting it with two torpedo tubes and a three-pounder gun. The ship was renamed the HMCS *Tuna* and sent out to patrol around Halifax, Nova Scotia.[6]

The other yacht, the *Winchester,* was an American ship Ross purchased for $100,000 in 1915. In keeping with its policies to remain neutral in the conflict, the US government tried to block the sale and export of the *Winchester,* but Ross managed to smuggle the ship out of American waters.[7] Renamed the *Grilse,* the ship was then converted into a destroyer, with two 12-pounder guns and a torpedo tube. Ross himself commanded both ships during his tenure in the Naval Volunteer Reserve.[8] When Prime Minister Robert Borden asked him to serve as chairman of the Pensions Board in Canada, Ross was relieved of duty in 1916 and then received the title of Commander of the Order of the British Empire.[9] From then on, John Kenneth Leveson Ross added the title *commander* to his name, that moniker accompanying him wherever he went for the rest of his life.

Now back on land for good and despite the demands of his new position, the commander turned his attention to his newest passion: horse racing.

The Ross men might have been "like father, like son" on the sea, but when it came to horses, racing, and gambling, the two did not see eye to eye. As an old-school Scot, James Ross abjured gambling, but after the war the younger Ross had wealth and time behind him, both of which allowed him to turn his attention to the pursuit that would immortalize him in the Canadian Thoroughbred Racing Hall of Fame but also would help to bankrupt him in only a few years.[10]

Jack Ross had always kept horses for riding wherever he lived and would attend races wherever he could, whether he was abroad in England or at home in Canada and the United States. Just as World War I broke out, he was in the process of dabbling in racing, contemplating starting his own stable, but his war service made that endeavor difficult. While on patrol along the eastern coast of Canada, Ross started communicating by letter with Captain William Presgrave, a native Canadian turned Marylander who trained horses in both Canada and the United States. Lieutenant Ross arranged to purchase a dozen of the captain's horses in training and then race them in the same colors that had graced the family yachts: orange and black. Presgrave trained Ross's string along with his own, and Linus McAtee served as the Ross Stable's first contract jockey. The Ross Stable was on its way, albeit on a smaller scale than Ross wanted.[11]

The first recorded entry for the Ross Stable was Yorkville at Laurel Race Course on October 13, 1914.[12] The next day, though, the *Daily Racing Form*'s form chart for the third race at Laurel showed that Yorkville had been scratched from that five-and-a-half-furlong sprint and then sold by Captain Presgrave.[13] So the Ross black and orange debuted instead at Havre de Grace's spring meet in April 1915.[14] On April 23, St. Lazerian finished fifth in a five-and-a-half-furlong allowance race, the sixth race on the day's card.[15] It was not the most auspicious of starts for what was to become the leading stable in the United States, but the fledgling Ross Stable would see its first victory a month later, when on May 17, 1915, Corn Broom came home as the winner of the Selling Handicap at Pimlico.[16] Second behind the four-year-old Corn Broom was another four-year-old, Bushy Head, owned by Harvey Guy (H. G.) Bedwell, the country's leading trainer in 1915.

In 1916, with America not yet in the war and Ross still patrolling the Dominion's seas, the Ross Stable under the management of Captain Presgrave soldiered on with its limited number of starters. However small his stable, Ross's horses started to make some noise. The success might have been small compared to that of other stables in 1916—$17,597 versus the $71,035 won by leading owner R. T. Wilson—but Ross nearly tripled the money he had won in 1915.[17] These few victories were enough to whet the commander's appetite.

Among the stakes wins for the orange and black were Damrosch's wins in the Preakness Handicap and the Woodstock Plate, Uncle Bryn's victory in the Connaught Cup, and Yellow Sally's win in the Juvenile Stakes in Canada, where she defeated some of the top two-year-olds in the country.[18] The Preakness victory for Damrosch did not carry the same weight as it would in a few short years; the race had returned to Pimlico in 1909 and had a purse of $1,500, far less than it would be years later.[19] It was a victory, though, enough of one to earn Damrosch the honor of being Ross's leading money winner in 1916.

In the autumn of 1916, Ross and his stable suffered a setback when Captain Presgrave died suddenly on November 29.[20] The death of his friend and trainer left Ross at an impasse. His operation was still small, only twenty-eight horses total, so Commander Ross had either to fish or to cut bait. He had jumped into racing while still at sea, literally, corresponding with Presgrave via letter and visiting whenever his leave allowed it. Now, though, the commander was back on dry land, relieved of his naval duty, and the head of the Pensions Board. With his time now his own again, he would have to be more systematic about his approach to owning and running a stable. The small success he had had to this point was not enough; the commander wanted to make his mark on the racing world in a big way. With that in mind, he laid out his plans and moved quickly to execute them.[21]

First, Ross purchased a sizeable tract of land outside of Montreal, Quebec, at Verchères. There, he wanted to build a large breeding operation not only to populate his own stable with quality horses but also to help improve Canadian bloodstock in general.[22] Next, Ross turned to Europe to pick up more good horses for his stable. With racing suspended on the continent because of the war, many stables in England and France were disposing of their stock. Prominent American owners such as Harry Payne Whitney and August Belmont Jr. were bringing European horses to race in the United States. When his European acquisitions were not successful, though, Commander Ross realized he needed more help to build the stable he wanted.[23]

Ready to make waves in the racing world, Ross needed to bring on the right trainer to handle his desired ascension. In June 1917, Ross struck a deal with H. G. Bedwell, a consummate horseman and a successful owner-trainer in his own right, to take over his upstart racing stable. Bedwell was the country's leading trainer from 1912 to 1917 and the leading money-winning owner in 1916.[24] He specialized in making silk purses out of sow's ears: taking average horses, training them up, and then winning with them enough to amass a reputation that would take him from the small-time West Coast to the big-time East Coast. He was the right man to help Ross realize his grand plan.

Bedwell's reputation as a consummate horseman started when he was a young man and remained the strongest part of his legacy long after he was gone from the track. Yet for every time his skills at conditioning impressed, questions about his methods for preparing his horses to run lingered.

Bedwell liked to say that his initials, H. G., stood for "Hard Guy," and his personality illustrated that nickname. Known for driving himself hard and his employees harder, the trainer once kicked an idle employee on his backside. When the young man inquired about what he had done to deserve it, Bedwell supposedly replied, "You're not doing anything."[25] The trainer valued hard work and perseverance; before he came on with Ross, he would train horses year-round, going from track to track, north to south, Canada to Havana or Tijuana. His life was about horses, their care, and their winning, and this is way it had been for him from his earliest years.

Bedwell was born on June 22, 1876, in rural Roseburg, Oregon, far away from cities and railroads, where horses were an indispensable part of life. His parents had moved west in the spirit of the Gold Rush of the mid–nineteenth century, but his father, Thomas Bedwell, died when H. G. was only eighteen months old, leaving his mother, Margaret, to raise H. G. and his three brothers by herself and in relative poverty.[26] As a young teenager, H. G. left his mother and brothers to cowpunch his way through the West, starting in his home state of Oregon and eventually ending up in Colorado.[27] For Bedwell and his fellow cowboys, horses were a fact of day-to-day life, and no doubt it was this constant exposure to horses' ailments, attitudes, and anatomy that made Bedwell such a complete horseman.

By the time the restless Bedwell was in his twenties, his work on the range had taken him from southern Oregon to western Colorado, where he finally settled in Grand Junction. He married Lotta Clark in 1896 and had two children, Nellie in 1898 and Leonard in 1903. After deciding to make Grand Junction his home, the young Bedwell worked first as a county clerk, but that desk job was not going to keep this former cowpuncher happy for long, so he returned to working with horses when he opened his own livery stable in the Grand Junction area. It was not long before the call of the track caught his attention; he got a taste of the racing life when a track opened up at the local fairgrounds.[28]

Although at this time racing might have been more famous for what was going on in the East, racetracks dotted the landscape nationwide, especially in the West. Bedwell translated his experience living with horses into training them for the track, and after meeting with success on the hardscrabble small-time circuits, he decided to aim higher and make racing a full-time occupation. What really spurred Bedwell into changing careers was a random encounter with a thrown shoe and a gelded Thoroughbred while at the races in Denver.

H. G. and his friend Frank Smith were driving through Denver when Smith's horse threw a shoe. They went to farrier J. L. W. Fisher to have the horse reshod, when Fisher, who also had worked for E. J. "Lucky" Baldwin, a California businessman whose estate later became the home of Santa Anita Park, started talking horses with the pair.[29] The farrier lamented the trouble he had had with a man who had leased one of Baldwin's former racers, Los Angeleno. Fisher had received the gelding from Baldwin as a reward for his work for the businessman and then had leased the gelding out to trainer J. W. McClellan. McClellan prepared Los Angeleno to run and claimed that Fisher had won $750 off the horse; he then sued the blacksmith for lack of payment. The court ruled in McClellan's favor and ordered Fisher to pay $120 plus costs to the trainer.[30] Still smarting from the case, Fisher eagerly showed off the gelding to Bedwell and his friend.

Intrigued by the horse's appearance, H. G., scarce on money, persuaded his friend Frank to buy the gelding.[31] The son of Baldwin's stakes winners Rey el Santa Anita and Los Angeles, Los Angeleno had had a mixed career in his three seasons of racing. Baldwin finally retired him at age four when he came up lame during the 1903 racing season.[32] The businessman gave the gelding to his smith, who had used him as a driving horse, until Bedwell encountered Los Angeleno that fateful day in 1905. By this point, young H. G. was already dabbling in training, with a few starters in races around the western Colorado area. After persuading Smith to buy the gelding, Bedwell started working with the horse, taking him to the races. When Los Angeleno won a race at odds of fifty to one, Smith was so happy with the result that he gifted the gelding to Bedwell, who used his success with Los Angeleno as an impetus to take his limited string and expand his territory.[33]

Now in his thirties, Bedwell packed up his wife and children and began the vagabond life of a trainer and owner. At first, he started small: Seattle, Butte, Memphis, New Orleans. Los Angeleno was not his only horse, but he became the symbol of what H. G. Bedwell was capable of as a trainer of Thoroughbreds.[34] The gelding won the Thornton Stakes, a four-mile race at Oakland, California, among many others, finishing his career with eighteen wins for his trainer-owner. Bedwell parlayed his success with Los Angeleno into growing his string of horses, most of them underachievers he claimed from other people, and building his reputation as a trainer who could take a lackluster performer and turn that horse into a winner.

Bedwell focused his efforts on the West Coast tracks, traveling up and down the Pacific coast. In December 1908, he claimed another gelding, Nadzu, for $1,200.[35] The chestnut had run against his horses previously, so no doubt Bedwell had already had his eye on Nadzu, especially since he no longer had a star like Los Angeleno in his string. Bedwell was winning and making a reputation for himself, but he lacked that stakes and handicap horse who would make people stand up and take notice. Nadzu became that horse.

Winless at two and three years old, Nadzu had only nine wins in thirty-four starts in 1908 for his previous owner. As a part of Bedwell's barn, however, he started thirty-one times in 1909, finishing in the money in 71 percent of his starts, the best year of his career.[36] By 1910, though, the six-year-old Nadzu had lost his winning ways, and Bedwell seemed ready to let go of him.

At Latonia on July 3, 1910, Bedwell entered Nadzu in a selling race at a price of $900—that is, the price another owner would need to pay to claim him. The gelding won the race, taking home a purse of $300 with no bids.[37] He was then entered for another selling race the next day, a turnaround time of only twenty-four hours.

Nadzu was already known for erratic behavior before previous starts, so much so that "his actions under colors on numerous occasions indicated dope," but "a thorough examination by a real veterinarian showed there was none."[38] On July 4, the gelding's behavior was again in question when he appeared for the day's last race, another selling race with a purse of $300. The race was delayed forty-five minutes because of the end of the Johnson-Jeffries heavyweight championship boxing match and the Latonia officials' desire to give the crowd additional time to bet on races at other tracks.[39] By the time the gelding got to the paddock for saddling, Nadzu appeared to be "in a frenzied condition."[40] Bedwell got the attention of the track veterinarian, Dr. William Keogh, reported his suspicion that the gelding had been tampered with, and requested a late scratch for his horse. Keogh excused Nadzu from the race, and the money bet on the gelding was refunded.[41]

Testing for stimulants was still years away, so any suspicion of stimulants was based on the judgment of Keogh, Latonia's veterinarian. When Keogh saw Nadzu acting erratically, he had to agree with Bedwell's request to scratch the horse. Bedwell's self-reporting, though, did not protect him from the suspension that the Kentucky Racing Commission handed down the next day.[42] However, the absence of scientific evidence meant that the grounds for the suspension were based on the track veterinarian's testimony and the affidavits provided by Bedwell and others involved.

Bedwell himself admitted to giving his horses arsenic from time to time, claiming that it was "a tonic for the blood, and with the blood in good condition my horses thrive and are able to race at their best speed."[43] Such concoctions were marketed for both humans and horses during this era. Willis Sharpe Kilmer, who would later own the great

Exterminator, derived his fortune from tonics his family had built their company on in New York. Even though others would later provide affidavits attesting to Bedwell's sporting cleanliness, rumors about stimulants followed him over the years.[44] In Nadzu's case, stablehand John Luthers claimed that he had accompanied another Bedwell employee, a young "negro," Kiel Williams, on a trip to Cincinnati, and there Williams had received a powdery substance from an unknown stranger who had asked Williams to give the substance to Nadzu in exchange for a large bet on the gelding.[45] Afraid of the consequences, Williams had then left the area, prompting Bedwell, who was determined to clear his name, to hire Pinkertons, the legendary detective and security agency, to find him.[46]

Bedwell's choice to self-report and then accuse one of his stablehands of slipping Nadzu something could have been an attempt to cover up any wrongdoing on the trainer's part. At its August meeting, the commission expressed their suspicion that Bedwell himself had given Nadzu a stimulant prior to the race's original post time, and, when the start was delayed, had to supplement that with more stimulants. As a result, the second dose "had an effect of an overdose and brought about the expose."[47] The commissioners did not buy Bedwell's story of the bribed stablehand. By their reasoning, if an unknown gambler could pay Williams off, then so could his employer.[48] The suspension remained in place while the investigation into the incident continued.

That meant that Bedwell and his string of twenty-two horses could not go anywhere. Not only was he unable to run them in Kentucky, but he could not run them anywhere else until the case was resolved. Desperate to gain reinstatement, Bedwell awaited the apprehension of Kiel Williams while also maintaining that Nadzu was a "crazy horse" who had previously been examined for stimulants because of erratic behavior and then cleared by veterinarians.[49] When Williams was finally located in early August, he agreed to swear in an affidavit to the story that Bedwell had put forth, but only after he was paid.[50] The trainer refused to pay, and the case dragged on for several more months. Bedwell applied to the Kentucky Racing Commission for the ability to sell his horses since he could not race them, but the rules disallowed that.[51] He shipped them to California anyway, hoping to do something with them there and find work for himself while he awaited reinstatement.[52]

Upon arriving at Emeryville, Bedwell found that there was no room for him. The track's officials informed the trainer-owner that they would adhere to the Kentucky Racing Commission's judgment and thus would not allow his horses at Emeryville. So Bedwell found a farm outside of the city to house his horses and waited out his suspension. He continued to apply for a reinstatement but was unsuccessful.[53]

In December 1910, Dr. Keogh, the veterinarian who had examined Nadzu and ruled that he had been doped, died from Bright's disease. With the veterinarian gone, H. G. Bedwell applied again for reinstatement. On April 29, 1911, the Kentucky Racing Commission, satisfied that the case was closed, reinstated the trainer. With thirty-two horses in his stable, worth upward of $100,000, Bedwell was eager to get back to the races and return to his winning ways.[54]

By the end of 1911, Bedwell was one of the top-ten money-winning owners in the country and fifth on the list of winning trainers for the year, not a bad showing for a man who had just gotten his license back at the end of April. By 1912, he was the leading trainer in the country for the second time and second on the list of money-winning owners. The incident with Nadzu might have been behind him, but that controversy and others like it would follow him for the rest of his career.

The cowpuncher from Oregon had become the leading trainer and owner in America by age forty. Bedwell raced year-round; his horses went north to Canada, south to Mexico, and as far west as California, eventually landing in the rich eastern racing circuit. In fact, when Commander Ross was trying to decide how committed he was to racing, Bedwell was the leading money-winning trainer *and* owner of 1916. At sunrise on December 31 of that year, he was second in money won to fellow owner R. T. Wilson. Bedwell was still running horses down in Havana, Cuba, on New Year's Eve. That day he had two horses finish in the money, one in third place and the other a winner, accounting for $425. That money put Bedwell over the top and gave him the leading-owner crown by $64.[55] Such was the career of "Hard Guy" Bedwell: he took small-time horses and won enough to attract the big-time money of someone like Jack Ross. What could he do with those greater resources behind him?

When Bedwell agreed to work for Commander Ross, he disposed of most of his own horses and then got to work looking for some quality racers for his new boss. He still finished 1917 as the leading trainer in wins because of his own horses but had already changed his focus to training the Ross Stable's string and acquiring more racing stock for his new boss.[56] Early on in their partnership, Bedwell recommended that Ross purchase Yarrow Brae, the farm Bedwell owned outside of Laurel, Maryland. By this point in the war, purchasing property in the United States was not a bad idea for Ross; Canada had recently halted racing, but the sport continued in the States. Ross's property at Verchères would be there for racing and breeding in Canada once the war was over and racing resumed, but until then the commander needed to focus on the American scene. Yarrow Brae was close to Laurel Race Course, so Ross would have a convenient spot for keeping his horses until his native land started racing again after war's end.

While Bedwell was helping Ross set up shop on American soil, he was looking for the right horses to represent this growing stable. He had his eye on a three-year-old named Cudgel, owned by John F. Schorr. Rumor had it that the war was going to mean a freeze on oats; supplies would instead be diverted to the war effort. That would mean horse owners would have to find other sources of food for their horses. This sort of uncertainty worked in Bedwell's favor. Bedwell had heard through a grapevine that went all the way up to President Woodrow Wilson's personal physician, Admiral Cary Grayson, who owned a Thoroughbred farm and racing stable, that the freeze on oats was not going to happen, but this information had not yet been released to the public. Bedwell played on Schorr's fears about the oats shortage and managed to finagle Cudgel from his owner for $30,000.[57] Soon after that, a report denying the freeze on oats came out in the papers, but by then it was too late for Schorr, who had already sold Cudgel. Ross now had a star for his 1918 season.

While at Saratoga Race Course campaigning Cudgel in August 1918, Commander Ross, still in pursuit of his blockbuster stable, was ready to buy. As Ross's trainer walked the Spa grounds, discerning eyes inspecting the horses on the track, Bedwell saw a chestnut colt with a white blaze and a bad attitude working out one August morning. John E. Madden had brought the son of Star Shoot to the Spa to find the right owner for his good colt. Madden's reputation as a consummate salesman and judge of horse flesh plus his familiarity with both Commander Ross and H. G. Bedwell made the Ross Stable the right target for selling this good colt, Sir Barton.

3

Our Hero Appears

In the summer of 1918, the chestnut son of Star Shoot and Lady Sterling was still part of Madden's stable, now two years old and ready for racing. He stood out, his connection to his half-brother Sir Martin, juvenile champion of 1908, marking him as one of the best that Madden had to offer.[1] To single out Sir Barton publicly as among the best of his juveniles was strategic: by dropping the colt's name in the press as he did, Madden was laying the groundwork for eventually selling Sir Barton. Madden saw the potential inherent in the son of Star Shoot, evident to many around Hamburg Place before the colt had even seen a saddle. The "Wizard of the Turf" knew he could find a buyer for this colt as long as he was able to sell his potential, and the easiest way to do that was to run Sir Barton in the biggest juvenile races.

The only problem? The colt's first few starts showed that it might take all of Madden's skills to find the right buyer to see the latent possibilities inherent in this chestnut colt with the wide white blaze.

To put Sir Barton on the road to new ownership, Madden decided to start the colt in his stable's cherry-red and white silks in the Tremont Stakes at Aqueduct. In an effort to draw attention to the colt, he chose the well-known stakes race rather than an allowance race. First run in 1887, the six-furlong Tremont was intended as a midsummer test for two-year-olds and drew plenty of attention on its own. Named for Tremont, supposedly the best two-year-old ever bred in the United States in the nineteenth century, this race marked one of the earliest opportunities for racing fans and pundits to see and then discuss the emerging juvenile class.[2]

The Tremont's field of nine featured Lord Brighton, the highly regarded favorite who carried the top weight of 125 pounds, and first-time starters War Pennant and Sir Barton, both carrying 112 pounds. At the start, Lord Brighton showed in front before My Friend eclipsed him to take the lead, pushing the favorite back into second. My Friend maintained her lead until the stretch, when she started to bear out. At this point, Lord Brighton took the lead again but stalled instead of pulling away from the field, allowing Sweep On to pass him. As the field thundered toward the wire, Lord Brighton made another run at Sweep On, retaking the lead. Despite jockey Lyle Lyke's assumption that his horse was safely in front, they nearly lost the race in the final yards, but his horse had enough in reserve to fight off his challengers and win by a length.[3]

Sir Barton, who spent most of the race at the back of the field in seventh, moved up to finish fifth. The *Daily Racing Form*'s chart for the Tremont included a comment on Sir Barton: he was "a good looker [and] raced green and is promising."[4] With Sir Barton's first race behind him, Madden pointed his colt toward a bigger and brighter stage: the Flash Stakes at Saratoga.

Saratoga Springs, New York, had been home to Thoroughbred racing since 1863, when organizers set up the first meet at the local Standardbred track.[5] More than fifty years later, racing at Saratoga had grown into one of the most prestigious meets in the country, where people came to see and be seen and, for some, to buy for the future. Horses were brought to the Spa to run and in some cases be sold to the highest bidder. Saratoga was the home of hope for both horse and human alike.

Among the attractions of the Saratoga meet were a series of races for two-year-olds, opportunities to see what the newest crop of horses had in store for the owners, trainers, and fans who might want to invest in them. Madden brought Sir Barton here to show him off, entering him in most of the prestigious juvenile stakes on Saratoga's schedule. If he were going to sell this colt, prospective owners needed to see him in action. The first of these races was the Flash Stakes.

Inaugurated in 1869, the Flash Stakes had become one of the premier stakes races for two-year-olds at Saratoga's summer meet. At five furlongs, the Flash tested the speed of these young horses as the year began to wane and speculation for the next season began. By Sir Barton's time, multiple well-known horses had won the Flash, including Hamburg, the namesake of Madden's breeding establishment; Old Rosebud, one of the five Kentucky Derby winners Madden would breed; and Fair Play, who would go on to sire Man o' War.[6] It was a show of Madden's confidence in Sir Barton—or perhaps his desire to sell the colt as soon as possible—that he decided to enter the colt despite his lackluster showing in the Tremont.

Prior to the Flash, Sir Barton attracted attention, "showing up well" in his workouts, alongside other top juveniles, such as Dunboyne.[7] In one workout in particular, Sir Barton ran a fast six furlongs in 1:14, catching the eye of H. G. Bedwell. The workout prompted the trainer to seek out Madden to put in a bid for Sir Barton.[8] Columnist Bert Collyer also took notice of Madden's colt, singling Sir Barton out the day of the Flash, predicting that the colt would "bring home the grapes" (i.e., win) despite the large field.[9] Even though Sir Barton, "one of the best Madden had raised this year,"[10] had raced only once, he had caught the eye not only of observers but also of potential buyers, setting the stage for the sale that was the start of a historic career in Thoroughbred racing.

Opening day at Saratoga, fifteen horses went to the post for the Flash Stakes, the third race on the card, immediately preceding the day's big event, the Saratoga Handicap. Commander Ross had Cudgel running in that feature, so no doubt he saw Sir Barton go to the post alongside another two-year-old of interest, the gelding Billy Kelly. Despite Billy Kelly's "awkward and scrawny appearance," his earlier races had brought him a reputation as a solid racer, with four wins already in 1918 for owner W. F. Polson. Polson had paid only $1,500 for the gelding, and Billy Kelly had already made back that money and more.[11]

At the barrier for the Flash, Billy Kelly stood in post position four, and Sir Barton was farther on the outside at post position nine. The race's start was "good but slow," with My Friend and High Time streaking to the lead.[12] Those two ran clear of the field for the first furlong, but Billy Kelly stalked them in third, waiting for the front-runners to tire. When the speed on the front gave way, Billy Kelly made his move, taking the lead and then drawing away to win by five lengths in track-record time. As Billy Kelly ran a race that made him one of the best in the East according to the experts, Sir Barton got off to a slow start and never factored, finishing in ninth after a trip in which he stayed in the back third of the field.[13] Sir Barton might have been on Commander Ross's radar still, but Billy Kelly's performance made the owner keen to add this gelding to his stable as well.

Immediately after the Flash, Commander Ross was anxious to put in an offer for the gelding, but Bedwell advocated for patience. "Weight will bring him to us," Bedwell assured his employer, predicting that the gelding would win the Flash and then the United States Hotel Stakes but lose in a handicap, which would make Polson more open to the commander's offers.[14] Eager to buy in an effort to meet his goal of the best stable in the country, Ross exercised patience in his pursuit of Billy Kelly, while John E. Madden continued to show his faith in Sir Barton by starting him alongside the gelding in the United States Hotel Stakes on August 3.

This golden age of racing had a sequence of prominent races for two-year-olds that became the basis of determining a champion for that age group. Saratoga's meet featured several of them, including the Hopeful Stakes, run on the last day of the meet, and the United States Hotel Stakes, which became Sir Barton's next test. Despite the short rest, Madden sent his colt to the barrier for the six-furlong race alongside, once again, Billy Kelly and a dozen others. Sir Barton received weight from the favorites, Dunboyne and Billy Kelly, getting a break of 10 pounds or more, which, coupled with their speed, made some sit up and pay attention.[15]

Billy Kelly was back in the news between races as W. F. Polson arrived in Saratoga to the report of an offer of $25,000 from Commander Ross, who was gambling that Polson would accept that offer plus the additional $5,000 that the Canadian would add onto the price if Billy Kelly won. Other top horsemen, including Exterminator's owner, Willis Sharpe Kilmer, and War Cloud's owner, A. K. Macomber, turned in bids of their own, but the $30,000 bid from E. B. McLean was the only number quoted in the newspaper coverage of the sale.[16] Polson turned them all down, declaring that he would not let go of the colt for less than $35,000.[17] While Polson batted away offers from Ross and Kilmer and Macomber, Billy Kelly, named for a sportswriter at the *Buffalo Courier*, entered the United States Hotel Stakes as one of the favorites, along with the colt Eternal and the filly Elfin Queen. He was to carry the second-highest weight, 127 pounds, behind Dunboyne's 130 pounds. The field of fourteen went to the post, with Billy Kelly on the rail, Sir Barton on the far outside, and other horses including Elfin Queen and Dunboyne in between.

High Time got the best of the start, jumping out in front of Billy Kelly and Dunboyne; Sir Barton, who was in post position eleven, hung out toward the back of the middle of the field, never factoring and not even garnering a mention in the race's form chart.[18] Despite the slow start, Billy Kelly's jockey Robert Simpson kept the gelding relatively close to the leaders, waiting for the front-runner to run himself out. As soon as High Time started to fade, Billy Kelly and Dunboyne surged past him, the former swinging wide as he moved toward the front.

The two leaders ran stride for stride for a time, but under the whip the gelding pulled ahead of Dunboyne and won the United States Hotel Stakes in 1:12⅖.[19] It was Billy Kelly's sixth victory in seven races, justifying Polson's reluctance to sell his star gelding. Now Ross would have to exercise patience a little longer and hope that the Albany Handicap would open the door for Billy Kelly to become part of his stable. The gelding was a hot commodity, a star who would fit in well alongside Cudgel and others in the orange and black, and Commander Ross was anxious to add him to his roster.

For Sir Barton, it was his third race and third out-of-the-money finish. He was still only two years old, and it was clear from his workouts that the potential was there for great speed. His pedigree promised that much; his half-brother's success at two promised still more. His performance on race day was not showing that latent talent—yet. Madden continued his colt on the campaign toward finding the right stable for him by sending him out in the Sanford Memorial Stakes eleven days later.

While Madden waited for the next chance to run Sir Barton at Saratoga, Billy Kelly went to the post for the Albany Handicap, another six-furlong test for two-year-olds, laden with 133 pounds. Running in his third race in a week's span, the gelding did his best under the heavy impost to maintain the lead he built early in the race. In the end, Star Hampton, carrying nearly 20 pounds less, stayed close to the rail when Billy Kelly went wide on the final turn and then took the lead in the waning strides of the race.[20] The day his horse was defeated, Polson finally relented. As H. G. Bedwell had predicted would happen when Polson turned down their initial bid, Billy Kelly's intrepid owner accepted an offer of $27,500 for the gelding, much to the dismay of his wife, who reportedly wept as the gelding was led away.[21] A bargain at $1,500, Billy Kelly had earned $19,000 in purse money for Polson and now brought in $27,500 from Ross. As a gelding, Billy Kelly would never generate breeding income, so it made sense for Polson to take Ross's offer. As his namesake sportswriter led him from his old barn to his new home, Billy Kelly became part of the loaded Ross barn, and William F. Polson was $45,000 richer than he had been before the gelding crossed his threshold.[22]

Sir Barton, though, was still in the Madden barn, but he remained on Ross's radar, despite his poor showing in his previous starts. Eager to provide Commander Ross with another brick to help him build that capital stable, Madden continued to demonstrate his faith in the colt by entering him in the Sanford Memorial Stakes, once again facing Ross's newest acquisition. Billy Kelly went to the post as the Sanford favorite despite carrying 130 pounds and ceding as much as 18 pounds to some of his competitors, including Sir Barton, who carried only 112 pounds and sported blinkers for the first time in his career.[23]

The field of eight met the barrier at 4:30 p.m., the fourth race on Saratoga's card for August 14. After standing at the post for a minute, starter Marshall Whiting "Mars" Cassidy dropped the flag, Lion d'Or jumping out to the lead, followed by Colonel Livingston. Rain earlier in the day had made the track muddy, but the favorite had no trouble finding his stride; despite a slow start, Billy Kelly hung out toward the middle of the field for the first part of the six furlongs, positioned for making a run at the leaders when it was time. As Lion d'Or's stride shortened, his front-running effort giving way, jockey Earl Sande urged Billy Kelly to kick into gear, first eclipsing Colonel Livingston and then Lion d'Or and finally pulling away as they thundered toward the finish line.[24] As the field passed the judges' stand, Billy Kelly was eight lengths in front, the rest trickling in behind him. Sir Barton maintained his seventh-place position throughout the Sanford, beating only Pastoral Swain by a neck.[25]

Newspapers continued to trumpet Billy Kelly's victory and his many accomplishments during this juvenile season, declaring him the best of that class. Each time he went to the post, the gelding faced better and better competition, beating them all. Sir Barton, despite his speedy workouts and purple pedigree, had yet to be seen in those same pages. Ever the consummate salesman, John E. Madden continued discussions with Commander Ross, who was still eagerly in pursuit of an elite stable and on the cusp of breaking through to become the leading owner in the United States. All Madden needed to do now was connect the latent potential of his son of Star Shoot with the owner and trainer best suited to tap into it.

After years of driving and racing and dealing, John E. Madden had built Hamburg Place into a breeding factory, turning out nearly a hundred foals each season. At sixty-two, he was one of the sport's elder statesmen, content to be a seller, not a buyer, making deals and always remembering that it was "better to sell."[26] He had built his reputation on his expertise with horses, so it was hard to argue with the "Wizard of the Turf" when he tried to sell any owner on a horse. In pursuit of that dream stable, Commander Ross was still buying horses and land in 1918, spending good money on both sides of the US-Canadian border. He had bought the excellent handicap horse Cudgel and now the promising juvenile Billy Kelly, who, though he was a gelding and ineligible for certain races, promised to make Ross more than he had spent. In Madden's eyes, Sir Barton was a natural fit for the ascendant stable, even if he had yet to win a race. The progeny of one of the country's leading sires and the mare that had produced Sir Martin, Sir Barton had shown promise in his workouts. He was small and deep chested, but trainer H. G. Bedwell clearly saw something in him because on August 21, 1918, Commander J. K. L. Ross purchased Sir Barton from John E. Madden for $10,000.[27]

Despite Sir Barton's maiden status, his pedigree, with Sir Martin and Isinglass in his tree, gave him some clout. Commander Ross's reputation for buying the best of the best and being willing to lay out money to build a great stable added to that clout, prompting newspapers to sit up and pay attention to the transfer of the chestnut colt. Billy Kelly, however, with his stellar record at two, overshadowed the still-maiden Sir Barton. Billy Kelly's price might have been nearly triple that of the chestnut colt with the wide white blaze, but in a year's time Sir Barton would overtake the gelding as the star of the Ross Stable and perform in ways that no one could ever have anticipated.

While Madden and Ross were negotiating, Major August Belmont Jr. had twenty-one yearlings for sale in a paddock at Saratoga. Because his war duties left him unable to race his horses, Belmont had decided to sell this group rather than allow them to race without his close supervision. Debt from investments such as the Cape Cod Canal had also left him in need of cash, and unloading these horses would net him enough of it to make the sale worthwhile. Before Belmont shipped them all to Saratoga, he offered the group to buyers such as Samuel Riddle, who turned down the offer after his trainer, Louis Feustel, inspected them. Belmont wanted too much for that group of yearlings, many of whom probably would not have netted the asking price on their own. In this pack of yearlings, however, one in particular stood out, despite a slightly narrower left forefoot, and caught Feustel's and then Riddle's attention. The chestnut yearling was already named—Man o' War, christened by Belmont's wife, Eleanor—and was for sure toward the top of their respective lists. As the gavel fell on his sale, Sir Barton's future rival became the property of Samuel Riddle for a respectable $5,000, half of what Sir Barton would cost Commander Ross.[28]

The sale of Man o' War might have been unremarkable at the time—his price the third highest, his name unmentioned in the sale's write-up[29]—but the son of Fair Play was destined to meet the son of Star Shoot in a match race that would shoot one horse to the highest heights of fame and push the other closer to obscurity.

4

Meet the New Boss

Commander Ross was going all in on building a powerhouse stable, and hiring H. G. Bedwell and purchasing horses such as Billy Kelly and Cudgel made it clear that the Canadian wanted to be a force in Thoroughbred racing and was willing to use his considerable fortune to make that happen. With all of the quality horses already in his stable, the recent purchase of the chestnut son of Star Shoot and Lady Sterling seemed like a footnote, another good horse added to a growing stable. But H. G. Bedwell was no slouch at finding and developing talent, and certainly buying Sir Barton made sense: the colt showed Bedwell something, an inkling of what was to come.

The problem was, Sir Barton did not make it immediately clear to everyone watching what that something might be.

The Ross Stable's newest addition contrasted with his new stablemate Billy Kelly in more ways than just his record on the track. Where Billy Kelly "was as sound as a bell and, moreover, had the disposition of an angel," Sir Barton had the misfortune of soft, shelly hooves and a bad attitude.[1] Sportswriters of the day made little comment about Sir Barton's temperament aside from a few remarks from time to time during his racing years. But Commander Ross's son, Jim, a teenager when the chestnut colt joined the stable, later described Sir Barton as "downright evil"; the colt kicked, nipped at passers-by, and seemed to take little interest in the people and other animals around him. His barn name, "Sammy," seemed to be a congenial oxymoron considering the younger Ross's take on his father's best horse.[2]

Profiles of America's Triple Crown winners draw on this description, arguing that young Jim Ross would have known this horse better than others. The younger Ross, though, was fifteen when Sir Barton joined the stable; in his memoir of this era, *Boots and Saddles,* he talks about his schooling, which might have kept him from the day-to-day life of the barn for a portion of those years.[3] In addition, the commander's son mentions that his father rode often and kept horses wherever they lived;[4] if the younger Ross's early exposure to horses consisted of more placid riding horses, then that less-than-flattering impression of Sir Barton's disposition is understandable. His description of Sir Barton contrasts with the description given in the horse's extended obituary in *The Horse* magazine in 1938. There, Margaret Phipps Leonard says Sir Barton was full of "vim and fire, and even a little headstrong at times." She attributes some of his "peculiarities" in temperament to his continuous stabling as a horse in training, an idea borne out by his last owner's report that Sir Barton was high spirited like a younger horse but not aggressive, likely a by-product of spending his final days on a ranch where he could roam free rather than face the claustrophobia of stabling.[5]

Of course, his trainer did not help Sir Barton's attitude. Whenever H. G. Bedwell would find the colt with his head sticking out of his stall, he "would teasingly slap him on one side and then on the other until Sir Barton acquired the habit of grabbing for his hand at each slap."[6] What the younger Ross might have interpreted as aggression or something sinister simply may have been a horse on the lookout for someone to tease him, an intelligent colt who liked to play roughly. The kicks and the disinterest in others were the by-product of a personality that was more horse than pet, unlike Billy Kelly, who was a stable favorite for his gentle personality. Few people, save for Sir Barton's devoted groom, "Toots" Thompson, seemed to earn that horse's consideration or regard.[7] Not even other animals, the proverbial menagerie around a backside barn, seemed to interest him. Whereas horses such as Man o' War and Exterminator had pets of their own, Sir Barton disdained that sort of familiarity with anyone outside of his groom. Sir Barton was no one's pet; he was "all horse," a personality that made the business of running his play.[8]

Like his new and more accomplished stablemate, Sir Barton stood only 15.2 hands at his withers. Both his sire and his dam had been chestnuts, and so their son's coat shone that burnished golden brown as well, and, like his sire, Sir Barton had a blaze that seemed to stretch from between his ears and down the left side of his face, stopping just below his left nostril. That blaze was the only white on him; the rest of his body was a sleek and smooth continuous sheen of golden brown over tight muscles. Although his owner's son might have thought of him as "evil," Sir Barton eyed his surroundings with curiosity and expectation, as if he needed to assess the situation before deciding how to deal with people and places. This colt was smart and fast, and he knew it, giving just enough to show those around him the depth of his talent but no more. He did not run for the love of those around him; no, he seemed more interested in asserting his dominance on the track than in gaining anyone's affection in the barn.

Regardless of how Sir Barton acted off the track, on race day he was the consummate professional. He might have been prone to nip at passers-by as he poked his head over the half-door of his stall, but his race-day attitude showed him to be focused on the task at hand. When facing the starter, Sir Barton "betrayed no nervousness; . . . his head held proudly erect as with bold, clear eyes he direct[ed] his gaze towards the far distance," or, in racing parlance, projected "the look of the eagle."[9]

The Ross Stable sealed the deal with Madden on August 21, 1918, when the chestnut colt officially went from Madden's barn to Ross's. Sir Barton's workouts upon changing stables and trainers seemed to encourage both his new connections and turf writers; the colt beat Foreground, one of his new stablemates in a workout in the days leading up to the Hopeful Stakes, running three-quarters of a mile in a decent 1:14.[10] Nominated also for the Belmont Futurity, Sir Barton had the potential to be "one of the topnotch juveniles of the year."[11] Sir Barton finally finding his form looked possible as he went to the post for the Hopeful at Saratoga with nineteen other juveniles on August 31.

On the last day of the Saratoga season, this next test would not include the Ross Stable's star gelding; Billy Kelly's original owner W. F. Polson had another of his two-year-olds, Vulcanite, in the race instead.[12] Without the dominant gelding, the field was wide open, highly regarded colts and fillies such as Eternal, Pigeon Wing, Sweep On, and others going after the rich $30,000 purse. Sweep On had won the Grand Union

Hotel Stakes after finishing second to Billy Kelly in the Grab Bag Handicap. Eternal, Terentia, and Hannibal had records that also put them in the mix as potential favorites for the race. The Ross Stable's newest acquisition, Sir Barton, drew the sixth post position, with long shots to his inside and the favorites on his outside. The chestnut colt stepped up to the barrier for his first start in the orange and black with odds of twelve to one, low considering his record to that point, but Bedwell and Ross had a reputation for finding and training up talent, and his morning workouts showed so much.[13]

None of it mattered in the end. At the start, Vindex and Grimalkin broke in front but burned off their speed as the field passed the half-mile mark. Shut off at the start, jockey Andy Schuttinger on Eternal moved up through traffic to third and then, on that final turn, took to the outside, going around the leaders to take the lead. Once clear, the crowd gasped as Schuttinger unleashed Eternal, the colt's burst of speed taking him farther away from the cavalcade of juveniles behind him in that last furlong of the race.[14] After the race, Daydue's jockey, Harry Lunsford, lodged a complaint against Schuttinger, accusing Eternal's jockey of grabbing Daydue's bridle and causing them to lose ground. Schuttinger countered with accusations that it was Lunsford who had committed the foul, grabbing Eternal's reins in an attempt to slow down the surging colt's move. The stewards ruled in Schuttinger's favor, dismissing the complaint, and the results stood.[15] Eternal had won the Hopeful and $30,150 over a crowded field of nineteen other horses.

Eternal's margin of victory was three lengths, his surge of speed in the stretch stamping him as one of the juveniles to watch. Comparisons to Billy Kelly and debates about the better horse began to swirl. Eternal's win made him the leading money winner of his age group, his camp calling him one of the best two-year-olds of the year. Racing officials began to talk about setting up a special race open to all juveniles, a chance to raise money for the Red Cross and its wartime work as well as to determine the best two-year-old of the year. Though Ross had not commented on the possibility of a match race, James McClelland surely would send Eternal up against Billy Kelly should Ross choose to participate.[16] Anticipation for a match race between the leading two-year-olds built as racing shifted back southward.

For his part, Sir Barton had rewarded his new owner with another clunker of a race, finishing sixteenth, not even factoring in the Hopeful. His workouts showed so much promise, his pedigree stamped him as one to watch, but none of his races had lived up to either. The best was yet to come, though, as Bedwell prepared a still-maiden Sir Barton for another of the big juvenile races of the year, the Belmont Futurity.

With Saratoga's meet concluded, the Ross horses decamped from the Spa back home to Maryland to prepare for the fall stakes races, including the Futurity at Belmont Park. Considered one of the most prestigious races of the Thoroughbred calendar during this era, the Futurity boasted a number of racing legends as winners, including Colin, Ogden, and more.[17] In this first part of the twentieth century, for the Futurity the breeder had to nominate a mare prior to foaling, so John E. Madden's nomination of his Lady Sterling colt meant that Sir Barton was eligible for the Futurity despite new ownership. Commander Ross had purchased the colt for a chance to have a starter in the Futurity, and in the colt's latest workout at Havre de Grace he raced close with Billy Kelly, who carried 105 pounds to Sir Barton's 127 pounds.[18] Sir Barton's time in the six-furlong workout was 1:15, a performance showing that he was ready for this next challenge.

From Maryland, Bedwell shipped the still-maiden colt to Belmont alone for the prestigious race, without his stablemate Billy Kelly. Had the gelding or his supposed rival Eternal started in the Futurity, it would have shrunk the field considerably. Their absence and the large purse of $30,000 instead meant that fifteen horses would vie for the Futurity title for 1918.[19] Among the hopefuls of note were Dunboyne and Purchase, both winners of multiple races, and Sir Barton, who might "spring a surprise" in his latest start.[20] With such a large field and the two best juveniles absent, the race was certainly wide open.

On September 14, with a fast track underneath them, the fifteen hopefuls lined up at the barrier, ready to claim their share of another large purse. Commander Ross stood among the largest crowd of the year at Belmont Park, hopeful that Sir Barton could break his maiden finally and do it in a big way. Dunboyne was first choice in the betting, followed by Purchase. Sir Barton had drawn post position thirteen, far on the outside of Dunboyne at post position four and Purchase on the rail at post position one. Dunboyne, who had a history of being fractious at the barrier, broke through twice, delaying the start for nearly eight minutes. The first time, he ran nearly two furlongs, and the second time about half that, carrying the race's highest weight of 127 pounds.[21]

Despite his bad behavior, Dunboyne got off to a flying start, as did Sir Barton, sixth behind Dunboyne and Pigeon Wing in first and second. Purchase did not start well, stopping when the barrier came up and then breaking toward the inside rail before swinging out toward the outside rail as jockey Lyle Lyke tried to straighten him out. By the time Lyke did, Purchase was eight lengths behind and next to last. In order to catch the field and have a ghost of a chance at the lead, Lyke had to use as much of Purchase's speed as he could to make up the ground they had lost.[22]

After a half-mile, jockey Andy Schuttinger had Dunboyne still on the lead, with the field shifting positions behind him, preparing to make a run at the leader. The Trump had moved up to second, passing Pigeon Wing, with Sir Barton stalking them in fourth. By the stretch, Sir Barton moved up from fourth to third and finally to second place, with Purchase—still wide toward the middle of the track—driving from the back of the pack to challenge the two front-runners, sitting third behind Sir Barton. Dunboyne pulled away to win by two lengths, with both Sir Barton and Purchase driving at the end.[23]

The Futurity was Sir Barton's best finish to date; he finally finished a race in the money and showed the speed that his workouts had promised. Commander Ross was as satisfied with the second-place finish as he would have been with a win because of the colt's burst of speed in that final furlong. Jockey Earl Sande's report about the race told the story of a colt ready to run who was obstructed by the traffic of a large field. Sande had to keep Sir Barton under wraps until they had space, but by then his move for the lead was too late. Had Dunboyne and Sir Barton been able to start on equal footing, the jockey assured his boss, the result would have been much different.[24]

Sure, Sir Barton had the pedigree, with two English Triple Crown winners in his lineage and a famous half-brother, but that was no guarantee that the promise he held would become reality. Now, though, Bedwell's training was starting to bring out something in the chestnut colt that he had not shown to that point. Hopes were high for the son of Star Shoot.

Hopes that might soon be dashed by a kick and a cut.

After the Futurity, Ross and company turned their attention to the remainder of the 1918 season, including a possible match race between Eternal and Billy Kelly. Sir Barton and Milkmaid, a two-year-old filly Ross also had purchased from Madden, were shipped from Belmont Park to Laurel in Maryland, where both looked forward to their next starts. But in mid-October an accident made it clear that Sir Barton was not going to make any more starts that year.

One mid-October morning Bedwell sent Sir Barton over the Laurel oval for a six-furlong workout. His time, 1:13, showed the colt was fit and ready for his next start in the upcoming Walden Stakes as well as in the other Maryland juvenile stakes for which he had been nominated. At some point that morning, however, Sir Barton got too close to one of his stablemates, Foreground, and Foreground kicked him, striking him in the stifle. The resulting cut soon became infected, with abscesses forming around the injured area, and suddenly the son of Star Shoot was running a fever of 105 degrees Fahrenheit.[25]

Septicemia, or blood poisoning, soon set in, the *Daily Racing Form* reporting that Sir Barton had "a bad attack of fever" in late October, a "case [that] was so severe and so alarming that everyone expected him to succumb." What seemed like a simple infection at first became such a threat to the colt's life that Bedwell himself nursed him, rarely leaving the colt's stall until it became clear that Sir Barton would recover. Ample experience with horses and their ailments made Bedwell the right person to see Sir Barton through this crisis, though the trainer credited the colt himself for the remarkable recovery.[26]

Though the crisis was averted, Sir Barton's two-year-old season was finished, with only one race in the money, an inauspicious start to the career of this good half-brother of Sir Martin. As he recovered, questions about his fitness after such an illness remained. Would he be able to return to form for his three-year-old season? Would such a debilitating fever leave him weak and unable to train?

As 1918 wound to a close, the year had one more race that mattered, one that Sir Barton would play no part in but that nevertheless would change the path of his three-year-old season and eventually racing history.

By September, the competition for the juvenile crown was down to two horses—Billy Kelly and Eternal, though colts such as Purchase and Dunboyne remained in the conversation as well. Both Billy Kelly and Eternal had shown themselves to be the best of the 1916 crop, with Billy Kelly winning their only meeting. The racing public was eager to see the two run against each other to settle the question of supremacy once and for all.

The clamor began in mid-September after Dunboyne's win in the Futurity. The Queens County Jockey Club struck first, offering a $2,500 purse for a six-furlong race at its Aqueduct racetrack, with a $2,500 subscription fee, meaning a purse of $10,000 or more for a match race among Billy Kelly, Eternal, and, potentially, Dunboyne and Purchase. As negotiations began, H. G. Bedwell made it clear that whatever the stakes decided upon for this race, the Ross Stable needed Aqueduct to guarantee payment of $2,500 if adverse weather canceled the race. Such conditions were necessary to justify putting Billy Kelly on a train and sending him from Maryland to New York. Shipping horses was already risky, but doing it in the later part of the year, with the three-year-old stakes looming in mere months, had to be worth the trip for Bedwell to take that kind of risk.[27]

Havre de Grace upped the ante for this juvenile playoff by offering $5,000 added money for the match race to take place there.[28] Bedwell was pleased with the offer; Havre de Grace was in Maryland, home ground, less of a trip than Aqueduct and New York. The latter, however, countered that offer with $5,000, rather than $2,500, and then granted the owners freedom to determine their own subscription fees, provided they paid at least $2,500. Queens County's latest offer, however, was contingent upon all three horses starting; the race would not happen with only two horses. George Smith, owner of Brighton Stable and Purchase, insisted upon a fast track, a difficult proposition in the fall in New York, whereas Bedwell assured everyone that Billy Kelly would run regardless of the track condition.[29] While all of this back and forth was going on, Colonel Matt Winn, the legendary promoter behind the Kentucky Derby, was working on bringing the race to his Laurel Race

Course, enticing the three owners with large sums of money as it became clear that the disagreement over track conditions was going to prevent a match race at Aqueduct before its fall season was over.[30]

Winn's offer was a $10,000 purse on top of a $5,000 subscription fee, which would bring the purse to $45,000 with three horses in the race and $30,000 with two. The race would be run in late October, with each horse carrying the same weight. Eternal's owner, James McClelland, upped the subscription fee to $10,000, while Ross pledged to pay the same; both men were wealthy enough that they could afford it. The resulting money was to be split between the Red Cross fund and Liberty Bonds.[31] The other two potentials, Dunboyne and Purchase, were no longer part of the equation. After Dunboyne won the Futurity in September, he developed a splint.[32] Recovery from that injury would require time, making additional starts in 1918 unlikely for Dunboyne. Purchase's part in the drama went away when his owner, Brighton Stable, sold its stock at a dispersal sale after going out of business. Famed trainer Sam Hildreth bought the colt for $12,500, but losses in races against lesser company had already pushed the colt out of the spotlight.[33] As Colonel Winn wanted, this dash to decide the juvenile champion became a two-horse race, Billy Kelly and Eternal, and thus in late September the race was on.

The race would happen rain or shine, with each horse carrying 122 pounds. Each owner was to pay a subscription fee of $10,000, and the Maryland Jockey Club would add $10,000 to the purse. The winner's portion would go to the American Red Cross, with Commander Ross stipulating that should Billy Kelly win, his portion would go to the Canadian Red Cross.[34] The match race was on, but no date had been set. Ross, who was competing with A. K. Macomber for leading owner of 1918, was impatient for a firm date because he had war work demanding his attention.[35] The race would be run whether the commander himself was present or not, but Ross very much wanted to watch Billy Kelly run—and win.

On October 12, Billy Kelly carried 109 pounds in the Columbus Handicap against three other horses, barely beating eight-year-old Leochares by a nose.[36] That same day the Maryland State Board of Health closed many public places, including Laurel, because of the Spanish influenza outbreak.[37] During the hiatus created by this closure,

Matt Winn tentatively scheduled the Billy Kelly–Eternal match race for October 24, and the owners agreed to put up $10,000 each plus the $10,000 from the Maryland State Fair. The winning owner would keep his $10,000, and the remaining $20,000 would go to buy Liberty Bonds for the Red Cross.[38] The misfortune of a public epidemic also was fortuitous for Billy Kelly, who needed extra time to recover from a cut ankle he suffered in his previous race. The cut refused to heal, forcing Bedwell to alter the colt's training regimen in the days leading up to the match race.[39]

The ban on public assemblies lasted long enough that the match race between Billy Kelly and Eternal was put on hold temporarily. When the flu epidemic abated, the Maryland State Board of Health lifted its ban on assemblies in public places on October 25, and racing resumed at Laurel. The match race was moved to Monday, October 28.[40] Billy Kelly and Eternal would meet in this much-anticipated and decisive six-furlong match race, with $30,000 and the juvenile crown on the line. It was finally time to run.

October 28 dawned sunny and dry, ideal weather for the crowd of twelve thousand that amassed at Laurel, its newly enlarged grandstand accommodating a larger crowd than at the previous year's match race between Hourless and Omar Khayyam.[41] Even the gelding's former owner, W. F. Polson, came down from Buffalo, New York, to witness the duel. The wagers for this match race were fast and furious, Commander Ross getting in on the action for upward of $50,000.[42] The time for excuses had passed, and neither the cut ankle nor the delay in getting to this match race mattered. About 4:00 p.m., the two competitors stepped onto the track for the John R. McLean Memorial Cup and headed for the starting barrier.

For owner James McClelland, jockey Andy Schuttinger was up on Eternal; for Commander Ross, Earl Sande was on Billy Kelly. Schuttinger was the more experienced of the two riders, but Sande was the Ross Stable's star jockey, a brilliant rider at age nineteen. Sande's task was to watch Schuttinger's every move; if Eternal set the pace, then Sande needed to keep Billy Kelly within striking distance. Sande needed to stay to Eternal's outside because the track was soft and deep toward the rail. Even if Schuttinger took Eternal wide on the turn or the stretch, Sande needed to stay to his outside. If Eternal broke slowly, Sande could take Billy Kelly to the lead, but Bedwell anticipated that Eternal would go to the front and try to set the pace.[43]

Twice Billy Kelly and Eternal broke from the barrier, only to be called back by starter James Milton. The third time, they got away cleanly, the two rivals even as they took stride.[44] The start favored the gelding, whose jump on Eternal gave him the chance to take the lead. Instead of using the advantage, Sande eased Billy Kelly's pace, heeding the advice to stay close. The two ran head to head for the first sixteenth, with Billy Kelly on the rail and Eternal to his outside.[45] Schuttinger, sensing the slow pace, gave Eternal some rein, taking a length-and-a-half lead after the first furlong. Billy Kelly was behind him, straining under a chokehold.[46]

By the end of the first quarter of the six-furlong race, Eternal was already two lengths ahead when Sande realized that he was too far behind his rival. He drove Billy Kelly faster, and the game gelding began to accelerate, but that hesitation had cost them both ground and time. The move came too late. The remaining distance did not give Billy Kelly much room to make up the ground Sande had given up in the first part of the race.[47] At this point in the race, Schuttinger's experience preyed on Sande's youth.

Of course, as Bedwell foresaw, Eternal bore out wide on the turn, and so Sande instinctually took Billy Kelly to the inside path to catch up. What Sande forgot was the advice against doing just that because of the slower going at the rail. Schuttinger then moved Eternal back inside, effectively cutting off Billy Kelly and Sande, which forced Sande to move back to the outside, losing ground and pushing Billy Kelly to accelerate even more in order to catch up to Eternal.[48]

As they closed in on the finish line, Billy Kelly, under Sande's frantic urging, started to inch up on his rival. Previously three lengths behind, Billy Kelly began to shrink Eternal's lead, calling upon his speed to collapse the gap between them. With each stride, that gap shrunk: Billy Kelly was at Eternal's flank, then his saddle girth, then his neck. At the wire, Eternal, clearly exhausted, had only a head on his rival. The defeated Billy Kelly passed him in the next stride, needing only a few more feet to get the win. The race's final time was 1:12; the track record was 1:11⅗. The two rivals had put on quite the show; the Laurel crowd accorded each an enthusiastic ovation after the race.[49]

Schuttinger's ride earned him the loudest proclamations, his skills trumpeted across the inches of newspaper copy written on the match race. Governor Emerson Harrington of Maryland presented Eternal's owner James W. McClelland with the gold cup that Edward McLean, owner of the *Washington Post* and the *Cincinnati Enquirer,* had donated to the race named for his father.[50] Andy Schuttinger received a bouquet of chrysanthemums and then a check for $1,000 from McClelland as thanks for the successful ride on Eternal.[51] Two-thirds of the $30,000 purse went to the American Red Cross, and McClelland got back his $10,000 subscription fee.[52] On that same day, Commander Ross pledged $2,000,000 to Canadian Victory Bonds, continuing his contributions toward the war effort.[53]

For some, the John R. McLean Memorial Cup had answered the question of the superior two-year-old of 1918, but, like so many rivalries in racing, the question of true superiority never had an answer. Billy Kelly passed Eternal in the strides just after the finish line; he had more starts and more wins than his rival. Billy Kelly versus Eternal—who was better? The racing world was determined to know.

Despite Eternal's victory over Billy Kelly, the consensus was that the two shared the honors. Commander Ross proposed a rematch, but Eternal retired for the winter after the match race, thus eliminating the chance to decide the matter once and for all.[54] James McClelland intended to point his colt toward the Kentucky Derby, so the next chance for Billy Kelly to face Eternal at the barrier would be in Louisville.[55]

As 1918 gave way to 1919, the Ross Stable looked forward to the Kentucky Derby for Billy Kelly. The great debate over the superiority of Ross's gelding or his rival continued on into the run-up to the Derby as the Winter Book opened with the two set as cofavorites; Sir Barton was far down the list, at fifty to one.[56] With Billy Kelly and Sir Barton, the Ross Stable seemed set up to dominate the three-year-old season, ready to prove its supremacy yet again.

Little did those at the Ross Stable know that the dominance they sought would come from an unexpected source.

5

Long Shot

At the eleventh hour on the eleventh day of the eleventh month of 1918, the great war that had killed millions and decimated parts of Europe was over. Realizing that defeat was imminent, its navy on strike and the long war taking its toll on its forces, Germany signed an armistice ending the conflict with Great Britain, France, and the United States. Its compatriots in war, Turkey and Austria-Hungary, had already made deals with the Allies to end their roles in the Great War, but the Germans had held out as long as they could. Once the armistice was signed, the Treaty of Versailles following in June 1919, soldiers began returning home, and the activities that had been curtailed during the fighting, such as horse racing, started up once again.

In 1918, American racing saw what an increase in purses could bring, with horses traveling more than in years past. No doubt the money that War Cloud, the first horse to run in (i.e., compete in but not win) all three of what would become the American Triple Crown classics, won going from Louisville to Baltimore to New York had the attention of a number of trainers and owners, especially H. G. Bedwell and Commander Ross. The prestige of those races was one thing, but the money they offered was another. Prestige *and* money? That made the Ross Stable stand up and take notice.

Little did they know that their inadvertent chase for the money in 1919 would become the ultimate chase for greatness in their sport for years to come.

Jack Ross was not, to put it mildly, his father. James Ross had considered gambling a low pursuit; his son, avid sportsman and jack-of-all-trades, reveled in the sport of Thoroughbred racing, seeking to own his own stable of champions. Alongside his love of racing was his love of a good bet. Ross regularly wagered on his horses, often for large sums. He was also unflaggingly honest. On one particularly memorable occasion, Ross's betting commissioner C. J. Enright misinterpreted a bet that the commander had wired to him: "Wish to wager twenty thousand SP my entry second race tomorrow." Enright thought that Ross's use of "SP" meant "straight and place" (first and second) rather than "starting price," the odds that bookmakers quote for a horse at post time. On behalf of Ross, Enright bet $20,000 on the horse, Welshman's Folly, to win and then another $20,000 for him to place. Welshman's Folly won the race, and with the bets that Enright had placed for him, Ross won $160,000. Commander Ross, though, anticipating that he would win $120,000, refused the extra $40,000 that he won. He told Enright to return to the bookmakers the portion that he should not have won. Commander Ross barely blinked an eye at sums in the five figures, especially when his horses were involved. Gambling was simply one of the pleasures of racing.[1]

As the debate over the better horse—Billy Kelly or Eternal—carried over from the old year to the new one, the commander and many others looked forward to the chance for the two colts to meet again, presumably in the Kentucky Derby in May. While having dinner one winter night in New York, Ross was approached by a gentleman he did not know, "an insignificant, yeasty-faced little man." The man offered his opinion that Eternal would beat Billy Kelly in the Derby and then proposed a wager. Ross agreed, expecting the wager to be $100 or less. When the commander asked the amount of the wager, the stranger replied, "$50,000." Ross replied that he would need some sort of guarantee of payment if the stranger lost, a demand met with annoyance on the stranger's part. The stranger then introduced himself as Arnold Rothstein.[2]

Rothstein already had a notorious reputation by this time, though the conspiracy to fix the 1919 World Series, also known as the "Black Sox scandal," was still months off.[3] He was also a racing fan, eventually owning his own stable as well as investing in Havre de Grace. As a horse-racing fan and a gambler, Rothstein had his own opinion about the Billy Kelly–Eternal rivalry, and, like Commander Ross, he was more than willing to wager big money on bets like this one. The two men settled on the terms for their friendly wager: Rothstein would win if Eternal finished ahead of Billy Kelly; Ross would win if Billy Kelly finished ahead of Eternal; and if neither colt finished in the top three, then the wager was off.[4]

Rothstein's bet was indicative of the mood of those early months of 1919. The focus was on the Billy Kelly–Eternal rivalry as sportswriters picked either one or the other for champion two-year-old of 1918. Although it was certain that those two would meet in Louisville, speculation ran wild as to who would accompany Billy Kelly to Louisville. With an embarrassment of riches in his barn, Ross could be satisfied that the money he had spent over the past two years of acquiring horses would give him the best shot at winning his first Kentucky Derby.

The Kentucky Derby had a rich and storied history, making it the perfect target for a man who wanted to become part of the elite of horse racing. Colonel Meriwether Lewis Clark, grandson of the famed explorer William Clark, had traveled to Europe in 1872, visiting such historic racing centers as Epsom in England and Longchamps in France. Determined to revive racing in Kentucky, which had had no significant racing operation since Woodlawn Race Course had closed in 1870, Clark sought to build an upscale racing facility much like Epsom Downs in England. He started the Louisville Jockey Club and Driving Park Association, with 320 members paying $100 each for the construction of a racetrack and grandstand on land leased from his uncles Henry and John Churchill. Modeled after the Epsom Derby, the Kentucky Derby was first run in 1875 at 1½ miles and then shortened to 1¼ miles. When Clark and Churchill Downs ran into financial issues in the 1890s, a syndicate led by W. E. Applegate and William F. Schulte bought Churchill Downs and instituted a number of changes, including building the iconic Twin Spires, hiring Colonel Matt J. Winn as their promoter, and in 1908 bringing pari-mutuel wagering machines. Because pari-mutuel wagering split the pool of money wagered among bettors based on the size of their wagers, it cut down on the unsavory aspects of using bookmakers for placing bets and made gambling more of an egalitarian pursuit. As long as fans had bet on the right horse, then they would take home money from that communal pool rather than taking directly from another person, as happened when placing bets with a bookmaker. With this newer, more democratic gambling system, Churchill Downs was able to withstand the wave of antigambling sentiment cascading across the United States, which virtually shuttered the sport in a number of places, except for Kentucky.[5]

By the first part of the twentieth century, these changes had brought Churchill Downs and the Kentucky Derby greater prestige and popularity. In 1913, August Belmont Jr. was one of those social elites whose presence made Derby Day a desirable destination, and that same year bettors cashed in to the tune of $184.90 for a $2 bet when long shot Donerail won the Derby that year, a record payout. In 1915, Harry Payne Whitney, son of financier and founding Jockey Club member William C. Whitney, brought his champion filly Regret to Louisville, where she beat a field of fifteen colts and geldings to become the first filly to win the Kentucky Derby. Whitney was thrilled that his filly had won "the greatest race in America"; no doubt Churchill Downs's owners were also thrilled at Regret's win, for Whitney's presence brought back some of that national profile the race had been missing in the previous two decades.[6] For Commander Ross, an increase in the Derby's purse from $14,450 in 1915 to $24,600 in 1919 as well as its ascendant social stature made Churchill Downs a desirable target for his three-year-olds.

With one of the Kentucky Derby favorites in the Ross Stable barn, the whole operation looked forward to the spring races for the stable's collection of three-year-olds. Geldings such as Billy Kelly had been declared ineligible for some spring stakes races because the industry was trying to promote breeding in light of the military's need for horses.[7] However, in January, likely owing to the potential hit to the pocketbooks at Churchill Downs if geldings were not allowed to start in the Derby, Charles Grainger, the track's president, announced that geldings could run in 1919.[8] The rematch between Billy Kelly and Eternal could now become a reality in the Run for the Roses.

Continuing his winning ways from 1918, Billy Kelly opened his campaign in 1919 with wins in handicaps against older horses at Havre de Grace. Eternal spent the early part of 1919 in Hot Springs, Arkansas, training at Oaklawn Park.[9] Sir Barton, fully recovered from his autumn illness, impressed in training; the colt's fitness showed him to be "as splendid a 3-year-old as can be found anywhere."[10] In order to have even more options for Louisville, Commander Ross had also purchased War Marvel and War Pennant from A. K. Macomber, giving him five potential starters for the Derby.[11] The stable's focus remained on getting Billy Kelly ready for Louisville. Who would go with him?

H. G. Bedwell's assistant trainer for the Ross Stables was the notorious former jockey Cal Shilling. Carroll "Cal" Shilling had grown up in Texas, riding on the bush tracks before moving on to riding professionally for trainers such as Sam Hildreth and winning a number of prestigious races, including the Kentucky Derby on Worth in 1912. His skills in the saddle, however, came with a temper and a habit of rough riding that cost him his jockey's license. He remained in the racing business, serving as an assistant trainer for Bedwell and even as an exercise rider. A future Hall of Famer, Shilling also mentored the Ross Stable's jockeys, including Earl Sande, who was a future Hall of Famer as well.[12]

Shilling grew intimately familiar with both Sir Barton and Billy Kelly in that run-up to the Derby and came to favor the Star Shoot colt, confident that he was capable of surprising everyone around him. For a while, Shilling stood alone in this opinion, until a workout in late April made everyone sit up and take notice.[13]

At Havre de Grace, H. G. Bedwell sent Sir Barton out with Cudgel and Billy Kelly on April 25 for a 1⅛-mile workout, a setup necessary to get the colt's best effort, with two other horses there to trick him into running. Cudgel ran with him for the first six furlongs, and then Billy Kelly jumped in for the last three furlongs; Sir Barton finished the workout with a final time of 1:54⅗ for the nine furlongs, nearly two seconds faster than Billy Kelly's and Dunboyne's recent times for the same distance.[14] Sir Barton had already attracted attention as a "full-fleshed and splendidly muscled chestnut," a horse fully recovered from his illness, one who "can do anything Billy Kelly can do—for fun."[15] If Bedwell was unsure up to that point about who would accompany Billy Kelly to Louisville, that workout and Shilling's advocacy must have changed his mind. When it came time to ship Billy Kelly to Louisville and Churchill Downs on May 1, Sir Barton would go, too.

Even though the gelding was getting much of the attention, Sir Barton became just as important to the stable's chances in the Derby as Billy Kelly himself. In fact, in the weeks leading up to the race, the son of Star Shoot seemed to be Ross's best shot for the race, especially given his maiden allowance of 12 pounds. Rather than carrying 122 pounds like many of his competitors, Sir Barton as a maiden was to carry 110 pounds, a significant advantage, making him "more dangerous than his stablemate."[16] Contrary to the idea that Sir Barton came along only to play rabbit for Billy Kelly, newspapers reported that Bedwell considered the colt the stable's "chief reliance in the Derby."[17] So, in addition to Shilling's consideration, Sir Barton had already caught the eye of others, though the focus remained predominantly on Billy Kelly, Eternal, and a handful of other notables, such as Vindex and Dunboyne.

Sir Barton impressed observers with his pre-Derby workouts, as horsemen commented again and again about his looks in comparison to Billy Kelly. Both had grown over the winter, but whereas Billy Kelly had maintained his somewhat scrawny and ungainly looks, Sir Barton was "big and powerful, with his speed backed by great muscular development."[18] His morning runs showed this development; his last workout before the Derby saw him go the 1¼ miles in 2:07 while carrying 120 pounds.[19] With the weight allowance and morning performances, Sir Barton was becoming in his own stable more of a favorite for the Derby than Billy Kelly.

With the speed Sir Barton showed in his workouts, it was no surprise that Bedwell wanted him to run in the Derby with his star gelding. If he burned out front-runners such as Eternal, that would leave Billy Kelly with a good chance to overtake tired horses to win. If Sir Barton did not fade, he could win in his own right, especially if the gelding could not maintain his speed over the distance; either way, the Ross Stable would come home in front. It was a sound and sensible way of looking at the race, especially given how much of a wild card Sir Barton was at the time. The workouts he put in, though, and the attention he had received from sportswriters as a result showed that he was a threat to every horse in the field, including his own stablemate.

In addition, questions and speculation abounded about all of the horses' ability to go 1¼ miles. All had workouts that were decent, logging times that were promising, but none of them had run a race longer than a mile, and the Derby came early in their three-year-old year. Those doubts allowed horses other than Billy Kelly and Eternal to enter the conversation, horses such as Vindex and Sir Barton. In all of the longer workouts prior to the Derby, four horses—Eternal, Vindex, Billy Kelly, and Sir Barton—showed the best times for one mile and longer. The field for the forty-fifth Kentucky Derby was considered among the best in nearly a quarter of a century because of the range of talent slated to meet the barrier on May 10.

Though Sir Barton had not run in almost eight months and had suffered through a serious battle with blood poisoning, the chestnut son of Star Shoot seemed to be fully recovered and full of run, ready to go. Despite the colt's status as a maiden, his latest workout, in which he ran the 1¼-mile route in 2:07, caught the attention of railbirds and turf writers alike. Among them was Sam McMeekin, writer for the *Louisville Courier-Journal*, who thought highly of Sir Barton, especially given his 12-pound weight allowance as a maiden:

> The selection of the probable order of finish is wholly a matter of personal opinion. The writer fancies the chances of Sir Barton. This son of Star Shoot has never won a race. But he ran second to Dunboyne in the Futurity and in private trials this spring has demonstrated that he is a high-class colt. With this as a hypothesis—a band of high-class performers, one of which is receiving a twelve-pound maiden allowance—the choice must fall upon the one so benefitted. A pound or two is often the margin of victory between horses of the same caliber. Twelve pounds given to a 3-year-old going a mile and a quarter in the spring is an enormous advantage. In the view of the figures Sir Barton has hung up in his work this spring, twelve pounds places him at the head of the list.[20]

Like Cal Shilling, McMeekin was so high on Sir Barton that he went out on a limb and picked the high-priced maiden, even with the twin pillars of 1918, Eternal and Billy Kelly, dangling before him. When the odds were published for the Derby on May 10, the Ross entries, Billy Kelly and Sir Barton, were cofavorites at three to one, while the McClelland entries, Sailor and Eternal, sat at five to two. With the rain sheeting down over Louisville, the dirt oval at Churchill Downs turned sloppy, inspiring even more questions about how the field would handle both the distance and the conditions.

Saturday, May 10, started gray and misty over the sloppy track that had absorbed at least a day's worth of rain. Dotted with puddles, the surface suited some of the elite horses set to start in the Derby that afternoon, including the favorites, Billy Kelly and Eternal. Sir Barton, however, reportedly did "not seem to like the mud," making his start an uncertainty despite the prognostications that held he had the best shot at the race.[21] Would the son of Star Shoot join his stablemate at the barrier for the Run for the Roses?

Unfortunately, Commander Ross and his family would not be there to witness one or both of his horses run for the rich Derby prize. The Ross contingent had rolled into Louisville earlier in the week, ready to enjoy all of the niceties the city had to offer, but the day before the Derby Commander Ross received news that his father-in-law, Wilmot Matthews, had suffered a stroke. Ross immediately left Louisville for Toronto to be with his wife, Ethel, and her family, but by the time he arrived, his father-in-law was improving. Getting back to Louisville for the Derby was impossible, however, and since the first radio broadcast of the Kentucky Derby was still a few years off, Ross would have to rely on telephone and telegram to hear news about his entry in the big race— news he was anxious to get, especially given his $50,000 bet with Arnold Rothstein. In order to win that wager, Billy Kelly did not need to win the race but simply finish in the top three and ahead of Eternal.[22]

The Ross Stable's regular contract rider was Earl Sande, who had ridden Billy Kelly in a majority of his starts for the stable.[23] The stable also had the services of Johnny Loftus, one of the country's leading jockeys, who had won the Derby on George Smith in 1916 and the Preakness Stakes the previous year on War Cloud.[24] As the stable's contract rider, Sande could choose his mount first, so he selected Billy Kelly; not only was he familiar with the gelding, but he was also confident that Billy Kelly was the right horse for that day. That left Loftus with the mount on Sir Barton; the veteran jockey had never ridden the colt in a race, but Johnny Loftus was one of the best jockeys in the country, a master of pace. Bedwell intended to take no chances when it came to executing his plans for the Ross entry.

Loftus, though, was having issues with the 110-pound impost slated for the maiden Sir Barton. Like most jockeys, Loftus often struggled with his weight; his normal riding weight was 115 pounds, and losing 5 pounds to ride Sir Barton became an impossible task. He got down to 112½ pounds, able to shed only 2½ pounds off of an already thin frame.[25] Thus, Sir Barton, a maiden, went to the post laden with only 112½ pounds, whereas accomplished horses such as Eternal carried as much as 122 pounds—definitely an advantage, as racing lore held that one pound equaled one length over a distance of ten furlongs or more. With that in mind, the 12-pound advantage meant that Sir Barton had the potential to finish far ahead of the field at the end of the 1¼ miles.

As Bedwell prepared his charges for the big moment, he relayed instructions to the two riders clad in the Ross orange and black. The strategy was still to let Sir Barton take the lead and run everyone out so that Billy Kelly could bring up the rear. Johnny Loftus's instructions were to allow Sir Barton to run on his own merits and Billy Kelly on his.[26] Bedwell knew what his horses were capable of; he might have loved Billy Kelly, but he clearly perceived the potential inherent in Sir Barton.

Derby Day might have been cool and dreary, but fans came from far and wide to watch and wager. As the crowd watched the twelve starters walk to the barrier, the Ross entries leading the field, the throng of thousands turned their attention to the best that East and West had to offer.[27] Little did they know that the race they were about to witness was the first step toward changing the course of racing history.

Despite the weather, chilly for early May, Kentucky's holiday had attracted a crowd of fifty thousand to Churchill Downs. The field of twelve—five geldings, six colts, and one filly—paraded to the post for the Kentucky Derby, the fifth race on the day's card. Included among that dozen were the two horses who had competed for the juvenile crown in 1918 and other notables such as Vindex and Be Frank, starters from prestigious owners H. P. Whitney, Willis Sharpe Kilmer, and W. F. Polson. Between these twelve horses and victory lay ten furlongs, a distance that each had yet to travel in their short careers. The heavy track, the Kentucky dirt still laden with days' worth of rain, sloshed under their feet as they strode to the starting barrier at the top of the Churchill Downs stretch. Sir Barton and Johnny Loftus took their place on the rail, post position one, while Billy Kelly and Earl Sande stood on the outside, in post position eleven. At 5:10 p.m., the crowd watched the horses in their positions at the barrier, "some of the horses excited and alert, others staid and controlled, ready to be turned loose when the word is given."[28] After four minutes, starter A. B. Dade sent the field away, the gathered multitude gasping, "They're off!," as the field took stride and passed the grandstand for the first time.[29]

Sir Barton broke cleanly from the rail and got to the front about six strides in, the other horses falling in line behind him. In order to avoid running in the muddy aftermath of other horses, Loftus needed to hustle the colt to the front immediately; by the first quarter, Eternal was second, two lengths behind Sir Barton, and Billy Kelly was third, just behind Eternal. At the half-mile mark, Schuttinger pushed Eternal to move within half a length of Sir Barton, but Loftus shook up Sir Barton and the colt pulled away, Eternal fading from the effort of trying to keep up.[30] Eternal fell back through the field, giving Sande and Billy Kelly, now in second, a chance to catch and then pass the gelding's stablemate. As the field swept into the stretch, the 1919 Kentucky Derby came down to its final furlongs, the two horses in orange and black leading the way.

If Bedwell or anyone else in the Ross party expected the front-running son of Star Shoot to fade at this point in the race, nine furlongs in and one more to go, Sir Barton, still under restraint, proved them wrong. Neither slowing nor fading, he went faster as the race went on, running his mile in 1:41⅘.[31] With Eternal beaten, fading to the back of the pack of twelve, Billy Kelly did his best to catch up; Loftus stalled on Sir Barton, looking around to see how close the gelding was. When he did not see Billy Kelly, Loftus tapped his mount with the whip, and Sir Barton responded as if this were the race's start rather than its end.[32] His lead grew larger in the stretch, and he hit the wire five lengths in front of his stablemate. It was the first time two horses from the same stable had finished one–two in the Kentucky Derby.[33] Sir Barton chose the Kentucky Derby, one of the country's most famous races, to break his maiden, and he did it in sensational style, despite the dreary weather and the heavy track.

Although Sir Barton may have shocked everyone with the decisive way he took the Derby, H. G. Bedwell did not betray any surprise at the colt's win, despite the fact that Sir Barton had beaten Bedwell's own admitted favorite, Billy Kelly. The only thing that dismayed the trainer was that the Derby win meant that Sir Barton lost his maiden advantage in the Preakness Stakes, which would be run four days later in Baltimore.[34] The "hard-luck" colt who had been winless in six starts to that point now brought home $20,825 for his owner; Ross also got the second-place horse's share of $2,500. Despite Billy Kelly's second-place finish, Commander Ross won the wager with Arnold Rothstein: Eternal finished tenth, well behind his rival. Not only did the commander come away with nearly $24,000 in purse money, but he also won $50,000 from Rothstein, more than double the purse money Churchill Downs offered for the Derby.

Sir Barton's win also validated the hunches of Sam McMeekin, who trumpeted his prediction in a reprinted paragraph from his May 10 article in the May 11 edition of the *Louisville Courier-Journal,* trumpeting, "I TOLD YOU SO!" in his write-up of the victory.[35] No doubt Cal Shilling, the lone champion of the chestnut colt in the colt's own stable, was feeling validated as well. Their time to celebrate was short, however, as H. G. Bedwell turned the stable's attention away from the twin spires of Churchill Downs and toward the familiar sights of Maryland and Pimlico.

The Preakness Stakes was scheduled for Wednesday, May 14, and the Maryland-based Ross Stable was eager to bring its horses back home to run in Pimlico's important stakes races. Duplicating War Cloud's route from the previous year, Bedwell declared Sir Barton for the Preakness Stakes, only four days hence.

In the wee hours of May 11, long before fans could venture to Churchill Downs to get a glimpse of the newly minted Derby winner, Sir Barton and Billy Kelly boarded a train bound for Baltimore, back to Maryland and a few miles closer to history.

6

Our Hero Heads East

After the dust—or rather the slop—had settled and the results were declared official, Sir Barton's Kentucky Derby victory was considered both a sensation and a fluke, simultaneously a by-product of his purple pedigree and of the maiden allowance and a muddy track. Only one other maiden had ever won the Kentucky Derby, so surely this one's victory had to be a fluke, right?[1] Billy Kelly supporters opined that his two starts prior to the Derby had sapped his speed. Eternal apologists cited the mud for the absence of one of the prerace favorites and determined that a fast track would have changed the result.[2] Either way, the result would not be the same the next time these horses met, they all declared.

The potentially fluky nature of Sir Barton's romp at Churchill Downs invited speculation about other horses and what they could do in the three-year-old stakes to follow. The human connections of horses such as Dunboyne, who had beat Sir Barton in the Futurity the previous fall, were claiming that the Preakness would give them a chance to shine.[3] The defeat of the two-year-old champions Eternal and Billy Kelly opened the door, at least in their eyes, to the chances for others to swoop in and do some dominating.

On the heels of his gelding's second-place finish, way ahead of Eternal's tenth place, Commander Ross got his $50,000 check from Arnold Rothstein, the bet between the colorful owner and the notorious gambler finally settled.[4] With his colt going from maiden to moneymaker, the commander was now nearly $75,000 richer because of Sir Barton. The colt's next start was to be the historic Preakness Stakes. Its $25,000 purse made it another rich target for Commander Ross and would give him another winner in a historic race.

The Civil War had forced Maryland, like Kentucky, to put racing on hold until 1868, when Governor Oden Bowie and a few others proposed restarting the sport with a new race, the Dinner Party Stakes, at a new racetrack, Pimlico. Located in Northwest Baltimore, Pimlico opened on October 24, 1870, with a horse named Preakness winning that first Dinner Party Stakes; three years later, former governor Bowie decided to sponsor a race named for that inaugural Pimlico winner, and thus the Preakness Stakes was born. Before 1919, the race had moved to New York and then back to Maryland, but the increase in purse money, from $4,800 in 1917 to $15,000 in 1918, had helped the Preakness raise its profile as a desirable destination for any three-year-old.[5] By the time Sir Barton arrived home in Maryland and stepped off the train at Pimlico, the Preakness Stakes was a stakes race with prestige and popularity, a worthy target for the Kentucky Derby winner.

Following a path that A. K. Macomber had set for War Cloud a year earlier, Bedwell entered Sir Barton for the Preakness Stakes. Though both the Kentucky Derby and the Preakness had been around for about the same number of years, before 1918 only three horses had made the trip from Louisville to Baltimore because the risks of shipping a horse that distance and the resultant changes to their schedules often made shipping impractical.[6] In 1918, after running in the Kentucky Derby, War Cloud made the trip to Pimlico and won one of the Preakness's two divisions. The increase in purse money from $5,000 in 1917 to $15,000 in 1918 resulted in the race's oversubscription, so the Maryland Jockey Club divided the starters into two divisions, offering $15,000 for each. On the heels of that success, $25,000 was added to the purse for the 1919 Preakness, thus attracting a field of twelve, including Derby starters Sir Barton, Vindex, Eternal, and Vulcanite.[7] That added money made the Preakness the richest race of the first half of 1919, worth more even than the Kentucky Derby. The large purse and the shorter distance in the Preakness—1⅛ miles—made this next prestigious stake an attractive option to several of those Derby starters, who had found themselves far behind Sir Barton at the finish line.[8]

Bedwell, now under the pressure of having to transport the Kentucky Derby winner on a train and run him again in four days after his win, watched anxiously as Sir Barton and other Ross horses boarded the train from Louisville to Baltimore in the wee hours of Sunday morning.[9]

Because the Preakness was four days hence, the group had to be on their way mere hours after Sir Barton crossed the finish line, with little chance to celebrate the victory before looking ahead to the next challenge. The trainer also had to contend with the risks inherent in such travel, including injuries incurred while being loaded onto and unloaded from rail cars as well as the exposure to germs from the sharing of close quarters. Rail travel also meant the loss of a day's worth of training and a disruption to the horses' routines. Sir Barton seemed to weather the six-hundred-mile trip to Baltimore just fine, arriving around noon the next day in good health, still in top condition, with nary a bit of stiffness.[10]

As anticipation for the Preakness built in the quick turnaround from one stake to another, the attention was not on the Derby winner but on the horses set to challenge him. Because the Preakness was one of the earliest prestigious tests of the season for three-year-olds, the race seemed wide open despite Sir Barton's win in Louisville. Purchase, who had skipped the Derby because of an injury, and Vindex were also in the mix, their names bandied about as everyone speculated who was the best of this class, but only Vindex would make it to Baltimore to contest the Preakness. The field numbered fifteen, including an unprecedented four starters from the Kentucky Derby.

Eternal, despite his lackluster showing in the Derby, was set to face Sir Barton again, and at a shorter distance, he was more likely to maintain his speed. His supporters were convinced that a fast track and even weights would mean their horse would finish in front of the upstart Sir Barton.[11] Dunboyne, who had skipped the Derby despite his good workouts in late April and early May, would face the barrier, too, his connections opting to save the colt for the Pimlico meet rather than putting him through the trip to and from Louisville. As the chestnut sun of Celt, a notorious bad actor at the barrier, prepared for that race, he lost his jockey when he stumbled at the start of his race before the Preakness. But jockey Buddy Ensor jumped back on the colt once the race was over and sent him a mile to work him out, his time a full second faster than the race he had just missed.[12] Despite his absence from Louisville, Dunboyne's previous starts and workouts, especially his win over Sir Barton in the 1918 Futurity, gave him a perceived edge over the Derby winner.

In addition to Eternal and Dunboyne, other horses of note, such as Vindex, who might run better on a dry track, and Sweep On, who had won the race that Dunboyne had missed, had their names bandied about as contenders for the Preakness.[13] Only Purchase, one of those colts who had shown potential at two, was still missing from the three-year-old scene, his injury set to keep him off the track until the meet at Belmont Park in New York.[14] With twelve named to start, the Preakness Stakes was shaping up to be as big of a challenge for Sir Barton as the Derby had been. Now saddled with 126 pounds rather than 112½ and tasked with being the favorite and the target rather than the dark horse, Sir Barton had to prove that his wire-to-wire Kentucky Derby victory was more than just a fluke.

As the short turnaround from the Kentucky Derby to the Preakness drew to a close, the rains of recent days gave way to sunshine, drying out the Pimlico surface just in time for the race. With a fast track, Dunboyne and Vindex were expected to be dangerous contenders, ready to challenge Sir Barton on their terms.[15] Was the Derby champion as capable on a fast track as he had been in mud? Bedwell would do his best to ensure that his colt would prevail in the next classic.

With all of these good three-year-olds in the Preakness, H. G. Bedwell knew that the key to winning the race would be to get the best start. The Preakness was an eighth of a mile shorter than the Kentucky Derby, which meant one less furlong for horses to execute their strategy depending on how the race unfolded. In this era, the start could make or break a race, especially at shorter distances, such as six furlongs, which made it harder to overcome a bad start.[16] Before the advent of the starting gate, horses would stand at the starting line before webbing, which would be thrown up when the starter dropped a flag. This type of start was an art; all of the horses had to be in line, pointing in the right direction, and *standing still* long enough to drop the flag and send them off. False starts were common enough that each jockey was familiar with how to get his horse back in line to start the race, and still others were familiar with a barrier tactic that Bedwell wanted to employ for the Preakness.

In addition to Sir Barton, the Ross Stable would send its winning filly Milkmaid to the starting barrier as part of the entry. Geldings were not eligible for the Preakness, but the stable had a number of eligible three-year-olds other than Billy Kelly to send with their Derby winner. Bedwell decided that the filly was the best companion for Sir Barton.

Her presence in the Preakness served one purpose: to ensure a good start for Sir Barton. Dunboyne and Vindex were notoriously bad at the start; if either one got a flying start over Sir Barton, it could be a disadvantage for the Derby winner. Earl Sande's job as Milkmaid's jockey was to keep an eye on Johnny Loftus and Sir Barton and ensure that the colt was on his toes and ready when the start came. If he was out of line, then Sande was to deliberately break the line with the filly in order to force a reset and do it in a way that escaped the starter's detection because it could mean a fine or suspension for the jockey. The idea was to secure as fair a start as possible for Sir Barton. Bedwell had already given Loftus his instructions, the same as those he had given before the Derby: "Get to the front and stay there!"[17]

Wednesday, May 14, 1919, was a sunny and dry spring day, making Pimlico's track a fast one. Prognosticators expected a record crowd for this midweek day of racing, which was to feature this second spring classic, its purse rich and its prestige growing. In addition to the Preakness's large purse, which had played a big role in raising its profile, the presence of the Kentucky Derby winner gave this spring stake a gravitas that it had not had before now. With a great crowd of nearly twenty thousand on hand, the stage was set for Pimlico to be number two on the list of must-run places for three-year-olds in the spring.[18]

A few minutes after 4:00 p.m., the twelve starters, including Dunboyne, Sweep On, and Eternal, jogged out onto the Pimlico oval, warming up before the 4:20 start.[19] Their competition trickled in, only twelve lining up at the barrier, including four who had run only days earlier at Churchill Downs: Eternal, Vindex, Vulcanite, and, of course, Sir Barton. As the field approached the start, Milkmaid took her place in post position six, with her stablemate Sir Barton to her right in the eighth position. Starter Mars Cassidy oversaw the twelve horses, as the record Pimlico crowd pressed forward, humanity covering every inch of the grounds, craning to see the start.

Before Cassidy could get them away, Eternal broke through the webbing, and then Milkmaid and Sweep On. After the field reset, Earl Sande must not have liked Sir Barton's position, so Milkmaid broke the line one more time.[20] Because Eternal, Dunboyne, Vindex, and Sir Barton preferred to run on the lead, getting a good start in this race was essential. Milkmaid's antics might have seemed problematic to others, but for the Ross camp she was doing her job beautifully. After five minutes, the field was finally still, all twelve with their toes on the line. With a drop of the flag, Cassidy sent the dozen away, but two horses missed their chance at a good start. Dunboyne, who had been standing next to Milkmaid, found himself knocked off stride when the filly bumped him at the start, leaving him unable to play a factor in the race.[21] Likewise, toward the outside, Vindex balked when the starter dropped the flag; left at the post, his jockey jogged to the first turn and ignominiously exited the track.[22]

Milkmaid and Sir Barton got away in first and second, but by the end of the first quarter the filly had given way to the Derby winner, who took the lead and never relinquished it. Eternal made his run at the Derby winner in the backstretch, doing his best to cut Sir Barton's two-length lead down inch by inch. As the field entered that final turn, Eternal fought his way to second, only two lengths behind Sir Barton and ahead of Sweep On and King Plaudit, but Loftus gave his colt some rein, and Sir Barton moved away from Eternal, who never factored again. No one came close to threatening the stranglehold of a lead that the Derby winner, dominant at every pole, had on his competition.[23]

The field stretched out behind Sir Barton as he ran, no one able to touch the show of speed happening on the front end. Johnny Loftus never showed him the whip and had him under hold for much of the race, easing the Derby winner in the stretch. Winless in his career only a week earlier, Sir Barton had dominated two races in a row, won $45,325, and did not look as if he had been extended or tested by any of his competition.

Most of all, he had done something no other horse had ever done: he had won both the Kentucky Derby and the Preakness. Only four horses had even run in both races between 1875 and 1918, and of those four only War Cloud had won one of the two races. Sir Barton was the first to win both. Much like War Cloud the previous year, he demonstrated the benefits of the trip from Louisville to Baltimore—that the short turn-around time and the risks inherent in shipping were worth enduring for a chance at the ever-increasing purse money, money that could not be won by staying at one track, but only in the chase from track to track. Unlike his predecessor, though, Sir Barton won both races, an unprecedented feat that showed just how profitable this route could be.

As Commander Ross accepted the Woodlawn Vase, a man climbed Pimlico's old clubhouse, his destination a weathervane on its roof. Painting the silks of the Preakness winner on the weathervane shaped like a horse and jockey had been a tradition for the past decade, another way to honor the race's winner.[24] Paint buckets in hand, the man carefully painted the orange and black of the Ross Stable on the vane, recognizing Sir Barton as the champion of the Preakness.[25] With this victory, Sir Barton not only had won another prestigious race but had become the first to show that this double was possible. His wins would go on to inspire a pursuit that quickly would alter the spring stakes schedule for years to come. This pursuit of the Kentucky Derby and Preakness Stakes would become one of racing's yearly focuses, eventually evolving into something even greater.

The plaudits for this new three-year-old sensation rolled in as soon as the field crossed the finish line in Baltimore. He was the top of his class, "some great race horse, with the accent on the great," especially if he could add other victories, such as the Latonia Derby, another prestigious three-year-old test to be run on June 7.[26] At this moment, Sir Barton was indeed "the king of them all," as Frank Brosche had foreseen when he showed off the son of Star Shoot at Hamburg Place two years earlier.[27]

The colt was not the only one to reap the rewards of victory. Commander Ross, already a rich man, was that much richer with the $45,325 won in two races plus what he collected from bets after both the Derby and the Preakness. In addition to the bet with Rothstein, the commander also collected on a bet with P. A. Clark, owner of Dunboyne, who had wagered that Dunboyne would show any Ross horse his heels.[28] Ross gave Johnny Loftus a check for $2,000, a grand for each victory.[29] Although the chestnut colt was certainly not the only winner in the Ross Stable, his wins in these spring classics had done quite a bit to fatten everyone's pockets.

Suddenly the colt who had gone into the Derby after showing only a flash of promise as a two-year-old in his last race of 1918 and had recently survived a serious case of blood poisoning was the top of the heap, "a great horse—a greater one than Billy Kelly," according to his own trainer, the one who had called the gelding his favorite.[30] Sir Barton was the name on everyone's lips, and his dam, Lady Sterling, was even more famous now than she had been from foaling champions such as Sir Martin.[31] Star Shoot's prowess as sire had produced a number of stars already, and many, including Commander Ross, were betting that Sir Barton could replicate his sire's success.

With horses such as Cudgel and Sir Barton in his string, Commander Ross wagered that breeding would be as profitable as racing and so bought a tract of land outside of Laurel, Maryland, intending to build a breeding establishment there, complete with a one-mile training oval. He already owned Yarrow Brae, formerly Bedwell's farm, and this new farm would become Bolingbrook, with the former to be used for breeding stock and the latter for horses in training.[32] And who would head his Maryland stud? Cudgel, his champion handicap horse, and, of course, Sir Barton, the new star of the Ross Stable.[33] Ross spoke of a desire to retire Sir Barton at the end of his season in order to avoid the downward slope so many other stars had taken when they stayed too long at the party.[34] It was a fitting way to reward this colt who had taken an already successful stable to even greater heights.

With a number of the spring stakes still to go, Ross and Bedwell decided to send Sir Barton and Billy Kelly north to New York for the spring meet at Belmont Park. The two left soon after the Preakness, destined for a longer stay in New York since both were nominated for several races there.[35] The Derby–Preakness double winner had been entered in the $5,000 Withers Stakes on May 24, the $10,000 Belmont Stakes on June 11, and several races at Jamaica Race Course. The Withers was another race featuring three-year-olds and had a number of horses of note among its potential starters, including Sweep On, Eternal, Vindex, and Dunboyne.[36]

The day before the Withers, though, the field whittled down to just three horses, including Eternal, who was apparently back for one more crack at the horse who had beaten him twice, and Terentia, a filly who had yet to break her maiden. Other than Eternal, none of the other good three-year-olds returned for another try at Sir Barton. Owner James W. McClelland wanted to show that Eternal was still the colt that had bested Billy Kelly the previous autumn, and so Bedwell, knowing the colt as he did, kept his eye on Eternal's workouts in the run-up to the Withers.[37] Prior to 1921, races at Belmont were run clockwise, as they were in England, rather than counterclockwise, which had become the custom in the United States.[38] Bedwell's keen eye spotted Eternal's tendency to bear out on the final turn going into the stretch, a little bit of information he socked away until Withers Day.[39]

Saturday, May 24, began warm and cloudless, but heavy rain in recent days had left the track less than fast. Officially, it was listed as good, but Bedwell called it slow more than anything else.[40] The original three starters had grown to six; Terentia had been scratched, and the third-place money was going to go unclaimed if no one else entered, so four colts—Pastoral Swain, Grimalkin, Sweepment, and Star Hampton—were added the day of the race.[41] All six horses would carry 118 pounds. The only horses anyone cared about, though, were Sir Barton and Eternal.

For this race, knowing that McClelland was taking one last shot at Sir Barton with Eternal, Bedwell gave Loftus different orders. Because of the shorter distance, he gambled that jockey Andy Schuttinger would send Eternal to the lead with Sir Barton from the get-go, hoping to set up a speed duel that would test Sir Barton's courage. Rather than take Sir Barton to the front as he had ordered in the Derby and the Preakness, Bedwell instructed Loftus to let Eternal set the pace and stay well back of him until the stretch. At that point, Bedwell predicted, Eternal would bear out wide, allowing Loftus to send Sir Barton toward the rail through the hole that Eternal's move would produce and then to the lead.[42] The tremendous crowd that had come to Belmont that day to watch the Withers would not be expecting this strategy, and, most likely, neither would Eternal.

Now, ten days after his most recent victory and two weeks since his first, Sir Barton walked out onto the sandy oval at Belmont Park to take on Eternal's challenge one more time.

The Withers was set to be the fourth of six races on the card that day, with nearly thirty thousand fans, the biggest crowd of the year, on hand to see Sir Barton and Eternal duke it out one more time.[43] The day was clear and warm, but heavy rain in the days before the race meant that the track was heavy with moisture and thus slow, especially at the rail. The throngs of race fans mobbed the paddock, forcing the track police to cordon off the area around the chestnut colt, who stood calm amid the activity. When the bugle's call to the post sounded, Sir Barton's ears pricked up at the sound, and when Loftus was boosted into the saddle, the colt was so eager to reach the track that Bedwell had to take his bridle to keep him from bursting through the crowd.[44]

As the six starters walked onto the track, the crowd burst into "a tremendous ovation" when Sir Barton stepped into sight. Johnny Loftus tipped the peak of his orange cap in repeated acknowledgment of their cheers. Sir Barton himself bobbed his head up and down as he strode toward the barrier, as if he recognized that the crowd's applause was for him. Eternal also received his fair share of applause, no doubt from the stubborn set of fans who still held on to the conviction that their horse was superior to this upstart. This was Sir Barton and Eternal's third meeting in 1919, and in the first two Sir Barton had more than gotten the better of Eternal. This might be Eternal's last chance to beat the Derby and Preakness winner, and everyone knew it. This last head-to-head meeting was going to define their rivalry from here on out. The fans who had come out to watch the Withers sensed this as well, for the air around Belmont Park seemed to undulate with the tension of the moment.[45]

Once Mars Cassidy had the six starters lined up at the barrier, the six broke cleanly after only a minute at the post, Sir Barton on the rail and Eternal next to him at the second post. Jockey Andy Schuttinger on Eternal was caught flat-footed at the start, giving Sir Barton the chance to jump out to the lead.[46] Schuttinger had to hustle Eternal closer to the front of the field in order to avoid getting caught in traffic, making up enough ground in 150 yards that he was head to head with Sir Barton.[47] Loftus then tightened up on the reins, slowing his mount and allowing Eternal to pass them to take the lead. Thinking that Eternal finally had the better of Sir Barton, the crowd let out "a mighty shout" at the sight of Eternal in front.[48] As the horses swept around the track, Sir Barton three lengths behind the leader, the idea that Eternal might beat the chestnut son of Star Shoot brought out a sustained roar that did not end until the field had crossed the finish line.[49]

The pace Eternal set sizzled with fast fractions, but Loftus kept Sir Barton under wraps, staying a length or two behind to maintain the charade. Possibly surprised initially at being held back, Sir Barton soon relaxed into his role running off the pace, waiting for his chance.

Approaching the half-mile, Loftus tapped Sir Barton in preparation for the move that would come on that last turn, rousing his colt to the task ahead of them.[50] As Eternal and Sir Barton swept one–two into that final turn, Eternal indeed bore out from the rail, just as Bedwell had predicted. At this moment, Commander Ross shouted, "Now! Come on with him, Johnny!" just as Loftus flicked his whip at Sir Barton and let loose on the reins.[51] Coming out of his wide turn, Schuttinger straightened out Eternal, but not before Loftus had guided Sir Barton through the hole on the rail, the chestnut colt striding out and running as he had been itching to do the whole time.[52]

Finally unleashed, Sir Barton shot forward and caught Eternal, the two running together for about a furlong. Then the Star Shoot colt overtook his rival, pulling out to an ever-increasing lead, Eternal's speed spent. With a sixteenth of a mile to go, Sir Barton was six lengths in front, Eternal a beaten second, the rest of the field struggling behind them.[53] At the wire, "Loftus was standing straight up in the stirrups," as Sir Barton simply cruised, plenty of run left in him.[54] The enthralled crowd erupted in cheers at the speed duel they had just witnessed: not only had Sir Barton bested Eternal for the third time, but he had done it in a time that was just two-fifths of a second off the Withers's record of 1:38⅖. On a fast track and with a license to run, the colt likely would have beaten that mark.

Three victories in three races. A grand total of $53,400 won in three of the richest and most prestigious races of the first part of the year.

Sir Barton was not even close to being done.

7

History Made

Three races in fourteen days: the Kentucky Derby on May 10; the Preakness Stakes on May 14; the Withers Stakes on May 24.

Three races in fourteen days. From Louisville to Baltimore to New York. More than eight hundred miles traveled on the American railroad system, loading onto and off of railcars, exposed to other horses and the elements.

Three races in fourteen days. From $4,113 to $57,513 won.

Three races in fourteen days. Defeating twenty-three different horses, including the two-year-old cochampions and other high-class three-year-olds.

Sir Barton was the toast of the racing world, superlatives hurled at him right and left. With his win in the Withers Stakes, his third win and third defeat of Eternal, Sir Barton had risen to a level that made him a *name.* H. G. Bedwell, who had professed to preferring Billy Kelly over Sir Barton, called the Derby and Preakness winner "the best horse I ever trained and one of the best any man has ever trained."[1] Turf writers had him on par with Colin and Sysonby, sure to win $100,000 in purses that year.[2] The colt who had started 1919 as fifty to one in the Kentucky Derby Winter Book was now the star of his stable, even more so than Billy Kelly and Cudgel. As Frank Brosche had seen two years earlier, Sir Barton was "the king of them all"—for now. Other horses always loomed on the horizon, speculative challengers to his supremacy, such as Vindex and Purchase.

As May gave way to June, the question of the new champion's next start became the focus of conversations between Commander Ross and trainer H. G. Bedwell. Two prestigious races were coming up: the 1½-mile Latonia Derby on June 7 and the 1⅜-mile Belmont Stakes in New York on June 11.[3] The Latonia Derby had a purse of $15,000, whereas Belmont's purse was only $10,000. The larger purse had to be attractive to both Ross and Bedwell, and to this point Sir Barton had shown that he was a good shipper. Billy Kelly also was in the conversation for the Latonia Derby. One likely would go in the Belmont Stakes, and the other would be shipped to Latonia. Who would go where?

A couple of days after the Withers, Bedwell informed Colonel Matt Winn that he would be shipping Sir Barton to Latonia on June 6.[4] The spring meet for Belmont would run through June 11, when the Belmont Stakes itself would be run, but signs pointed toward the newest racing sensation heading back west to Kentucky instead of staying put in New York.[5]

But something simple would keep Sir Barton at Belmont Park. That something simple would help Sir Barton make horse-racing history.

After his win in the Withers, not only had Sir Barton attracted a cavalcade of superlatives, but he also had gained another bit of notoriety: the attention of the Wizard of the Turf—his former owner, John E. Madden.

Madden had made his reputation breeding, buying, selling, and then sometimes reselling or rebuying horses. Hamburg Place turned out a number of good horses each year, including Sir Barton's half-brother Sir Martin. Star Shoot, Sir Barton's sire, had been one of the leading sires in America over the past decade. Madden also had bred, broke, and raced Sir Barton before selling him to Commander Ross in August 1918 for $15,000.[6] Now, though, Madden wanted Sir Barton back, and he was willing to pay a tidy sum to get him. Hamburg Place would be the logical place for the chestnut colt to retire once his racing career was done; he had been bred there, and his sire was part of the roster of stallions. So after Sir Barton's sensational win in the Withers at Belmont Park, Madden approached Commander Ross to talk terms.

The Wizard of the Turf offered Commander Ross $1,000 for Sir Barton right there on the spot and upon the colt's retirement would pay $50,000 more. His offer thus allowed the colt to race for Ross until he was ready to retire; the commander would keep whatever purse money Sir Barton might win and then collect another sizeable sum when Sir Barton retired, regardless of his condition. Madden did not care if the colt broke down while in training and could not race again; he just wanted the chance to breed him.[7] The offer was attractive: Win more races and more money and then collect another $50,000 on top of that? Commander Ross, though, politely turned down Madden's offer, already intent on making Sir Barton the head of his stud when his three-year-old season was done.[8]

The offer was big enough to make the newspapers, owing to the interest that Sir Barton was generating with each win. Madden was not successful in reacquiring his former charge at that particular moment, but his influence on Sir Barton's life was not done yet.

While Sir Barton was ramping up for the Withers at Belmont, Ross's excellent handicap horse Cudgel was at nearby Jamaica Race Course, running in the Kings County Handicap. Carrying 132 pounds, he finished third behind Royce Rools and Straight Forward, both of whom were carrying between 20 and 30 pounds less than Cudgel. Within days of his turn at Jamaica, Cudgel and Milkmaid arrived at Churchill Downs on the morning of May 21, ready to prepare for their starts in the Kentucky Handicap and the Kentucky Oaks, respectively.[9]

Cudgel came to Kentucky in the care of assistant trainer Cal Shilling, while H. G. Bedwell remained in New York with Sir Barton and Billy Kelly. Shilling prepped the star handicap horse for the Kentucky Handicap with a one-mile workout two days before the race while they waited for Bedwell to arrive. Cudgel was set to carry 135 pounds in the Kentucky Handicap, which he had won the previous year, but if the weather did not cooperate and the track was muddy, the heavy impost and the quality of the field would make Bedwell unlikely to send Cudgel to the starter.[10]

Sure enough, May 24 featured heavy rain in the Louisville area, which meant that Cudgel would not be defending his 1918 victory in the Kentucky Handicap. Shilling sent the horse back to New York while keeping Milkmaid at Churchill Downs for the Kentucky Oaks the following week. After that race, Shilling and Milkmaid would meet the Ross representative for the Latonia Derby at Latonia one hundred miles away in northern Kentucky, near Cincinnati. Originally, Bedwell had declared Sir Barton for Latonia; on June 4, however, a couple of days after the colt was to arrive in Kentucky, the trainer indicated that the Derby and Preakness winner would start in the Belmont Stakes instead, without giving an explanation for the change.[11]

In addition to his nominations for the Latonia Derby and the Belmont Stakes, two of the season's biggest three-year-old stakes, Sir Barton also had his name down for races such as the Suburban Handicap at Belmont Park alongside his stablemates Cudgel and Billy Kelly. With Latonia's spring season just starting and Empire City's and Saratoga's seasons coming up, Sir Barton had a number of potential starts on his calendar, giving him ample opportunity to dominate the latter half of 1919 the same way he had dominated the spring to that point.

Neither Cudgel nor Sir Barton were going anywhere, though. Cudgel had returned from his aborted trip to Churchill Downs with a little souvenir—"a bad cold."[12] This cough reportedly lingered and spread to stablemate Sir Barton, and thus a trip west to Latonia was out of the question.[13] None of the Ross horses shipped to Latonia for its Derby; the biggest star featured in the race was Sir Barton's thrice-defeated rival Eternal, who led the race for the first half and then faded to sixth.[14] Sir Barton recovered from the cough that Cudgel had brought back from Kentucky, preparing for his next start in the Belmont Stakes, eighteen days after the Withers Stakes and thirty-two days after his first sensational win in the Kentucky Derby. This call to the post was about to become the call to history.

For Americans, the Belmont Stakes was the closest thing to the European concept of a derby run on this continent.[15] Much like Colonel Clark and the Kentucky Derby, August Belmont Sr. modeled the Belmont Stakes, his namesake race, after races such as the Epsom Derby.[16] Belmont also wanted to create New York's own version of the English Triple Crown, intending the Withers Stakes and the Lawrence Realization to make up the other two legs.[17] Although that sequence did not take hold in the consciousness of racing in America, the Belmont Stakes maintained its position as a prestigious stakes race, even as it lagged behind the Derby and the Preakness in purse money, with a total purse of $14,200.[18] By 1919, the Belmont Stakes, run in early June, had become the perfect test of maturing three-year-olds' capacity for stamina, much as August Belmont Sr. had intended. In addition to the challenge of its 1⅜-mile length, a furlong longer than the Kentucky Derby, Belmont Park ran its races clockwise rather than counterclockwise, as most American races were run.[19] Having already won the 1¼-mile Kentucky Derby and the

Withers on Belmont's clockwise course, neither issue posed a challenge to the ascendant Sir Barton.

With the presence of the Kentucky Derby and Preakness winner in the list of starters, the Belmont Stakes enjoyed renewed attention in 1919 that foreshadowed the intense focus it would see in years to come. The news that Sir Barton would start in the Belmont scared off much of his competition; although his win streak might be a tantalizing challenge to spoilers, his condition showed that he also was in peak form. His erstwhile rival Eternal had flailed in the Latonia Derby just days earlier, so he would not be in New York to face the barrier with Sir Barton. Purchase, whose injury had forced him to miss both the Derby and the Preakness, was in New York, but owner and trainer Sam Hildreth had sent the colt in a one-mile allowance race a few days before the Belmont. He wanted to avoid a confrontation with Sir Barton at even weights, opting to save his colt for a chance at the champion when weight would favor Purchase.[20] Both Dunboyne and Vindex were no-shows owing to health issues: Dunboyne had injured himself at the start of the Preakness, when he was caught behind the crowd of horses at the start and got away poorly, and Vindex was sidelined with a cough.[21] The Belmont field became Sir Barton and four others, three from the stable of William R. Coe, insurance executive and owner of a number of Thoroughbreds. None was expected to give the champion any real challenge.

For the midweek crowd assembled at Belmont, Wednesday, June 11, was warm and sunny, the track fast and dry, perfect conditions for this classic. Of the original four other horses named, two, Pastoral Swain and Over There, were scratched overnight, leaving only two horses to accompany Sir Barton to the barrier, Natural Bridge and Sweep On. He had beaten all comers to this point and had scared off the rest, save for these two. The only thing left was the running.

The crowd thronged Sir Barton as soon as he entered the paddock, craning for a look at this sensation that seemed peerless. Twice the usual number of fans for a Wednesday had ventured out to Belmont Park to watch this race, twenty-five thousand straining to see this new star.[22] Commander Ross, his wife, Ethel, daughter, Hylda, and son, Jim, were all in attendance, along with a box full of friends, ready to watch Ross's newest star dominate his competition.[23] From all accounts, the look of the colt, "superbly muscled, with quarters that indicate strength and strong, straight legs that taper to the fine point desirable in a horse bred for speed,"[24] mirrored his looks before the dominating performances of his earlier races. He was the epitome of class, his burnished chestnut coat covered with a saddlecloth and Loftus's small saddle. H. G. Bedwell secured the customary blinkers over the wide blaze on Sir Barton's head, and then young Johnny Loftus was boosted onto the colt's back. No wonder the masses were pushing into the paddock to get a glimpse. This was a Thoroughbred of the highest class, and he was about to make history.

The sandy Belmont track was fast on this warm summer's day as the field trickled from the paddock to the track to stand at the barrier. Sir Barton stood on the rail in the first post, with Sweep On and Natural Bridge to his right in the second and third posts. They stood at the barrier for only a minute, and when Mars Cassidy sent them on their way, Sir Barton leaped into the lead, but, as in the Withers, Johnny Loftus pulled him back, allowing Natural Bridge to take over, with Sweep On bringing up the rear.[25] Loftus kept his colt two or three lengths behind Natural Bridge for the first three-quarters of a mile until the field reached the stretch.[26] Then the jockey gave Sir Barton his head and let the colt fly.

As they rounded the turn into the stretch, Natural Bridge began to tire, and Sir Barton started his move, bounding up to a three-length lead. Behind him, Sweep On, who had been sitting several lengths back as he waited for a chance to make a move of his own, began to overtake Natural Bridge.[27] The horses swept into that wide final turn, Sweep On's challenge quickly becoming futile as Sir Barton's lead stretched to five lengths.[28] As they hit the wire, the first Triple Crown was complete. In the process, Sir Barton ran the 1⅜ miles in 2:17⅖, bettering the stakes record by two-fifths of a second and the American record by one-fifth of a second. Had Loftus not had him reined in for the majority of the race, his time likely would have been even faster.

The crowd of twenty-five thousand greeted the champion with enthusiastic applause as he passed by the judge's stand on his way to the winner's circle. He was compared to the great Colin, fans calling Sir Barton the "horse of the decade" and even the horse of the century, a racing wonder. Commander Ross, "bubbling over with joy," shook hands with Johnny Loftus and patted his champion colt.[29] The resplendent Canadian accepted the sterling silver plate and a purse of $11,950, his colt well on the way to reaching and maybe even breaking Colin's record $100,000 career earnings mark.[30] With plenty of races still remaining in 1919, Sir Barton certainly had ample opportunities to make that happen.

The war over, horse racing was back with a vengeance, both attendance and purses increasing, thanks to horses like its newest star. Sir Barton set the stage for so many memorable moments yet to come, but another chestnut colt would do his share to make 1919 a year to remember and bring racing into another golden age.

In thirty-two days, May 10 to June 11, Sir Barton had won four of the biggest races of the first half of the three-year-old racing season, amassing $65,350 in purses, and in the process, though no one knew it at the time because the feat had no name and no precedent, winning the first Triple Crown. The Derby–Preakness double was already a first, but the chestnut colt who had done almost nothing at two years old had dominated his peers and had become the talk of the racing world at three, inspiring a championship pursuit that remains the goal of many a breeder, owner, trainer, and jockey to this day. The following year, 1920, racing officials at Churchill Downs and Pimlico adjusted their calendars to accommodate those who wanted to travel from Louisville to Baltimore to attempt the Derby–Preakness double. The purses for each of these races grew. The sport had been forever altered by the victories of a horse who often teetered on the brink of unsoundness but turned in performances that would make him the choice to challenge the century's best horse.

The twenty-five thousand who witnessed the 1919 Belmont Stakes would be a fraction of the ninety thousand who would bring down the house at Belmont Park when American Pharoah in 2015 and then Justify in 2018 duplicated Sir Barton's triple. The instantaneous celebrations that erupted across the world as the newest Triple Crown winners crossed the finish line contrast greatly with the world Sir Barton inhabited. In 1919, America had no radio broadcasters to describe the scenes to ready listeners, and no television cameras to show how he romped home with hardly a challenge. Sir Barton won his Triple Crown in a different time, when reputations were made by the photographers and writers who observed and chronicled these moments.

In the words of the *Daily Racing Form* on June 12, 1919, words that presaged the moniker "Triple Crown," Sir Barton "added another jewel to his crown" with his win in the Belmont Stakes.[31] It would be a decade before Gallant Fox would repeat this triple, but, unbeknownst to everyone present at Belmont Park that day, the trip from Louisville to Baltimore to New York in the late spring would become the ultimate test of the champion, the measuring stick for Thoroughbreds for years to come.

On June 6 at Belmont Park, Purchase, the only top three-year-old whom Sir Barton had yet to meet and beat, won an allowance race by four lengths. His was the third race on the card of six on a quiet Friday as the Belmont spring meet grew closer to its end. The last race of the day was a five-furlong dash for two-year-old maidens. The field had seven starters, four of whom were making their first starts, including a gangly chestnut with a white blaze named Man o' War.

The previous year this colt had been sold at Saratoga for $5,000 while John E. Madden was in negotiations with Commander Ross for the sale of Sir Barton. Over the months since that August day, trainer Louis Feustel had been getting the young colt ready for the track, with none other than jockey Johnny Loftus trusted to help school Man o' War for the track in the mornings.[32] Now that Man o' War was two and the juvenile season was gearing up, it was time to give the colt his first try at running with competition. Rather than choose a more prestigious first race for his charge, Feustel put him in a no-name sprint to give the colt a little racing experience before pushing him to bigger things.

With Loftus up, the big red colt strode to the post, standing on the rail and positively towering over his competition. He was fractious at the start, though, where "he kicked and fussed so much that it was feared he would leave his race there."[33] Loftus, though, accustomed to the colt's antics, waited patiently for the starter to drop his flag, and when he did, Man o' War got away flying. With practiced hands, Loftus held the colt back, allowing the filly Retrieve to pass him and take the lead by a neck. They stayed just behind the filly until the stretch, when Loftus let the colt have some rein, and he took off like a shot, head high as his long stride stretched out over the Belmont track.[34]

By the time Man o' War crossed the wire, he was six lengths in front before anyone knew what had just happened. Loftus was practically vertical in his stirrups in his effort to pull up the colt and save his bountiful energy for another day. Retrieve staggered across the finish line well beaten, much like the rest of the field. It was an auspicious start for Samuel Riddle's newest racer and augured well for the future if the colt could stay healthy.[35]

Man o' War's dominant debut was the first step on the path that would take him toward a date with Sir Barton and a match race that would forever alter both horses' legacies.

8

Bumps in the Road

Unbeknownst to his connections or to anyone present at the Belmont Stakes, Sir Barton's win there had made history. The magnitude of the accomplishment would become obvious as the three races eventually coalesced into the now well-known championship sequence. Whereas American Pharoah's and Justify's wins would be greeted with worldwide elation and glee nearly one hundred years later, Sir Barton's accomplishment raised a far different fanfare, the celebrations limited to print comparisons to great horses of earlier eras and praises such as "horse of the decade." His Derby–Preakness double was a monumental achievement in itself and for the first part of the next decade would become the standard that others would try to duplicate. When Gallant Fox added the Belmont to his double in 1930, writers harkened back to Sir Barton's triple triumph, and thus the concept of the Triple Crown began to coalesce in the minds of everyone involved with racing, from fans to owner to trainers and many others. Until then, though, Sir Barton's wins in the Kentucky Derby, the Preakness Stakes, and the Belmont Stakes would remain separate wins, not the symbol of supremacy they would together become in later years. Even as Sir Barton crossed the finish line in New York, his dominance had its doubters, especially those who were fans of another chestnut named Purchase.

In the wake of his triumphant month of domination, Sir Barton was now pointed toward the latter half of the year, with meets at Empire City, Saratoga, Laurel, Havre de Grace, and Pimlico still to come. The Travers Stakes, the summertime derby, was one target, as were starts in the Empire City Derby and the Kenner Stakes. The $100,000 total winnings mark was just a start or two away, practically a fait accompli provided Sir Barton stayed sound.[1] Most importantly, with the handicap season on the horizon, New York handicapper Walter Vosburgh assigned Sir Barton the highest weight of 135 pounds for the Stuyvesant Handicap, a preview of things to come.[2]

Four wins in four races in thirty-two days might have been an ambitious streak for any horse, but for a horse as precariously sound as Sir Barton the load of those starts started to wear on his champion legs. Star Shoot had notoriously difficult soft hooves and passed that trait on to many of his progeny, including Sir Barton.[3] Those thin-walled hooves were difficult to shoe and caused the colt quite a bit of discomfort in his racing career. His inconsistent performances in races might be attributed to that discomfort.[4]

Sir Barton had already begun to show signs of soreness before the Belmont, but Ross and Bedwell ran him anyway, and the colt easily defeated the only two competitors who joined him at the post.[5] After the Belmont, though, the diagnosis for the soreness was bucked shins, also known as microfractures, in the front cannon bones.[6] The cannons are the larger bones in a horse's lower legs. Because the front legs strike the ground first when a horse is running, they are candidates for issues like this, especially when a horse runs so much in a short time, as Sir Barton had. The best treatment for this type of condition is rest, but with the number of rich stakes still to come in 1919 neither Bedwell nor Ross seemed keen on a protracted layoff for their champion.

With the colt's record-setting month complete but his soundness questionable, Bedwell gave him a short break, going for the Dwyer Stakes at Aqueduct on July 10. In order to make that start, Sir Barton had to continue his workouts, though Bedwell eased up on the colt as they prepared for that next start.[7] He thought the month between starts would be enough to keep the newly minted Triple Crown winner in fighting shape. He was wrong.

As Sir Barton prepared for his next start, he hit himself during a workout in early July, just days before the Dwyer.[8] The misstep did not cause any obvious injury, but Bedwell could tell that the colt had bruised a hoof. Sir Barton missed five days of training as a result, leaving his fitness for his next start in doubt.[9] As the day of the Dwyer approached and

Purchase's star ascended throughout June, it became apparent that Sir Barton's claim on the three-year-old division still needed defending and that he would have to defeat Purchase to do it.

Purchase had been considered among the top two-year-olds of 1918, but after his loss to Dunboyne and Sir Barton in the Futurity, the colt had fallen by the wayside, and the competition for the 1918 juvenile crown had come down to just Billy Kelly and Eternal. Purchase had two more starts in 1918, winning one and finishing third in another before being retired for the winter. Just before the end of the year, his owner, Brighton Stable, went out of business, and the colt was sold to Sam Hildreth.[10] As 1918 turned into 1919, Purchase was among the shortest-priced horses in the Kentucky Derby Winter Book.

Hildreth had been pointing his chestnut colt toward those spring stakes races that Sir Barton dominated, but Purchase got one of his hooves caught in a hayrack in his stall and injured himself just as the season was starting.[11] This injury meant that the colt did not have his first start of 1919 until early June, right as Sir Barton was finishing up his record-breaking run. Because Purchase missed all of those prestigious spring races and had yet to meet Sir Barton on the track, observers had no metric for comparing the two colts. As Sir Barton's spring campaign was winding down, Purchase was starting his season in style, leaving pundits antsy for the two to meet.

Recovered from his April injury, Purchase reeled off a win a week in June, first in an allowance race and then in the Stuyvesant and Southampton Handicaps. In his first start, Purchase was characteristically fractious at the barrier and even swerved out in the turn but easily took down a field of other three-year-olds by four lengths in a time that was less than a second off the track record.[12] Then, he faced six other three-year-olds, including Billy Kelly, in the Southampton Handicap, giving weight to all except the Ross gelding, and beat them all, despite being boxed in on the rail early on and forced wide to make up ground.[13] Those first two starts were enough to make everyone sit up and take notice, especially those who thought Purchase might be the only three-year-old left in the country with the potential to take Sir Barton down.

Purchase continued his winning ways, facing Eternal in races only days apart, winning the Stuyvesant but finishing second in the Brooklyn after a fractious start. In four races in less than four weeks, Hildreth's colt had racked up three victories and a second-place finish, demonstrating that the injury that had kept the colt out of the spring stakes races was behind him. It also opened up questions about the status of the three-year-old division. With that age group showing such depth, who was the best of the best? Could Purchase dethrone the "king of them all," Sir Barton? Or could the son of Star Shoot outrun another rival and prove once and for all that he was the best of 1919?

It was time to find out.

The game of racing has its hiccups that can appear at a moment's notice. Perhaps it is something as innocuous as a misstep during a workout that turns into a bruise that becomes an interruption to a workout schedule. Maybe it is an owner who feels the pressure of having the best horse of his age in his stable and a list of big-money stakes to come. For jockey Johnny Loftus, the hiccup was a suspension for rough riding that threatened his chance to ride Sir Barton in the Dwyer.

On July 7, just three days before the Dwyer, Johnny Loftus had the mount on a horse named Ting-A-Ling in Aqueduct's first race of the day, a six-and-a-half furlong selling race for three-year-olds and up. It was a no-name race, a paycheck really, but Loftus was arguably the best jockey in the country and prone to giving it his all. On Ting-A-Ling, he drove stride for stride with jockey Tommy Davies on Housemaid, the two of them far ahead of the field. The gelding continually pushed Housemaid out from the rail as Loftus pushed his mount harder and harder in the duel.[14] As the jockey whipped and drove Ting-A-Ling, the gelding began to bear out even more, pushing Housemaid toward the outside rail, effectively interfering with the latter's ability to run her race. As the two flashed under the wire, it was difficult to tell which horse had come out ahead. Some thought that Loftus had managed to get Ting-A-Ling a nose in front; the judges thought that the finish did not matter because Loftus and his mount had interfered with Housemaid, and thus they disqualified Ting-A-Ling and placed him second.[15]

Not only did Loftus lose the race via disqualification, but the judges also decided to suspend him for rough riding. With only three days until the Dwyer, the jockey who had ridden Sir Barton in all of his wins thus far in 1919 potentially could miss his chance to ride the Triple Crown winner in this next start. Fortunately, the Aqueduct judges decided that two-day suspension was enough of a punishment for his performance on Ting-A-Ling.[16]

Loftus did not excuse his performance but did try to explain himself. Ting-A-Ling, prone to bearing out, usually ran with a burr bit to keep him straight but lost the burr when one of the assistant starters knocked it out at the barrier.[17] Without it, Loftus found it more difficult to keep the gelding straight. He accepted his punishment with grace and waited for his chance to ride Sir Barton in the Dwyer Stakes.

Formerly known as the Brooklyn Derby, the Dwyer Stakes was a midsummer race for three-year-olds at Aqueduct. First run at Gravesend Race Course on Coney Island, the race moved to Aqueduct when racing resumed after the Hart–Agnew ban on gambling in 1908 forced New York racetracks to cease operations, and Gravesend, among other tracks, never reopened. When the race returned, officials renamed it the Dwyer Stakes after Michael and Phillip Dwyer, the brothers who had built Gravesend.[18] By 1919, the race was 1⅛ miles, offering a purse of $6,000. With Saratoga's late-summer meet and its prestigious races coming up, the Dwyer was a nice tune-up for Sir Barton.

Other potential starters for the race included Eternal, who had bested Purchase in the Brooklyn Handicap nearly two weeks earlier; Purchase, who had yet to face Sir Barton in 1919; and three others. The intrigue for this particular confrontation was high. Sir Barton had beaten Eternal three times already. Eternal had just beaten Purchase in the Brooklyn Handicap, but Purchase had spotted his rival 12 pounds in that race and still managed to finish a couple of lengths behind him despite the bad start. In this case, that victory meant that Eternal would now carry more weight than Purchase for this 1⅛-mile race.[19]

With his stellar record behind him, Sir Barton was assigned the heaviest impost, 127 pounds, giving weight to every other starter, including 6 pounds to Eternal and 9 pounds to Purchase. Surely, though, the Star Shoot colt, who had won more than one race cantering, had this race in the bag, especially when the day of the Dwyer dawned with rain sheeting over New York City, turning a hard track into a soft and sloppy one.[20] That might have turned off some horses' connections, but this dreary day shone bright for Commander Ross.

The commander knew that his colt had a bruised hoof after striking himself during a workout. He also knew that his champion had been showing signs of soreness before the Belmont, but Commander Ross was confident that the wet going could make Sir Barton and his shelly hooves more comfortable, especially with these question marks about his condition. The wet start to Dwyer Day became the deciding factor: Ross opted to start the colt, despite Bedwell's apprehensions about Sir Barton's soundness. The trainer agreed to run his charge provided his boss did not bet on the race.[21] Ross agreed; he might not be able to gamble on the race, but the $6,000 purse was difficult to pass up, especially with the mythical $100,000 mark within sight. Thus, a sore and tired Sir Barton went to the post on a dreary summer day in New York, with only two others at the barrier with him, Purchase and Crystal Ford.

The crowd that had braved the rainy weather wanted to see this triumvirate—Sir Barton, Purchase, and Eternal—confront each other finally but were soon disappointed to see that one would decline the issue. Eternal, whose presence had promised to make the Dwyer the most exciting three-year-old race since Sir Barton's dominant run had started, scratched at the last minute, scared off by the off-and-on showers that July day. Trainer Kimball Patterson did not want Eternal to run against both Sir Barton and Purchase in the slop, especially when Eternal would be giving weight to the upstart Purchase.[22] That withdrawal made the race a three-horse affair, the intermittent rain tapering off just as they took the track.

The three stood at the barrier on Aqueduct's sloppy dirt oval—Purchase on the rail, Sir Barton on the outside, Crystal Ford in between them. Purchase engaged in his usual misbehavior, but starter Mars Cassidy got the three away within two minutes despite Purchase's antics. Sir Barton won the start, taking the lead in this 1⅛-mile race, with Crystal Ford behind him and Purchase stalking them both, only a half-length behind. Johnny Loftus had to tap his mount a couple of times; he knew Sir Barton could be sluggish at times early in races, and today was one of those days. This running order, Sir Barton–Crystal Ford–Purchase, stayed that way for the first six furlongs, with the son of Star Shoot maintaining a lead of a length or two throughout. His early fractions were fast for a sloppy track, but as they exited the final turn and straightened out into the stretch, it was clear that the pace was taking its toll on the Triple Crown winner.[23]

At the top of the stretch, fans could still see daylight between Sir Barton and his competition, with Purchase looking beaten as he was still pinned on the rail, a length or so back of the other two. Then, as they approached the mile mark and with one more furlong to go, Purchase made his move. The rail cut off as a possible route to the front, jockey Willie Knapp took to the outside, giving Purchase his head and summarily passing the outclassed Crystal Ford. Knapp had his sights set on the front-running Sir Barton, determined to catch and then pass him. As they crossed into the last furlong of the race, Purchase caught up to Sir Barton, despite the sting of Loftus's whip on Sir Barton's flank. The Triple Crown winner tried to stay with Purchase in this final drive, head to head with Purchase for about a sixteenth of a mile before he finally gave way to the fresher colt, who finished three lengths in front.[24] Purchase's time was 1:52⅗, two-fifths of a second faster than Sir Barton's Preakness time, which was run on a fast track. Since Sir Barton led the race for the first mile, losing his lead only in that last furlong, the time tells a story itself.

Sure, Sir Barton did not mind running on a sloppy track. Sure, in theory, a muddy track suited his shelly hooves better because it was softer, as Commander Ross had assumed. Bedwell had instructed Loftus to take Sir Barton to the front, despite Loftus's own instincts that the colt might have preferred to run from behind.[25] Loftus tried to keep Sir Barton more on the outside, where the track was firmer, but as Sir Barton ran, he "splashed the water and ooze backward," the track perhaps sloppier than Loftus might have liked.[26] In order to run those fractions, Sir Barton, carrying 9 more pounds than Purchase, had to expend more energy to overcome the slower track and keep his lead. On any other day, that might have been enough to beat even Purchase, a fresher horse with a longer stride and carrying less weight. Yet on this day Purchase was able to pull ahead of the Triple Crown winner. Tired from a long campaign, Sir Barton had to work harder to run as he had in the past, and the deep going further increased that workload. The slop was deep enough that the colt came back to the barn missing a shoe.[27] Already difficult to shoe, Sir Barton was prone to shedding shoes in races; in this case, the muck had forced the shoe on his left front leg loose, another impediment to success that the colt had to overcome to finish second.[28] Ultimately, the going, the weight, and the shoe were all too much, but

Sir Barton had held on gamely, surrendering only in that last furlong of the Dwyer Stakes. The margin did not matter, however; the loss to Purchase did.

Commander Ross was philosophical about his champion's defeat, understanding that the colt was not as good as he had been in his previous starts and satisfied that his star had finished the race sound. Bedwell acknowledged that Sir Barton was off his game and waxed positive that his horse would beat Purchase if and when the two met again.[29] After this performance, it was clear, though, that Sir Barton's spring campaign had left him tired and sore. In order to be sound and ready for the fall, he needed a layoff, and thus the Triple Crown winner was put on the shelf for the remainder of the summer.

What this performance in the Dwyer did not do was seal Sir Barton's status as the champion of his age group.[30] His record of four wins and one second in five starts were all in prestigious races, the most famous and richest of the spring. Purchase, though, had five wins in six starts, with only a second to Eternal in his loss column. Sure, Purchase's wins were all in races that were not nearly as prestigious or as rich as the Kentucky Derby or the Preakness Stakes, but they all had come just after Sir Barton's dominant month of racing.[31] Turf writers were itching for a rivalry, and since most of the 1919 crop of three-year-olds had yet to inject intrigue into the division, the writers created that intrigue. Despite his four wins in four weeks and the large amount of purse money that came with those wins, Sir Barton was still apparently not quite the "king of them all," even with all of the praise heaped upon him after his Belmont win. Purchase's presence was enough to cast doubt on Sir Barton's dominance until the two met again. With half of the year still to go, the chances of another meeting between the two were good—as long as both stayed sound.

9

Ups and Downs

Humbled by Purchase, the ascendant Sir Barton found his rise arrested, done in by a turned shoe and a slow track. While the rest of the Ross Stable continued racing, Sir Barton got a well-deserved two-month vacation. Though he went with the rest of the stable to Saratoga for that late summer meet, he did not start a race there, despite endless speculation about his return to the track and his next confrontation with Purchase, a meeting that supposedly would decide the three-year-old division once and for all.

As Sir Barton's absence lengthened, Purchase's star ascended even higher. Rather than being "the king of them all" still, Sir Barton had not just been dethroned. No, his defeat was "worse than that, for no Bolsheviki could have knocked a reigning monarch from his pedestal more rudely than Purchase upset the Canadian's colt."[1] Hannibal's win in the $12,500 Travers Stakes brought out more detractors, who saw the race for the best three-year-old to be more wide open than ever.[2]

And while Purchase and Sir Barton had their merits debated in print, a two-year-old named Man o' War threatened to eclipse them all with his own stellar performances at the Spa.

Purchase's defeat of the Triple Crown winner brought him to the front of the pack in the debate about the three-year-olds' championship, and the performances he turned in during Sir Barton's absence only added fuel to the fire. Nine days after the Dwyer, Purchase faced only two others in the Empire City Derby, winning the 1⅛-mile race with ease despite giving more than 10 pounds to the other starters.[3] Next, he set his sights on the Spa, joining War Cloud and three others in the 1¼-mile Saratoga

Handicap. He gave weight to every other horse and came home in front in 2:02⅖, just one-fifth of a second off the record for that race.[4]

Nearly three weeks later, Purchase continued his dominance in the one-mile Saranac Handicap for three-year-olds, defeating his only two opponents after six others scratched. He gave more than 25 pounds to The Trump and Passing Showers and still made the race look like nothing more than a workout.[5] Neither of his competitors ever threatened him, and in his next start just six days later, the Huron Handicap, Purchase faced another field of his peers—again minus Sir Barton—and dominated once again. Included in his list of vanquished competitors this go-round was Hannibal, whose performance in the Travers had aroused some talk of his own share of the three-year-olds' championship, but, despite his 8-pound advantage over Purchase, Hannibal was not able to challenge the ascendant Hildreth colt over the 1³⁄₁₆-mile course.[6] It was Purchase's fifth victory in his past six starts, demonstrating yet again why he was in the conversation for the three-year-olds' crown.[7]

Then, only four days later, as the Saratoga meet was set to conclude, Purchase faced the great gelding Exterminator and others in the Saratoga Cup, a long-distance event of 1¾ miles. In this weight-for-age event, three-year-old Purchase was assigned only 116 pounds, whereas four-year-old Exterminator carried 126 pounds, a decided advantage for a horse on a hot streak. Despite the advantage, though, the gelding was too much for Purchase; Exterminator was the master of the long-distance race, and the 1¾-mile race was his easily.[8] Purchase apologists blamed the sheeting rain that had mucked up the track and jockey Willie Knapp for dropping his whip just a furlong before the finish.[9] Despite the loss, it spoke to Purchase's quality that the only horse who had beaten him in this stretch of starts was the legendary Exterminator.

While Purchase was burning up the track and Sir Barton remained barn bound, another chestnut colt was dominating the juvenile set at Saratoga and, unbeknownst to all around him, building a legend to last many lifetimes.

As the summer of 1919 went on, New York racing went from Belmont Park in early June to Jamaica and Aqueduct and then finally to Saratoga for the month of August. Samuel Riddle sent Man o' War on the summer racing trail in New York, his trainer Louis Feustel working hard to keep the big red chestnut on edge as his dominant wins at Belmont and Jamaica earned him the unprecedented honor of carrying 130 pounds each time he took the track at Aqueduct and Saratoga. The heavy weights, though, did not seem to matter to the two-year-old; he put away his competition with ease each time he set foot on the track.

From the get-go, the son of Fair Play and Mahubah grabbed everyone's attention. Debuting at Belmont in June certainly gave him a prime racing audience; his maiden race came just days before Sir Barton's dominant win in the Belmont Stakes. After his maiden win in his first race, Man o' War was noted as "one of the finest looking two-year-olds in some time."[10] He continued dominating the competition through his starts in June and July, but once he made it to Saratoga, people looked for a dark horse to emerge and challenge Man o' War. By the time he vanquished his competition in the United States Hotel Stakes on August 2, it was clear that this two-year-old was unlike any other seen in recent memory.

Man o' War was so singular that Phil Chinn, well-known breeder and trainer, and Montfort Jones, Oklahoma oil magnate and recent entry into the racing world, went to Samuel Riddle with an outrageous offer: $100,000 for his two-year-old.[11] When Riddle turned Jones down, Jones upped the ante to $150,000, an unprecedented price for a two-year-old.[12] Riddle was a businessman, though, and no doubt he saw the long-term benefits of his initial $5,000 investment in the Belmont-bred son of Fair Play.

The colt looked unbeatable; in six starts, he had carried progressively more weight and given much more to his competition but still had beaten all of them. Certainly no one could blame Riddle for wanting to hold onto Man o' War, imagining the possibilities of what one so talented on the racetrack could do once he entered the breeding shed. He was the new Colin incarnate, on his way to winning exorbitant sums of money. The praise sounded familiar; this was the same acclaim that had been laid upon Sir Barton in May and June. The $50,000 that Madden had offered for the Hamburg-bred son of Star Shoot paled next to the $150,000 Jones had laid on the table for Man o' War.[13] Sir Barton's loss in the Dwyer and his time off to recoup had put the Triple Crown winner on the proverbial backburner, and the racing world had found its next star in his absence.

If Sir Barton's loss dimmed his star this much, what would a loss do for Man o' War? Was it possible that any horse could beat Big Red?

Less than a decade earlier, the *Titanic* had set sail on its maiden voyage with the supposition that it was unsinkable—until the ship hit an iceberg in the North Atlantic and took fifteen hundred passengers to the bottom of the ocean with it. Man o' War might have looked as unsinkable as the *Titanic*, but August 13, 1919, was proof that, like the *Titanic*, nothing in life is a sure thing.

Marshall Whiting Cassidy was the well-known New York–area starter and racing official, so well-known that jockey Johnny Loftus knew the small tells that preceded Cassidy's lift of the barrier. On August 12, Cassidy was seen celebrating his birthday with friends at hotelier Tom Luther's lakeside home, a party that featured a number of well-known faces from the Saratoga community, including some horsemen of note. When it was clear that the birthday boy was not going to make it to work the next day, Saratoga had no understudy for the legendary starter. Plucked from his duties as a placing judge, Charles Pettingill suddenly found himself dropped into the role of starter for the day.[14]

Pettingill had experience as a starter, but it had been nearly three decades since he had had a go-round—a notorious day in 1893 in which his inability to control the jockeys had resulted in the horses running in the American Derby endured ninety minutes of false starts.[15] Wednesday, August 13, 1919, had only seven races on the card, including the Sanford Memorial Stakes. The day was supposed to be one like any other: some claiming races, a couple of handicaps, and another juvenile trial. Man o' War was among a field of seven in the Sanford that featured at least two other good colts, Upset and Golden Broom, whose previous start had tapped him as having the potential to challenge Big Red.

By the time the horses lined up for the start of the Sanford, Loftus had already had to deal with Pettingill in the previous race, the Watervliet Handicap. The substitute starter was having difficulties getting the jockeys to behave; whereas Cassidy would not tolerate the tricks that jocks might employ to get the coveted flying start, Pettingill could not muster the authority to keep everyone in line, an already tough task given the fractiousness of horses at the start.[16] Man o' War was known to break through the barrier more than once before settling down long enough for a race to start. Today, though, Big Red was not the one breaking through; it was the horse that was supposed to be his only competition, Golden Broom.

Golden Broom's false starts meant that it took a minute or two to settle everyone back down once the horse was brought back into line. Johnny Loftus kept his colt quiet and attentive rather than stirring him up for a fast start; his orders were to fall in behind Golden Broom, who the Man o' War team anticipated would go to the front in this six-furlong race. Finally, Pettingill was satisfied that everyone was in place and ready to go, and he pulled the trigger—leaving Man o' War a second behind.[17]

How Man o' War missed the start is a source of controversy nearly a century later. Some accounts had the colt being moved back a couple of steps by an assistant starter as they were trying to get everyone in line at the start. Another had Loftus turned toward the inner rail, waiting for a chance to get back in line.[18] Speculation and retellings even had the horse turned around backward. The mistake likely came when jockey Willie Knapp on Upset moved his colt in the right position for Pettingill to think that they were all in line right, but Loftus happened to have his head turned away, still awaiting his chance to line up again.[19]

Despite the bad start, the twenty-eight-foot stride Man o' War possessed helped him make up the ground he lost. He could have easily overtaken or at least come alongside his quickest challenger; Loftus, though, stuck to Riddle's strategy and kept the colt behind. By the second furlong, the field started to close in around Man o' War, and suddenly Loftus found himself boxed in. As front-runners Golden Broom and Upset blazed through the first quarter and then the half-mile, Man o' War had nowhere to go. Golden Broom was on the rail, Upset to his right; despite his best efforts, Loftus's only option was to go around them. On a two-year-old carrying 130 pounds, even Loftus, who knew Man o' War intimately from five previous races plus months of schooling, worried about the colt's limits.[20]

As the field rounded the final turn into the stretch, Golden Broom reached his limit. Also carrying 130 pounds, the colt could not carry that much weight and continue to battle Upset. He was on the rail, though, which meant that avenue was still closed to Loftus on Man o' War. Knowing that Big Red was on his heels and that Golden Broom was done, Knapp desperately called on Upset to move faster. Carrying 15 fewer pounds than Man o' War, Upset sprinted those last yards, Knapp pleading with the colt to hold on.[21] Man o' War was closing fast, but the distance to the wire was shrinking as quickly as he was covering it. The big red colt possessed everything he needed to pass Upset except the very thing that he needed most: distance.

They flashed under the wire, Upset maybe a half-length or even a neck in front. Just after the wire, Man o' War caught and then passed Upset, but it was too little, too late.[22] The legend that the *Titanic* was unsinkable had not originated with White Star Lines, and the idea that Man o' War was unbeatable did not come from Riddle or Feustel, but from the turf writers who heaped the same acclaim on Man o' War as they had on Sir Barton mere weeks earlier—that is, until the Dwyer. Now, would Man o' War suffer the same from the exposure of his fallibility?

The defeat, however, seemed to have the opposite effect, enhancing the Riddle colt's reputation. The crowd might have cheered Upset when he returned triumphant, walking into the winner's circle, but they also cheered for the red Riddle colt, their enthusiasm for him undiminished.[23] For Man o' War, the heroic nature of his loss, overcoming a poor start and a bumpy trip to nearly overtake Upset, garnered him even more praise and heaped blame on jockey Johnny Loftus, who stood accused of a bad ride, a reputation that followed him even after his death in 1976. Sir Barton's performance in the Dwyer came despite losing a shoe in the heavy going; he had been in the lead, though, and overtaken by Purchase. In the Sanford, Man o' War had come from behind, powering through a bad start and a challenging trip, and nearly caught Upset. No doubt the Dwyer had left fans feeling diminished, but the Sanford left the throng at Saratoga thrilled despite their disappointment at Man o' War's loss. His performance was heroic, whereas Sir Barton's had been more of a letdown, his reputation deflating when he was unable to duplicate his past striking performances.

Man o' War now was Sysonby, the colt who had lost only once because his groom had drugged him, the only way that colt could have met defeat. For Man o' War, the horse was not at fault; forces external to him were. Ten days later Big Red reinforced his claim on the two-year-olds' championship when he met Upset in the Grand Union Hotel Stakes and beat the Whitney colt. The win put the Sanford in the past, making it a footnote on the red colt's record, but Johnny Loftus suffered that air of blame throughout his remaining starts on Man o' War and for years afterward.

Not quite a month after losing a shoe and the Dwyer at Aqueduct, Sir Barton returned to training at Saratoga as H. G. Bedwell watched and waited to decide the colt's next move.[24] The trainer wanted to take it slow in his effort to get the colt ready for the fall stakes. As his supposed rival Purchase came and went at Saratoga, turf writers speculated that the two would meet again there, but that confrontation never materialized. Sir Barton stayed on the comeback trail, but Bedwell decided to save his racing for September.

With a win in the Hopeful Stakes on closing day at Saratoga, Man o' War continued his devastation of the two-year-old division, devouring all challengers, including a promising filly named Constancy acquired by Ross in an attempt to derail the big red train. The Hopeful marked the end of the summer meet at Saratoga, which meant it was time to make a pit stop in New York before heading back to Maryland for the fall meets. Bedwell shipped the Ross horses to Belmont, where Milkmaid won the Belair Handicap, and then Billy Kelly and Cudgel finished in the money in their starts. Their stay in New York was not long, though, and the Ross Stable returned home to Maryland in early September.[25]

Eight weeks had passed since Sir Barton's first loss of 1919, and now Bedwell had determined that his champion colt was ready to run. At $65,350 in purse money won, Sir Barton needed to add more victories to his record to try for the $100,000 mark that Colin had reached in his third year. It was time for the little big horse to make his mark on the racing world again.

The September 1919 issue of *Vanity Fair* magazine featured an article by sportswriter O'Neil Sevier titled "Sir Barton, the Chestnut Hope," in which Sevier called the colt "the new racing idol [who] deserves his fame."[26] Though the article came out in September, Sevier clearly wrote his missive on Ross's champion colt before the colt's defeat in the Dwyer.

In the eight weeks since then, the dominance that Sir Barton had shown in winning the Kentucky Derby, the Preakness, the Withers, and the Belmont seemed to dissipate in the harsh light of the Saratoga performances by both his conqueror Purchase and the upstart juvenile Man o' War. Sir Barton still held the lead in money won for 1919, but he could not catch a break in terms of reputation, for many spoke of handing the three-year-old-of-the-year honors to Purchase, especially after the colt ran away with the Saratoga Handicap.

After the stint in New York, the Ross Stable was back in Maryland and readying for the fall meets on its home turf. Sir Barton was ready to come back and stake his claim to the three-year-old division one more time. On Sunday, September 7, the cusp of the opening of the fall meets, the stable arrived back in Maryland. Sir Barton and stablemate Billy Kelly hit the track for three-furlong workouts that saw both colts going the distance in 0:37.[27] Clearly the stable's top two three-year-olds were ready for the barrier at Havre de Grace. Next up for both was the Hip Hip Hooray Purse on September 11, Havre de Grace's opening day.

Recent rains had the track rated a vague "good," but showers that came in during the day's racing made the going muddier.[28] Scratches abounded, disappointing the crowd of seven thousand that had come out to see the opening-day features.[29] The field for the Hip Hip Hooray had included Milkmaid, Ross's good filly; Sun Briar, Willis Sharpe Kilmer's good handicap horse; and a number of other horses with subpar records and low imposts. By the time the horses went to the post, the field was down to seven horses from the original fifteen entries: Billy Kelly, Sir Barton, and five others. Sir Barton carried 120 pounds, as did Billy Kelly, giving 15 pounds or more to each of the other horses in the race, who carried 105 pounds or less.

The field stood at the barrier, with Sir Barton on the rail and Billy Kelly in the middle of the field in the fourth post.[30] The track in front of them was muddy, the same sort of going in which Sir Barton had sloshed his way to a rousing victory over Billy Kelly in the Kentucky Derby nearly four months earlier. Today's route was four furlongs fewer, however, a distance more suited to Billy Kelly's running style than to Sir Barton's.[31] With that layoff behind him, the son of Star Shoot was the fresher horse, in theory, but how would he race this time, ready or rusty?

At the start, Billy Kelly took the lead for a few strides, but on the rail

Sir Barton jumped into the fray, sticking his head in front of his stable-mate. Earl Sande held Billy Kelly back just enough to allow his stable-mate to set a speedy pace and run on the lead until the last quarter, when Sande gave the gelding some rein. For a furlong, the two battled for the lead, Sir Barton a neck in front. In the last yards, though, as the six-furlong sprint came to a rapid end, a tired Sir Barton yielded to Billy Kelly and held on just long enough to finish second, a head in front of a surging Midnight Sun.[32]

The Hip Hip Hooray showed that Sir Barton still had some of that Triple Crown form, though "he seemed unable to fully extend himself in the murky going."[33] Winning would have been an ideal way to start off the second half of Sir Barton's three-year-old season, but his trainer had taken the shelly-hooved champion's return to training slowly; this second-place finish was a good sign that the colt was rounding back into form.[34] With that sprint under Sir Barton's belt, H. G. Bedwell carded his champion colt for another start just two days later in the Potomac Handicap.

Now that Sir Barton was back on the track, he could reclaim his rightful place as the top three-year-old in the nation. Purchase had already staked his own claim to that status. With his loss in their only meeting, Sir Barton seemed to be at a disadvantage, and certainly the loss in the Hip Hip Hooray did not help. Fans and turf writers alike were spoiling for a chance to settle the matter once and for all. The day before the Potomac, Sam Hildreth wired racing officials at Havre de Grace that he was sending a three-year-old to run in that race. Speculation abounded that Purchase would be the one coming to town to meet Sir Barton at the barrier. Both would carry 132 pounds.[35] It would be the perfect time to decide who was king of the threes for 1919.

That confrontation was not to be. Two days after the Hip Hip Hooray, both Billy Kelly and Sir Barton were back for the Potomac Handicap, a 1 1/16-mile race for three-year-olds with a $10,000 purse. With them in the field were the filly Milkmaid and only two other horses, Be Frank and Clean Gone. Hildreth's starter, whoever he had intended it to be, was absent, and the question of supremacy was tabled for another day.

Another large crowd was on hand this Saturday, expecting more great racing and disappointed to see that the Potomac was going to be light on competition for the Ross Stable.[36] As a handicap race, the imposts were assigned according to achievement; of course, Sir Barton had the heaviest impost, 132 pounds, despite his recent losses. Billy Kelly, who had run more races and had more wins to his name, carried 125 pounds, and Milkmaid 117. Sir Barton gave as much as 32 pounds to the lightest-weight horse, Clean Gone, who carried only 100 pounds.[37] With Johnny Loftus away riding Man o' War at Belmont, Sir Barton once again was without his usual pilot, so one of Ross's other contract riders, Tommy Nolan, had the mount for this race.

With three starters in this race, the Ross Stable had scared away any other horses that might have been tempted to challenge the stable and its deep roster of three-year-olds, leaving only two entrants from other stables. Sir Barton stood on the outside in the fifth post, Billy Kelly to his left, and Milkmaid on the rail. Billy Kelly got the best of the start, followed by Sir Barton and Milkmaid. Though both Milkmaid and Billy Kelly broke in front of Sir Barton, their riders, Schuttinger and Sande, "waited for Nolan on Sir Barton," allowing the colt to pass them both for the lead.[38]

The Triple Crown winner had a two-length lead before the first quarter had passed and never relinquished that front-running position. Sure, Billy Kelly could have been taken back to hang just off the pace and stalk, and the slower fractions that Sir Barton was running gave Billy Kelly ample room to make such a move. Yet Sande held back, opting instead to form a pocket with Milkmaid. On the rail, Milkmaid stayed just ahead of Billy Kelly, who ran toward the outside, forming a barrier to keep any other horses from making a run at the front-running Sir Barton.[39] As a result, Be Frank's jockey, Harold Cassity, took to the outside to go around both the gelding and the filly. Though Cassity was not able to catch the leaders, his move brought Be Frank closer to the trio than if he had he stayed more to the inside.[40]

In the end, the 132 pounds Sir Barton carried made little difference in his performance as he flashed under the wire a length and a half in front of Billy Kelly, who had made up ground in the stretch to nip Milkmaid at the finish.[41] The Potomac was a one–two–three finish for Commander Ross, with his best three-year-olds duking it out over the 1$\frac{1}{16}$ miles. Interestingly, though, the fractions plus the strategy employed by the three jockeys in this race suggest that Ross and Bedwell might have declared Sir Barton to win. That information was not posted, as the rule would have obligated Commander Ross to do, but the way those three ran made it clear that Earl Sande on Billy Kelly and Andy Schuttinger on Milkmaid had orders.[42] Whatever the intent behind the arrangement, the win "showed great improvement," as Sir Barton seemed to benefit from his previous start in the Hip Hip Hooray.[43]

Having the top-three finishers in the Potomac netted Commander Ross $9,900, a nice payout for one race. However, not everyone was so excited about the Ross Stable's performance in the Potomac; the *Washington Post* complained about the one–two–three Ross finish, calling it "not good for the turf and hardly [representative of] good sportsmanship."[44] Continuing the commander's good fortune, the stable won two other races with Constancy and Boniface on that day's card.[45] The stable was enjoying another banner year, leading in purses won and standing at the top of most of the standings, with a top handicap horse, Cudgel, and the top three-year-old, Sir Barton, in its barn.

While Sir Barton and company were dominating the Potomac at Havre de Grace, two other horses of note were bringing down the house at Belmont Park. On the same day, September 13, Man o' War met the barrier for the six-furlong Futurity with nine other two-year-olds and blew them away as he had in nearly every start in his brief career. He hung just behind Dominique and John P. Grier until the stretch, when Johnny Loftus moved him around the front-runners to take the lead at his leisure. Man o' War made his last start of the year a memorable one, taking home $26,650 for his romp.[46]

In winning the Belmont Futurity, Man o' War sealed his place as the greatest of two-year-olds to that point, even more so than Colin had. Handicapper George Gonzalez had seen every running of the Futurity from its inception in 1888, and he declared the son of Fair Play "in a class all by himself."[47] Johnny Loftus's ailing mother, Eleanor, had come in from Chicago to see her son thunder home on the back of the greatest, sobbing in the winner's circle as her son celebrated his victory on the big red colt.[48] The Futurity capped off a thrilling year for the colt and his jockey, who was finally back in favor after the debacle in the Sanford— or so he thought. As prognosticators looked forward to Man o' War at three, Loftus hopped a train back to Maryland, the best jockey in the country ready to ride for the Ross Stable once again.

On the same day, Purchase had his next start in the newly inaugurated Jockey Club Stakes, a race limited to three-year-olds. No one, not even Dunboyne, who had beaten Purchase and Sir Barton in the 1918 Belmont Futurity, dared challenge Purchase, resulting in a walkover.[49] That result brought him to nine wins in eleven starts, with only two second-place finishes to blemish his record. His wins had come in races with less prestige than those Sir Barton had won, but these performances were enough to earn Purchase a place in the conversation about the best three-year-old of the year. The only way to decide which colt was the best was to have the two meet on the racetrack one more time. Sam Hildreth sent Purchase on to Laurel in preparation for the fall stakes races there, including another possible meeting with his rival, Sir Barton.[50]

Modern fans are familiar with the incentives that organizations will use to drive fans to spend their money on an event. Nearly a hundred years ago, race tracks faced the same need to attract fans to the races on any given day, especially as the antigambling legislation of the previous decade evolved into the postwar era of diversion. Americans were looking for distraction, a chance to lose themselves in something light when the news had been dark for so long. Attempting to capitalize on this search for entertainment, Havre de Grace decided to add a new race to its card for September 24: the Record Purse.

The idea behind this race was simple: open up a race to entries three years old and older, use an allowance format to give top horses a break in weights, and then add the incentive of doubling the purse if a horse finishes with a certain time. This format allowed Sir Barton to carry only 110 pounds and Cudgel 115 pounds, even though they had winning records. If the winning time were 1:36⅖ or better, the purse would have an extra $2,500 added to it.[51]

So eleven days after his win in the Potomac, Sir Barton was back on Havre de Grace's dirt oval for the Record Purse, the track mucky after the recent days' rain. As the barrier flew up, Midnight Sun and The Porter got away in stride, but the Triple Crown winner stumbled at the start, needing a few strides to settle in behind Midnight Sun and Sinn Feiner.[52] The Porter stayed at his flank as they stalked the front-runners. As the two on the lead began to tire, the opportunity to take the lead and close out the win came, and Sir Barton took it. He had company, though, with The Porter making his run at the lead as well. As the two leaders rounded that last turn toward home, The Porter was able to kick into another gear and pass the struggling Sir Barton.[53]

In the end, despite the name "Record Purse," the fractions for the mile fell well short of the record of 1:36⅖ that organizers were hoping for, owing in large part to the slow going at Havre de Grace that day. For Sir Barton, it was his second defeat in three races. With that defeat came the inevitable speculation that the colt had fallen off the form that had brought him his earlier wins.[54] With Havre de Grace's fall meet coming to a close and the focus moving to Laurel, however, the Triple Crown winner still had a number of chances to return to form and prove he deserved his place at the top of the heap.

A start in the Havre de Grace Handicap and the chance to face older, more experienced horses were the perfect opportunity for him to do just that.

In this era of racing, the handicap was the king of all of the races, and because the racing scene was smaller, a handicap could feature multiple prestigious horses in the same field.[55] Champions such as Exterminator and Cudgel would often cross paths in such races at Havre de Grace, Belmont, and Saratoga. The Ross Stable was deep in handicap talent, with 1916 Preakness winner Damrosch, Triple Crown winner Sir Barton, top-rated sprinter Billy Kelly, and champion older horse Cudgel, who possessed an impressive record in handicaps. Commander Ross, thanks to his profligate spending and sage advice from his trainer, had amassed a stable that had a hand in many of the day's big handicaps. It was no surprise, then, that Ross entered a number of his top racers in the Havre de Grace Handicap, one of the features of the fall meet at Havre de Grace.

Billy Kelly, Sir Barton, and Cudgel were originally to start in the Havre de Grace Handicap, but Bedwell sent Billy Kelly to the Susquehanna Handicap instead, where he carried top weight and set a track record in the win.[56] That left Sir Barton and Cudgel to go to the post for the 1⅛-mile Havre de Grace Handicap. Also in the field with the two Ross horses were the 1918 Kentucky Derby winner Exterminator and The Porter, the conqueror of Sir Barton in his previous start. Owing to his superior handicap record and reputation, Cudgel carried the top weight of 129 pounds, with Exterminator assigned 126 pounds, and both The Porter and Sir Barton 124 pounds.[57] The field had four other horses, all assigned lighter weights, including Midnight Sun, but the attention was on four names in the race.

Johnny Loftus was back from New York and returned to his duties with the Ross starters, but he was not on the back of the horse who had carried him to those springtime classic victories.[58] Instead, America's best jockey had the mount on Cudgel, and Joe Metcalf was assigned to Sir Barton. Were these jockey assignments an indication of Bedwell's strategy for the race, a signal that Cudgel was the preferred Ross starter over Sir Barton? With Exterminator in the race and getting a weight break of 3 pounds, Ross would need the best jockey in the business to help him get Cudgel by the 1918 Kentucky Derby winner. For Sir Barton, this was his fourth start in less than three weeks. How would he hold up under the demands of this schedule and this field?

At the start, Sir Barton stood on the outside, in the eighth post, with Cudgel, Exterminator, and The Porter all in the middle of the pack at posts four, five, and six.[59] Away from the barrier, the Triple Crown winner jumped out to the front at the start of the race.[60] Loftus kept Cudgel at the back of the pack, content to trail the field as Sir Barton set fast early fractions. As the field rounded into the final turn, the Triple Crown winner still led, but Loftus cued Cudgel to move, the two going around the field on the outside, eating up ground. As they rounded into the stretch, Cudgel started to overtake Sir Barton, followed by Exterminator, but Metcalf held the colt in position, cutting the Kilmer gelding off.[61] This gave Cudgel a lane to take the lead while keeping Willie Knapp and Exterminator at bay. Finally, in the last furlong, Exterminator was able to inch past a tiring Sir Barton and then attempted to overtake Cudgel, jockey and horse straining for every inch.[62]

At the wire, Cudgel held on to his half-length lead over Exterminator, with Sir Barton only a neck back of the 1918 Kentucky Derby winner. The race time, 1:50, set a new track record for 1⅛ miles. Cudgel's triumph capped off another three-win day for Commander Ross, after Billy Kelly's and His Choice's wins earlier in the day.[63]

Immediately after the race, Willie Knapp went to the judges with a claim of foul against Joe Metcalf on Sir Barton, charging the jockey with herding.[64] The claim was denied, however, but the unseemly nature of Cudgel's win, with the clear use of Sir Barton as the pacemaker for his stablemate, left a bad taste for some. The Ross horses dominated yet again, and the depth of the talent within Ross's roster did afford Bedwell a chance to manipulate the end result to some extent.[65] As with the Ross triumvirate in the Potomac, it looked as if the other Ross starters were in the Havre de Grace Handicap only as insurance for the preferred entrant. For Harry Price of the *Washington Post,* this performance was problematic, as "patrons of racing . . . like to see contests and trainers who pick such soft spots for their horses are rare fortunately," no doubt leveling his charge at Bedwell.[66] Indeed, Sir Barton seemed not only up to the task of pacemaker, but the close finish between Cudgel, Extermi-nator, and Sir Barton implies that perhaps the colt could have done more had Metcalf allowed him to compete rather than give preference to Lof-tus on Cudgel.

Whatever the perception of both Sir Barton's and Cudgel's perfor-mances, the closing of Havre de Grace and the start of racing at Laurel shifted the focus back to deciding the champion three-year-old of the year. Hildreth had already sent his string to Laurel, meaning that Pur-chase stood in wait for another confrontation with his supposed rival, the only two horses left standing for the title.[67] Now, all that remained was for the son of Star Shoot to meet the son of Ormondale one more time. How and when that would happen remained the source of endless speculation into October and the fall meet at Laurel.

10

Break-Up, Shake-Up, Hop

On Wednesday, October 1, 1919, more than thirty thousand fans crowded into Cincinnati's Redland Field, with the overflow of eager fans standing when seats were unavailable. The Chicago White Sox were in town for the first game of the World Series, ace hurler Eddie Cicotte on the mound. The game was scoreless in the bottom half of the first inning when lead-off hitter Morrie Rath came to bat for his first appearance in the World Series after spending several seasons in the minors. Cicotte's second pitch hit Rath in the ribs, sending the Reds' lead-off batter to first base. Surely, that wayward throw was not nerves; Cicotte had been here before, pitching in multiple World Series games in previous seasons. As Rath trotted to first base, Cicotte stood on the mound, the world around him unchanged, except for one thing.[1]

Cicotte's errant pitch signaled that the fix was on, with gamblers such as Arnold Rothstein giving the players involved monetary incentive to cheat. The White Sox would soon turn black, coloring 1919 in a way that could never be undone for the eight players who were in on the fix. Soon the year would also leave its black mark on one jockey and one horse for generations to come.

With the three-year-old stakes races mostly behind him, Sir Barton was now part of the handicap circuit, taking on the challenge of running against older horses under weights that might not be in his favor. New York handicapper Walter Vosburgh, in discussing the current crop of racing stars, cited Sir Barton and Purchase as the best of the current three-year-olds, horses that promised to make the next year's older division exciting.[2] Outside of the two-year-olds rounding into form and the three-year-olds running in rich stakes, the handicap division was the focus of the preponderance of the racing season across the sport. Sir Barton's transition into this phase already had begun, but the biggest challenge for H. G. Bedwell and company would be training this colt for such high weights: Sir Barton teetered on the brink of unsoundness on a regular basis, and that much weight could become problematic quickly. What would Ross and Bedwell decide to do with their great three-year-old? Would they keep him on this path for another year's worth of racing in 1920 or retire him after his stellar season?[3]

The handicap circuit was also the path that could put him in the conversation with the best juvenile champion America has ever known, the two-year-old whom Vosburgh could single out as being the top of his crop—Man o' War.[4] If Sir Barton continued racing as he had in 1919 and Man o' War dominated at three as he had at two, was a meeting between the best of his generation and the best ever to set foot on a track inevitable? Or would other forces intervene and leave fans to wonder "what if"?

The Ross Stable made its way north to Laurel and the second half of its fall season. With only three months left in 1919, the time left to settle the score between Purchase and Sir Barton was dwindling, the title of three-year-old champion on the line.

The move to Laurel for the fall season was a coming home of sorts for H. G. Bedwell and the horses he trained. The stable's home track was Laurel, near Yarrow Brae and Bolingbrook, the farm that the commander was outfitting with a one-mile training track and other facilities for preparing the Ross horses for 1920.[5] Sir Barton had wintered in the area the previous year as he recovered from the blood poisoning that had nearly taken his life. Laurel's dirt oval and white fences were familiar ground for him and Bedwell, who wanted to take advantage of the colt's form right away and entered Sir Barton in the Maryland Handicap on October 4. Conspicuously absent from that race? Sam Hildreth's good three-year-old Purchase. Hildreth had shipped his stable to Laurel already but chose not to enter Purchase in the Maryland Handicap. When would the top-two three-year-olds meet the barrier together and finally show everyone who was number one?

In addition to Purchase, Sam Hildreth had another good three-year-old in his barn, a relative newcomer named Mad Hatter, who had earned his name through his temperamental antics, familiar to everyone who knew his sire, Fair Play.[6] Hildreth had leased Mad Hatter from his breeder August Belmont Jr., opting to bring the colt along slowly; Mad Hatter made his first start of 1919 in September, finishing second and then wheeling off two wins in a row. He was another hot horse despite his lack of experience, especially after he beat Travers winner Hannibal and other good three-year-olds in the Minneola Handicap.[7] Hildreth's stable overflowed with talent, and now he was set to send another challenger to face the barrier with Sir Barton.

At 1¼ miles, the Maryland Handicap was a test of three-year-olds at a long distance and at handicap weights so that the field stood a chance against first-tier horses such as Sir Barton and the absent Purchase. The rivals were assigned the highest weight, 133 pounds, giving weight to other good horses such as Billy Kelly, Hannibal, Milkmaid, and Mad Hatter. The race was a test exclusively for three-year-olds, so the competition should not have been much of a problem for Sir Barton even at such a high weight; he had dominated the division for much of the year already. In addition, the race had a $10,000 purse, with a winner's share of $7,750. Man o' War was retired for the year, so Sir Barton had another chance to pad his lead in money won and get closer to that elusive $100,000 mark. The lightly raced Mad Hatter, who had carried 118 pounds in his previous win, got a paltry 106 pounds in an effort to even the field for the Triple Crown winner's competition. Could the 27-pound difference between the newcomer and the Ross horse be enough for an upset?

Saturday, October 4, was sunny and warm, the track fast—ideal conditions for good racing for the crowd of more than ten thousand at Laurel. As the six horses for the Maryland Handicap trickled up to the barrier, Sir Barton took his place on the outside, Johnny Loftus back on him for the ride. The two Hildreth starters stood to the inside, Mad Hatter on the rail and Thunderclap next to him. In between were only three horses, quality runners Be Frank, Audacious, and Sweepment. Only two horses mattered, though, as rival owners Ross and Hildreth were set to battle once again.

Starter James Milton kept them at the post for only a couple of minutes, the field getting away clearly; Mad Hatter made the best of the start, taking Thunderclap with him to the front.[8] Rather than go straight to the lead and duel with the Hildreth pair, Loftus held Sir Barton in check, hanging back behind the front three, allowing the lighter-weight horses to dominate with speed while he waited for them to tire.[9] Mad Hatter and Thunderclap hung out on the front, Audacious just behind them, for the better part of the race. Loftus and Sir Barton sat back patiently, much as they had in the Withers while waiting for Eternal to bear out; as they passed the three-quarters mark, Loftus began to inch Sir Barton forward, gaining ground in anticipation of the front-runners tiring.[10] With Mad Hatter on the rail, Thunderclap sat to his outside, forcing Loftus to take Sir Barton out wider in order to have space to move on that final turn. As they entered the final stretch, "the leaders opened like a fan coming home, with [Sir] Barton on the outside."[11]

At first, the Triple Crown winner sat in third, behind Thunderclap and Mad Hatter. Then Sir Barton was second, only a length behind Mad Hatter. The Hildreth colt seemed to stall as Sir Barton's rush of speed overtook him and took the lead.[12] As Sir Barton and Loftus hit the wire, they had a two-length lead, their patience rewarded in that last quarter of a mile. The race's final time was a speedy 2:02⅖, only two-fifths of a second off the track record. Johnny Loftus and Sir Barton returned to the judges' stand to a raucous ovation from the Laurel crowd, who "had seen a great race and one of the greatest Thoroughbreds of all time."[13]

Carrying the highest weight of 133 pounds, Sir Barton had toyed with the field, showing once again the same speed and versatility as his record spring starts. The near-record time at such a weight facing fresher horses signaled a return to form for the Triple Crown winner. The son of Star Shoot won the Maryland Handicap "in such an impressive manner that it stamped him perhaps the greatest three-year-old of his time, unless Purchase can beat him."[14] Sir Barton had risen to the occasion under a heavy impost to win a handicap, while Hildreth had sent out only two lightweights to face the rival claimant to the three-year-old division. Perhaps it was time to crown the king of the three-year-olds after all.

Sir Barton's win in the Maryland Handicap was called his best performance of the year, a return to the dominant form that he had had before the Dwyer.[15] His position at the top of his age group after such a performance came with a caveat, however: only a race at equal weights would decide who was at the top of the heap. Purchase might lead in the number of wins (nine), but Sir Barton led in money by tens of thousands of dollars. Raced conservatively, Sir Barton had taken a path where the money lay, much like War Cloud the previous year. Purchase may have won more races, but the quality of his competition varied from start to start, unlike the situation for his rival.

In this new phase of his career, Sir Barton was one of those names that fans went to the track for. His performance in the Maryland Handicap reinforced that reputation and added more fodder to the argument of his supremacy over Purchase. All that remained was another meeting between the two at the barrier.

Five days after the Maryland Handicap, Purchase danced onto the track for another workout, Hildreth trying to keep his star three-year-old in shape as they waited for a chance to meet Sir Barton to decide the king of their division for the year.[16] Opportunities to take to the track to meet the fleet son of Star Shoot had come and gone, but Hildreth was holding out for an advantage. He knew that meeting Sir Barton in a handicap meant weight. He had seen what the Triple Crown winner could do even at the heavy impost of 133 pounds. Hildreth was no dummy: he wanted to meet Sir Barton under weight-for-age conditions, which would put both colts at the same weight and likely avoid the heavy burden that handicapper Walter Vosburgh would assign them.[17] In the meantime, Purchase was under the saddle for another workout.

Hildreth gave the order to Laverne Fator, the jockey serving as Purchase's exercise rider, to work the colt for a mile. After three-quarters of a mile, however, Fator pulled the colt up. Purchase was limping and his ankle reluctantly bearing weight as they walked back to the barn. The next morning the ankle was badly swollen, a blow to Purchase's chances at the three-year-old crown.[18] He would not race again in 1919. The question of who the better three-year-old was would go unanswered still; with Purchase out, as long as Sir Barton held onto his form, he would be king of the division by default.

Hildreth was not discouraged, though, for he still had his good Mad Hatter, who would meet Sir Barton again on November 5 in the Autumn Handicap at Pimlico.

As the Laurel meet concluded, racing shifted its focus northward to Baltimore, where Pimlico promised to showcase the year's talent in the last major meet of 1919. This meet held opportunities for all of the Ross talent to shine, especially the stable's elite three-year-olds. One of the primary attractions of this particular meet was the Weight-for-Age Serials for all ages. The three races graduated in length, from ¾ mile to 1⅛ miles, and though each purse had a guaranteed $3,000, another $1,000 bonus was there for a horse who won two of the three races. Those races were an ideal fit for Billy Kelly and Sir Barton, especially since the Triple Crown winner was only $1,225 behind Man o' War for the year's money title.

Since his win in the Maryland Handicap on October 4, Sir Barton had stayed busy with workouts but had not followed up his stellar performance with another visit to the barrier. After a month off, Sir Barton's next start was to be the Autumn Handicap at Pimlico on November 5. The layoff went unexplained; Bedwell kept whatever cards he had close to the vest. The Triple Crown winner had reeled off five starts in less than four weeks, and no doubt he needed the break. The problem was that after his previous layoff and subsequent return he had showed that he needed a race before he was back at peak form. Was he due for another clunker, a race to shake off the rust?

As in the Potomac Handicap, the Ross Stable was looking to dominate again in the Autumn Handicap with Sir Barton, Billy Kelly, and Milkmaid all entered. Despite his win in the Latonia Championship Stakes, Mad Hatter was still sporting the light impost of 111 pounds, 5 pounds more than the 106 he had carried in that first meeting with Sir Barton but still a significant weight advantage. None of the starters, not even the venerable Billy Kelly, was to carry more than Sir Barton, who was again laden with the most weight.[19] Despite the time off and the weight, observers believed that "Sir Barton, even with 132 pounds up, seems to have a mortgage on the race."[20]

The rains that had soaked the mid-Atlantic had left the Pimlico oval muddy, and cloud cover on the previous day had not allowed the track to dry enough to make it any better. In this case, since water drained downward toward the infield, the rail was much deeper and therefore slower than running in the outer lanes.[21] The track condition plus the 21-pound difference between Mad Hatter and Sir Barton had to give H. G. Bedwell pause. His horse had lost a shoe and the Dwyer on a similar track.

As the field strolled onto the Pimlico oval, it numbered five instead of seven because Billy Kelly and Hildreth's Lord Brighton had scratched. Mad Hatter stood in his post on the rail, Sir Barton on the outside.[22] At the start, Loftus moved Sir Barton to the rail rather than staying in the middle of the track; stalking the pace on the rail and taking the inside route had worked in the Maryland Handicap. To Loftus, who had not ridden any of the earlier races on the card, the track might have looked dry on top, but that masked the slow going underneath.[23]

Mad Hatter broke in front with Bridesman, but rather than go straight to the lead and expend his colt's speed early, jockey Laverne Fator took Mad Hatter back behind the leaders. Bridesman and Milkmaid set the pace, both Mad Hatter and Sir Barton stalking. At six furlongs, Milkmaid's speed gave away, but Bridesman kept a hold on his lead. Behind him, Mad Hatter made his move, gaining ground on Bridesman, who hung tenuously onto his fast-fading lead. Running in the middle of the track, Mad Hatter eclipsed Bridesman in the stretch, leaving the crowd looking for the Triple Crown winner to make his move as well. But while Mad Hatter had accelerated and taken the lead in the easier footing toward the middle of the track, Loftus still had Sir Barton laboring on the rail. As the field closed in on the finish, Loftus sensed that he was unable to pass the tiring Bridesman, easing up on his efforts to urge Sir Barton. Bridesman hung on to his second-place position, with Sir Barton finishing eight lengths behind him and twelve lengths behind the winning Mad Hatter. The Triple Crown winner and leading three-year-old had turned in his worst performance of 1919.[24]

After the race, H. G. Bedwell was livid at the ride that the jockey had just given the Derby winner.[25] Loftus was an experienced rider and should have known the track's condition, even if he had no other mounts that day.[26] In the paddock, away from the Pimlico crowd, the trainer and jockey argued, loud enough for bystanders to hear, exchanging words that did not make it into the papers the next day, outside of a couple of oblique references to their verbal tussle.[27] What transpired in the paddock after the Autumn Handicap at Pimlico, though, was no thrashing of a jockey who had ridden poorly. It was the clash of two titans, one who made his living riding the best and knew horses like the back of his hand and one who had fought and worked hard to ascend to a position of prestige.

In that battle of words flew accusations, ones that would resonate beyond that day and that race and that horse.

For Johnny Loftus, the Autumn Handicap capped off a series of questionable rides that had plagued him throughout the year. Turf writers might have had short attention spans, but they had long memories, and this particular turn on Sir Barton prompted a rehashing of the sins Loftus had committed in 1919. For Sir Barton, the issue started with the Dwyer, where Loftus had kept the colt on the Aqueduct rail, which had been deep and harder to navigate that day, resulting in his first loss of the year. Sure, Purchase received a break in weights and was a fresher horse, but Loftus's decision to keep his mount in the deeper going was a poor choice by an experienced jockey. It was well known that Sir Barton was more likely to lose a shoe because of his shelly hooves on even a dry track, but that wet dirt played a role in the wrenched plate that the colt suffered in the Dwyer, and Loftus should have been more aware of the track's condition.

In addition, Loftus had been accused of poor decision making in the Sanford Stakes, Man o' War's only loss that year and ultimately the single loss of the colt's career. Accounts of how Man o' War missed the start differed, and the Sanford's scant six furlongs was not enough room for even Man o' War's twenty-eight-foot stride to overcome the poor start. The problem arose in that Loftus had positioned his mount off the pace, as ordered, but also on the rail, which meant that the colt was boxed in and unable to change his position unless Loftus was willing to take the colt wide to get out of it. If he took Man o' War wide, he was not sure if the colt possessed enough stamina and speed at his heavy impost to overcome the gap between him and the leaders. In the end, Man o' War's only loss might have been laid at the feet of Johnny Loftus, even with the substitute starter and the tactics of other riders in the Sanford, especially Willie Knapp.

Ultimately, when Bedwell and Loftus butted heads in the Pimlico paddock, Bedwell's accusations about Loftus's ride called the jockey's very character into question. The trainer bandied about the idea that the jockey had "pulled" Sir Barton in the Autumn, keeping the colt under wraps so that he would not perform as well as he could have.[28] To "pull" a horse was a deliberate decision, something that took both skill and nerve. If Loftus had done that, he put his reputation on the line because if such behavior were discovered, he could easily lose his contract with Ross and then possibly risk his standing with other trainers and owners. Who would trust their horse to a man willing to cheat, whatever the reason? To make matters worse, the horse who won the race was Mad Hatter, trained by Sam Hildreth. It was Hildreth's own Purchase that Loftus had ridden in two victories in the past year, the same horse who had been the burr in Sir Barton's side since their confrontation in the Dwyer. Bedwell knew Hildreth well; both had cowpunched their way through the West, their practical and lifelong education on horses bringing them to this point in their own racing careers.[29] Accusing Loftus of colluding with Hildreth, even if such an accusation proved to be untrue, had more downside for the jockey than for the trainer. The jockey's employment was at the pleasure of the owners and trainers he rode for; with no union or similar organization on his side, this employee had little recourse.

Loftus, though, had a trump card—or so he thought. He knew something about H. G. Bedwell that could have ramifications far greater than even Loftus could have imagined—a dirty little secret that might not have been all that secret after all.

"I'm going to tell Commander Ross," Loftus declared.[30] That was a threat that H. G. Bedwell did not take lightly.

Not quite a decade before that argument at Pimlico, another incident in a paddock put H. G. Bedwell in a troublesome spot. When his horse Nadzu acted erratically at Latonia in July 1910, it was clear that something untoward had happened to Bedwell's horse. Had the trainer slipped the gelding something, accidentally overdoing it because of a delayed start? Or, as Bedwell alleged, had a stablehand doped the horse after a gambler had bribed him to do so? It took ten months and the death of the track veterinarian before H. G. Bedwell was cleared of all charges. The specter of hop, though, stuck to the trainer throughout his career.

Johnny Loftus had started riding Thoroughbreds in 1909 and met Bedwell in South Carolina a couple of years later as the young jockey began his own ascendency through the ranks of riders.[31] Loftus would know what Bedwell did to prepare his horses for race day because Loftus had known H. G. Bedwell for years and had spent 1919 as one of the Ross Stable's contract riders. Even though doping a horse was technically against the rules, the United States lagged behind Europe in terms of detecting any illicit chemical enhancements and thus much more infrequently punished any horseman caught engaging in such a practice. The Nadzu incident had threatened Bedwell's career, but almost getting caught did not seem to curb the trainer of that behavior, or so Loftus implied in the paddock at Pimlico.

What, though, did Bedwell gain from running Sir Barton cold, or without hop, as Loftus implied? Any sort of attempt to manipulate Sir Barton's odds in his next start would not yield enough profit to make that worthwhile; such a betting coup would be easier to pull off with a lower-profile horse with higher odds. Or was this charge Loftus's way of deflecting the accusation of pulling Sir Barton in the Autumn? The jockey would know how detrimental that accusation could be to his reputation: it did not matter if it was true or not, only that it was out there. With at least three other questionable rides that year, all well known, the jockey stood to lose plenty if he did not challenge Bedwell or find a way to undercut whatever he might say. Johnny Loftus could threaten to go to Commander Ross and tell him what his superstar trainer was doing with the superstar horses that Ross had spent a fortune on, but what did the jockey expect could come of such a conversation?

The conflict between Bedwell and Loftus over two racing sins with potential long-term repercussions put the commander in a tight spot. If he sided with his trainer, he stood to lose faith with the nation's leading jockey. If he sided with the jockey, the implication that H. G. Bedwell was hopping his champion three-year-old and possibly others in the Ross Stable affected more than just the trainer. Not only could Bedwell face penalties as serious as a ban from racing, but Commander Ross could as well. The Jockey Club had denied Cal Shilling a license to ride for years because of rough riding, among other sins. How would they react if they found that the leading owner and leading trainer were giving their horses stimulants?

If the Jockey Club found that the commander knew that Bedwell was hopping his horses, then Ross himself risked losing all of his investment in the sport. He had spent hundreds of thousands of dollars on his stable, from buying horses to building farms in two different countries. For his investment, he had the leading stable in the United States for the second year in a row and had won more than $200,000 that year alone—all of it based on the guidance, labor, and input of H. G. Bedwell. Whether the commander was willfully ignorant or not, he was not going to risk everything to give Loftus what he wanted and save the jockey's reputation. After all, the young man was merely a jockey, an employee expected to subjugate his will to that of his employer without turning a hair. Loftus was no shrinking violet, though, and in the end he forced Ross to side with Bedwell. Johnny Loftus was left out in the cold, losing the mount on Sir Barton and facing the possibility that his contract with the leading stable in the country would not be renewed for 1920.[32]

The center of all of this conflict was the horse, Ross's leading money winner for the year and the de facto three-year-old champion, the colt who had made history before anyone had a name for it. Despite sportswriter Red Smith's assertion in 1960 about Sir Barton winning on hop,[33] which was likely founded on rumor, no evidence ever existed that Bedwell drugged Sir Barton—except for this argument between the trainer and Johnny Loftus. Nevertheless, if even the merest scent of a pulled-horse accusation could cost a jockey, what would this association with a trainer who had a reputation for using hop do for a horse? Quite a bit it seems, even fifty years after Smith's columns originally ran and a hundred years after Sir Barton raced. To this day, despite the absence of hard evidence, the specter of hop follows not only H. G. Bedwell but Sir Barton as well.[34]

Stimulants cannot make a bad horse good, nor can they replace the will to win. If anything, there was always the chance of their having a deleterious effect, as in the case of Nadzu.[35] Sir Barton showed his potential every time he bested his stablemates in the morning. He would not have won the favor of Cal Shilling and *Louisville Courier-Journal* writer Sam McMeekin had he not possessed something worth fighting for. Sir Barton would not have been the star of the stable if he were so unreliable. The Autumn Handicap came toward the end of the long year's campaign; perhaps the issue was less that Bedwell had started a cold horse and more that he had sent a weary Sir Barton, who was entering the final phase of a hard campaign, against a fresher colt such as Mad Hatter.

Whatever the behaviors of the humans around him, Sir Barton had showed his innate talent and speed time and again, enough to make history with his wins in the Kentucky Derby, the Preakness Stakes, and the

Belmont Stakes in 1919 and only a year later to be tapped as the perfect challenger to the Horse of the Century.

Two days after the Autumn Handicap debacle, Sir Barton returned to the Pimlico oval for the Serial Weight-for-Age Serial 2, a one-mile race worth $2,300 to the winner. His twelve-length defeat by Mad Hatter just two days earlier left Loftus on the ground; how Sir Barton ran today would determine if that grounding was justified.[36] If Sir Barton ran poorly, the loss in the Autumn was on H. G. Bedwell. If the colt ran well, eyes would turn back to Loftus again, those questionable rides still dogging him.

The Pimlico track for this race was fast, unlike the Autumn Handicap, and for once the Triple Crown winner got a break in the weights.[37] In the Pimlico Weight-for-Age races, older horses carried more weight, with four-year-olds and older carrying 126 pounds and the three-year-olds only 120.[38] Bypassing another go at Mad Hatter in the Bowie Handicap, Sir Barton and Billy Kelly, who had won the first Serial, strode to the post with two others, Lucullite and The Porter.[39] Lucullite was another Hildreth starter, winner of several handicaps carrying high weight at the New York tracks that year. The Porter had set a record for a mile and seventy yards at Churchill Downs that year and had won the Harford County Handicap as well as other races. Each was a good horse in his own right, all winners of multiple races, but today none was real competition for the Triple Crown winner.

As the field of four trotted to the barrier, the most notable difference between that moment and forty-eight hours earlier was the man astride the three-year-old star. H. G. Bedwell had tapped twenty-year-old Clarence Kummer to replace Johnny Loftus on Sir Barton.[40] Breaking from the second post position, Kummer sent Sir Barton to the front within the first quarter, Lucullite and Billy Kelly just behind him, and The Porter trailing. As the field rounded that last turn, The Porter went to the outside, moving past a fading Lucullite and bearing down on Billy Kelly. After six furlongs, The Porter passed Billy Kelly, who was laboring on the rail, and set his sights on Sir Barton. He managed to stick his head in front for a beat before Kummer gave Sir Barton rein and the colt took off, the speed that was his hallmark carrying him away from the field. Sir

Barton won going away, his mile in 1:40, only one second off the track record. The turnaround was remarkable and did not go unnoticed.[41]

Four days later Sir Barton answered those questions one more time with another win, this time in the last of the Weight-for-Age serials at Pimlico, this one a 1⅛-mile race. Only Billy Kelly and Lucullite, Hildreth's good older horse, accompanied Sir Barton to the barrier.

The day was rainy and chilly, classic November weather in Maryland, but the crowd for the day's racing at Pimlico swelled as the country celebrated the first anniversary of the armistice that ended the Great War the previous year. With the grandstand decorated in the Allies colors and a band poised to play the national anthem, the Serial was the day's feature, but, with Sir Barton having only two other challengers, those in attendance were betting on a romp rather than a race, putting enough money on the entry of Sir Barton and Billy Kelly so that the payouts would be minimal at best.[42]

Again carrying 120 pounds, Sir Barton lined up on the outside, with Billy Kelly to his left and Lucullite on the rail. At the break, Billy Kelly jumped out to the lead, Kummer keeping Sir Barton right on his stablemate's shoulder. They formed a barrier in front of Lucullite, trying to keep the older horse from making a run at the lead. At the half-mile mark, Laverne Fator on Lucullite took a chance and gunned within half a length of the leaders. Kummer nudged Sir Barton, and the colt took off, taking over the lead, never looking back. The sloppy track impeded any sort of sizzling fractions, but Sir Barton did not need his speed; the three-length lead he had over Billy Kelly left no doubt about who was going to finish in front this day.[43]

As Sir Barton stepped off the muddy oval at Pimlico, one of the Ross stablehands proclaimed, "Bang the cymbals! Beat the drum! Sir Barton is a champion and Lucullite is a bum!"[44] Lucullite, winless in all of his confrontations with the Triple Crown winner, pulled up lame at the finish, a metaphoric embodiment of most challengers' effectiveness against the Ross Stable in 1919.[45] After going winless at age two, Sir Barton bookended his three-year-old season with wins in the Kentucky Derby and in the last Serial. He won $3,250 for his efforts in this last race, including a $1,000 bonus for winning two of the three Serials.[46] That brought his total money won in 1919 to $88,250, short of the mythical

$100,000 mark that people had speculated he could earn but still the most money won for the year. Right behind the Triple Crown winner was Man o' War, with nearly $5,000 less.[47] It was to be the last time Sir Barton would beat Man o' War at anything.

As the year came to a conclusion and a new decade loomed on the horizon, the turning of the calendar meant that Sir Barton was now classed among older horses like Cudgel and Exterminator, destined for the handicap circuit that would see him continue carrying the highest weights wherever he went. The new year also meant that the dominant Man o' War was now three years old, poised to take on the same races that had made Sir Barton a star. Questions about Man o' War's ability to continue his dominance hung in the balance. If the big red colt ran in the new year as he had in the old, who could possibly be his equal?

11

New Year, Same Rivals

While in New York for the National Horse Show on November 18, 1919, Sir Barton's breeder, John E. Madden, received news from Hamburg Place that Star Shoot, the leading sire in the country for five of the past ten years, was ill with pneumonia.[1] By the next day, the chestnut son of an English Triple Crown winner was dead, and Hamburg Place now lacked a flagship sire. The operation did not lack for good horses, but the death of his excellent sire no doubt started Madden thinking about the future. Ross had already turned down his offer to buy Sir Barton and have him stand at Hamburg Place after he retired. What was next for the Wizard of the Turf?

In his sixty-fourth year, Madden decided that focusing on the business side of his interests rather than the breeding side was the answer. In 1919, he was the leading breeder in the country, and in January 1920 Hamburg Place announced a sale where seventy-eight broodmares and thirty yearlings were to go on the auction block, the first of a series of sales of breeding stock.[2] Getting out of the breeding business cleared the way for Madden to concentrate on his other businesses while continuing to advise others on the business of horses, which would give him chances to touch Sir Barton's life again and again.

Sir Barton's wins in the Serials put him over the top of Man o' War in terms of money won in 1919. In thirteen starts, the son of Star Shoot had won eight times, finished second three times, and third twice. Throughout 1919, Sir Barton did not finish out of the money in any of his starts, amassing $88,250 in purse money. He led the Ross Stable's roster of runners, besting the money won by Billy Kelly, Cudgel, Milkmaid, and others. Some called the colt the three-year-old champion for 1919, while others continued to debate his merits versus those of his rival, Purchase. Purchase had run eleven times and won nine of those times, but the purse money he won was only a third of what Sir Barton brought in. James McClelland, owner of Eternal, declared Sir Barton to be "the best three-year-old I've ever seen in my thirty years on the turf, and I've seen some great horses."[3] Eternal's trainer, Kimball Patterson, echoed those sentiments: "Sir Barton is one of the greatest racehorses ever seen on the American turf. He can carry any kind of weight on any kind of track and does not need a pacemaker. He makes his own pace and seems to say, 'Come and get me.'"[4] This kind of respect followed the colt into the new year, the maiden-to-monarch quality of his three-year-old season making his accomplishments all the more thrilling and impressive.

His accomplishments had made enough of an impression that he even merited a profile in *Vanity Fair* magazine, one of the Jazz Age's cultural chronicles,[5] where sportswriter O'Neil Sevier extolled his virtues and recounted his accomplishments.[6] An article syndicated in a number of newspapers in late November 1919 advised that those seeking wealth should invest in the Thoroughbred, a tip that came from "the season's record of Sir Barton, star of the Commander J. K. L. Ross stable and the leading money winner of this season."[7] Despite the ongoing debate about whether he deserved the "three-year-old of the year" crown, still an unofficial designation but one that turf writers assigned to their choice nevertheless, Sir Barton's unprecedented run in 1919 put him in the highest echelons of his sport, high enough that Sevier called him "a horse of truly epic stature."[8]

In any other year, the Triple Crown winner would have been called not only the three-year-old of the year but also the best *horse* of the year to boot, but Sir Barton shared 1919 with a lightning-fast two-year-old named Man o' War.[9] Sir Barton might have been the leading money winner, but Man o' War's performances on the track attracted more attention and more praise, despite the long list of prestigious races that Sir Barton had won in the past year.[10] This duality in in the attention Sir Barton received—reaping praise yet playing second fiddle—dominated the coverage of racing through the quiet winter into the chattering spring of 1920.

Even as Sir Barton's claim to the three-year-old crown was debated, the Fairgrounds in New Orleans decided to honor the son of Star Shoot by naming a race for him.[11] Run on January 5, the race was a one-mile dash for three-year-olds, with a purse of $1,000.[12] On the muddy track, General Glenn hustled out to the front and stayed on the lead for the majority of the race, until Damask came from far back and made a run at him, taking the lead. Damask could not hold on, and General Glenn inched back up, sticking a nose in front as they flashed under the wire.[13] The value to the winner was $700; the value to history was this: not even a year from completing the first Triple Crown, Sir Barton had secured his reputation enough to have a race named after him, not just while he was still alive but also *while he was still racing.*

His dominance on the track also made Commander Ross's stable the leading money winner for the year. The stable more than doubled the total money it won in 1918, from $99,179 to $209,303.[14] As a trainer, H. G. Bedwell came in second in number of wins, with sixty-three, but he far outpaced any other trainer in money won. In less than five years, Commander Ross's liberal spending on horses and land and personnel had shot him to the top of the turf world.

Once the racing year concluded, the Ross Stable decamped to its Maryland farms, outside of Laurel, for the winter hiatus. Billy Kelly and Sir Barton officially turned four on January 1, shifting their focus from the classics that had dominated their three-year-old season to the handicaps that made up the majority of the racing options for older horses. At Bolingbrook, the Maryland farm outfitted especially for the training side of the Ross operation, Billy Kelly, Sir Barton, Milkmaid, and the rest of the racing stock wintered with the jockeys who were under contract to the stable, including rising star Earl Sande and veteran Tommy Nolan. Nolan had charge of the Triple Crown winner, whom the *Daily Racing Form* called "a stallion of some stubbornness,"[15] as the horses exercised under cover during the long winter. Sir Barton seemed to be ready to run, his impatient nature spoiling for some time on the track rather than being cooped up in the barn.

As the new year opened and brought with it speculation about who would dominate in the coming months, Sir Barton's name came up in the mix, of course. Walter Vosburgh complimented the three-year-old champion, saying that, "despite apparent soreness, [he] showed high class."[16] Writers such as W. C. Vreeland anticipated that Purchase and Sir

Barton would renew their rivalry on the track in 1920 and do so at even weights, thus proving once and for all who was the better of the two.[17]

Ross had toyed with the idea of retiring the champion, knowing what imposts the handicappers would burden him with if he raced in his fourth year. For a man who was trying to build on the success he had had in 1919, sending both Cudgel, who was already slated for stud in 1920, and Sir Barton into the breeding shed was a great temptation. Retiring his top two racers, though, would leave the Ross Stable without a star. Commander Ross had a fleet of good horses getting older, a crop of younger horses still untested, and an industry full of owners and trainers aiming to challenge him. The Ross Stable needed one champion still on its roster for 1920, so he kept Sir Barton in training while sending Cudgel to his second career in the breeding shed. Having already turned down an offer of $200,000 for his Triple Crown winner, the commander demonstrated that he "had faith in Sir Barton, even against these heavy odds, and he had that spirit of the sportsman which made ducking a challenge unthinkable."[18]

In 1919, Sir Barton had not only duplicated War Cloud's path from Louisville to Baltimore to New York but surpassed it by winning all of those races, a historic accomplishment. The following year, promoters wanted to capitalize on the popularity of racing that postwar America had adopted as one of its diversions of choice. In Kentucky, Colonel Matt Winn announced that the 1920 Kentucky Derby would add $30,000 to its purse, bringing the total purse up to $50,000.[19] In addition, Pimlico scheduled the Preakness for May 18, ten days after the Kentucky Derby, another effort to attract the Kentucky Derby winner and, of course, use that to bring fans to the track.[20] Was this change another by-product of Sir Barton's Derby win? The maiden allowance of 10 pounds, which had allowed Sir Barton to carry only 112½ pounds in his wire-to-wire victory, was eliminated. Colts and geldings would carry 126 pounds and fillies 121 pounds from here on out, regardless of their record.[21]

The increase in the Derby's purse money and the change in the races' calendar should have attracted the best of the three-year-olds, but the Riddles declined to ship Man o' War to Louisville for the Derby, thus scuttling one chance for the two-year-old champion to win a big-money race.[22] Owner Samuel Riddle, wary of running any horse 1¼ miles too early in its sophomore year, passed up Louisville for Baltimore, where he declared Man o' War would make his first start of the year in the Preak-ness Stakes. The colt had wintered there in Maryland, and the trip to Pimlico was much shorter than the trek out to Louisville and back.[23] Although Man o' War had wintered well and appeared more than ready, the colt's abilities and burgeoning superstar status were more points of anxiety than boons for the longtime Thoroughbred owner. He lived in fear of something happening to the best horse he had ever owned, and he was not about to risk the colt's soundness for even the Run for the Roses.

Thoroughbred racing in America had its governing body in the Jockey Club, the group of officials who maintained the American Stud Book and issued licenses to jockeys and trainers. Whenever the Jockey Club with-held a license, it generally offered little in the way of public comment, often leaving applicants in the dark about why.[24] In March 1920, as win-ter was giving way to spring and the new year's racing in the East was on the horizon, the news out of the Jockey Club's meeting was that Johnny Loftus, the most famous jockey in the country, who had ridden both Sir Barton and Man o' War, among other top horses, had his application for a license in 1920 denied.[25] The Jockey Club gave no comment about the news, following its usual modus operandi, but its silence on the matter made the speculators the loudest voices in the room. For fans who might only follow racing through the papers, the news that Loftus was set down would come as a surprise. For those in the know, it would not.

That shouting match in the paddock at Pimlico was a shot across the bow; Bedwell, famous for being a demanding boss, was not going to let an employee railroad him, even the great Johnny Loftus. Loftus's threat to speak to Commander Ross about the trainer's practices was a show of insubordination and a violation of the position Loftus had accepted when he signed a contract with Ross. Ross was not going to entertain any notion that his trainer was doing something untoward because it would put the commander himself in the position of aiding and abet-ting Bedwell's crimes. No, it was easier to let the Jockey Club see that maybe Loftus, especially after the debacle in the Sanford, among other strikes against him, was the one who had done wrong. After all, racing's best rider did not have any recourse. Loftus had been in an especially privileged position because he had contracts with both Samuel Riddle and Commander Ross and also rode for Sam Hildreth, but that position did not insulate him from consequences. His win percentage in 1919 was 37 percent, with 65 wins in 177 mounts, earning $215,418 in purse money.[26] Johnny Loftus was not the leading rider in terms of number of wins, but he was in prestige. Now, though, all of that prestige could not protect the country's best rider.

Johnny Loftus had intended 1920 to be his last year in the saddle, anticipating that he would earn as much as he could in that final season and then retire from riding and apply for a trainer's license the following year. He was fighting a losing battle with his weight and decided that he could parlay his reputation as a great rider and horseman into the training side of the business.[27] All he needed was just one more year of riding, one more year of purses to help him transition from one side of racing to another.[28] He had won more than $200,000 in purse money in 1919. What could 1920 bring him?

He would never know. Before Loftus lost his license, Samuel Riddle had renewed his contract with a raise, a bonus, and even a place to live on the Riddle farm in Berlin, Maryland.[29] Now Loftus was on the ground, set down with nowhere to go, unsure about what was next.

In 1908, when the Hart–Agnew Act did not end gambling in New York, the state took it a step further and passed even more restrictive legislation that could fine and imprison any racetrack owners and other track officials if patrons were found betting on their premises. When amendments limiting the liability of racing officials failed, racetracks closed, and a number of stables took their stock elsewhere, down to Kentucky and Maryland and overseas to Europe.

The result of the Hart–Agnew Act and its accompanying restrictions was that racing in New York died for two years until a New York court ruled that the law applied only to bookmakers and not to the average patron. Even though racing in New York was able to restart as early as 1913, some of the horses, owners, trainers, and jockeys who had ventured out of state and even overseas never returned. The bill also had the effect of bolstering racing in other states. At the turn of the century, Maryland had only one track, Pimlico, but by 1920 the state, which had a population of a little less than two million, had four racetracks: Bowie, Havre de Grace, Laurel, and, of course, Pimlico. With racing flourishing there, the Maryland legislature was trying to lasso the industry and take control of the flow of money whirling around the tracks.

In early 1920, Maryland state senator Harry H. Nuttle proposed a bill similar to that of the Hart–Agnew Act. His bill would ban pari-mutuel wagering in Maryland, a system that pooled the money that bettors put in and then paid it out after taxes and the "house take" based on odds. In 1919, the state's four tracks had taken in more $30 million in wagers over one hundred racing days.[30] Bettors had to pay cash to place a bet in the pari-mutuel system but could operate on credit in the book-maker system, which was popular in Britain. Opponents of Nuttle's bill argued that the pari-mutuel system was fairer than using bookmakers; people who chose to gamble had to use cash rather than credit. Nuttle and supporters of the gambling ban only saw the millions and millions of dollars taken in and lamented the immoral diversion that so many people engaged in each day of racing. Like the Hart–Agnew Act in New York, Nuttle's bill sought to end gambling in Maryland, another front in the battle between the Prohibition-era moralists and the diversion seekers of postwar America.

In response to Nuttle's legislation, Lieutenant Colonel Stuart S. Janney,[31] partner in the same law firm as Governor Albert Ritchie, proposed the Burke–Janney bill, which established a tax of $6,000 per racing day for each track and stipulated the tax would be paid to the track's municipality rather than to the state. Such a move would ensure that some of the money each track took in would stay in the area and be used for public benefit. However, such a tax did not benefit the state as a whole; sure, Baltimore and its population of nearly 750,000 would reap benefits, especially with its status as the center of the majority of the state's population, but the money stopped there. Most of the tracks were around Baltimore, so the trackless part of the state would see little of that income.

Another benefit proposed by the Burke–Janney bill, however, would be the establishment of a state commission to oversee racing in Maryland. This commission would enable the state to have some regulatory power over the sport, which would lend the sport some credibility in that it would be willing to submit to some oversight. Whereas the Nuttle bill wanted to shutter racing altogether—an amendment was added at one point that would completely outlaw horse racing for a prize—the Burke–Janney bill would allow racing to continue with oversight and with the industry contributing money to the counties that the tracks resided in, $6,000 *each day* of racing, limited to one hundred days. The fight continued in the legislature, both bills at the center of the discussion, and the idea of allowing the voters to have a say was bandied about as those in the racing industry made their voices heard.

Among those advocating for racing's continuance in Maryland were Colonel Stanley Koch of the United States Army Remount Service, which depended on the Thoroughbred industry for breeding stock; Arthur Hancock, owner of Claiborne Farm and citizen advocate for the Remount Service; O'Neil Sevier, sportswriter; and Commander Ross. The commander discussed his investment in Maryland, which totaled nearly $1 million to that point.[32] Not only did he own property in the state and use it as his American headquarters, but his stable frequented the tracks in the area, using Laurel as a training base during the racing year. Just as the commander was eager to see racing return to the Dominion, he wanted to see racing continue in Maryland. The spring meets were only a month away; passing the Nuttle bill could put a halt to them and drive horsemen and their money away from Maryland, achieving the same effect that the Hart–Agnew Act had in New York. Much like Prohibition, these laws on horse racing made it inconvenient to engage in this pursuit, but not impossible. Enforcement would be problematic, and the repercussions potentially devastating.

On March 31, the Burke–Janney bill cleared the Maryland State Legislature and went to Governor Ritchie for his signature. The governor and Lieutenant Colonel Janney had been part of the law firm that had served as regular counsel for Pimlico.[33] The Burke–Janney bill established the Maryland State Racing Commission and provided for one hundred total days of racing in Maryland. The law also established a tax of $6,000 per racing day, a yearly tax revenue of $600,000.[34] The commission was to have three members, all appointed by the governor.

The number of racing days allotted was fewer than what the four Maryland tracks had run in the years leading up to the passage of Burke–Janney, so dividing up the one hundred days between the four was going to be a challenge. At least the state had avoided the two-year stoppage of racing that New York had seen, from which New York was still recovering. Governor Ritchie took several months to appoint his three-member commission, while the individual tracks worked on dividing up their available dates over the four tracks and eight remaining months. Once the commission was in place, though, its authority over the four tracks within its jurisdiction was going to face a challenge in the coming months that would change the makeup of the state's largest and winningest stable.

Despite the severe winter on the eastern seaboard, Bedwell and company kept the Ross Stable's racing stock, including Billy Kelly and Sir Barton, in training, working them under sheds and on the farm's covered quarter-mile track until Laurel opened for training.[35] This star-studded stable would make its 1920 debut at Havre de Grace in mid-April, with a formidable roster of fifty-three horses total, including a number of good older horses and an uncertain crop of two- and three-year-olds among its ranks.[36] Both of Ross's champion horses were ready for the new season, growing in girth (Billy Kelly) and energy (Sir Barton) as their first starts approached. Trainer Bedwell was especially effervescent about Sir Barton: "I'll give $500 to anyone who can find a blemish on him."[37] The champion was apparently raring to go, tearing a sweater and shirt from an unfortunate stable boy and then trying, unsuccessfully, to chew the light bulb in his stall.[38] Per usual, Sir Barton was willing to give only as much in workouts as Bedwell could extract from the reluctant exerciser, approaching his works with his characteristic verve and "pep."[39] Based on Bedwell's confidence and Sir Barton's crankiness, the champion appeared spoiling for another racing season.

Billy Kelly was still the wiry and businesslike racer he had been in 1919. He beat Sir Barton to the barrier in 1920, winning his first start in the Harford Handicap on April 16, before meeting Sir Barton in the Belair Handicap on April 19. This race, at six furlongs, was more of a sprint, which favored Billy Kelly's racing style more than Sir Barton's, though both had more than enough potential speed to dominate. The Triple Crown winner carried the most weight, 133 pounds, and Billy Kelly was similarly burdened at 132; the other contestants were lightly weighted, of course, carrying up to 30 pounds less than the two Ross horses.[40]

The Belair had attracted the largest crowd of the Havre de Grace meet so far, with fans turning out in force for the four-year-old debut of the Ross entry.[41] The field for this feature had only six horses, none of note outside of Billy Kelly on the rail in the first post position and

Sir Barton toward the middle in the fourth post. Before the race, Commander Ross had declared Sir Barton to win, exercising his privilege as owner of the entry to say which of his horses should finish first.[42] The only downside to such confidence was the trend over the colt's career to throw in a clunker when coming of a layoff. Earl Sande, the stable's main contract rider, had the mount on Billy Kelly, while Clarence Kummer—who also rode for Samuel Riddle—was again astride Sir Barton.

At the break, Billy Kelly jumped out ahead of his stablemate by a half-length, while Sir Barton worked to fend off a lightly weighted Ticklish. The Triple Crown winner stayed close to Billy Kelly, Ticklish on his heels, until the stretch, when Sir Barton started to tire and Kummer eased him, as they were overtaken by War Mask and then Ticklish. Fading to third and then fourth as the field flashed under the wire, the champion three-year-old of 1919 finished out of the money for the first time since the Hopeful Stakes in August 1918. Sande appeared to have Billy Kelly under restraint, as if he were trying to adhere to the Commander's declaration that Sir Barton should win, but Sir Barton could not hold his speed for the whole of the six furlongs, losing ground to horses who carried 25 to 30 pounds less than he did. Billy Kelly might have won the race for the Ross Stable, but Sir Barton's lagging performance showed an unexpected layer of rust on the Triple Crown winner.

After the Belair, Ticklish's jockey Jimmy Burke went to the Havre de Grace stewards to lodge a complaint that Clarence Kummer on Sir Barton had interfered by calling out instructions to Sande while they were running together down the backstretch. The stewards overruled the objection, unwilling to interfere with or regulate any jockey's speech during a race.[43] Clearly, the Ross jockeys, both aware of the declaration to win, would have had to communicate because Sande was supposed to surrender to Kummer on Sir Barton when the time came. Kummer likely had told Sande to go on, sensing that his mount was not up to the task. Both horses had been working well, showing that they were more than ready for a new season of racing, but as in the past Sir Barton showed that he needed a race to round into form.[44] Expectations for the Triple Crown winner were high, though, and a clunker of a race, especially finishing out of the money, was not in the plan for fans. However, with his next start in only five days, past history augured well for his backers.

Five days later, on April 24, both Billy Kelly and Sir Barton returned to the Havre de Grace oval, this time in different races. Billy Kelly started in the Circle Purse, a one-mile race with a small purse, finishing second behind Star Master. In the race before that, Sir Barton and Clarence Kummer went to the post for the Climax Handicap, a six-furlong sprint with a purse of a little more than $1,300. Carrying 133 pounds, the champion gave more than 10 pounds to every horse in the race, including his stablemate, Milkmaid.[45] Historically, the follow-up start after a layoff was generally a good spot to bet on the Triple Crown winner because he had previously shown that he needed a start to get his motor running. With one start already in 1920, would he be gassed up and ready to go?

For the Climax, Sir Barton had post two, with Ticklish, the lightweight who had finished in front of him in the Belair, on the rail and Milkmaid way on the outside in post seven of a seven-horse field. At the start, Fruit Cake jumped out to the lead, with Ticklish and Milkmaid just ahead of the champion. Right behind Sir Barton was the H. P. Whitney filly Panoply, ridden by future Hall of Famer Frank Coltiletti. A furlong in, Panoply started to rush toward the front, but her saddle slipped, unseating Coltiletti, who tumbled to the dirt, knocked unconscious by the fall. Unburdened of her rider, Panoply ran ahead of the field while Sir Barton rushed to the front of the lightweights. By the half-mile mark, Sir Barton was a length in front of the field, then two-and-a-half lengths, and in the end flashed under the wire a length and a half in front, "never fully extended," Panoply running with him the whole time. Panoply's performance made observers think she might have had enough speed, especially carrying 27 fewer pounds, to challenge Sir Barton, but losing her rider meant she lost her chance to count in the official finish. Milkmaid managed to come home second, Ticklish behind her in third.[46]

The win for Sir Barton was so good and Bedwell so confident in the horse's form that he decided to send him out again three days later in the Marathon Handicap, Sir Barton's third start in nine days.

With the news that Man o' War was declining a trip to Louisville for the Kentucky Derby on May 8, the race and its $30,000 purse were up for grabs to any horse who could come home first at Churchill Downs. The field meeting the barrier would be large—seventeen in all, with five scratched—and run the gamut of the three-year-old talent outside of the dominant red chestnut staying home that day. H. P. Whitney had more than one Derby starter up his sleeve, including Man o' War's erstwhile conqueror, Upset. In addition, Whitney had Damask, the colt who had come in second in the inaugural Sir Barton Purse at the Fairgrounds, and Wildair, who had just lost to long shot Sandy Beal the same day Sir Barton won the Climax. To prepare Wildair for his trip to Louisville, Whitney's trainer, James Rowe, entered the brown son of Broomstick in the Marathon Handicap at Havre de Grace.

At 1¹⁄₁₆ mile, the Marathon was a perfect tune-up for the Derby, only three-sixteenths of a mile shorter than the classic route. In addition, the three-year-old Wildair was getting a weight break from the field, all of whom were a year or so older than he. Wildair's 110 pounds were not the lightest weight in the field—that was Bolster's 106 pounds—but with this weight Wildair would have the chance to get in a preparatory start for the big race and do it without carrying the 126 pounds he would have to tote in Louisville. This setup made the Marathon a win–win for Whitney and Wildair.

For Sir Barton, the Marathon was about two and a half furlongs longer than his previous two starts, and since he had won under restraint in his previous race, the longer distance should give the champion a chance to stretch his legs and use his speed and endurance to win handily. For this three-year-old champion with a stellar reputation, expectations held that he would have the race in hand, especially when three horses scratched, leaving only Sir Barton, Wildair, and a long shot named Bolster in the field. Yet he was giving the other two starters enormous weight advantages, and the 135 pounds he carried just begged for something improbable to happen.

Commander Ross had considered retiring Sir Barton at the end of 1919, wanting, he said, to avoid the inevitable decline that happens when horses stay too long at the party. After the Marathon, perhaps he should have listened to that instinct. Another heavy impost in another start so close to the one before it appeared to be too much for the chestnut colt over the longer distance. On a chilly spring day, Sir Barton and Earl Sande went to the post with his two competitors, standing on the outside, with Wildair in the middle and Bolster on the rail. A steady rain had turned the Havre de Grace dirt into mud, heavy going that proved problematic for several favorites that day.

At the break, Sir Barton showed his nose in front briefly, but Earl Haynes on Wildair moved to the lead within strides. The Triple Crown winner stayed with Wildair for the first six furlongs, sitting a couple of lengths off as he "appeared to be able to go to the front when he pleased." Sande took Sir Barton wide on the final turn into the stretch, opening up a hole on the rail. Sir Barton made his run at Wildair as they turned for home, but the heavy impost and the quick turnaround left him empty of effort. Bolster passed him on the inside, nearly catching Wildair, who had been running under restraint on the lead. Earl Haynes shook up Wildair and pulled away from Bolster, managing to stay a neck ahead of the lightly weighted challenger. Sir Barton straggled home third, four lengths behind. His performance was lackluster, as he appeared unable or unwilling to respond to Sande's urging in the stretch. The flagellation he took in print was easily as sharp as the lash that Sande had used.[47]

The Marathon was "the fall of the mighty," as the best son of Star Shoot "staggered in four lengths behind Bolster, with weary legs and badly besmirched reputation."[48] The "great" Sir Barton had suffered "an ignominious defeat," able to hold onto his speed for only the first six furlongs and clearly not ready for anything beyond that.[49] Were the imposts too much for even this Thoroughbred, the champion of the previous year? In his first three starts of 1920, Sir Barton had carried 133 pounds twice and then 135 pounds, with only one win in three. Weight was supposed to be the great equalizer, and these assignments appeared to do the job. The heavy imposts that his three-year-old season earned him might have been a badge of honor, but so far they also seemed to be his downfall.

As Havre de Grace wound down its spring meet, H. G. Bedwell looked to reward his champion colt by starting him again, trying to take advantage of the star handicapper's apparent soundness even with the heavy weights assigned to him. Three days after his lackluster performance in the Marathon, Sir Barton was back at the barrier, now for the 1¹⁄₁₆-mile Philadelphia Handicap. For the fourth time in less than two weeks, the champion carried more than 130 pounds, giving his competition as much as 37 pounds! Even Billy Kelly, a champion horse and no stranger to handicap imposts, carried only 127 pounds. After two starts at six furlongs, with strong performances and then an embarrassing loss at 1¹⁄₁₆ mile, the Triple Crown winner was again trying the longer distance. What Ross and Bedwell were looking for in these performances was unclear, but they appeared determined to enter their two star older horses in as many handicaps as they could before the meet's end.

Perhaps owing to the exposure of Sir Barton's fallibility, eight other horses went to the post with the Ross duo, the largest field of the champion's spring campaign so far. Clarence Kummer was back on Sir Barton, and Earl Sande took his usual place astride Billy Kelly. Other than the Ross entry, the only horse of any stature in the field was A. K. Macomber's good handicapper Star Master; the other horses were mostly lightweight platers, horses running above their class. Sir Barton stood in the ninth post position, on the far outside, with only War Mask on his right, and Billy Kelly was toward the middle, in the sixth position.[50] At the break, Billy Kelly and Star Master went to the lead, with Sir Barton in third, lying in wait just a length ahead of the crowded field.

A half-mile in, Sir Barton had moved back to fourth; War Mask had slipped into the lead, leaving Billy Kelly fighting on the front end to keep up with the leaders. Just behind Sir Barton was a lightly weighted gelding named Crystal Ford, carrying 100 pounds and a lackluster past record, which explained his 106 to 1 odds. In the stretch, as War Mask, Billy Kelly, and Star Master tried to outrace each other, Sir Barton on their heels, Laverne Fator took Crystal Ford to the outside of the dueling trio. The gelding, who had shown very little in his past two starts at Havre de Grace, passed the tiring leaders in the last furlong of the 1¹⁄₁₆-mile race, his light weight and speed carrying him to win by a neck over Star Master. Billy Kelly finished in third place, a neck back of Macomber's horse, and Sir Barton, burdened by his 132 pounds, followed his stablemate.[51] The Triple Crown winner barely outlasted the lightly weighted Cromwell to finish fourth. It was another poor showing by the champion, who had finished out of the money twice already in 1920, breaking his streak of top-three finishes that had lasted all of 1919.

For the Ross horses, the Philadelphia was another ignominious loss. For Crystal Ford, in contrast, there had been an amazing reversal of form. After finishing behind other average horses in his previous starts, where he was unable to maintain his speed, the four-year-old gelding had pulled something akin to what Royce Rools had done at Pimlico in 1919. Royce Rools, trained by Andy Blakely and owned by T. H. Cross, had surprised everyone when he beat 1917 Kentucky Derby winner Omar Khayyam and Ross's good handicapper Boniface to win the Pimlico Spring Handicap at one hundred to one. The Maryland Jockey Club suspected something fishy about the sudden change in Royce Rools's form and suspended both his trainer and owner.[52] Cross was forced to liquidate his holdings, and A. K. Macomber bought Royce Rools; Blakely continued training and owning horses in Maryland.

Crystal Ford's reversal of form did not attract the same attention as Royce Rools's; the latter went on to win other handicaps and show that perhaps beating Omar Khayyam was not a fluke after all. The surprise winner of the Philadelphia attracted less attention than the horses that he beat or the price that he paid out for the win. Going off at odds of 106 to 1, Crystal Ford paid $214.40 to win, but the horses he beat, especially the Ross horses, dominated the copy devoted to the Philadelphia. Turf writers cited the role that the weight both Sir Barton and Billy Kelly had carried and the absence of weight on Crystal Ford had played in his surprise victory. Sure, the Triple Crown winner had run "courageously," but, again, the weight told the tale.[53] When it was time to make his move as his stablemate started to struggle, Sir Barton "found the weight too great a burden," unable to find that gear and take his place at the front of the field.[54] He seemed to lack "the dash or stamina that he had last season."[55] He and Billy Kelly straggled home, close enough to the top two finishers that another gear could have won either of them the race, but neither horse finding it.

As Havre de Grace closed, Pimlico opened for its spring meet, which was to include Man o' War's 1920 debut in the Preakness, scheduled for May 18. For Sir Barton, it was the home of his next stop, the Rennert Handicap, a one-mile race for four-year-olds and older, with a $2,500 purse. Despite the mixed results of his races so far that spring, he was still the heavyweight, once again toting 132 pounds and still spotting his competition almost 20 pounds or more. None of the other horses entered in the Rennert was of consequence, and, again, it was a given that Sir Barton should dominate this field. Bert Collyer, in his column of picks for the day, even said that bettors should "toss out [the] recent efforts of

Sir Barton, they have been too bad to be true, he's a stake horse and can beat anything they send out against him when the checks are in."[56] At this level, horses like Sir Barton had to be unbeatable, and any off performance could kill a reputation.

Collyer's analysis was accurate. With Sande back in the irons, Sir Barton returned to his winning ways, stalking the pace before taking the lead on the final turn to win the Rennert by a length. The Rennert was one of the three Ross victories of the day, with King Thrush, Ross's Derby hopeful, dominating an allowance race in preparation for his trip to Louisville, and Intrigante, one of the Ross two-year-olds, finally breaking her maiden over other juveniles.

With that victory, Sir Barton had won two of the five races he had run in two weeks, with one third-place finish and two finishes out of the money. Then Bedwell found a possible answer to the champion's inconsistency: a wrenched ankle.[57] Sir Barton was out indefinitely as his trainer decided to rest him and his stablemate Billy Kelly, who had been battling through his own spring starts. Commander Ross and his connections acutely felt the loss of these two lynchpins of the entire stable. With Cudgel sent to stud and the stable's younger horses continuing to develop, Sir Barton and Billy Kelly were meant to be the focus of the stable's collective glory in 1920 as they had been in 1919.

But this was a new year, and as Sir Barton exited the stage at Pimlico, another dominant chestnut made his three-year-old debut.

Star Shoot, Sir Barton's sire.

Sir Martin, Sir Barton's half-brother.

John E. Madden,
Sir Barton's breeder.

H. G. Bedwell
and Commander
J. K. L. Ross at
Saratoga, 1918.

(*Top, left*) James Ross, Commander Ross's father, 1901. McCord Museum, II-138346.

(*Top, right*) William Walker. Keeneland Library Collection.

(*Right*) James Kenneth Leveson Ross, 1914. McCord Museum, II-202470.

Sir Barton.

Sir Barton, Kentucky Derby winner, with trainer H. G. Bedwell (*holding bridle*) and jockey Johnny Loftus, 1919. Churchill Downs, Inc./Kinetic Corporation.

Kentucky Derby general admission ticket, Sir Barton's maiden win, 1919. Ken Grayson/Sutcliffe Collection.

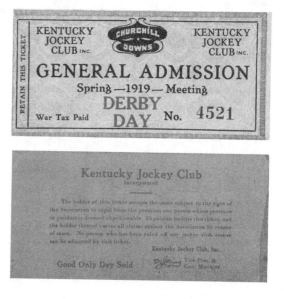

Earl Sande on Sir Barton, August 1920.

Sir Barton wins the Saratoga Handicap, August 2, 1920.

Sir Barton duels with Gnome in the Merchants and Citizens Handicap, August 28, 1920.

$ 75000. Match Race, won by Man O'War.

Sir Barton trails Man o' War in the Kenilworth Gold Cup, October 12, 1920. Ken Grayson/Sutcliffe Collection.

Ticket for the Kenilworth Gold Cup, October 12, 1920. Ken Grayson/Sutcliffe Collection.

Earl Sande on Billy Kelly, undated.

Johnny Loftus on War Cloud, the first horse to run in all three races that would become the Triple Crown, 1918.

Eternal, undated.

Dunboyne with Earl Sande, 1921.

Willie Knapp on Purchase, 1919.

Milkmaid with Earl Sande, undated.

Boniface with Earl Sande, undated.

Cudgel with Johnny Loftus, 1919.

Mad Hatter with Earl Sande, undated.

Exterminator with Albert Johnson, undated.

Man o' War with Earl Sande, 1920.

Frank Keogh, undated.

Cal Shilling, undated.

Left to right: Earl Sande, Frank Keogh, Albert Johnson, and Andy Schuttinger at the Saratoga scales, undated.

Earl Sande, undated.

Johnny Loftus, undated.

Clarence Kummer, undated.

Samuel Riddle and Elizabeth Dobson Riddle, undated.

Louis Feustel and Samuel Riddle, undated.

Sam Hildreth, undated.

B. B. Jones and his wife, Ethel, undated.

Sir Barton at Audley Farm, 1921. ©Jones/Feild Family Photograph Collection.

Sir Barton at Audley Farm, undated. ©Jones/Feild Family Photograph Collection.

Sir Barton with Price Sallee at Audley Farm, undated. ©Jones/Feild Family Photograph Collection.

Sir Barton on Dr. Hylton's ranch outside of Douglas, Wyoming, 1934. Courtesy of *Casper Star-Tribune*.

Portrait of Sir Barton with Johnny Loftus by Franklin Brooke Voss. Courtesy of the National Museum of Racing.

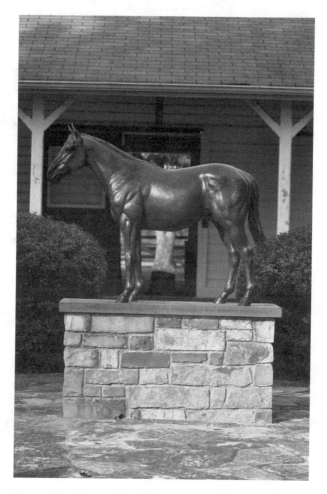

Statue of Sir Barton at Audley Farm's Stallion Barn.
Photograph by Corey Kirk.

Sir Barton's grave in Washington Park, Douglas, Wyoming. Photograph provided by the City of Douglas, Wyoming.

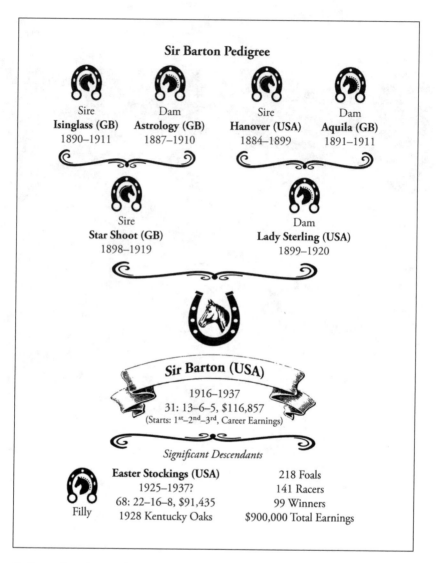

Sir Barton Pedigree

Sire	Dam	Sire	Dam
Isinglass (GB)	**Astrology (GB)**	**Hanover (USA)**	**Aquila (GB)**
1890–1911	1887–1910	1884–1899	1891–1911

Sire	Dam
Star Shoot (GB)	**Lady Sterling (USA)**
1898–1919	1899–1920

Sir Barton (USA)

1916–1937
31: 13–6–5, $116,857
(Starts: 1st–2nd–3rd, Career Earnings)

Significant Descendants

Easter Stockings (USA)	218 Foals
1925–1937?	141 Racers
68: 22–16–8, $91,435	99 Winners
1928 Kentucky Oaks	$900,000 Total Earnings

Filly

Sir Barton's pedigree. Graphic by Jamie Kelly.

Records and Matches

After five races in fifteen days, Sir Barton landed on the proverbial shelf a wrenched ankle the result of all of that training and racing. H. G. Bedwell knew his Triple Crown winner inside and out; he was a horse that gorged on his feed and disliked workouts. Sir Barton needed to *race,* so it took staging his workouts as races to get him ready for anything. Bedwell had tried running the champion in a handful of starts close together in an effort to ready him for the rich handicaps that came in the summer and the fall. But Sir Barton teetered on the brink of lameness with every start, and that kind of schedule was too much for a horse with such uncertainty in every step.

His recovery might have kept him out of sight, but he was not out of mind by any stretch. In early June, handicapper Walter Vosburgh put out his weights for the Suburban Handicap, which had the son of Star Shoot at the top of the list at 129 pounds.[1] He was ranked above Purchase, who had yet to make a start in 1920, at 128 pounds; Exterminator, a Kentucky Derby winner and great distance horse, at 123 pounds; and Man o' War at 114 pounds.[2] Vosburgh established with this ranking that Sir Barton was better than Purchase, though some, including sportswriter W. C. Vreeland, maintained that Purchase surely could beat the Triple Crown winner if they were ever to meet on the track again.[3] As 1920 went on, though, one horse's performances in the Belmont Stakes, the Travers, and more would make the name of Sir Barton's true rival clear.

The difference in how Vosburgh saw Sir Barton and Man o' War at that point in the year was stark; Sir Barton still held his place as the best of the best, even after his mixed start to 1920; although juvenile champ

Man o' War's performances to this point were impressive, they were not enough, because of his age, to unseat the son of Star Shoot—yet.

As Sir Barton rested, though, Man o' War ran and ran and ran and set the whole world on fire. Could anyone battle those flames and not be consumed in the process?

Not one of the three-year-olds in the Ross Stable was ready for the Kentucky Derby in 1920, so, the year after his historic win, the commander was out of the mix for the Run for the Roses. The stable instead entered King Thrush in the Preakness, its lone representative in that rich stake.[4] Absent from the Preakness, though, was Kentucky Derby winner Paul Jones: Ral Parr's Derby winner was a gelding, and, as in 1919, geldings were still ineligible for the Preakness.[5]

As Pimlico looked toward the Preakness and the debut of Man o' War, Commander Ross not only brought King Thrush to the barrier but also the Woodlawn vase, the Civil War–era trophy that had become one of the rewards of a Preakness victory. Tradition held that the owner who took the trophy home could offer it to the winner of any race at Pimlico the next year, but in this case it had been passed down to the winner of the Preakness since the trophy's return in 1917.[6] In addition, the Maryland Jockey Club prepared for another Preakness tradition: painting the almost life-size, horse-shaped weathervane on the Pimlico clubhouse cupola each year with the colors of the winning owner. For the time being, the orange and black of Ross Stables still hung supreme over Pimlico.[7]

It would be the last time those colors would reign supreme.

In bypassing the Kentucky Derby, Man o' War had yet to show what he could do at three years old. The juvenile races limited horses to running less than a mile; the colt had shown that he could blaze through six furlongs with no trouble. What would that speed look like over a mile and an eighth? A mile and a quarter? His pedigree suggested that he possessed the stamina for a distance, and, sure, trainer Louis Feustel could work his colt out at those distances, but those longer workouts seemed to indicate that the colt tired toward the end of one mile.[8] So many horses who had shone in those shorter races at two years old dulled in the longer distance events at three. What would 1920 bring for Samuel Riddle's Man o' War?

Ten days after the Derby, five horses made the trip from Louisville to Baltimore to run in the Preakness, including Man o' War's conqueror from the Sanford, Upset. Wildair, the colt who had beaten Sir Barton in the Marathon Handicap, also came to challenge Man o' War. The Ross representative, King Thrush, stood next to the big red colt at the barrier, the stable's only challenger to Man o' War. In all, eight horses faced the barrier with Man o' War, "the best 3-year-olds of the season in all probability, certainly they were the best 2-year-olds of the last season."[9] Despite the big red colt's promising last workout at Belmont before shipping to Pimlico, the doubts about his ability to carry his speed over a distance brought out a slew of good horses to test him.[10]

In the end, he made them all look ordinary. Any remaining doubts about his speed and stamina evaporated as the colt dashed to the front three strides out from the barrier and then seemed to be running easy with the field trailing behind him, doing their best to keep up. When Kummer saw first King Thrush and then Upset make their runs at Man o' War, he let his horse have some rein; Man o' War increased his lead to three lengths before Kummer wrapped him up again.[11] The winning margin for the Preakness was a length and a half in a time of 1:51⅗, just three-fifths of a second off the record.

Both margin and time could have been even better than that had Riddle allowed Kummer to let his mount run freely the whole race. The record crowd of thirty thousand rained down "a storm of cheers" as the colt returned to the judges' stand, the spectators still marveling at the performance of the "King of the 3-Year-Olds."[12] While the Riddles collected the Woodlawn vase and celebrated their big red colt's victory, a man climbed the cupola and painted over the Ross orange and black with the Riddle yellow and black, Man o' War replacing Sir Barton both literally and figuratively.

Those new colors on the Pimlico weathervane were a portent of things to come.

After only one start in 1920, Man o' War continued to shine, the comparisons to stars of old inadequate in light of his demonstrations of how fast and far he could run. Sir Barton might have been "king of them all" in 1919, but in 1920 Man o' War was making a case for his own claim to the throne.[13] Indeed, one turf writer claimed that he was "the greatest colt this country has produced in a score of years, if indeed he is not the greatest racer the country has ever seen."[14]

While Sir Barton readied for late summer racing, Man o' War rode the momentum of his Preakness victory to New York, the same route that Sir Barton had plotted the previous year. In the Withers, Man o' War faced only two other horses and left them both many lengths behind him as he clocked the fastest mile in American history, 1:34⅘, and looked as if he could have lowered the record by many more seconds.[15] That performance, only his second start of 1920, attracted another crowd of thirty thousand and, with them, another round of praises from the elite of the racing world for the horse that had dazzled them all. "I never saw his equal," said R. T. Wilson, who owned Hannibal, the Travers Stakes winner in 1919.[16] Even Man o' War's breeder, August Belmont Jr., was impressed: "I always thought Tracery was the best horse I ever bred, but this colt appears to be a wonderful performer."[17] In 1919, the praises had been for the chestnut son of Star Shoot, who had swept the Triple Crown and the Withers Stakes in only thirty-two days. In 1920, these words landed on Man o' War, and they were destined to remain there for the rest of the century and beyond.

Man o' War's victory tour continued in Gotham as he went to the barrier next for the Belmont Stakes. Only one other horse met him there—Donnacona, who also had run in the Kentucky Derby and the Preakness—but it did not matter who stood with Man o' War at the barrier. Kummer and Man o' War navigated the zig-zag course at Belmont Park with ease, lowering the American record for 1⅜ miles to 2:14⅕. The crowd at Belmont, numbering twenty-five thousand as they had the previous year when Sir Barton won the same race, saw the performance of a century.[18] August Belmont Jr. lauded the Fair Play colt as the best seen in this country, though not the best that Major Belmont himself had ever seen.[19]

The colt's abilities seemed limitless, and the potential for any other horse to challenge him waned with each start. Horsemen looked for situations where they could provide a real test for the greatest horse the American turf had ever seen. While they all marveled at his apparent infallibility, they also want to see more and to test the limits of the colt's speed and stamina.[20] Could any other horse truly push him the way eager racing fans craved?

Much as in 1919, when Purchase had pushed Sir Barton to the limit in the Dwyer Stakes, the 1920 Dwyer would provide another epic confrontation and answer the question about what Man o' War would do when faced with a horse who looked him in the eye and did not flinch.

Like Sir Barton the previous year, Man o' War came to Aqueduct for the Dwyer ready to continue his winning ways. Of course, at this point, he had won so often and so emphatically that precious few owners wanted to pit their horses against a colt so dominant "that [he took] the heart out of the opposition."[21] H. P. Whitney, though, dug deep into his stable of horses and entered John P. Grier, a fresh three-year-old whom trainer James Rowe had been pointing toward this confrontation with Man o' War. The two were the only horses entered in the Dwyer, with Man o' War assigned 126 pounds to John P. Grier's 108.[22] These two colts had met as two-year-olds in the Futurity, where John P. Grier had, of course, finished second to Man o' War. So this meeting in the Dwyer would not be their first, nor would it be their last, but it was about to become their most memorable.

As the only two horses on the track for the Dwyer, Man o' War had to face John P. Grier with no other horses to distract and draw this new rival into a speed duel and clear the way for Kummer and Red to make their move. Aqueduct was packed with almost forty thousand fans eager to see if Louis Feustel's prediction about a speed record would come true. With the start of the Dwyer obscured by the trees near the chute, fans did not see how Man o' War nearly lost the race just as it began, slipping on a wet spot in the Aqueduct dirt.[23]

The advantage of a twenty-eight-foot stride was that once the colt had his feet under him, he could make up ground with only a few pumps of his legs. As the two colts came out into the clear, the crowd saw the red Fair Play colt but could not find John P. Grier. Jockey Eddie Ambrose was not about to let Kummer settle Man o' War on the lead and so had John P. Grier look his rival in the eye as they rolled over the dirt course. Kummer had no choice but to stay put; John P. Grier had the weight advantage, and Ambrose was betting that the colt's speed could hold out because of it. The result of this strategy put the two colts so even that the crowd could not see John P. Grier next to the larger Man o' War.[24]

Their fractions sizzled: a half-mile in 0:46, besting the track record by two-fifths of a second, and three-quarters in 1:09⅖, one-fifth of a second faster than the world record. The two matched strides, coming out of the last turn together, John P. Grier giving up nothing to Man o' War. They entered the long homestretch, nearly a half-mile, eye to eye. Truly, it was the first time that Man o' War had had another horse look him in the eye and not flinch, a new sensation for the most dominant horse in recent memory, his first real test. They burned through a mile in 1:35⅗, bettering the track record by four-fifths of a second. With only an eighth of a mile to go, Man o' War flinched, and John P. Grier nosed in front of him. That advantage was soon a head and then a half-length, and Ambrose tried to give his mount a breather so that he could collect himself and prepare for the final rush toward the wire.[25]

A crack resounded between the two of them: Kummer stung Man o' War with the whip, a sensation the champion horse had not felt since the chaotic Sanford nearly a year ago. The red colt reacted, picking up his stride, and in two or three pumps of his great legs took back the lead. Ambrose tapped John P. Grier, again bringing his mount level with his rival. Kummer's arm flew again, the leather coming down on Man o' War's flank and tapping into that deep reserve within his great colt. John P. Grier had no answer for that final surge. The lead at the wire was a length and a half for Man o' War, the hardest-fought length and a half of his career.[26]

Their last furlong was a walk compared to the rest of the race: 0:13⅕ seconds, a sign that the two horses had been slowing the whole way, even as the stakes ramped higher. Regardless, the Dwyer's final time was 1:49⅕, a world record. W. C. Vreeland, sportswriter for the *Brooklyn Daily Eagle,* proclaimed Man o' War "a super horse of all times" and the Dwyer "one of the greatest races that has ever taken place in this or any other country," demonstrating to the world once again why Man o' War deserved the superlatives.[27] Riddle's colt stood alone atop his division— indeed, atop the racing world as a whole. With his epic vanquishing of John P. Grier, what horses were left to challenge him? John P. Grier was the second best of his age. Man o' War faced threats from no other horses within his division. Who else could hold a candle to this "Horse of the Century"?

Perhaps the answer lay outside of the three-year-olds, within the next echelon up: older horses, handicappers such as Exterminator and

Sir Barton. Truly, they were the only challenge remaining. Where and when were the only questions left to answer.

By mid-1920, the Ross Stable already had amassed $120,000 in purse money. Unlike 1919, the purses did not come from the stable's three-year-olds but instead from its older horses, such as Boniface, who racked up a number of wins in 1920.[28] Even with the success of Boniface, the stable as a whole was not performing as well as it had by the same point in 1919. The two- and three-year-olds were not showing up the way that Billy Kelly, Milkmaid, and Sir Barton had the previous year. The Ross Stable could lose its place at the top of standings if those good older horses were not replaced with younger talent of the same caliber.

Nearly three weeks after his win in the Rennert, Sir Barton appeared at the top of the list of weights for the Kentucky Handicap. His impost for the 1¼ mile was to be 135 pounds, Boniface's 132 pounds.[29] Cal Shilling came westward to Louisville with surging Boniface, and Earl Sande followed after his ride on King Thrush in the Preakness.[30] Sir Barton was to come to Louisville, too, but he never did arrive there. The reason? H. G. Bedwell had been unable to secure an express railcar for Sir Barton.[31] More than once during this layoff because of the wrenched ankle, speculation held that the four-year-old would be sent here or there to run, and more than once he stayed put, Bedwell working on making over his charge to return him to form. The goal? Saratoga and the prestigious and rich races to be run there.

Sir Barton was not the only horse aimed in that direction. So many other great Thoroughbreds were headed toward the Spa for the late summer's racing there: Exterminator, Lucullite, Man o' War, and more. Absent, though, would be Sir Barton's supposed rival, Purchase, who after suffering another injury while training for the Metropolitan Handicap in late May had not made a single start in 1920.[32] This injury would delay their meeting yet again, leaving Sir Barton alone at the top—for now.

His mixed results that spring threatened to tarnish the hard-won reputation the Triple Crown winner had earned in 1919. As May turned into June and then July and now with August on the horizon, Sir Barton was out of the spotlight long enough that the poor performances in Maryland had been explained and put aside. His entry in a number of handicaps and the heavy imposts assigned to him for each kept his name in the papers, but really he had not given anyone anything to write or gush about—yet. His eagerly anticipated return to the barrier would set the stage for an epic confrontation that would make the reputation of one horse and break the reputation of the other for years to come.

With the Ross Stable now in Saratoga, Sir Barton continued to work out, showing that he was ready to go after his recovery from that wrenched ankle in the spring; in the week leading up to his start in the Saratoga Handicap, he ran 1¼ miles in 2:05⅗ under a hard hold.[33] The champion was ready to run, and the racing world was happy to see him.

Sir Barton's reemergence onto the scene was celebrated with the news in late July that he was awarded the top impost for the Saratoga Handicap: 129 pounds. The mixed results of his spring campaign had not dampened handicapper Vosburgh's respect for the Triple Crown winner.[34] Getting top weight in the Saratoga Handicap showed that the champion three-year-old of 1919 was still respected at four. Man o' War might be the first name on everyone's lips, his ceiling still the subject of speculation, but Sir Barton had shown his talent and speed time and again and was ready to show the depth of both again at Saratoga.

In early August, the crowds came to upstate New York from South America, Canada, Cuba, and other parts of the United States, all seeking diversion amid the glorious backdrop of the Spa—and a glimpse of the big red colt who had the racing world a-flutter.[35] The historic track featured a new fountain in the center of the sunken star in its infield as well as a new and now faster track surface, anticipating the battles to come.[36] The town was spick-and-span, ready for the throngs that would fill its idyllic grounds and lavish hotels as they descended for this month-long celebration of the Thoroughbred. Even though Man o' War would not be seen at the barrier until the Miller Stakes on August 7, Saratoga treated the incoming masses to a star-studded Saratoga Handicap on opening day.

Eight horses made up the handicap's field, with such notables as Exterminator, the 1918 Kentucky Derby winner and great long-distance runner; Mad Hatter, Sir Barton's conqueror in the Autumn Handicap; and Boniface, Sir Barton's stablemate and noted handicap contender.[37] Sir Barton's return to racing was not going to be a cakewalk with these horses standing next to him at the barrier. Carrying 129 pounds, Sir Barton also shouldered the heaviest weight in the field, even more than another classic winner, Exterminator, who carried 126 pounds. Those workouts earlier in the week gave everyone a glimpse of a horse who was ready to dominate again, so bettors made Sir Barton the favorite going into the race. His spring starts and long layoff, though, left some with doubt about his fitness, speculating that he would need a race to round into form once again.[38]

On a lovely summer day, the first day of Saratoga's celebrated meet, a record crowd turned out to enjoy the fruits of the improvements made both to the town and to the track. The wealthy and fashionable filled the stands, the who's who of racing in attendance as the five horses made their way onto the fast track around 4:30 in the afternoon for the day's feature, the Saratoga Handicap.[39] Boniface and two others had scratched, leaving Exterminator, Wildair, The Porter, and Mad Hatter, "the outstanding cracks of the handicap division," to face the Triple Crown winner at the barrier.[40] Earl Sande and Sir Barton took their position, standing in the second post, one off from the rail. Wildair, who had beaten Sir Barton in the Marathon, stood to his left, and the great Exterminator on his right. He was giving each of these horses weight, as little as 3 pounds and as much as 14 pounds. Each of those challengers, horses deep in experience and talent, had a chance to beat him. How would the four-year-old reward Vosburgh's estimation of his deep talent and speed?

The five stood at the barrier for only a minute, starter Mars Cassidy getting the field away cleanly. With the drop of the flag, the five broke almost in sync, but by the first quarter Sir Barton had pulled into the lead, Sande chilly and patient on his back. Jockey Andy Schuttinger allowed Exterminator to trail, content to reserve his speed. The Porter and Wildair flanked Sir Barton as they passed the first quarter in a moderate 0:24 seconds and then the half-mile in 0:47⅘. As The Porter and Wildair gave up their chase, Mad Hatter made his move, forcing Sir Barton to greater speed, completing three-quarters of a mile in 1:11. When Mad Hatter was spent, he fell back, and Sande gave his mount a breather; their mile time was 1:36, the pace slowing some as they approached the race's end. With Mad Hatter's challenge repelled, Sir Barton then faced a challenge from the venerable Exterminator, Schuttinger riding the rail in his attempt to inch his mount past Sir Barton. Sande gave the Triple

Crown winner a tap, and Sir Barton turned on the speed again, repelling Exterminator's efforts and pulling away from the field in the stretch. At the wire, after Sir Barton's fast fractions had burned off all of his competition, including the venerable Exterminator, Sande eased up on Sir Barton as they flashed under the wire two lengths ahead of the field. The final time? Sir Barton covered the 1¼ miles in 2:01⅘, a track record and potentially the best ten-furlong time clocked to that point.[41]

In 1913, H. P. Whitney had brought his horse Whisk Broom II back from Europe to run in New York as racing tentatively restarted in the state after its two-year hiatus. After winning the Metropolitan and Brooklyn Handicaps, Whisk Broom II strode onto the Belmont oval for the Suburban Handicap, laden with 139 pounds and giving significant weight to all of his competitors.[42] In the end, the massive impost did not impede the speedy Whisk Broom II from covering the 1¼ miles in a flat 2:00, smashing the world record by nearly three seconds. From the moment the Whitney horse vaulted across the finish line, though, his time was in doubt. Aside from the incredulity of such a performance, which instantly inspired doubt about the spectacle, people suspected that the track's official clocker had misjudged the Suburban's special finish line and thus had stopped his watch too early.[43] An investigation by Belmont's stewards supported clocker W. B. Barretto's official time of 2:00 for the ten furlongs, though others present had their watches stopped at a second or two slower than what Barretto posted.[44] Regardless, the record still stood, though many present when Sir Barton turned in his own speedy performance claimed that his ten furlongs was faster—and more significant.

Among the cheering throng in the expansive Saratoga grandstand in August 1920 was Commander Ross and his family as well as trainer H. G. Bedwell, fresh off of his three-month remake of his demanding champion horse. Years later, a middle-aged J. K. M. "Jim" Ross would look back on that memorable day from his youth, when his father's Triple Crown champion demonstrated how he had earned the moniker "Horse of the Century" the previous year: "I cannot believe that there was a time when my father and Bedwell—all of us—were more exultant. Any number of Billy Kelly's two-year-old races? Perhaps. Sir Barton's Futurity? His Withers? Perhaps. There must have been other races in which our horses produced a comparable joy, but there were few, if any that gave us the sensation of supremacy that this one did."[45] Years later Earl Sande would cite this performance as "the best performance of a horse—time, weight, and class of opponents considered—I have ever witnessed. He gave the best handicap horses of his day weight and decisive beatings after setting his own pace all the way."[46] Sir Barton's performance from barrier to wire was better than his wins in the Kentucky Derby and the Maryland Handicap, which Johnny Loftus himself had cited as one of his favorite races of his career.[47] In the Saratoga Handicap, Sir Barton bettered his own personal best time by four-fifths of a second. The show of speed he put on inspired exuberance that gushed from the broad Saratoga grandstand into the next day's papers.

His performance was "perhaps the greatest race of his career," as he had conquered the likes of Exterminator and Mad Hatter and Wildair in emphatic fashion.[48] The record crowd for Saratoga's opening day greeted the winning Sir Barton with cheers from all sides, "not that he had been heavily supported, but because he is a horse that has become more or less of a turf idol."[49] His showing in the Saratoga Handicap "broke the heart of such a grand Thoroughbred as Sam Hildreth's Mad Hatter," similar to the effect that Man o' War had on his own conquered challengers.[50] After a spring's worth of lackluster starts, this return to form in the Saratoga Handicap renewed those memories of his form in 1919, when he was "the greatest Thoroughbred in the world."[51] Henry King called his win "more than a record breaking performance. It was wonderful, little less than phenomenal, and, when he stepped past the judges he was proclaimed the greatest handicap horse in the world, and the equal, if not the superior, of the invincible Man o' War at weight for age."[52] Sir Barton's display of great speed in the Saratoga Handicap, especially given the impost and the competition, seemed to be the better performance over those that Man o' War had turned in to that point, even the duel in the Dwyer. When the wooden blocks spelling out that record time were hung on the board in the Saratoga infield, those numbers ignited a spark in the collective minds of those present.

The next day Man o' War added some kindling to that nascent fire. The big red colt trotted out for a 1⅛-mile workout before his next start, the Miller Stakes, on August 7. Big Red's time for the workout was 1:49⅘; the American record for the same distance was 1:49⅕, a record Big Red himself had set in the Dwyer Stakes in July. Observers were blown away by the workout. The day before, as Sir Barton flashed under the wire in record time, he was "a turf idol," his form echoing that of his record-breaking three-year-old season.[53] Man o' War's workout, though, showed that the Triple Crown winner certainly did not stand alone atop the racing world. The talk began of bringing the two horses together on the track, preferably in the Saratoga Cup set for Saratoga's closing day. That race was 1¾ miles, ample distance for both horses to demonstrate this overwhelming speed that they had been showing in their separate starts. What could they do if they were to meet on the hallowed Saratoga oval? Great crowds already thronged Man o' War each time he emerged from the barn, a spectacle of humanity doing anything to catch a glimpse of this marvel. A meeting between Man o' War and Sir Barton would be an exhibition unlike any other, sure to attract crowds eager for the diversion.

"I hope he won't duck us," H. G. Bedwell said, anticipating the questions about facing the big red colt. "I would have liked to see him run yesterday against Sir Barton on a weight for age basis. However, don't make any strong statements on the subject because you have to take them back."[54]

Louis Feustel, tired of hearing about Sir Barton's performance, said of his own colt's workout, "Red worked as fast as Sir Barton ran. . . . He could have gone a mile and a quarter in record time if I had sent him that distance at full speed."[55]

The rivalry talk had begun.

13

Lighting the Match

Archaeological evidence shows that humans first domesticated horses as early as 6000 BCE, spreading this new breed rapidly across Eurasia as they became an integral part of the proliferation of cultures and civilizations. Along with the domestication of the horse came one of the oldest sports known to humans: horse racing. The question of whose horse is the fastest became as essential to the pursuit of sport as the questions of who was the strongest or fastest person.

With the evolution of horse racing came the evolution of the breeds meant for racing, whether it was trotting, pacing, or running. The essential pursuit of breeding Thoroughbreds, horses created specifically for running, has been balancing speed with stamina. Every so often the sport is graced with horses who possess both in abundance, and when that happens, the primitive drive to determine supremacy kicks in once again.

This time, though, in 1920 the drumbeat came not from one man's challenge to another but from the crowd around them, the fans who thrilled at watching these horses run and the turf writers who were as invested in those horses as the average fan who stood next to them at the rail. The men behind the horses shied away from the challenge, their own fears keeping their horses away from each other. When one horse dominated every other horse his own age, his owner feared the unknown depth of his colt's talent and the inevitable frailty of any animal. The owner of another exceptional horse saw and heard more than he let on, reluctant to pit the already iconic speed and stamina of his rival against the fallible talent of his own champion.

The beat of the drum resounded with each headline, each inch of ink devoted to speculation that shared newsprint with facts. As August ticked by into September, the beat grew louder and more insistent, the percussive pressure weighing on Samuel Riddle and Commander J. K. L. Ross.

The match was lit by words, and only by deeds would it be doused.

Man o' War's start in the Dwyer showed the depth of talent and gameness that Riddle's red colt possessed, staring John P. Grier down and besting him in the final strides. Two days after the Dwyer, jockey Clarence Kummer was at Aqueduct trying to move a filly named Costly Colours into the lead as the field sprinted toward the finish of the day's last race. The filly stumbled, going to ground with Kummer pinned beneath her, his feet still in her irons. Quick thinking on the part of two other jockeys kept Kummer from being trampled, but the colt Flying Cloud was not so lucky. He tripped over the filly, his jockey landing clear of the melee and rolling under the rail to get out of the way. Temporarily knocked senseless, Flying Cloud recovered and walked away. Costly Colours lay on the track still; once they were able to free Kummer from her saddle, it was clear that the filly would not be able to rise despite her efforts to respond to her trainer's call.[1]

Despite being pinned underneath Costly Colours, Kummer seemed to escape the spill with only a few cuts on his arm and the inevitable shock involved with the proximity of death and injury amid flying horses. Two hours later, though, he walked into a local hospital to find that his shoulder was fractured.[2] His injury knocked him out of the saddle for several weeks, so when it came time for the Miller Stakes at Saratoga, Kummer was still a no-go for riding Man o' War.[3] Trainer Louis Feustel knew that they would need a jockey who was experienced and skilled enough to be able to keep Man o' War from overdoing it on the hard Saratoga track, so they "borrowed" Earl Sande from the Ross Stable.[4] The young Idahoan was on a streak at Saratoga, winning three races in one day that week and proving to be the most capable, if not the most popular, jockey on the circuit. Sande agreed and showed up in the Riddle black and yellow on race day, Feustel and Riddle telling the jockey to let the horse win comfortably and not try to set any speed records. Sande—the same jockey who had ridden Sir Barton just days earlier to a track record—nodded and was boosted up onto Man o' War's back, his charge restless and ready to run.[5]

Sande's job of winning the race comfortably was not a challenge; neither of Man o' War's competitors, Donnacona and King Albert, wanted to confront the big red colt, so getting to and holding onto the lead were easy at every point in the race. The hard part was following the trainer's other instruction: to win at a comfortable speed. Man o' War challenged Sande's hold on him at every turn. The young jockey "was pulling at the reins as hard as he could and calling to Man o' War to slow up" as they hurtled down the stretch toward the finish. By the time the pair crossed the finish line—in first, of course—Sande was worn out from keeping Man o' War under wraps, but he still won the Miller in near-record time, just three-fifths of a second off the record set by Ross's own Cudgel.[6]

Sande for his part publicly praised Man o' War's prowess but told Feustel privately that he would not ride the colt again. "He damned near pulled my arms out of their sockets," the young rider told the trainer afterward.[7] In talking to the press, Sande said, "I never felt anything like that horse in my life. He is a regular machine. He strides further than anything I ever rode and does it so handily that you would not know he was running at all."[8] Sande had called his score on Sir Barton in the Saratoga Handicap one of his greatest rides, but these comments about Man o' War had to poke at Ross's pride. His contract jockey praising his own champion's supposed rival? Ross's dismay might not have been apparent at that moment, but Sande's comments would come back to haunt the jockey soon enough.

Though the war in Europe had been over for more than a year, horse racing in Canada had taken longer to recover from the cessation prompted by the fighting. By the end of 1919, limited racing meets had come and gone, but 1920 saw racing return to full strength in the Dominion, with Commander Ross in the mix, of course. On August 10, the specter of a potential meeting between Man o' War and Sir Barton hanging over them, Cal Shilling, Earl Sande, and Commander Ross accompanied the champion west to Fort Erie Race Track, just over the Canadian border.[9] There, the champion had a date with the barrier in the Dominion Handicap.

Sir Barton's train arrived one day before the race, greeted by summer rains and a small field for this romp.[10] The trains that brought the swelling mass of people to the track for his appearance needed two extra cars to accommodate the overflow.[11] Fort Erie's opening day greeted its patrons and starters with a heavy track for its feature, the 1¼-mile Dominion. The lack of competition and the 134 pounds Sir Barton had to carry demonstrated that he was one of the elite in racing.

His performance in the Dominion lived up to that billing. Breaking from the third post, the champion jumped out to the lead and "set a dazzling pace," hugging the rail while The Porter trailed on his outside, staying right on Sir Barton for seven furlongs. At that point, Sande decided that they were done toying with the competition and pushed his mount to lengthen his lead and seal the win for good. The Porter faded, and Bondage passed him after stalking the two front-runners for the majority of the race. Sir Barton, unpressed and hand ridden (without use of the crop), finished two lengths ahead, with Bondage closing the gap in the stretch.[12]

Sir Barton's time for the race was slower than his performance in the Saratoga, but the heavy track and easy trip meant that he did not need to turn on all of his speed to win on his first trip to Canada. The crowd that packed Fort Erie for the race did not care about the final time; they were excited to see the Ross horse in action, cheers ringing out as the winning horse and jockey returned to the judges' stand.[13] Sir Barton was, after all, not only Canadian owned but also still considered Man o' War's only rival. Commander Ross was jubilant, happy to be "a Canadian owner introducing to his native land his adopted son."[14]

The champion was back in a big way, racking up another big win and then hopping on a train to Saratoga, where the racing world was still clamoring for a meeting between the son of Star Shoot and the son of Fair Play.[15]

While Sir Barton rested from his Canadian jaunt, H. G. Bedwell decided to pass the time by needling Louis Feustel about matching Sir Barton against Man o' War. Every time Feustel demurred and refused to take the bait, Bedwell knew that others would see the big red colt's owner and trainer as fearing the great handicapper. To this point, Man o' War had stayed within his age group, facing and besting every horse he met at ages two and three. Riddle had shied away from running his champion against older horses, paranoid of what could happen to his once-in-a-life-time horse if he ever had to face the likes of Sir Barton and Exterminator—and had to carry the weight imposts that would come with those races. Feustel, though, finally reached his limit with Bedwell's teasing.

On August 16, five days before Man o' War's start in the Travers and five days after Sir Barton's domination in the Dominion, Bedwell passed Feustel on the track at Saratoga and tossed out a "How about that match race?" at his supposed rival.[16]

"I've been waiting for you," Man o' War's trainer snapped back. Feustel, whose level head and patience had been the right fit for the temperamental red colt, threw Bedwell's challenge back in his face. "I'll race you this morning," Feustel shot back, "and I'll bet you $100 or $500 I beat you. If that's not enough, I think Mr. Riddle will back me for $5,000."[17]

That ended Bedwell's teasing for good. Feustel's challenge left the trainer "nonplussed for an instant, then made a joke of it and walked away," not ready to pick up the gauntlet Feustel had just thrown down.[18] As Bedwell walked away, Feustel could be heard yelling at his retreating back, "I'll meet you soon enough. I'll meet you in the Cup and if you don't run out I'll show you that you only think you have the greatest horse."[19]

Feustel's remarks all but guaranteed that Man o' War would run in the Saratoga Cup on the meet's final day. "The only thing that would keep my horse out is an accident. I don't think Bedwell is overanxious to meet me and he might have an engagement for Sir Barton in Canada about that time," the trainer declared.[20]

If Bedwell shied away from Feustel's remarks before the Travers, Man o' War's performance over that 1¼-mile track had to give even the most ardent Sir Barton supporter pause. Facing Upset and John P. Grier, the only two horses who had ever challenged or bested Riddle's big red colt, Man o' War flew to the lead at the start, cutting off both horses' chance to hem him in one way or another. Jockey Andy Schuttinger, subbing for a still-injured Clarence Kummer, kept a strong hold on his mount, even slowing his colt enough to invite John P. Grier and jockey Eddie Ambrose to come up alongside them. The Whitney colt would not move, preferring to stay back of Man o' War's heels. John P. Grier recognized his rival from their lockstep confrontation in the Dwyer, where

Man o' War had looked him in the eye and bested him, and was apparently loathe to reengage. Upset hung behind both horses, waiting for his chance to make a run.[21]

Man o' War ticked off the fractions in record time while carrying 129 pounds, moving so easily away from John P. Grier that the crowds that lined the rail on both sides gasped. As the 1¼ miles shrunk to less than a quarter-mile, Upset made his move, his sights on the finish line, where he had once come home in front of the big red colt. Schuttinger let Upset creep up on them, but never once did either of the Whitney colts threaten the dominant Man o' War. Under a hand ride, the sting of the whip unnecessary, Man o' War had slowed down over that last quarter-mile, but his speedy early fractions nevertheless guaranteed that he would come home in a fast time for the ten furlongs. On Saratoga's infield board, the wooden numbers spelled out the final time for the 1920 Travers Stakes, 2:01⅘. Man o' War had equaled the track record Sir Barton had set only nineteen days earlier.[22]

The *Daily Racing Form*'s headline the next day said what the thirty thousand present for Man o' War's victory must have been thinking: "Man o' War Is Invincible."[23]

Feustel's guarantee about the Saratoga Cup stoked the excitement of turf fans everywhere. Anticipation of a meeting between Sir Barton and Man o' War, any meeting, dominated American sports pages. Man o' War's performance in the Travers saw him equal the time Sir Barton had posted in the Saratoga Handicap, a race that seemed to up the stakes in the rivalry between the two. The Triple Crown winner, with his next start on the horizon, the Merchants and Citizens Handicap, had another chance to show everyone, including those backing Man o' War, why he was the right horse to challenge the big red colt.

Hot streaks can knock an average horse into a new bracket, bringing him from also-ran to horse-to-beat in the blink of an eye. But Man o' War's winning record was more than a hot streak; his dominance was the stuff of legends. Sir Barton had had his own hot streak going in 1919 until he met Purchase in the Dwyer, but he returned to form later in the year, as he would do again and again throughout his career. He occasionally would meet horses who had streaks of wins that garnered them mentions in the columnar inches of newspapers. In late August 1920, one such horse on a hot streak was Gnome.

Sired by Whisk Broom II, the horse who held the disputed record of 2:00 for the 1¼ mile, Gnome was one of those horses whose pedigree came with great expectations and whose lackluster performances promptly erased them. Unraced at two, Gnome's three-year-old season was one spent racing behind better horses, but at four he was experiencing something of a renaissance at Saratoga.[24] Now part of the Virginia farm owner Samuel Ross's stable, Gnome caught everyone's attention when he finished third behind the good handicap horses Naturalist and Boniface by a couple of lengths in the Lake George Handicap early in the Saratoga meet.[25] Then he won a mile allowance race by five lengths and followed that win with a victory in the Champlain Handicap by looping around the outside of a crowd of good handicap horses, including Exterminator and Mad Hatter, and pulling away to win by a length and a half.[26] By the final week of Saratoga's August meet, Gnome had made enough of a name for himself that the *Daily Racing Form* remarked that "it would not surprise anyone to see the speedy Gnome give the Ross champion the battle of his life."[27]

A week after Man o' War had equaled Sir Barton's track record, Sir Barton trotted onto the Saratoga oval for the 1³⁄₁₆-mile Merchants and Citizens Handicap. This last week of August saw the end of Saratoga's meet, and a meeting between Sir Barton and Man o' War in the Saratoga Cup was anticipated with rapture, especially as inches of newsprint traded speculation about what the big red dynamo had to fear from the older horse. Like Sir Barton's most recent start in the Dominion, this handicap had another small field, including Gnome, who was carrying 115 pounds to Sir Barton's 133 pounds. Bettors made Gnome the favorite, the break in weights enough to assume he held an advantage, especially given rumors that the Triple Crown winner had not shipped back well from Fort Erie.[28] At the barrier, Sir Barton stood with Gnome on his left and the lightweight Jack Stuart on his right.

When Mars Cassidy sent the field away, the champion dashed to the front, grabbing a one-length lead, with Gnome and then Jack Stuart on his heels. Around the first turn, jockey Johnny Callahan moved Jack Stuart past Gnome, Frank Keogh content to let his mount sit a couple of lengths behind to conserve energy. Sitting chilly on the back of the chestnut champion, Earl Sande kept Sir Barton on the lead, staying a length ahead of Jack Stuart, whose weaving kept Gnome behind him in last. They stayed that way on the backstretch and into the final turn, Sir Barton appearing to pull at the reins with Sande holding him steady.[29]

On the final turn, as the stretch opened up before the field, Callahan called on Jack Stuart to press Sir Barton, getting as far as the champion's saddlecloth before the lightweight faltered. Seeing Jack Stuart's challenge fail, Frank Keogh decided it was time to move. As the three came into sight of Saratoga's grandstand, he took Gnome to the outside, around Jack Stuart, and bore down on Sir Barton, intent on using Gnome's speed to challenge the front-runner. Sande knew that Keogh was bearing down on them, glancing back to see the challenger coming at them in a rush.[30]

Nearly two years earlier, Sande's inexperience had allowed Andy Schuttinger to fool him into a move that lost Billy Kelly the match race with Eternal. Now, with steely resolve coursing through his veins, Sande urged Sir Barton on, determined to hold off the oncoming challenge. He kept his mount on the rail, forcing Gnome to come at him on the outside; staying on the rail allowed Sande to keep Sir Barton straight and prevented Gnome from pushing Sir Barton out. Sande knew that his mount, already pushed to a frenetic pace, could not let up now and so urged him with hands and whip and voice, staying just a head in front of Gnome as they thundered toward the wire.[31]

As the challenger closed in on Sir Barton, as the margin shrunk inch by precious inch, the speed was such that a tiring Gnome bore out ever so slightly, unable to maintain the straight course necessary to keep pressuring Sir Barton. The crack of Keogh's whip brought the colt back into line, but it was too late. The momentary bobble was enough to allow the Triple Crown winner to reach peak gameness, sticking his nose in front. As they came down to the wire, each stride had one horse or the other in front, so close that half of the crowd swore Gnome took it, while the other half knew Sir Barton had it. Sir Barton and Gnome had battled to the wire, an epic confrontation that only added to the Triple Crown winner's legacy.[32]

They hit the wire together, the great crowd filling the Saratoga air with cheers and shouts at the spectacle that they had just witnessed. When Sir Barton's number went up on the board, the crowd burst with clamor again, still arguing over the finish. Even Commander Ross and H. G. Bedwell, both of whom had been standing by the finish line at race's end, were not sure of their horse's victory until his number was posted on the board. The stirring finish and sizzling time marked the Merchants and Citizens Handicap as "one of the best, if not the best race of his career," showing that Sir Barton was "one of the very best handicap horses in training."[33]

When the race's time hit the board, the clamor for a meeting between the Triple Crown winner and the younger and supremely dominant Man o' War began to intensify.[34] Sir Barton's time of 1:55⅗ set a world record for the 1³⁄₁₆ mile, bettering by a full second Man o' War's time for the same distance in the Miller Stakes. Man o' War had equaled Sir Barton's record for the 1¼ mile in the Travers. In the summer of 1920, no other horse could come anywhere close to Man o' War—except Sir Barton. Ross's great champion had set two records in the month of August, beating the best of what Saratoga had to offer. In the eyes of fans and writers alike, Sir Barton was the only horse with a ghost of a chance of looking Man o' War in the eye—and then passing him.

The chance for the two rivals to meet slipped away from Saratoga as both Man o' War and Sir Barton declined to start in the Saratoga Cup. Feustel's guarantee that his red colt would start in that feature on the last day of the meet at the Spa gave way to Riddle's preference to keep the colt on schedule for the remainder of his three-year-old season.[35] Citing uncertainty about getting a railroad car for his champion colt if they stayed too long in upstate New York, Feustel put Man o' War on a train back to New York City.[36] In the meantime, turf writers and fans alike lamented the Ross and Riddle reluctance to meet, judging that "the owners of Sir Barton and Man o' War are afraid of each other and do not care to risk a meeting."[37]

Instead, Man o' War was back at Belmont, ready to face his age group again in the Lawrence Realization. By the morning of September 4, Man o' War had only one competitor, Sea Mint. The lightly raced colt was a maiden, though, and his connections wanted a spot where they could show him that winning was possible, so they scratched. The scratch left Belmont Park with the possibility of a walkover; the crowd might have wanted to see an exhibition of Man o' War's speed, but Samuel Riddle wanted to avoid the crowd's possible scorn at the absence of competition for the big red colt. Instead, an hour before the race, Sarah

Jeffords, the Riddles' niece, entered her own horse Hoodwink, who had run six furlongs the day before and now came into the race at the odds of one hundred to one. The race was literally Man o' War's to win, barring injury or other disaster, attracting a crowd of twenty-five thousand to Belmont Park for the spectacle.[38]

And a spectacle it was. Hoodwink led for only a second as the flag came down and the two horses flew away from the barrier. After one hundred yards, Man o' War passed Hoodwink; by the first quarter, he was twenty lengths ahead. Kummer, back in the saddle after fracturing his shoulder, let the champion colt run, giving the throng of people present the show they were hoping to see. In his recap of the Lawrence Realization, W. C. Vreeland effused that "poor old Father Time was as badly beaten as Hoodwink," such was the colt's speed.[39] By the time Man o' War crossed the finish line, one hundred lengths in front, he had set a world record for the 1⅝ mile, 2:40⅘, bettering the old record by nearly two seconds.[40]

Prior to the race, the Belmont management had persuaded Samuel Riddle to allow Man o' War to run as full out as possible in order to measure the colt's stride. The track's caretakers harrowed the dirt course, smoothing over the hoofmarks from the previous races, and after Man o' War came back from his world-record race, racing officials ran out onto the track, measuring the hoof prints that the great red colt had left behind. Man o' War's stride measured twenty-five feet when he was not pressed, shortening to twenty-four feet, eight inches when he was sprinting. He covered the ground "like some great bird in full flight," running so effortlessly that "he showed no signs whatever of being tired."[41]

As the racing world buzzed about the Lawrence Realization, August Belmont Jr. pursued still something even more elusive than a three-year-old willing to face Man o' War on a racetrack: Sir Barton versus Man o' War. Sir Barton had been entered for the Manhattan Handicap on September 2, but Bedwell decided that his champion had spent too much time on a train and not enough time in training.[42] Bedwell knew that his horse was not ready to meet Man o' War just yet, admitting that Sir Barton "was not himself when he ran against Gnome at Saratoga, although he won that race."[43] The trainer would have to be careful with his Triple Crown winner if he wanted to keep him in racing shape for the fall. Belmont, though, dangled an additional $10,000 for the Jockey Club

Stakes, trying to entice Commander Ross to send Sir Barton to the barrier alongside Man o' War.[44]

H. G. Bedwell declined the offer. "Sir Barton has been on the [railroad] cars a lot and as he is a gross horse and fills up quickly he requires more work than any other of my string. . . . It is going to take a long time to get him where I think he will be at his best."[45] In addition, the Jockey Club Stakes was a weight-for-age affair, meaning that Sir Barton could give Man o' War 8 pounds or more, a significant advantage for the big red colt. Both had turned in performances at significant weights, but weight seemed to tell more on the older Sir Barton than it did on the younger Man o' War: thus, in the judgment of writers such as W. C. Vreeland, the older horse could not concede weight to the big red three-year-old and expect to have a chance.[46] Louis Feustel assured the world that Man o' War would be at the Jockey Club Stakes, no matter who the other starters were. Man o' War again faced only other three-year-olds there, though, no older horses willing to meet him in this Belmont feature. None of them was able to give Man o' War anything close to a challenge.

Sea Mint once again entered a race with Man o' War and then scratched the day of, but at least Damask was still in the race, ready to provide some sort of competition for the Riddle colt. Man o' War barely acknowledged his challenger's existence. After the first quarter, Red was four lengths ahead; in the stretch, his lead was twelve lengths, and at the finish fifteen.[47] Even under Kummer's steady hold, Man o' War ran the 1½ miles in 2:28⅘, a new American record.[48] To this point in 1920, Man o' War had vanquished every horse who faced him, setting records left and right. With winnings of $162,465, the colt was on track to pass $200,000, given the right opportunities. Riddle certainly would not risk his singular three-year-old for any old race. Indeed, the Riddles passed on meeting Exterminator in the two-mile Autumn Gold Cup four days after the Jockey Club Stakes, opting instead to send their big red colt back to Maryland for the richer and shorter Potomac Handicap.[49]

As Man o' War was loaded onto a rail car bound for Maryland, the offers for a match race that would pit him against the best of his elders flew back and forth as fast as the trains that crisscrossed the country around him.

In 1919, Sir Barton had won eight of his thirteen starts, including the

Kentucky Derby, the Preakness Stakes, the Withers Stakes, and the Belmont Stakes, never finishing out of the money. In 1920, he won five of his eight starts, in most carrying more than 130 pounds. He set records at the 1¼ mile and the 1³⁄₁₆ mile. All of these accomplishments came while running on the brink of unsoundness, the shelly hooves he had inherited from his sire likely leaving him sore more often than outsiders knew. At 15.2 hands, he was more compact than many of his contemporaries, but barrel-chested with well-muscled back legs, capable of great speed but also a gluttonous appetite. Even as a yearling, he had stood out as "the king of them all," as Frank Brosche had declared at Hamburg Place.

Man o' War might have been taller, won more money, set more records, and even captured more fame, but in the fall of 1920 only Sir Barton possessed the potential to look him in the eye and pass him.

That was why Colonel Matt Winn, the master promoter of American Thoroughbred racing, spent time at Saratoga trying to convince Samuel Riddle, who had never allowed Man o' War to race in Kentucky, to bring the colt to the Bluegrass State to run against Sir Barton. He offered $25,000 plus a $2,500 gold cup to both Riddle and Commander Ross. Ross, ever the sportsman, agreed to Winn's terms, eager to have his champion face Riddle's.[50] Then Laurel chimed in with an offer of $30,000.[51] Ross and Riddle agreed to hold out for $50,000, neither willing to risk their precious champions for anything less.[52] For Riddle, that kind of money would push Man o' War past Domino in terms of money won. For Commander Ross, $50,000 was a bet, a gamble akin to the one that Arnold Rothstein had proposed prior to the 1919 Kentucky Derby. That kind of money had prompted him to start Sir Barton alongside Billy Kelly and put them on the road that had led them here. Commander Ross was a wealthy man, a philanthropist, a lover of the undulating seas and fast horses. That kind of money might not mean that much to him in the long run, but beating Man o' War? That was priceless. If those were the terms that would bring the opportunity, so be it.

As the days wore on, offers poured in, and serious discussions between the owners began. At first, the match race discussions included just Samuel Riddle and Commander Ross. The first $50,000 bid came in, but its source might have been a surprise to some: A. M. "Abe" Orpen, the owner and promoter of several tracks on the Canadian side of the

Detroit River, including Kenilworth Park. H. G. Bedwell had trained for Orpen in 1913, during Orpen's brief stint as an owner,[53] and later Bedwell had had success with his own horses as well as a few of Commander Ross's at Kenilworth Park in the track's early days.[54] Perhaps owing to Bedwell's familiarity with all of the men involved, Orpen had sent an emissary, E. G. Vivelle, to New York to personally meet with the two owners and extend the offer. Upon hearing that New York racing officials were considering a bid of their own, Orpen wired that he would top any offer by at least $10,000.[55]

Orpen also suggested that they extend an invitation to Willis Sharpe Kilmer and Exterminator. The negotiations continued anew, with Kilmer included in the mix. Colonel Winn was to be in Maryland by Sunday, but news about Orpen's offer and the owners' acceptance was broadcast before Winn got there, the terms settled forty-eight hours before Winn could present his in person.

Orpen's proposed race was 1¼ miles in October at Kenilworth Park, located just across the Detroit River from the city of Detroit, Michigan. Neither Ross nor Riddle had a preference about the distance, but Kilmer wanted the race to be at least 1⁵⁄₁₆ miles. Feustel and Riddle argued for weight-for-age conditions, meaning that Sir Barton and Exterminator, four and five years old, respectively, would carry more weight than the three-year-old Man o' War. Kilmer argued instead for handicap weights, with handicapper Walter Vosburgh to set the weights.[56]

The distance and the weight were sticking points for Kilmer; Exterminator was known for his wins at long distances, building up momentum the longer he had to run, in contrast to the front-running speedier styles of his two rivals. Riddle knew that weight-for-age conditions favored Man o' War, a relief from the higher weights he had carried in previous races. The same went for Sir Barton; he had been the heavyweight in all of his races for all of 1920, carrying around 130 pounds or more each time. Both horses had had long campaigns in 1920, with demanding performances on more than one occasion. Weight for age meant a break from handicap weights. Ross sided with Riddle on these terms, prompting Kilmer to bow out of the proceedings. Exterminator would not meet Man o' War and Sir Barton at Kenilworth.

As Ross's and Riddle's stables settled in at Havre de Grace, Orpen upped his offer again, this time to $75,000, with a $5,000 gold cup.[57]

Behind Orpen's aggression was news of Matt Winn's anticipated similar bid for a match race at either Latonia or Churchill Downs, an offer announced on September 23, based on reassurances from H. G. Bedwell that Winn would have the last word.[58] As far as Winn knew, Orpen's last offer was $50,000, and Winn had the blessing of the Kentucky Jockey Club to make any offer for the match race. Orpen was determined to have this match race at his Kenilworth track, and so to beat Winn's advances toward the two owners, the promoter traveled from Toronto to Maryland to deliver his bid in person.[59] The three—Orpen, Ross, and Riddle—met about three o'clock on September 24 in the directors room of the clubhouse at Havre de Grace, Orpen immediately letting the two men know that he would up the amount of his original proposal.[60] Commander Ross and Samuel Riddle shook on the terms: 1¼ miles, weight for age, winner-take-all purse of $75,000 plus a $5,000 gold cup. An hour later, the trio received word of Colonel Winn's similar offer, but it was too late.[61] The most desired match race in many years would take place between these two stars of American racing on Canadian soil.

Both Sir Barton and Man o' War had run the match race's distance of 1¼ miles in the same time within the same month. Both had looked the best horses in their respective divisions in the eye and then pushed past them, effectively establishing themselves as the best of the best. With Exterminator out of the picture, the match race was set to answer the question that had inspired it in the first place: Who was faster, Man o' War or Sir Barton?

On October 12, 1920, at a Canadian racetrack that was only twenty miles from the country that had clamored for it, "the Race of the Century" would answer that very question and establish one horse as "the Horse of the Century" and the other as an almost-forgotten champion.

14

Rendezvous with Destiny

By a trick of geography, Windsor, Ontario, home to Kenilworth Park and the "Race of the Century," is south of Detroit, Michigan. In 1920, the area was more flat prairie and less urban cosmopolis than the nearby manufacturing hub. To Jim Ross, Commander Ross's son, Kenilworth was more a "wilderness" than the site of a grand spectacle.[1] The match race everyone had been clamoring for would play out on a not-so-grand stage, with Kenilworth nearly three miles from the center of the city of Windsor, alone on the flat, undeveloped land that ringed the city. It was most definitely not the grand stage of Saratoga or Havre de Grace, but it is what Riddle and Ross had agreed to when they shook hands with Abe Orpen.

American turf writers decried the site of the match race, lamenting that the two champions, both of whom were bred in Kentucky and raced primarily in the United States, would travel to Canada to do battle.[2] Colonel Matt Winn, the man who almost single-handedly would make the Kentucky Derby one of the premier sporting events of any year, withdrew his equivalent offer of a $75,000 purse and $5,000 gold cup. Orpen was determined to bring the match race to Kenilworth in an effort to contribute to the reinvigoration of Canadian racing. Even if he did not make a profit on the venture, he wagered that the attention brought to racing in Canada would be worth any losses.[3]

Man o' War's speed and stamina made him a formidable foe on any given day; although Sir Barton possessed both in abundance, his soreness after three starts in August lingered, threatening his ability to hold his own against the big red colt. H. G. Bedwell's statement about the Triple Crown winner's fitness was the truth: he would need some time to get the champion ready to face Man o' War, time that he truly did not have. Ross's and Riddle's negotiations put a deadline on the battle preparations: October 12, 1920. Only eighteen days.

As his father's champion walked off a railroad car to face the challenge ahead, the young Jim Ross felt that Kenilworth Park, as he later described it, was "both a battleground for greatness and a breeding ground for disappointment and distortion."[4]

A prescient assessment of what became a make-or-break moment for Sir Barton, America's first Triple Crown winner.

With Exterminator and Willis Sharpe Kilmer out of the mix, the match race between Man o' War and Sir Barton was to be a 1¼-mile, weight-for-age event, scheduled for October 12, Columbus Day, at Kenilworth Park in Windsor, Ontario. The three-year-old Man o' War would carry 120 pounds, whereas the four-year-old Sir Barton had to carry 126 pounds. If one horse did not make it to post, the race would be a walk-over; the winner would have to run the 1¼-mile route to get the $5,000 gold cup that Orpen had commissioned.[5] To earn the $75,000 winner-take-all purse, both horses would have to start from the barrier.

Once the particulars were decided, the next issue became jockey assignments. Clarence Kummer had ridden Man o' War in most of his starts since Johnny Loftus had lost his license in March 1920. Ross held second call on Kummer's services; the jockey also had ridden Sir Barton in several of his starts, though Earl Sande was both Ross's contract jockey and the usual jockey for the Triple Crown winner. Legally, because Ross held Kummer's contract, he could deny the jockey's services to Riddle.[6] However, Riddle held a trump card as well: Man o' War did *not* have to run in the match race. The whole spectacle was built on the sportsmanship of the two owners and their willingness to give into the clamor that had brought them to this point in the first place. Commander Ross acquiesced, and thus Kummer would ride Man o' War, while Earl Sande was to ride Sir Barton.[7] Riddle sweetened the pot for Kummer, rewarding him with the promise of a $5,000 bonus for riding Man o' War in the match race.[8]

Ross initially had wished for either Kummer or Johnny Loftus, who had ridden Sir Barton in his Triple Crown races the previous year, but Loftus was still officially on the ground, with no jockey's license for the foreseeable future.[9] Even if Ross felt that he could get Loftus reinstated, the jockey still could expose Bedwell with his accusations about the trainer's alleged use of hop. That alone would jeopardize quite a bit for Ross, not to mention betray the trainer who had gotten him to this prestigious position in the first place. Earl Sande was tapped to ride Sir Barton almost by default. If Ross offered up an incentive similar to the one Riddle gave Kummer, the offer was not public knowledge. Kummer's bonus, though, got its fair share of press, perhaps signaling confidence in Man o' War from both the Riddles and the media.

The details for the match race, officially named the Kenilworth Gold Cup, were announced to the public on September 24, leaving both horses and their connections eighteen days from that point to prepare for their meeting. Man o' War's most recent start had been the Potomac Handicap at Havre de Grace on September 18, so he would have in total just twenty-four days to prepare. Sir Barton's most recent start had been August 28 in the Merchants and Citizens Handicap, where he had scored that narrow victory over Gnome. Bedwell had admitted that the stretch battle had taken its toll on Sir Barton. Would the extra time be enough for Bedwell to get his horse ready for this ultimate test?

Once the details were hammered out and the match race was officially on, the focus of the racing world became the confrontation between Man o' War and Sir Barton. Matt Winn was disappointed to hear that Orpen had beaten him; Winn was going to make the same offer, but for the Kentucky tracks, keeping the race America clamored for in America.[10] He had sent a telegraph and then telephoned to ensure that the message was there. According to H. G. Bedwell, Winn's bid was miscommunicated as a $5,000 purse plus the gold cup.[11] But, in truth, Winn had been prepared to offer up to $100,000, given the chance.[12] He instead somehow lost the opportunity to land the "Race of the Century" despite Bedwell's assurances that Winn had last call for Ross and Riddle's attentions.[13]

The New York tracks had made no offers for the match race, which frustrated racing fans in that state, home to spectacular wins for Sir Barton and Man o' War. One sportswriter even called out those in charge of racing in the state, saying that "it would do no harm if the men who run the tracks in this section really woke to the fact that the war is over, that New York is the biggest city in the world and the biggest racing centre and that the race of a right belonged in New York." August Belmont Jr. had offered to bump up the purse for the Jockey Club Stakes as an incentive for the two horses to meet there. Somehow, this same sportswriter complained, New York lacked promoters willing to woo Ross and Riddle, and thus New Yorkers lamented their missed opportunity to see "two of the greatest horses of all time—one of them without a doubt the greatest of all time."[14]

The teeth gnashing over that missed opportunity was matched by the Dominion-side frustration with Commander Ross for agreeing to race at Kenilworth. Ross was ecstatic that the race was coming to Canada because he had worked to improve and promote racing there now that the war was over. But the Ross family was from Montreal, and the French/English divide made some question the race's location at Kenilworth Park rather than at the swankier and larger Woodbine. The criticism rankled Commander Ross, but in the end it was Orpen and Kenilworth who had pursed the commander and Mr. Riddle, not the officials at Woodbine.[15]

The choice of Kenilworth also sparked rumors that the two owners were getting a percentage of the track's take for the match race. Fans and writers alike had no idea that the two owners had already agreed to take the first offer of $50,000 or higher, neither of them necessarily needing the money and Riddle pursuing the match race only because he wanted Man o' War to retire with winnings of more than $200,000.[16]

Immediately after the announcement, racing fans flew into action. Special trains would run from all over up to the Detroit–Windsor area.[17] Bettors made Man o' War, getting 6 pounds from the Triple Crown winner, the immediate favorite.[18] To those in the know, railbirds who watched the horses day in and day out and horsemen who had seen the two run, the odds did not look good for Sir Barton. Sure, he was a champion in his own right and likely would be the best horse in any other year. Against the three-year-old wonder, though, Sir Barton's disadvantages were clear: he was older, his stride was shorter, and, as even Jim Ross noted, he did not look as sharp as he had in his August record starts. Rumors began to circulate about the Triple Crown winner's fitness, ones that H. G. Bedwell needed to address sooner rather than later.[19]

With only eighteen days between contract and clash, if Sir Barton were sore, preparing him to run against Man o' War was going to be a titanic task.

For Samuel Riddle, the rumors about his take from the match race were just one issue that he had to deal with. The other was the safety of his champion Thoroughbred. Even though he had assured everyone that Man o' War would run in his fourth year, a bruised tendon from the Potomac plus the implicit threats involved in a race of this magnitude and the money to be made on it, especially through gambling, showed Riddle how vulnerable even a superhorse like Man o' War really was.[20] The safety of the horses was just one part of the equation, though. With the recent revelations about the Black Sox scandal,[21] Kenilworth wanted to protect its investment and keep everything connected to the race on the up and up by protecting the horses and their people from outsiders. To ensure his horse's safety, both on the track and off, Samuel Riddle announced on October 3 that the Kenilworth Gold Cup would be Man o' War's last race, saying that the sport would get more from his time at stud than if he continued to race.[22] The news added another layer of meaning and urgency to the forthcoming match race.

Meanwhile, preparations for the meeting of two great horses continued. Kenilworth anticipated that up to fifty thousand people would come to witness Man o' War versus Sir Barton on October 12, an assumption borne out by the profusion of hotel bookings and requests for box seats at Kenilworth. Both Riddle and Ross had requested their own boxes big enough to house friends and luminaries, and requests for grandstand boxes came from as far away as Louisiana. The track saw new bleachers going up, accompanied by Orpen's remarks about the price of wood, as well as steps to rope off the infield so that the twenty acres there could hold any overflow from the grandstands.[23]

While A. M. Orpen ruminated on the price of lumber, H. G. Bedwell kept his own grumblings about his charge close to the vest, choosing to keep Sir Barton mostly out of the spotlight during their preparations.[24] He did work Sir Barton on the oval at Laurel on October 3, sending the champion over the race's distance of 1¼ miles with Cal Shilling and the 126 pounds assigned. Sir Barton worked best with company, so Bedwell also sent out, first, Billy Kelly and then Motor Cop to run with him. His time was fine, finishing the 1¼ miles in 2:09; observers called it "the most phenomenal ever seen at Laurel," despite the slow track.[25] At the same time, his stride was "choppy," and when his stablemates got a significant lead on him, "he resented it and did not care to run after [them] as he considered it love's labor lost."[26] What did a choppy stride indicate so close to this massive challenge? Was it a sign of soreness or a by-product of temperament, much like the apparent sulking that Sir Barton demonstrated during the workout?

Between workouts at Laurel and Bolingbrook, Commander Ross's nearby farm, rumors swirled that Sir Barton was running lame, training poorly for the "Race of the Century."[27] Unlike Man o' War, who was openly training at Belmont Park, keeping Sir Barton at Bolingbrook lent an air of furtive secrecy to the training that aroused suspicion. If he were sound and ready to run, why not be more open in training? To combat the rumors, John A. Payne, who had recently bought a horse from Commander Ross, announced that he had seen Sir Barton at Bolingbrook and that "Sir Barton was in perfect condition for the race with Man o' War."[28] Bedwell pronounced Sir Barton ready to race and communicated that to Commander Ross, a sentiment J. K. M. Ross echoes in *Boots and Saddles:* "Had [my father] been told the colt was not in perfect racing fettle, he definitely would have withdrawn him."[29] But some in the racing world echoed observations that Sir Barton had lost some of his edge, despite not starting for nearly a month.[30]

Louis Feustel, upon hearing the rumors about Sir Barton's condition, told reporters that he would not put Man o' War on a train until Sir Barton had boarded one of his own. "'No use in making this trip unless Sir Barton is ready,'" he told W. C. Vreeland.[31] Man o' War was working out in public at Belmont, his recovery from the possible injury from his start in the Potomac evident.[32] Feustel sent Man o' War out for a 1¼-mile workout, giving him a chance to stretch his legs and demonstrate his readiness for the match race. Clockers stood by, watching the red colt's fractions fly by, his pace on track seeming equal to or better than the 1¼-mile record, a mythic 2:00 flat. Instead, he finished with a time of 2:02⅗, just over the 2:01⅘ mark both he and Sir Barton had run in August.[33]

As the two champions and their contingents readied to head westward out of one fray and into another, Kenilworth finished its preparations for their arrival. With the final nail driven into the bleachers that extended the grandstand by eight hundred feet, A. M. Orpen felt that the $125,000 the whole match race would cost, including the expense of nails and wood and labor, were well worth it: "I have seen Domino and Henry of Navarre and Tenny and Salvator and Simmons and Dr. Rice in dual contests. All of these horses provided race turf entertainments, but I sincerely believe Man o' War and Sir Barton will accomplish what none of these performers in the past have, and that is establish a new record for the distance over which they are contesting."[34] This expectation of speed from both champions spoke to the heart of the challenge: the catharsis that comes from watching two champions battle it out in their arena. Orpen expected something exquisite, as did the throngs of celebrities and fans descending upon Windsor.

The special railroad car that would take Sir Barton to Kenilworth from the Ross Stable's home base near Laurel awaited the Triple Crown winner and his entourage. First, though, Bedwell needed to send him over the route again, this time an easy gallop to stretch his legs before spending a day in the confines of his box car. He covered the ten furlongs in 2:16, his trainer "express[ing] confidence in the ability of the Star Shoot colt to beat the three-year-old champion."[35] Despite the rumors that abounded about Sir Barton's condition, Bedwell continued to pronounce his horse ready to hold his own next to the dominant Man o' War. Contrast this certainty with the younger Ross's opinion—echoed in the perceptions of other turf writers—that "his time was very satisfactory, but [Sir Barton] was not as sharp as he had been at Saratoga."[36] If H. G. Bedwell had any reservations about his horse, he did not share them with anyone either publicly or privately.

With that, at noon on October 6, Sir Barton strode up the ramp into his special railcar, accompanied by H. G. Bedwell; the stable's farrier, A. S. Dodd; his groom, "Toots" Thompson; Cal Shilling; and Wolf, a Belgian Wolfhound the papers called Sir Barton's canine companion.[37] When they arrived in Detroit, the "king of Thoroughbred four-year-olds" had a chance to "poke his head out of the open door of the car and briefly [take] a survey" of the scene as Bedwell arranged his entrance into Canada.[38] They crossed over the invisible line into the Dominion and a few steps closer to the "Race of the Century."

A few hours later, about six o'clock in the evening, Man o' War trotted up a similar ramp into his own special railcar, built with "special doors designed to fool anyone not trained to operate them."[39] Enclosed with him in this roomy, two-stall home were his pony companion; four stablehands; his grooms Frank Loftus and Barney Tate; his exercise rider Clyde Gordon; and bags of the great colt's feed and casks of distilled water from his home at Belmont Park. Louis Feustel met them at Grand Central Station in New York City and pronounced Man o' War ready to travel, the journey to Windsor to last a day. At least two of the men in the car would stay awake to make sure the colt was comfortable, his accommodations befitting a titan of the turf.[40] Man o' War was on his way.

Alone on the prairie, beyond where city gave way to country, stood Kenilworth Park. Absent the glamor and gilt of tracks such as Woodbine or Saratoga, A. M. Orpen's operation was more functional than spectacular, an upstart racing plant whose record for the 1¼ mile was 2:09, nowhere near the record times that both Man o' War and Sir Barton had run. Kenilworth had never seen the likes of these two champions. Upon first viewing, the track did not seem like the site fitting the "Race of the Century."

In addition to the bleachers and other accommodations for the racegoers, Kenilworth also had constructed stables styled like bungalows, with quarters for the grooms and trainers above the stalls. Around these stables was a short dirt training track, good enough for jogging, but not for a significant workout. Enclosing this track was "an eight-foot wire fence and . . . Pinkertons day and night," ensuring that no one could get in without permission, cutting down on the risk of sabotage.[41] For two horses whose careers had proved that they were a world apart from their competition, they were now literally in such a world, a microcosm of pressure inside a macrocosm of anticipation.

Sir Barton arrived first, just before the first race of the day on Thursday, October 7. Not quite two hours later, as Man o' War was pulling into Kenilworth, Sir Barton emerged from the champions' complex to jog under saddle. Cal Shilling let him jog up and down to stretch his legs, while Man o' War stepped out of his special car and down the ramp into the newly built barns.[42] Feustel declined to send the colt out, opting to keep him in the barn until the next morning. The last big workout for both horses was scheduled to be on Sunday, October 10, but Friday saw the two champions out on the oval to get a feel for the track and stretch their legs.

After a good night's sleep, both horses made the one-hundred-yard walk from bungalow barn to backstretch for a short workout the next morning, October 8.[43] Man o' War strode onto the Kenilworth oval with Clyde Gordon on his back, working a quarter of a mile in a quick 0:22⅘. Sir Barton followed a little later for his own short workout, Cal Shilling in the saddle as he went a half-mile in 0:49, his first quarter in 0:24⅗. Throngs of spectators hovered outside Kenilworth, trying to get a glimpse of these two monarchs of the turf before the day of the race, when forty thousand people or more were expected to pour into Windsor and descend upon Kenilworth, all wanting to be a part of the spectacle.[44]

In the meantime, the horses' human connections continued to field questions about their equine stars. Samuel Riddle, Louis Feustel, and Clarence Kummer projected confidence whenever they spoke about their big red colt. Kummer, who had ridden both Man o' War and Sir Barton, had no trouble sharing his assessment of the colt he was to ride: "I have ridden both Man o' War and Sir Barton and I know that Man o' War is the better horse."[45] In contrast, Commander Ross and H. G. Bedwell measured their words and were realistic but confident. "While I am making no predictions," Bedwell said, "I believe that our chestnut will not be disgraced in the contest at hand. He will try his best and that's all we can expect."[46]

Commander Ross projected confidence in his horse but was no fool in terms of understanding Sir Barton's chances against Man o' War. He was a sportsman and spoke as such, praising his horse to the media and not shirking what might have seemed to be an immense challenge: "I have always felt that Sir Barton would give Man o' War a race, provided we could get him to the post right. I believe that we should do that and I am confident that if Man o' War is to beat us at Kenilworth Park he will have to run faster than he has run so far." More significantly, though, unlike his trainer, under the veneer of confident showmanship necessary to pull off this spectacle, the commander said, "If we are beaten, well and good, Sir Barton will suffer no diminution in prestige if he is beaten by Man o' War."[47]

Sunday morning, with the race only forty-eight hours away, two trainers sent two horses on two very different workouts. Bedwell sent the Triple Crown champion out under Cal Shilling and 130 pounds for the match race's distance, 1¼ miles. As usual, he needed companions to motivate him. Sir Barton was not going to give his trainer or anyone else anything on any other day but race day. First, Baby Grand strode next to him as his coworker for the first five-eighths, followed by His Highness to finish out the training run.[48] The 1¼ miles clocked by the only older horse willing to meet Man o' War at the barrier was 2:09, more than seven seconds slower than his record at Saratoga only eight weeks earlier, but two-fifths of a second faster than the Kenilworth track record. Over the course of the workout, again with Cal Shilling on his back, Sir Barton was "under slight restraint" toward the workout's end, and Bedwell was "well pleased and pronounced [the champion] ready for the big race."[49] If the chestnut champion appeared to feel the impact of the track on his tender hooves or any touch of soreness at all, Ross and company did not let on. He accomplished this workout outside the watchful eyes of a crowd of fans. Like the days spent preparing for this race before boarding a train, Sir Barton trained outside of the gaze of those who wanted to see him challenge the supposed "Horse of the Century."

New York Tribune writer W. J. Macbeth, though, felt otherwise about the workout, observing that "Sir Barton seemed a trifle sore Saturday morning and that he was inclined to be a bit proppy, even though nothing like his best was asked of him."[50] The Triple Crown winner's feet danced over the surface, awkward and stiff, indecisive about striding over the Kenilworth surface. Was it antipathy for the track, which Orpen was preparing for a speed duel that might result in a record? Had Bedwell been able to get Sir Barton back in top form, as both the trainer and his boss claimed? The four-year-old had not run a race in more than a month, supposedly ample time to recover from his previous three grueling wins. Macbeth's assessment was but one in a sea of media coverage, lost in the inches and inches of newspaper columns devoted to the "Race of the Century."

Man o' War went out for his final workout before the day's first race, a larger crowd than usual already there in anticipation of seeing one or both of the main attractions. Feustel also sent his champion colt 1¼ miles, and, according to the *Daily Racing Form,* exercise rider Clyde Gordon kept him under "stout restraint until the last quarter, when he began to lengthen his stride and run some."[51] Man o' War covered the distance in a slightly faster time, 2:07⅗, sprinting that last quarter. The colt returned to an ovation from the early throng of the day's fans, the *Daily Racing Form* pronouncing him in "superb condition."[52] The trainer said his colt "was never in better condition. . . . I will have no excuses to offer if Sir Barton proves the better."[53]

After watching Sir Barton work the 1¼ miles, Bedwell exuded more confidence than he had been willing to share in earlier comments, acknowledging Man o' War's excellence but also Sir Barton's status as a horse apart from any three-year-old Man 'o War had met to this point. "This track suits Sir Barton," Bedwell shared. "He is ready for the race of his life."[54] Meanwhile, A. M. Orpen had the track continually harrowed and even scraped, sending a roller over it to tamp down any loose dirt and make the track fast. Orpen wanted to see speed, and he prepared his track's surface in the hopes of getting it.[55] If Sir Barton was ready to meet Man o' War, he was going to have to do it on a hard, fast track, not on the soft, harrowed surface he had been working on to that point.

As the stage was prepared for the onslaught of this spectacle, the horses at its center rested and ate as if it were any other day. Their preparations were done. All that was left was the running.

15

Spectacle

On July 4, 1919, Jack Dempsey entered a boxing ring with Jess Willard to challenge Willard's title as World Heavyweight Champion. In Toledo, Ohio, the six-foot-one Dempsey fought Willard, who towered over him by five and a half inches and about 60 pounds, for three rounds, beating him to a bloody pulp. Seven times in the first round alone, Dempsey sent his opponent to the mat, more than once rendering the towering but now obviously former champion senseless. The victory had been unexpected; Willard had gone into the fight heavily favored over the smaller Dempsey.[1] By the time Dempsey was done, he had earned the nickname "Giant Killer," a moniker that would stick with him long after he was gone.

Similarly, Frank Hankett, once the stable agent for Commander Ross, had bestowed the nickname "Dempsey" upon the stable's own giant killer, Sir Barton.[2] Time and again, the chestnut son of Star Shoot, only 15.2 hands at the shoulder, had taken on bigger horses and beaten them to the wire. In Man o' War, he was again confronted with another equine version of Jess Willard, and observers speculated whether this "Dempsey" had the stuff to take him down.

Clarence Kummer and Earl Sande rolled into Windsor Sunday evening, October 10, about the same time as Commander Ross and his party. The two jockeys were the picture of seriousness, the best of America's jockeys, ready to ride the two best horses the country had to offer.[3] In contrast to the serious focus of these professional athletes, the mood of Commander Ross and his party of friends and family, staying on Ross's private rail car, was ebullient and relaxed as they reaped the fruits of his wealth and privilege.[4] Jim Ross, the teenage son of the Canadian sportsman whose later memoir preserved the moment, saw the setting for this spectacle as "a bleak and gloomy wilderness on the outskirts of the industrial city of Windsor," the opposite of the grandeur of places such as Saratoga and Belmont and Havre de Grace.[5] As workers prepared special boxes for the connections of both racers—one clad in Riddle yellow and black, the other in Ross orange and black—Jim Ross despaired at the "low, skeleton-bare racing plant with a hard-surfaced mile track," a setting that didn't inspire confidence in the Ross party.[6]

If the track inspired distress among the Ross party, no doubt Earl Sande's evident anxiety did the same. When Commander Ross arrived at Kenilworth, he was met by H. G. Bedwell, who was experiencing doubts about Sande's mental state: "'The boy can't handle it,' Bedwell informed his boss. 'He's not himself and I'm worried.'"[7]

Two years earlier, Bedwell had attributed Billy Kelly's loss in a match race with Eternal to the young jockey's nerves. Sande had been outmaneuvered by Andy Schuttinger, an older jockey, who had fooled the young man into going against the instructions he had been given, a move that had cost Billy Kelly the race. Sure, Sande was older now, but he was facing Clarence Kummer, another older, more experienced jockey who had ridden both Sir Barton and Man o' War, the latter in most of his starts in 1920. Sande had replaced Kummer on Man o' War in the Miller Stakes, so he would know what Riddle's colt was capable of, especially after fighting him throughout the entire race. Sir Barton had had more than one jockey in 1920, but Sande had been on his back for his most recent four starts. History being what it was, Bedwell became deeply concerned about Sande's state of mind as the big day approached. The trainer's admonitions to young Sande to take care and not injure himself in the days leading up to the race likely had not helped.[8]

With the match race set for Tuesday, October 12, and Sande's mental health in question, Commander Ross tried to improve their jockey situation by telephoning Algernon Daingerfield, the Jockey Club's assistant secretary, on Monday, October 11. The Jockey Club had denied Cal Shilling a jockey's license for nearly a decade, but Ross wanted the organization to overlook that small detail and allow Shilling to ride in the match race, with the condition that no promises of a license or anything else were necessary beyond that date. Algernon Daingerfield, the Jockey Club's assistant secretary, could not make policy like that, though, and the stewards of the Jockey Club would not meet again before the match race.[9] Ross was fast running out of options.

Without Loftus as an option, Bedwell and Ross decided to bring in Frank Keogh, a middle-aged jock on a career upswing, as the backup rider for the match race. Keogh's contracts belonged to Admiral Cary T. Grayson and Samuel Ross, both prestigious owners and both friends of Commander Ross. After riding the Saturday afternoon card at Laurel, Keogh got the message that he was to board a train to Windsor and needed to report to A. M. Orpen when he arrived. The jockey was not to be informed about why he was traveling to Kenilworth, but presumably he knew the reason as soon as he learned the destination.[10]

So the jockey who had ridden Gnome in his epic confrontation with Sir Barton in the Merchants and Citizens Handicap six weeks earlier headed to Kenilworth and what he assumed was backup status for both Sande and Kummer. His trip would instead become more than simple substitution.

Monday morning, both horses had taken to the track for a short workout, blissfully unaware of the ongoing debate about the choice of rider for the orange and black. Today's exercise was no blowout, but a jog to keep the legs limber. Man o' War went a half-mile in a leisurely 0:51; Sir Barton's five furlongs came in at 1:04.[11] While the horses placidly moved over the oval, the humans were in high gear. A third horse, Wickford, mysteriously appeared on the roster for the match race, now officially named the Kenilworth Gold Cup. Baffled reporters soon learned that the heretofore unknown horse was nothing but an official figment, a third horse entered to satisfy the Canadian regulation against match races.[12] Officially assigned 126 pounds and then officially scratched the morning of the race, Wickford passed into history as a horse of no consequence save for his status as trivia.

While A. M. Orpen was attending to official business, Kenilworth was preparing to receive the spectators ready for racing history. Boxes had sold out long before the race itself, so the only spaces left for those unlucky enough not to secure one were the standing-room-only area at the end of the newly lengthened grandstand and the overflow into the infield.[13] The gates would open at 9:00 a.m. on race day; the race itself would not happen until 4:00 p.m.[14] Even with the admission set at $5, a high price in those days,[15] Orpen was expecting up to forty-five thousand for the day's racing, a crowd that could rival those at Churchill Downs on Derby Day. Not only would trains run at regular intervals to ensure that fans could arrive at the track in plenty of time, but Kenilworth would also have extra attendants on duty to take tickets and see to the crowd's needs.[16]

The gold cup that accompanied the $75,000 purse was on display at the track, still blank and awaiting the name of the winner. Upon hearing this, the crowd present cheered, the Canadians favoring Commander Ross's champion over his big red challenger. With the owners' boxes draped in their appropriate colors, the faces that would join Ross and Riddle arrived in Windsor for the show. John E. Madden and August Belmont Jr., the breeders of the combatants, had been invited to Kenilworth, but only Madden could attend, with Belmont unable to get away. Other guests gathered with the men of the hour in their private cars, each parked on sidetracks at Kenilworth.[17]

As Ross and Bedwell debated jockeys and Riddle strode confidently through the race preparations, Johnny Loftus was hanging out at Jamaica Race Course in New York, writer Vincent Treanor finding him in the last row of the grandstand. The man who had ridden Man o' War to all of those two-year-old victories and Sir Barton to his Triple Crown sweep sat idly debating the match race with Treanor. "They're both great horses," the former jockey said, "and it will be a horse race." As the man who had known both horses in victory and defeat, Loftus went on to say of Man o' War, "Some horse, I'll say."[18] No prediction, but plenty of praise for Man o' War. No one at Jamaica and few anywhere save for Canada would predict a victory for the Triple Crown winner.

On Monday, the day before the "Race of the Century," Kenilworth ran a seven-race card, mostly claiming and allowance races. Commander Ross had two starters that day. In the third race, a claiming race for horses foaled in Canada, Aconi ran next to last under the Ross Stable's newest jockey, Joe Gruniesen. Later, the sixth race was an allowance for three-year-olds and older. The commander's filly His Choice had the stable's contract jockey, Earl Sande, on her back. Sande kept His Choice just back of the leaders for most of the six furlongs, but when he had the chance to close on the front-running The Boy, he did not do it, leaving the filly to finish second. Instead of an easy win, Sande had not been able to make the move that could have put the filly on the lead.

Between Bedwell's admonitions not to get hurt and the pressure of being at Kenilworth finally, were nerves bogging down this elite rider?

As the Riddle party enjoyed a dinner with friends in anticipation of Tuesday's spectacle, the Ross party argued and debated the merits of the jockeys in front of them: Keogh or Sande? Sande or Keogh?[19] The discussion went long into the night, leaving the Sir Barton connections haggard and no closer to an answer. Jim Ross, always arguing the side of the young jockey, hoped that the morning would find Sande standing out as the right choice.

"Several times I spoke out, and I spoke for Sande," Ross recalled later about his role in the discussions that night. "I longed to say more, but in that group my pleadings were largely ignored. I felt as though this were a jury room and that a friend of mine were being tried."[20]

The next morning Earl Sande's fate would be in hands of one man, Commander Ross, the impulse to win warring with the commander's desire to be fair, a conflict with no good resolution.

In the early-morning light of October 12, anonymous faces stood in the fog around Kenilworth Park, waiting for the chance to enter the grounds and take their places in the stands. These hundreds of patrons had skipped breakfast in an effort to beat the crowd to the track and would take advantage of the restaurant on the premises once they were admitted. As the bulk of the crowd trickled in once the trains began to run in earnest, the atmosphere turned festive, as if the circus were in town.[21]

In the same fog, the quiet was broken by the presence of two horses and their entourages. Rather than allow Man o' War to sprint a furlong or two as he often had done before, Feustel had his big red colt jog a slow mile, while Samuel Riddle and his guests looked on. Riddle then took them all behind the barbed-wire fence and armed guards to the barn where his prize horse had been housed for the past several days. Despite the show that his horse had put on again and again, Riddle was nervous about the possibility of *losing,* about finding out that this horse, to which so many people had attached words such as *invincible,* actually was fallible. Bruised tendons and security threats aside, the looming shadow of a Triple Crown winner caused the usually confident owner to give "no predictions other than that the best horse would win."[22] The anxiety of the moment was becoming epidemic as the crowd grew larger and the time to the race grew shorter.

That same tension had already settled onto frayed nerves in the Ross Stable. Earl Sande mounted Sir Barton for this last morning workout, trotting the champion out to the match race's starting line; the 1¼ miles on Kenilworth's mile oval had the pair starting on the turn. Bedwell ordered his jockey to send Sir Barton two furlongs, a quarter of a mile, which the four-year-old did in 0:24⅘.[23] The Ross men watched the pair work, Jim straining for any sign that Sande would hold up under the pressure. "Sir Barton didn't seem razor sharp but he moved well," the younger Ross later reported. "Sande, on the other hand was in an extreme state of anxiety."[24] Nothing in the jockey's demeanor did anything to allay Commander Ross's concerns about his ability to handle the race to come.

Ross's options were few: no Cal Shilling, no Johnny Loftus. Commander Ross had given up his chance at Clarence Kummer early in the negotiations for this spectacle. The dilemma: stick with a nervous Sande, who might calm down once on the track for the race, or go with Frank Keogh, who had ridden Gnome to a close finish next to Sande and Sir Barton only six weeks earlier. In the end, as Jim Ross reflected, "my father, with excruciating reluctance, gave into Bedwell."[25]

Finally, Commander Ross told Earl Sande, "You've been unlucky lately."[26] Sande cried, of course, heartbroken that he was not going to be able to ride the Triple Crown winner in the biggest race of the year.[27] After days of anticipation and admonitions from H. G. Bedwell to avoid injury, Sande had been denied the opportunity to ride without any warning. Perhaps Ross's decision to take Sande off of Sir Barton was not just because of the nerves; though Ross never publicly said that Sande's lack of confidence in his horse bothered him, and certainly no such motive was expressed after the fact, the implication that Sande's comments may have piqued his boss is possible, even if Commander Ross himself might not have been aware of it.[28]

Even though Ross opted to take Sande off his prized Sir Barton, he also did not want to sully the jock's reputation while the young man was still under contract. Ross released a statement at noon on race day:

I have determined to substitute Jockey Frank Keogh for Earl
Sande on Sir Barton in today's race for the reason that my
boy is not in good form, as his recent performances will show.

My action is taken without prejudice to Sande and in making the change I am only exercising my prerogative as owner
of Sir Barton. I would rather win this race today than all the
other races in which Sir Barton may participate. Keogh is at
the top of his form at present and I want to take advantage of
it so there will be no excuse after the contest is won or lost.

I have the utmost confidence in Sande, but feel I would be
doing myself and Sir Barton an injustice if I did not send him
to the post with every avenue safeguarded.[29]

Frank Keogh expressed surprise at the decision. He knew he had been
dispatched to Kenilworth in case either Kummer or Sande became inca-
pacitated, but he never expected to ride for a reason like this. Now,
though, he was charged with the task of piloting Sir Barton, a horse he
had never ridden, in a match race against Man o' War. Not six weeks earlier, Henry King had credited Earl Sande's ride on Sir Barton with being
the difference in their win over Keogh and Gnome in the Merchants and
Citizens Handicap.[30] Now, bare hours before the "Race of the Century,"
Commander Ross put his Triple Crown winner, the horse tapped as the
best challenger for the supposed "Horse of the Century," in the hands of
the man who had pushed Gnome to look Sir Barton in the eye but at the
last moment had flinched.

By the time Algonquin won the third race of the day, Kenilworth undu-
lated with a sea of humanity, parted only by the dirt arena where the
two champions would meet. After the gates had opened at 9:00 a.m.,
the atmosphere around the track quickly grew carnivalesque—people
streaming in from the trains that ran at regular intervals throughout the
day; games designed to fleece fans of their wagering money cropping up;
track police patrolling to keep the criminal activities at a minimum.[31]
People streamed in from both sides of the border, determined to get a
glimpse of history and willing to pay for the privilege.

Orpen announced that the official attendance figure was more than
twenty-one thousand persons. Kenilworth had prepared for a crowd of

forty-five thousand, so the actual number was well short of what Orpen had hoped for, but it nevertheless set a Canadian record.[32] The track collected more than $100,000 in admissions, which more than paid for the $75,000 purse and $5,000 gold cup, and on top of that were the monies collected from wagering. J. K. M. Ross remembered the crowd was "tremendous. The grandstands and lawns and paddocks were taxed as they never have been and would never be again; the mob flowed over into the infield; the pari-mutuel windows were almost impossible to reach and any movement at all was at times impossible."[33]

The big names in racing were there, too: John E. Madden, the man who had bred Sir Barton; William Woodward, Belair Stud's breeder and owner who would later own and breed two Triple Crown winners of his own; Foxhall Keene, the son of Colin and Sysonby's owner, James Keene; and opera star Enrico Caruso.[34] The two owners sat with their assembled parties in their specially draped boxes, the gold cup within their sight. With two Pinkerton agents flanking its perch, the mahogany-mounted Tiffany gold cup promised to the winner sat glinting in the autumn sunlight, awaiting its inscription. With a value of $5,000, this prize stood fourteen inches high, fifteen inches across, and eight inches deep, an impressive prize unto itself, dwarfed only by the $75,000 purse, winner take all, that A. M. Orpen had promised. Around the track, on stands of their own, the Educational Films Corporation had set up multiple cameras, ringing the Kenilworth oval, to capture the race in its entirety, the first film of its kind.[35]

The only space left to move on at Kenilworth was the dirt oval itself. Orpen wanted it in "perfect condition," anticipating that a speed duel might develop between the two champions. Rolled and packed, the lightning-fast surface might promise speed, but for Sir Barton it would bring nothing but misery.[36] Shorter, older, and now forced to run on a surface antithetical to his sore feet while carrying more weight than his fleet rival, the track in front of him promised that this battle would be unlike any other he had ever experienced.

After Algonquin won the third race, H. G. Bedwell sent Sir Barton out onto the track to warm up, a slow gallop around the mile oval, and then over to the paddock for his final preparations. Rather than saddle Man o' War in the barn as they had done for the Potomac Handicap, Feustel bypassed any warmup and brought Man o' War out to the paddock, groomed and saddled him, and walked him around the ring while they waited for post time.[37] Pinkertons agents kept the pressing crowd away from the saddling area, allowing only the horses' trainers, owners, and their guests inside the ring.

With the bugle's call, Keogh and Kummer received their instructions and a boost into the saddle. On edge, nerves ramped up to maximum as they had been all week, Bedwell instructed his new rider "to do his best at the barrier and ordered him to use the whip freely. 'Shake him up all the way,' he said, 'Give him the whip hard and often and keep him going at his best all the way. If you can get to the front, do so. This colt is game and will do his best if you urge him.'"[38] Trusting that Sir Barton would respond, Bedwell had chosen to have him play the aggressor, to take the lead and then gain enough ground at least to make a race out of it. More than once the Triple Crown winner had won wire to wire. Why not on this day as well?

As Feustel tightened the girth on Man o' War's saddle, he seemed more serene and confident than his anxious counterpart nearby. Kummer, clad in the distinctive gold and black, knew his horse and knew his opponent, trading his nerves for the certainty of the horse beneath him. "Ride as you would in any selling race," Feustel told the rider next to him. Then both Samuel Riddle and Feustel told their man, "Don't worry about being beaten, Clarence. If he beats you, it will be all the same. We know you will do your best so don't worry about us being peeved at you if the unexpected happens." "Thanks," Kummer said, ready for his boost into the saddle. "I'll win."[39]

Only two horses paraded from the paddock onto the Kenilworth dirt for the fourth race, but they were no ordinary horses running in an anonymous allowance race. They were the best of what Thoroughbred racing in America had to offer: Man o' War in Riddle's yellow and black, wearing the number 1, and Sir Barton in Ross's orange and black, wearing the number 2. The crowd of twenty-one thousand greeted their emergence onto the track with "a tremendous ovation," the sound following the horses from the paddock to the barrier.[40] Man o' War, despite the cavalcade of sound, strode along calmly; Sir Barton tested Keogh, giving his substitute jockey plenty to do as they walked to the starting line. Whereas Man o' War seemed calm and ready, Sir Barton "appeared nervous, anxious and strung-up," no doubt leaving some to speculate whether Johnny Loftus really was right about H. G. Bedwell's methods.[41]

As the two horses walked toward the starting line, the difference between them was striking. Both were chestnuts with white markings, but Man o' War, more red than gold, towered over the Triple Crown winner by nearly a full hand.[42] With black and gold ribbons braided into his mane to match the festive occasion, the beauty of Man o' War and the power and muscle of his form were clear to the world. The Triple Crown winner, who would have outshined every horse on the track any other day, "beside the champion of champions . . . looked rather insignificant."[43] Henry V. King's description of the Triple Crown winner would come to ring true for many days beyond this one.

The two horses approached the barrier at the top of the homestretch; the dirt oval at Kenilworth was one mile, so in a 1¼-mile race they would cross the finish line twice. Starter Harry Morrissey had visited both Kummer and Keogh in the jockey's room before the race, warning them that he would not drop the barrier unless both horses were standing still.[44] No flying starts for either of these front-running champions. They took up their positions at the line, Sir Barton on the rail, Man o' War to his outside. The big red colt, always fractious at the start, threatened to break through a couple of times, Kummer keeping sure hands on his mount to quiet him.[45] Sir Barton had calmed after showing nerves on the walk over from the paddock, standing still at the barrier as he had done so many times before. Finally, after about a minute, both horses were still, and, *finally,* the moment that the entire crowd—the entire racing world—had clamored for arrived. The barrier flew up, "the shout 'They're off!' went up from thousands of throats [and] they sprung forward together, head and head, neither having an advantage."[46]

With Man o' War unaccustomed to standing still at the start, Sir Barton got a jump on the big three-year-old colt, leaping out to the lead. The Triple Crown winner hugged the rail, the shortest path, with a one-length lead on his competitor.[47] Both horses were front-runners: Sir Barton's style was to take the lead and hold onto it, wire to wire as in many of his best wins, and Man o' War was the same way. The four-year-old led for "approximately two hundred yards and for a few fleeting seconds it looked as though we were to have a duel of the first magnitude," in which these two speed horses would stare each other in the eye until one succumbed.[48]

Instead, as J. K. M. Ross recalls, "by the time they had passed the judges' stand for the first time, Man o' War, galloping well within himself, was two lengths in front and was able to take the rail. Keogh was already applying the whip."[49] If any horse got a jump on him, Man o' War's long stride allowed him to catch up within a short distance. Even though the Triple Crown winner held the lead at first, as he had done so many times before, that lead dissipated with a couple of Man o' War's strides. Clear of Sir Barton, Kummer opened up the lead to a length and then to three. Keogh followed the instructions from H. G. Bedwell, using the whip and urging Sir Barton on, but Sir Barton's "short, choppy stroke which, apparently was twice as rapid as that of his competitor, was leaving him constantly farther behind."[50] It was at this point that J. K. M. Ross noticed that, despite Keogh's urging, "Sir Barton seemed to sulk. In any event, he was not striding out in his usual manner." Even his father, the game sportsman and eternal optimist, noticed Sir Barton's antipathy: "He's not himself. I think his feet are hurting him, but he certainly is game!"[51] Man o' War fought for his head, while Sir Barton fought to do something, anything, to catch up to the long-striding colt in front of him.

Perhaps it was the hard, fast track or the incessant whip or even the fact that Man o' War had passed him, but, whatever it was, Sir Barton did not look like the horse he could be. Compared to the big red colt fighting to fly, at this moment the Triple Crown winner looked like any other horse. But as they entered the final turn, Sir Barton seemed to be running more like the champion he was. For a few seconds, he no longer lost ground but instead threatened to gain on Man o' War.[52] He was taking this second chance to gain on Man o' War, showing "how far he would withstand extreme pressure."[53] Sensing this, Kummer gave Man o' War his head, and suddenly what had been a three-length lead became six in just a few strides. Rather than pressuring his opponent, Sir Barton fell farther behind. Kummer reined Man o' War in again when it was clear that the Triple Crown winner was losing ground, despite being under Keogh's incessant urging. The six lengths became seven and then no more as the three-year-old crossed the wire and Sir Barton straggled home, still gamely working, still struggling despite the hard track and the clear and definitive defeat.[54]

Not only was Man o' War's victory decisive, but his time, despite Kummer's hold on the reins for the majority of the race, was a track record 2:03, bettering the previous record by more than six seconds and just one-fifth of a second off the Canadian record of 2:02⅘ for the 1¼ mile. Man o' War could have bettered that record time had he been able to run a straight path; as Kummer looked back to see where Sir Barton was, his vision was impeded by the throng of humanity that had moved from one rail to the other as they rounded the track, some of them even coming onto the dirt oval near the end of the race. To avoid the trespassers, Kummer had to take Man o' War wider, covering more ground than necessary along the way. His mile time was 1:37⅖; the record at Kenilworth for a mile was 1:39⅖. "Vanquished but trying hard," Sir Barton came home at 2:04⅖, five full seconds better than the track record even though *he had come in second.* Man o' War could easily have bettered all of the attendant records, but "only consideration for a fallen rival had prevented it."[55] The eternal lament issued from the big red colt's last race was that no one would ever know the true limits of his speed.

"What a marvel!" Commander Ross exulted as he watched the match race's finish, his horse straggling home behind Man o' War. Like the true sportsman, the commander "quickly turned towards Mr. Riddle, and with a broad smile grasped him warmly by the hand. Then the two owners left their boxes and proceeded, arm in arm, down the steps to the front of the judge's stand where Mr. Riddle accepted the magnificent gold cup amidst a storm of applause, and for the benefit of the cameramen, was once again congratulated by my father."[56] Despite Man o' War's emphatic triumph over the best horse he would ever own, Commander Ross remained the good sport, celebrating with Riddle and company as the cameras rolled and the champagne began to flow.

The noise of thousands of fans expressing their unceasing admiration followed the victor as he trotted up to the judge's stand, Kummer hopping off to weigh in officially.[57] Man o' War nuzzled and sniffed the gold cup his owner now held in his hand and posed for the movie cameras that were there to capture the whole event.[58] Riddle filled the cup with water and offered it to his champion colt. "He won it for me," Riddle said, "and he should be the first to drink out of it."[59] Man o' War drained the gold cup, thirsty after his decisive victory. Out of sight of the cameras now, his defeat preserved for all time, Sir Barton returned to his barn. Giddy from victory, Louis Feustel said, "Sir Barton isn't dead, but he is dizzy, and if he had attempted to follow our horse much further he would have dropped dead."[60]

After both the victor and the vanquished were bedded down to recover from their confrontation, Commander Ross and son Jim joined the party in Samuel Riddle's private railroad car, next to Ross's own, sharing in the exultation. The gold cup was filled yet again, this time with "a most potent punch," and passed around the car for guests to share.[61] Commander Ross was trying to talk Riddle into sending Man o' War to England to run in the Ascot Gold Cup, then considered the greatest race in the world. Riddle demurred, Man o' War's soundness and security unrelenting concerns for him.[62] The pressure of owning the best Thoroughbred in the country was enough to deter him from extending his horse's career. With his victory in the match race, Man o' War had become the leading money winner in the United States with $249,465. The world mark was $280,675, held by none other than Isinglass, Sir Barton's grandsire. Tempting as it was to go for that record, Riddle nevertheless declared Man o' War retired for good and ready for stud in Kentucky.[63]

Though Bedwell had pronounced the four-year-old Sir Barton ready to race in the days leading up to the match race, J. K. M. Ross later expressed regret that the champion was "not at his best at Kenilworth."[64] He echoed the going wisdom from that era that the Triple Crown winner was not completely sound prior to the match race and therefore did not meet his supposed rival on even terms. Even if he had been, as even Ross himself admits, it was improbable that Sir Barton could have beaten Man o' War, but he might have given his rival more of a fight if he had been the same horse as he was at Saratoga in August.

Offering no excuses, sharing no details about his horse's fitness or any compromises thereof, Commander Ross simply said, "There is no horse in the world that can equal Man o' War."[65]

16

Aftermath

As newspapers across the county trumpeted Man o' War's victory, the details of his every move were reported to eager fans everywhere. The "Horse of the Century" departed Kenilworth for the United States to do a sort of victory tour, appearing first at the Rose Tree Hunt Club in Pennsylvania and then ceremoniously retiring to Hinata Farm in Lexington, Kentucky. Riddle eschewed a parade and opted instead to allow his prized colt to put on a show as he galloped under Clyde Gordon one last time at the old Kentucky Association track.[1] The last moments of the big red chestnut colt's public life were splashed across the country in print as the "Horse of the Century" was celebrated into retirement and stud duty. Racing fans were privy to the spectacle thanks to the turf writers eager to chronicle every moment.

No such accolades were accorded his competitor. When the Ross Stable decamped from Kenilworth back to Maryland, their departure and arrival were met with little fanfare outside of a mention in the *Daily Racing Form*.[2] A week after the race, Sir Barton's name started to appear next to Man o' War's in advertisements for *The Race of the Age,* a film about the race by the Educational Film Corporation of America that showed footage of the Kenilworth Gold Cup's preparations as well as the race itself and had started to play in theaters all over the country. About the same time, one newspaper ran a photo of the Triple Crown winner, his head hung low, with the headline, "Sir Barton, Canadian Horse, Loser to Man O' War in Winsor [*sic*] Race."[3] He was an outsider now, Canadian despite being bred by the leading American breeder and running all but two of his races in the United States. The horse that had made history in 1919 with a streak of victories that would become the kingmaker for so many other horses was relegated to literal second-place status, a loser, an afterthought next to the big-striding colt who outran him again and again on movie screens everywhere.

While Man o' War said good-bye to racing with praises and attention galore, Sir Barton and his entourage returned to Laurel and resumed racing, back to the routine of morning workouts and afternoon races. As the second-best horse in America returned to the track, the question that followed him was: Which horse would be racing after the spectacular defeat—the great heart that had dug deep to beat Gnome by a nose or the broken heart that remembered being bested by the very best there ever was?

The fallout from the match race landed not on the Riddle camp, but on the Ross connections, beaten and now broken up as they loaded up for home after their defeat. Earl Sande, who had ridden for Commander Ross for a good part of his young career, asked for his contract, ready to sever ties with the stable after being set down for the match race.[4] Several days after the match race, the Commander gave Sande his contract and then offered him more money if he would stay on with the stable.[5] Sande turned down the offer, knowing that if he continued riding for Ross, the moment one of Ross's horses lost he would be blamed for a bad ride and face accusations of trying to get even with the owner who had humiliated him.[6] Sam Hildreth had already offered him a contract of $12,000 per year, and other owners expressed interest in adding Sande's services to their own stables.[7] On October 21, Earl Sande signed a contract to ride for Hildreth, Commander Ross's rival, the man who owned and trained both Mad Hatter and Purchase, for a retainer of around $20,000.[8] The breakup of the Ross Stable had begun.

Eleven days after the match race, Sir Barton was back on the track at Laurel, ready to resume racing after his defeat. Despite his showing at Kenilworth, he was still considered the best of his age group, still listed as top weight in many of the handicaps to be run that fall alongside horses like Exterminator.[9] Even better, the Ross Stable was on track to make even more money that year than in 1919, though Sir Barton factored for far less of the total in 1920 than he had the previous year.[10] With the horse that dared challenge Man o' War running in the day's feature, the crowd at Laurel numbered twenty-two thousand, one of the largest crowds there to date.[11] On October 23, the Triple Crown winner returned to the barrier in the Laurel Stakes, his connections hoping that he would add to the commander's purse as 1920 grew closer to its end.

As one of the older horses in the field, Sir Barton carried 125 pounds, giving weight to the other starters but also carrying less than he had in previous starts. The large Laurel crowd made the Triple Crown winner the favorite, demonstrating that his loss to Man o' War had not completely erased his status in his home state.[12] A race like this one should have been right up the champion's alley, a chance to return to his winning ways; instead, it proved another disappointment.

Prior to the race, jockey W. J. "Jack" O'Brien took Sir Barton out to the track for his warmup, but the horse whose trainer H. G. Bedwell had praised prior to the match race looked "stiff and drawn."[13] Perhaps the trip to Kenilworth had taken more out of the son of Star Shoot than first thought.[14] The Porter and Sir Barton, the race's heavyweights, had the outside posts, all of the inside starters carrying less weight. At the barrier, Sir Barton broke in third, hanging out behind the front-runners until they straightened out into the backstretch. O'Brien sent the champion after Blazes, but he could not get the Triple Crown winner to challenge the three-year-old. Unable or unwilling to catch the front-runner, Sir Barton faltered, allowing The Porter to catch and then pass him.[15] O'Brien gave up the chase and hung on to finish third in a race with a brisk though not record-setting pace.

The champion was "thoroughly but not disgracefully beaten," and O'Brien was accused of an inefficient ride compared with what Earl Sande could possibly have done.[16] For the horse who seemed like the best that racing in America had to offer next to Man o' War, Sir Barton appeared to be a shadow of what he had been in his magical August races.

Prior to the match race, the Educational Film Corporation of America had paid the Kenilworth Jockey Club $100,000 for the exclusive rights to film both the race and the preparations for it. In order to keep the footage that the filmmakers collected exclusive, guards patrolled the track to prevent any outside cameras from capturing any of the competitors and their training and routines in the days leading up to the race.[17] The end result, a film titled *The Race of the Age*, hit screens across the country in the months after the race but made its debut at a dinner given by Samuel Riddle at Glen Riddle Farm at the end of October.[18] Those present were treated to a panoramic view of Kenilworth as well as a slow-motion capture of Man o' War's great stride.[19]

As Sir Barton's defeat was splashed across movie screens all over the country, as the iconic photo of Man o' War pulling away from him appeared in rotogravures everywhere, the dark cloud that would come to obscure America's first Triple Crown winner began to descend and settle, and he would be hard-pressed to find his way out of it.

Twelve days after straggling home third in the Laurel Stakes, Sir Barton faced the barrier once again, this time at Pimlico in the Fall Serial Number 2. The Serials were the stakes races that he and Billy Kelly had dominated in 1919, and expectations held that they could do it again, especially after Billy Kelly won the first Serial four days earlier. Running a mile, Sir Barton was to carry the same weight as all of his competitors, 126 pounds. Among them were his stablemate Billy Kelly and an old foe, Mad Hatter.

Commander Ross still held second call on the services of Clarence Kummer, who sat astride Billy Kelly for this one-mile test. Back on Sir Barton was Frank Keogh.[20] Starting from the rail, Sir Barton showed a flash of his old form, his early speed pulling him out to a two-length lead over his stablemate.[21] At the half-mile mark, Buddy Ensor sent Mad Hatter on a tear, this son of Fair Play dashing past both Ross horses and squeezing a neck in front.[22] Was Sir Barton flinching at the oncoming assault of speed, the memory of Man o' War beating him more than Mad Hatter? Ensor and Mad Hatter widened that lead to four lengths, while Billy Kelly began to overtake his stablemate. Sir Barton came on again at the last, narrowing the gap between Billy Kelly and himself, but it was no use.[23] As the three horses flashed under the wire, Billy Kelly barely edged him out at the end. Pushed by the quick pace Sir Barton had set in the first half of the race, Mad Hatter ran the mile in 1:38, a new track record. The Serial Number 2 was Mad Hatter's sixth straight victory, showing that he was "twenty pounds better than he was at any period in his career, whereas Sir Barton has deteriorated from his best form by at least twenty pounds."[24] These lackluster starts did nothing to raise Sir Barton's profile in print, especially with the omnipresent advertisements for *The Race of the Age* running in so many newspapers around the country.

Five days later, in the last of the Serials, Sir Barton again faced his stablemate Billy Kelly, Blazes, and Mad Hatter, the latter with Earl Sande on his back.[25] Frank Keogh sat astride the Triple Crown winner one more time. Sam Hildreth's horses were on an upswing, while Commander Ross's seemed to be on a downward trajectory. Earl Sande's latest victory in the Bowie Handicap had been the first time he had ridden against his former boss's horses, and, to his delight, he and Mad Hatter had been able to run down Boniface for the win. That race, though, had been run only two days before this latest Serial. Would Mad Hatter have enough to continue dominating the Ross horses?

Starter James Milton sent the field off on a bad start, with Dr. Clark turned sideways and Mad Hatter starting to wheel as they were sent away.[26] Sir Barton, though, was able to get a jump on the field, battling Blazes through the early part of the race. Billy Kelly, as he had in the past, was supposedly there to set the pace for his stablemate and burn off any speedy competition over the first part of the 1⅛ miles, but Keogh and Sir Barton had beaten him to it.[27] A half-mile in, as Blazes started to fade, Sande on Mad Hatter made his move, passing a wrapped-up Sir Barton, Keogh biding his time. As the field thundered toward the finish line, Mad Hatter stayed on the lead, but his recent starts and fast pace took their toll on the Hildreth colt. As he started to fade, Billy Kelly came on to pass Mad Hatter and then draw away from the field. Sir Barton followed on his stablemate's heels, passing a tiring Mad Hatter to come in second.[28]

The race was a fast one, just three-fifths of a second off the record of 1:51. It was Sir Barton's third race since the match race with Man o' War on October 12. In the bare month that had elapsed since his defeat at Kenilworth, he had finished third twice and then second. He had shown flashes of the horse he had been before, but the form that had made him the horse tapped to match with Man o' War continued to elude him.

He was still the best older horse racing, even if he was not quite showing the same form in these latest starts, but his reputation was built on those brilliant performances at Saratoga only three months earlier. These recent losses, though, "[brought] up the question as to whether or not he had his heart broken through chasing the superhorse in that particular race."[29] John P. Grier, the colt who had pushed Man o' War to his limit in the Dwyer Stakes, was not the same horse after that epic confrontation. Could it be that Sir Barton was suffering from the same malady? In addition, as the *Daily Racing Form* noted, he "was not always kept at his best," a subtle indictment of his conditioning throughout the 1920 season. The Sir Barton who had beat Exterminator and Mad Hatter in the Saratoga Handicap and then outlasted Gnome in the Merchants and Citizens "was quite a different animal from the Sir Barton beaten so ignominiously by Man o' War at Kenilworth and since then by worse race horses."[30]

Fall Serial Number 3 at Pimlico was Sir Barton's last race for 1920. He had run twelve times that year, with five wins, two seconds, three thirds, and two finishes out of the money.[31] The match race had left the Triple Crown winner with no obvious physical issues, but clearly he was not the same horse he had been in August. If Man o' War broke the hearts of his opponents, as J. K. M. Ross contemplates in his memoir,[32] those last three races of 1920 showed that it was possible Sir Barton could be counted among the broken-hearted.

In 1920, the Ross Stable finished second in the money won, despite the fact it had surpassed its total for 1919, winning $250,586. Sir Barton won only about a quarter of what he had won in 1919, his purses totaling only $24,494 as opposed to the $88,250 won the previous year.[33] The match race was winner-take-all; Sir Barton's loss meant that, despite the hoopla, the Triple Crown winner and the Ross connections came home empty-handed, with only the memory of the moment to show for it all. Even though 1920 was not as good as 1919 for Sir Barton, he still led his division, having bested many of the other horses listed in the *Daily Racing Form*'s assessment of his peers.[34] The Ross Stable looked forward to another year of racing with its roster of star horses in 1921, but the departure of Earl Sande and another controversy brewing on the horizon dimmed the brightness of the stable's future.

When the Jockey Club was incorporated in 1894, its purpose was "not only to encourage the development of the Thoroughbred horse, but to establish racing on such a footing that it may command the interests as well as the confidence and favorable opinion of the public."[35] Among the founding stewards was August Belmont Jr., the breeder of Man o'

War, Mad Hatter, and many others. As the ruling body for Thorough-bred racing in America, the Jockey Club maintained the American Stud Book and issued licenses to trainers and jockeys. Throughout the coun-try, it was the recognized authority over the racing industry, so that if it set aside or denied a trainer's or jockey's license application, as it had Johnny Loftus's in March 1920, he would be unable to work at any track in the country. No owner could run a horse with an unlicensed trainer or jockey.

Carroll "Cal" Shilling had been the best jockey in the country early in the century. Born in Texas in 1885, he and his four brothers were jock-eys who got their start riding on the bush tracks of the American South-west. Cal became a professional in 1904 and then moved east to ride in the more elite and lucrative New York and New Jersey areas. In time, he was leading the country in earnings, contracted by owners such as Sam Hildreth and H. C. Hallenbeck, who owned Shilling's lone Kentucky Derby winner, Worth. Shilling's stature as the country's leading jockey saw him with enough money to buy several businesses in his hometown, Paris, Texas, as well as to absorb any downturn in his fortunes.[36]

Along with his good luck, however, came moments in which Shil-ling's temper got the best of him. The Jockey Club set aside Shilling's application for a license in 1910 after the jockey stabbed his former boss, R. L. Thomas, in a dispute over his contract. Shilling claimed that he stabbed Thomas in self-defense after the owner struck him while they argued over Shilling's refusal to renew his contract.[37] Although Shilling avoided jail time for that incident, it was not the only time the young man faced repercussions for his hotheadedness. In 1912, he won the Kentucky Derby on Worth, but he also lost his license for good after he struck another jockey with his whip during a race at Havre de Grace in September.[38] His action grounded him permanently in the United States, although he could go to Europe or Canada to ride if he chose.

Shilling stayed in the United States, training and owning horses of his own while he attempted to persuade the Jockey Club to reinstate his jockey's license. Even John E. Madden tried to intervene on the jockey's behalf, but to no avail.[39] Shilling went to work for H. G. Bedwell some-time in 1918, their friendship forged when Shilling had ridden for the trainer years earlier. The former jockey came on board as an assistant trainer and an exercise rider. He was one of the few voices advocating for Sir Barton in the run-up to the 1919 Kentucky Derby, certain that Sir Barton had more potential than he had been given credit for to that point.[40]

In the waning days before the match race, the doubts that Commander Ross had about Earl Sande led him to inquire with the Jockey Club about granting Shilling a temporary license to ride so that he could entrust the former jockey with the monumental task of riding in Sir Barton against Man o' War.[41] The request was denied, leaving Commander Ross to make his ill-fated choice. For eight years, the Jockey Club had held fast to its ban of Cal Shilling the jockey, although it was totally fine with Cal Shilling the trainer and owner. Over the years, Shilling had not relented in his pursuit of his jockey license since his initial ban in 1912. Now, with the owner and trainer of one of the most prestigious and high-profile stables in America on his side, Shilling made a final play for reinstatement.

After Earl Sande's severance from the Ross Stable, the commander was left with no good lead jockey for his stable. Sure, Tommy Nolan was still under contract to Ross, and the stable held second call on Clarence Kummer's services, but the owner and trainer of one of the country's leading stables wanted an ace in the hole.[42] They sought an advantage they felt only one man could bring: Carroll Shilling.

In the paddock prior to the Pimlico Fall Serial Number 3 on November 10, 1920, H. G. Bedwell saddled Billy Kelly and then stood awaiting his jockey. Earlier in the day, the Maryland State Racing Commission had held a meeting in which Cal Shilling was granted a temporary license to ride in the state of Maryland. Sam Hildreth, H. G. Bedwell, and Commander Ross, all of whom knew Shilling intimately after his years of working with them, had advocated for his licensure. The Maryland State Racing Commission, despite the Jockey Club's permanent suspension, granted their request. Shilling appeared ready to ride, but if he did, the clerk of scales would not be able to weigh him out, and Frank J. Bryan, the steward who represented the Jockey Club, would have to step aside.[43] That was when the trouble began.

Shilling could not ride Sir Barton or Billy Kelly that day because of a technicality. Even though the Maryland State Racing Commission had granted the license, the Maryland Racing Association was running the

Pimlico meet under the sanction of the Jockey Club, of which a majority of the horsemen in the area—stewards, trainers, and owners alike—were either licensees or members. The Maryland State Racing Commission was a relatively new governmental agency, created that year as part of the effort to regulate racing in Maryland; it had yet to draft rules of its own for conducting racing in the state. Because the association was under the authority of the Jockey Club, and the Jockey Club had denied Shilling a license, if he insisted on riding in that race, two of the three stewards and the clerk of scales could not participate in the certification of the race. In addition, a number of owners of horses running at Pimlico were members of the Jockey Club as well and so likely would pull their horses from the meet in protest of this violation of the Jockey Club's rules. With Commander Ross absent from that day's racing at Pimlico, Bedwell had to pull Shilling and substitute another jockey in his stead.[44]

The next day Shilling tried again, this time slated to ride Manoeuvre for Buck Foreman. If Shilling were not allowed to ride, the Maryland State Racing Commission declared it would revoke the Maryland Racing Association's license to run the Pimlico meet and then the association would be obligated to cancel the remainder of the day's racing and possibly other cards after that. The association did not want to violate the commission's order, but it also could not violate the rulings of the Jockey Club, to which a number of association members belonged. To avoid the calamity of canceled racing, Commander Ross had Shilling stand down. While the stewards, Shilling, and Commander Ross were working out the situation, Algernon Daingerfield, assistant secretary to the Jockey Club, conferred with the group to help reach a solution.[45] The Jockey Club had a meeting the next day, at which it would rule on a resolution that would grant the Maryland State Racing Commission the authority to grant licenses if it would adopt the Jockey Club's rules for racing rather than write its own.[46]

When the crowd at Pimlico heard that Shilling would not be riding in the last race of the day, his admirers set upon Maryland commission official Joseph P. Kennedy as he walked from a meeting with Commander Ross, Shilling, and the stewards back to the Pimlico clubhouse. First, a woman hit him, her folded program striking him on the front of his hat. Then a man in the crowd lunged at Kennedy, and soon Kennedy felt blows from several persons, including a blow behind the ear, as he elbowed his way through the crowd to escape the melee. He ended up with a broken finger, a few bruises, and a terrific headache and was sent to bed that evening to recover, vowing that he would be back at Pimlico the next day, even if he had to be on crutches to do it.[47] The incident was over quickly, but the attack on Kennedy indicated the feelings roiling under the surface. Shilling had popular sentiment on his side, but would that be enough to convince the Jockey Club to reverse eight years of policy?

Now that the Maryland State Racing Commission had collided with the Jockey Club, the very question of who was to grant any sort of license in Maryland exposed a flaw in the creation of the commission: it controlled the number of days of racing in the state as well as where the money generated went, but it also controlled the licensure of trainers and jockeys operating within the borders of the state. The Jockey Club supposedly held sway over licenses not only for trainers and jockeys but also for meets held at tracks across the country.[48] The question became, then, whose authority superseded the other's? Should the rules of the Jockey Club, which was based in New York, govern racing in Maryland when that state already had its own racing commission? If the Maryland Racing Commission granted a license that the Jockey Club would not recognize, what effect would that have on those racing in Maryland who also were members of the Jockey Club? If the conflict over jurisdiction could not be resolved, then it was entirely possible that racing in Maryland could shut down altogether.

The Maryland State Racing Commission's authority over all of Maryland racing meant that it was not necessarily privy to the information that the Jockey Club, based in New York, had regarding Carroll Shilling's case, but it had requested the evidence that had kept the stewards of the Jockey Club from licensing him for eight years, a request that had not been answered until this incident occurred.[49] Known to the crowds at Pimlico and Laurel and Havre de Grace, Shilling had his advocates, including his current boss, Commander Ross, and Sam Hildreth, one of his former bosses. Even Governor Ritchie and other government officials had advocated for Shilling's reinstatement, trying to persuade the Jockey Club to relent and allow the ruling of the Maryland State Racing Commission to stand.[50] Their voices might have reached the commissioners' ears, but they had little effect on the steadfastly deaf and immovable stewards of the Jockey Club. However, in order to avoid cancelling the last two days of racing at Pimlico, Ross told Shilling, his employee, that he was not allowed to ride despite his pro tem license.[51] In asking Shilling to stand down, he was siding with the Jockey Club for now, but that caused the Maryland State Racing Commission to rebuke him for siding with New York rather than with Maryland.[52] But after the incident with Kennedy and the threat of a shutdown in Maryland, the Maryland State Racing Commission and the Jockey Club decided to meet and resolve the conflict once and for all.[53]

One week later, on November 18, the Jockey Club met with William P. Riggs, representative for the Maryland Jockey Club; Joseph P. Kennedy, representative for the Maryland State Racing Commission; and George Brown Jr., representative for Bowie Racetrack. Present at the meeting was Commander Ross, while Cal Shilling, nearby in an anteroom, waited to hear the final decision about his fate.[54] The conflict between the Maryland Jockey Club, beholden to the Jockey Club, and the Maryland State Racing Commission, the authority over all Maryland racing, required resolution and the idea was that bringing all of the parties together here would give them a chance to reach it.

The question at hand was who held the authority to grant Cal Shilling a license to ride in Maryland, but, before they could hash that out, Commander Ross withdrew his application for Shilling's reinstatement.[55] Ultimately, Ross decided to back off of his pursuit and assured the Jockey Club that he would not submit any further requests for Shilling's licensure as a jockey. Cal Shilling still retained his license to train, but, as long as he remained with Commander Ross, he would not pursue another chance at being a jockey.[56] The Ross Stable remained in good standing with the Jockey Club, though the outfit found itself still without a lead contract jockey.

If Commander Ross had not relented, he would have forced all of the parties involved to decide right then and there who had sovereignty in the state of Maryland. Even if Ross won, he risked his reputation and his ability to run his horses in New York and elsewhere, possibly forcing other racing associations to have to choose between remaining in good standing with the Jockey Club or allowing Ross's horses to run on their tracks. If he withdrew from the battle, however, he avoided that potential conflict. Ending this conflict meant that Ross at least could keep Shilling on in the role he had played to that point for the Ross Stable, as exercise rider and assistant trainer.

The Maryland State Racing Commission and the Jockey Club agreed to hold a series of meetings for "a much better and broader understanding of turf matters in general, turf law, turf decisions and the reason for them" once racing had concluded for the year.[57]

The next week, racing went back to business, the turf war avoided, and the waning days of racing in 1920 able to go on without a hitch. As the furor over Cal Shilling and his attempt to reinstate his jockey's license died down, C. Edward Sparrow, sportswriter for the *Baltimore Sun,* took a moment to send his readers back in time. On September 25, 1912, trainer Frank M. Taylor and the late H. C. Hallenbeck, the owner who held Shilling's contract, decided to cancel Shilling's mounts for that day's racing at Havre de Grace. "The weather was bad and we had colds," Taylor remembered, "and I cancelled Shilling's mounts for that day." As the holder of Shilling's contract, Hallenbeck was able to tell Shilling what he could and could not do. But Shilling rode his five mounts that day anyway, despite the fact that the owners he was riding for knew that Taylor had cancelled his mounts, which was a violation of turf ethics. In the fifth race, Shilling rode a mare named Jacquelina in a selling race with a purse of $400. In the stretch, Shilling had his mount catch up to the front-runner Royal Meteor, ridden by Jack Diggins, when Diggins supposedly grabbed the mare's bridle, prompting Shilling to do what he could to fight off Diggins's interference. Then both jockeys struck each other with their whips. The fight ended with both horses being disqualified and the jockeys suspended for the remainder of the Havre de Grace meet.[58]

At its meeting in October 1912, the Jockey Club set Shilling down for life. Although Cal Shilling might have been one of the best jockeys in the country, in an earlier incident he had attacked his former employer and nearly killed him, and now he had hit another jockey with his whip on a day when he also violated his employer's edict that he was not to ride. Rough riding was one thing—Diggins was suspended, too—but the consistent insubordination Shilling showed was not something that the Jockey Club wanted to tolerate.[59] Eight years later, it held firm in its position.

Because of the ban on Shilling, his lone Kentucky Derby winner Worth went to the barrier for the 1912 Stafford Handicap with Tommy McTaggart instead. On the first turn, McTaggart tried to cut to the rail in front of the leader Nonpareil but misjudged the distance between them. This caused Nonpareil's front legs to strike Worth's hind ones as Nonpareil fell, taking two other horses with him. Two tendons were severed in one of Worth's legs, ending his career and putting his life in danger. The colt eventually had to be euthanized, costing Hallenbeck one of the best horses he had ever owned. The stable's fortunes were never the same after that.[60]

Shilling's mount on the fateful day that ended his riding career was not a champion horse like Worth, but a common plater named Jacquelina. Her owner and trainer? H. G. Bedwell, the man who made Shilling his assistant trainer and advocated for him to the brink of a turf war. His advocacy for the former jockey before and after the match race would not go unnoticed. Neither would another prematch race incident that involved H. G. Bedwell and the winner-take-all part of the Kenilworth Gold Cup.

In early December 1920, Cal Shilling decided not to renew his trainer's contract with Commander Ross and instead stayed on at the Ross Stable solely as an exercise rider so that he could pursue a jockey's license once more. Knowing that Commander Ross had pledged not to apply for a license for the former jockey while he was under Ross's employ, Shilling had to sever that relationship officially, even though he continued to live on the Ross property.[61]

Meanwhile, as the Ross Stable looked forward to a new year of racing in 1921, rumors of friction between H. G. Bedwell and Commander Ross abounded, speculation that likely resulted from the Shilling scandal and the supposed bad advice that Bedwell gave his boss during the uproar.[62] In late March came word that Louis Feustel had received his trainer's license despite having his application set aside at an earlier Jockey Club meeting.[63] Even though Bedwell had yet to submit his own license application, the Jockey Club stewards made it known that they would not accept H. G. Bedwell as the authorized agent for the Ross Stable.[64] Although newspapers did not share the reason behind this decision, August Belmont Jr. clarified it in a letter addressed to William P. Riggs, secretary of the Maryland Jockey Club, in late April 1921.

The Kenilworth Gold Cup was a winner-take-all event: the loser's connections received nothing from the race except a trip to Windsor, Ontario, and their regular salary. H. G. Bedwell, reading the writing on the wall, approached both Samuel Riddle and Louis Feustel in an effort to make some sort of arrangement in which the trainer would get something more out of the race.[65] In doing so, Bedwell violated turf ethics: one simply did not ask an opponent for a reward should his horse lose.[66] Riddle and Feustel, confident in their horse, had no reason to act on Bedwell's suggestion; Bedwell, also confident in their horse and realistic about his, acted like far less of a sportsman than his boss had.

Bedwell's action created yet another sticky situation for Commander Ross. Because Bedwell now had no license, the trainer could not sign for the Ross Stable's entries, and the Maryland Jockey Club turned down all of those entries into its spring races because Bedwell's signature was on the entry blanks. The Maryland State Racing Commission had accepted Bedwell as Ross's authorized representative on April 1, but, again, the question of sovereignty came up. Who was the ultimate authority here: the Maryland Jockey Club and the Jockey Club or the Maryland State Racing Commission?[67] Sure, the Maryland State Racing Commission could rule that Bedwell could serve in that capacity in Maryland, but that ruling did not apply out of the state—to the tracks in New York City, for example. Indeed, the Jockey Club said that it would not accept the Ross Stable's entries on metropolitan tracks if the commander insisted on keeping Bedwell in his employ.[68]

Bedwell had taken Commander Ross's fledgling stable and turned it into a powerhouse. He had acquired most of the stable's star horses, including Cudgel, Billy Kelly, Sir Barton, and Milkmaid. He had conditioned those horses to a number of brilliant victories, including Sir Barton's Triple Crown as well as his record performances in races such as the Saratoga Handicap and the Merchants and Citizens Handicap. In their tenure together, from 1917 through 1920, Bedwell had helped the stable win nearly $556,000 in purse money. It was H. G. Bedwell who got the ball rolling on the match race, which ended in a bitter disappointment for Commander Ross. Not only did his horse lose the race, but he also lost his stable jockey and likely discovered that his trainer had approached Man o' War's connections to get something out of the match race even if Sir Barton lost. It was H. G. Bedwell who recommended standing Earl Sande down and pursuing a license for Cal Shilling, a pursuit that forced Ross to end the former jockey's quest in order to avoid long-term repercussions. Again, the commander was on the cusp of becoming an outsider. Again, his trainer was at the center of the issue.

On April 16, 1921, Commander Ross hired Henry McDaniel to take charge of the Ross stable of stars starting May 1. The Jockey Club had forced Commander Ross to sever his relationship with Bedwell in order to keep the Ross horses running on tracks sanctioned by the Jockey Club. Bedwell received his salary for 1921 as part of his severance and was able to buy Ross's share of two horses they co-owned.[69]

With Bedwell's and Sande's exit, the Ross Stable underwent a tremendous change in less than a year. As J. K. M. Ross remembers in *Boots and Saddles*, "Those illustrious days were past."[70] With McDaniel now in charge, would Sir Barton be ready for racing in 1921?

Henry McDaniel was no rookie trainer. Commander Ross had brought on a savvy, experienced man to take charge of his horses. McDaniel had trained both Sun Briar and Exterminator for Willis Sharpe Kilmer, so "Uncle Henry" was the perfect man to get champions such as Sir Barton and Billy Kelly ready for racing in 1921.

However, on the same day the *Daily Racing Form* shared news of McDaniel's hire, Sir Barton's workout at Havre de Grace showed that he was "big and huge, not ready from all appearances."[71] Sir Barton was notorious for being an enthusiastic eater and a lazy exerciser; Bedwell had noted in the past how it would take more than one horse running with the champion in order to get him to work because he had to be tricked into running as if it were a race. McDaniel decided that getting Sir Barton back into racing shape, after thirty-one starts in three seasons and with already questionable feet, was going to take too much work to risk his soundness. On April 23, 1921, the Triple Crown winner was officially reported as retired.[72]

Back to Bolingbrook went Sir Barton, this time for good. His first service was to be with Constancy, who was also newly retired.[73] Commander Ross now had two good sires at his Maryland farm, with Cudgel already standing stud there. Replete with new blood coming in through both sales and breeding, Ross was looking toward the future, his champion horses there to bring forth more colts and fillies to fill his stalls.

In August, Montfort and Bernard B. (B. B.) Jones, brothers who had made their fortune in oil, offered Commander Ross a tidy sum for his champion Sir Barton. The brothers were looking for good stallions to bring to their breeding operation at Audley Farm in Virginia, a nascent operation similar to Ross's own five years earlier. On the advice of John E. Madden, Sir Barton's breeder, the Jones brothers offered an unnamed sum for the Triple Crown winner to become part of their lineup of stallions.[74]

With that, Sir Barton began a new phase of his life, the final phase of many Thoroughbred stallions' careers: stud duty. In September, he was shipped from Bolingbrook outside of Laurel, Maryland, to Audley Farm, outside of Berryville, near the Maryland–Virginia state line.[75] His exit from the racing scene did not come with the fanfare that Man o' War's had, but his career had forever changed the sport he had dominated. A symbol of the peak of possibility inherent in every Thoroughbred, Sir Barton was now a name eternally etched in the highest echelons of racing.

17

Good-bye, Sammy

By the time Commander Ross retired Sir Barton from racing, his name was often seen in tandem with Man o' War's, most notably on advertisements for the film *The Race of the Age* and in articles extolling and retelling the legendary season that the big red colt had had in 1920. For all that Sir Barton had done in 1919 and 1920, none of his accomplishments was enough to push the Triple Crown winner out of the big red colt's shadow. Instead, the shelly hooves that had plagued America's first Triple Crown winner throughout his racing career, which his owner's son, Jim Ross, was "convinced [was the cause of] a large percentage of defeats he suffered," finally caught up to him.[1] After teetering on the brink of lameness for three racing seasons, Sir Barton bid farewell to the racetrack, his exit lacking the fanfare of his rival Man o' War's. In late 1921, the Triple Crown winner was sold to B. B. and Montfort Jones and then retired to Audley Farm in Virginia, where he headed their new breeding operation.

At five years old, Sir Barton turned away from the grind of racing life and toward the breeding shed, his new owners gambling on whether he could sire horses who could duplicate his speed and stamina. His golden age was over, as was that of many of those who had been on the journey with him. His accomplishments would record their names for all time, but few would reap the benefits of that notoriety in their own lifetimes.

Like Commander Ross, the Jones brothers had money, and they were willing to use it to dive with gusto into the sport of kings. B. B. and Montfort Jones were sons of a Virginia doctor and his wife who had relocated from southern Virginian to Noxubee County, Mississippi, after the

Civil War. Both brothers were born in Mississippi, two of nine children for Dr. Montfort and Sallie Jones, but made their fortunes in the Oklahoma Territory. Montfort moved west first, opening a bank in Bristow, and then convinced B. B. to settle there as well. Through relationships with oil speculators in the area, the brothers were able to purchase leases on lands rich in oil, investing in the Cushing Oil Field with famed speculator Tom Slick in 1912. The brothers eventually sold their properties and created the Bermont Oil Company to pursue their other interests, including philanthropic work.[2]

The Jones family had spent time at the spas in Hot Springs, Arkansas, and on one trip to the area in 1919 Montfort decided to visit Oaklawn Park, where he spied a horse named Thelma E. He bought the two-year-old filly on the spot, the first horse in what was to become the Audley Farm stable.[3] Later that year Thelma E. won the Beldame Handicap at Aqueduct, and the Jones brothers were hooked.[4] That early success at the track inspired them to buy more horses, including a half-brother to Sir Barton, a colt named St. Henry,[5] and a number of others from John E. Madden, who was slowly getting out of the breeding business and expanding his interests into other areas. As Montfort and B. B. Jones got their start in racing, Madden served as their mentor, helping them acquire horses as they moved to establish Audley as both a racing and a breeding operation.[6]

B. B. Jones purchased Audley Farm from Archibald Cummins on April 28, 1921. The farm was 515 acres; the brothers wanted to turn the majority of it into a training and breeding facility for their stable and then use the rest for crops, an apple orchard, and cattle, all consumables they could use to sell or supply the farm. Montfort bought half of Audley in 1922 and then purchased an adjoining farm, Buena Vista, in 1923 to expand their holdings even farther. As the brothers worked to make Audley fit their vision, they added a number of barns, a training track, fenced paddocks, an equine hospital, and gravel roads. When they were done, Audley was the largest Thoroughbred farm in Clark County, Virginia, and the only one training horses for the track in addition to breeding and selling yearlings.[7] The Jones brothers had made Audley a place for breeding, training, and wintering their horses, not unlike Commander Ross's Maryland properties.

Early in the brothers' racing career, Audley got horses from breeders like John E. Madden, but as they built their roster of stallions, they were able to race homebreds as well. One of their most successful early racers, Princess Doreen, was bred by Madden; she went on to win the Kentucky Oaks in 1924 as well as the Coaching Club American Oaks in 1924 and the Saratoga Handicap in 1926. No doubt it was Madden's influence that brought the brothers to Sir Barton as his racing career ended and stud duty lay before him. He was brought on as their lead stallion—Ormondale, Royal Canopy, and Rockminster standing with him. Later, St. Henry, Sir Barton's half-brother, came to stand stud at Audley as well, his racing career shortened by his limited success on the track. In addition to the stallions, the Jones brothers brought on a number of mares from Madden's farm Hamburg Place, including several sired by Star Shoot, Sir Barton's sire.

In August 1921, Commander Ross's sale of Sir Barton to the Jones brothers and John E. Madden made the papers, but the price went undisclosed.[8] However, the commander had supposedly turned down an offer of $100,000 for the Triple Crown winner, so the Jones brothers' offer must have been higher than that to secure the services of Man o' War's only rival.[9] In addition to the money he received for the horse, Ross also secured the rights to breed five of his mares to his former champion each breeding season. Within a month of the sale, Sir Barton left Ross's Maryland properties and was sent westward to Audley. His stud fee was $1,000, and "his book was full most every year."[10]

At stud, Sir Barton seemed to be much the same horse he had been on the track. Never one to be a pet, the retired racer transitioned into stallion duties with ease but still maintained that quality of keeping the people who worked with him on their toes. Whatever bad habits he might have picked up as a horse in training, cooped up in a stall for hours on end, might have abated, but he was still "a headstrong, mischievous boy—no particular harm in him if one knew how to handle him," as Margaret Phipps Leonard describes him in her profile of Sir Barton in *The Horse* in June 1938. Bedwell's habit of slapping at Sir Barton's muzzle every time he saw the horse with his head out in the barn had led to the horse's habit of grabbing anyone nearby without cause. In the article, B. B. Jones told the story of Sir Barton grabbing a guest's uniform and tearing it; the stallion was only being playful, ripping the man's clothing but not hurting the man himself. According to Leonard,

Sir Barton had even caught one of B. B. Jones's fingers in his teeth more than once but always let go after his owner admonished him.[11] Whatever devil young Jim Ross had seen in Sir Barton could have been the disposition of a smart horse who did not want to be stabled, a horse who liked to bully and intimidate if one allowed him to do so but also inclined to back down rather than hurt those around him.

Much like Man o' War and Cudgel, Sir Barton did not truly bond with people. Billy Kelly might have been easygoing enough to be H. G. Bedwell's favorite, but Sir Barton was the most accomplished horse he ever trained. That drive to compete might have made it hard for the Triple Crown winner to get along with humans, but it was exactly that drive as well as his speed and stamina that the Jones brothers were gambling would show up again and again in the foals he produced.

At stud, if a successful racehorse does not reproduce himself in some form or fashion, then his failure as a sire becomes part of the conversation about that horse. Sometimes reputations can be rescued through that horse's influence later in pedigrees, as the generations expand from immediate progeny outward. For Sir Barton, his mixed legacy at stud mirrors that of many Triple Crown winners. At Audley, Sir Barton was the star sire, a Triple Crown winner, a horse who had won more than $100,000 and had set speed records on the track. Unimpressive at two, nearly legendary at three, and uneven at four, he also proved to be inconsistent at stud. Much like Star Shoot's other progeny, Sir Barton's effectiveness as a sire was nowhere near his success on the track. Star Shoot was not known for being a good sire of sires but instead exerted his strongest influence as a broodmare sire,[12] and Sir Barton seemed to follow in his footsteps, siring fillies who fared better on the track (and later as breeders) than many of his colts did.

He had stakes winners such as Donna Barton, Chancellor, Nellie Custis, and Easter Stockings. Easter Stockings (1925, out of Irish Lassie, by Celt) won the Kentucky Oaks and Latonia Oaks in 1928 as well as the Kentucky Handicap in 1930. She also was named champion three-year-old filly of 1928. Cudgeller, part of Sir Barton's first crop of foals, won the Fort Miami Derby and the Independence Handicap and finished in the money in other stakes races during his career. Nellie Custis (1926, out of Minerva, by Black Toney) was also a winner, with the Fort Thomas and San Francisco Claiming Handicaps among her wins. In the end, Sir Barton sired 218 foals, 141 of which started on a racetrack somewhere and 99 of which were winners. His progeny won a little more than $900,000 total in their careers.[13]

Though the horses Sir Barton sired did well enough, he was not able to produce a horse that rose to the same heights he did in his racing career. The idea that a son of Star Shoot could not go on to success at stud became the going wisdom about pedigrees as time went on, and so, despite his get (i.e., his progeny) winning $100,000 each year from 1928 to 1930, the idea that he was a failure as a sire dogged Sir Barton.[14] Ultimately, his greatest contribution to his sport became that storied spring of 1919 when his Triple Crown win raised the bar for Thoroughbreds for years to come.

Saratoga held its usual sales during its August meet in 1927, attended by many of the country's elite owners, including Montfort Jones. On August 11, Montfort spent the day at the Spa, taking in the sale of yearlings and the day's racing before returning to his room at the United States Hotel. He retired to his room and never woke up. Admiral Cary Grayson, President Woodrow Wilson's physician and fellow Virginia Thoroughbred breeder, was called to Montfort's room but found him unresponsive. Montfort Jones, the face of the racing arm of Audley Farms, was gone, and now B. B., who to this point had been more involved with the breeding side of the operation, had to balance both the breeding and the racing. He did the best he could with what he and his brother had built, but by 1935 he had started to slow down.[15]

In the midst of the Great Depression, Jones and Audley remained steadfastly successful, with the Jones fortune from oil and other ventures keeping them insulated from the economic devastation of that era. By the time B. B. Jones decided to stop racing and focus solely on breeding, he had spent $2.5 million on the stock that had been part of Audley since the brothers started the farm in the early 1920s. In 1939, after the death of Bright Knight, one of B. B. Jones's favorite horses, Fasig-Tipton, the premiere auction company for the racing industry, came to Audley to help Jones sell off his remaining breeding stock. From 1939 to 1953, Audley was home to a dwindling number of Thoroughbreds and other livestock, with occasional dispersal sales up until B. B. Jones's death in 1953. Over the years, Audley would not only sell its horses at auction but would also sell others, including Sir Barton himself, to the United States Army Remount Service. Sir Barton became part of the Remount Service in late 1932, B. B. Jones likely selling the Triple Crown winner for $500.[16]

Why, though, did America's first Triple Crown winner, the only horse deemed worthy of challenging Man o' War, end up in the Remount Service rather than elsewhere to continue his stud career?

One reason: John E. Madden.

John E. Madden got his start in racing because of his hearty physique, parlaying his prize money from boxing into prize money from horses. But even the hearty can be vulnerable to the physical infirmities of old age. In late October 1929, after walking from his office on Wall Street back to his suite in the Philadelphia Hotel, Madden came down with a cold that quickly developed into pneumonia. He had always prided himself on his physical vigor, so the Wizard of the Turf demurred when his sons recommended he go to the hospital. Determined to beat his illness on his own, he sent sons Joseph and Edward away and went about his business. Alone in his suite, the seventy-two-year-old John E. Madden suffered a heart attack on November 2, his death coming within months of famed trainer and owner Sam Hildreth's.[17]

Over the years since Madden had sold Sir Barton to Ross and then lost both Star Shoot and Lady Sterling, the breeder had held several dispersal sales, gradually drawing down his Thoroughbred holdings while also increasing his investment in other ventures.[18] Neither of the Madden sons went into breeding, opting instead to sell off the last of the Hamburg Place horses in 1931. Years later, John E. Madden's grandson, Preston, would take up the mantle of breeder, eventually breeding his own Kentucky Derby winner, Alysheba (1987), to go alongside the five his grandfather had bred on the same bluegrass estate.[19]

In his will, John E. Madden provided for Sir Martin, his champion horse who still remained at Hamburg Place even after being retired from stud duty. With Montfort Jones's death in 1927 and then Madden's in 1929, Sir Barton had nowhere to go once B. B. Jones decided that the Triple Crown winner was no longer useful to Audley. Owing to the influence Madden had over Jones and other breeders, the Remount Service became an option; Madden had championed the Remount Service's mission, going so far as to write an essay on the Thoroughbred's suitability for breeding cavalry horses, published in the *Thoroughbred Record* in 1913.[20] Had Madden still been alive in 1932 when Jones decided to sell Sir Barton, he might have brought the great son of Star Shoot back to where he was born. But with Madden gone and interest in the stallion's services dwindling, Sir Barton, America's first Triple Crown winner, became part of the Remount Service.

He was in the army now.

During World War I, the British, American, and French Allied forces had faced shortages of cavalry mounts. These shortages had made news during and after the end of fighting as the US military took steps to deal with them at the time and to prevent them from happening again should a similar conflict arise. The United Sates Army Remount Service had been established in 1908 in an effort to centralize the procurement of mounts for both cavalry and artillery regiments. During the Civil War and after, individual regiments and then the Cavalry Bureau had been charged with obtaining mounts, using a system that was fraught with corruption and fraud. After World War I, the Remount Service, a division of the Quartermaster Corps, formalized its breeding operations to prevent the issues that had plagued the system of obtaining needed horses in previous conflicts.[21] The Remount Service preferred Thoroughbreds for its breeding operations, wanting a combination of that breed's stamina and speed for its horses. Thoroughbred sires were bred to mares of other horse breeds to create the ideal Remount horse, "a functional, well-balanced horse that stood 15–15.2 hands and weighed between 1,000 and 1,200 pounds."[22]

Prior to the Army Horse Breeding Program's inception in 1913, the military had a difficult time finding the right number of well-bred horses suited to its purposes. Without consistent standards for horses and programs for breeding them, the stock available was spotty; horses might have been plentiful, but those well suited to the military's purposes were not. Thus, the breeding program sought to take Remount stallions, mostly Thoroughbreds, and place them with civilian agents in a variety of areas around the country. These stallions were listed for reasonable fees for other civilians to breed their mares to, in many cases $5 or $10. The horses produced as a result of mating mares with Remount stallions could either be purchased by the military for its use or sold by the breeder for private use. This program encouraged the breeding of military-grade horses to ensure ample supply during wartime and to give breeders quality horses they could sell during peacetime. Thoroughbreds of note helped the Remount Service even more. What private breeder could resist paying such a small fee for the chance to breed his mare to a horse that had won the Kentucky Derby?

The racing industry was on board with the Remount Service. Beginning in 1918, the newly formed American Remount Association worked with and encouraged owners of Thoroughbreds to donate or sell their stallions to the Remount Service in order to ensure a supply of quality sires. Famous horses and classic winners such as George Smith, American Flag, Behave Yourself, Donerail, and Sir Huon were either gifted to or purchased by the Remount Service to stand as stallions. The American Remount Association and racing associations encouraged owners not to geld their horses, discouraging the practice by barring geldings from participating in a number of races. Exterminator and Billy Kelly, Sir Barton's stablemate, had been barred from running in the Preakness Stakes because they were geldings. The association also recruited owners to donate or sell their Thoroughbreds to benefit the Remount Service. B. B. Jones's sale of Sir Barton to the Remount Service gave the breeding program its most elite stallion yet.

In late 1932, Sir Barton's tenure in the Remount Service started at Fort Royal, Virginia, the service's headquarters and one of its eight depots. Before the end of the year, he was transferred west to Fort Robinson, Nebraska, and then was placed with Dr. Joseph Roy Hylton, a ranch owner and Remount agent located outside of Douglas, Wyoming.[23]

Born in 1883 in Kansas, Dr. Hylton was one of Wyoming's renowned surgeons, educated at Bennett-Loyola Medical School in Chicago and later consulting with the Mayo Clinic on a number of cases. In addition to being a husband and a father of three, he was a member of the Democratic National Committee and owned ranches in both Converse and Albany Counties, Wyoming, including La Prele Creek Ranch, where Sir Barton was stationed. Hylton was a Remount agent, his ranches housing several Thoroughbreds of his own as well as quarter horses, cattle, and sheep.[24] He bred Sir Barton to his own mares and as a Remount agent allowed other breeders access to the Triple Crown winner's services, resulting in the possibility that a number of horses of multiple breeds in the western United States may have Sir Barton in their pedigrees.

For Sir Barton, life on the Hylton ranch in Wyoming was a far cry from the excitement of his racing days. The people who had accompanied him throughout his racing career soon found themselves beyond those halcyon days as well.

After the departure of Sande and Bedwell, Commander Ross's stable continued racing throughout the 1920s, but the stable never returned to the success it had in 1918–1920.[25] The match race and the ensuing controversies over Cal Shilling's licensure and H. G. Bedwell's violation of turf ethics before the race cost Ross the services of the trainer who had taken him to the top of the racing world. Despite the resources available to him, Ross was not able to duplicate the success of those early years and the prestige that a horse like Sir Barton had brought to his stable. Billy Kelly ground out several more seasons of racing, finally retiring in 1923 with a record of 39 wins, 14 second-place finishes, and 7 third-place finishes in 69 starts. He died in 1926 at Ross's farm at Verchères, outside of Montreal, Quebec.[26]

A mixture of philanthropy, racing expenditures, and extravagance for many years drained the Ross family of the wealth that the commander had inherited from his father. In 1921, Commander Ross sold Bolingbrook, outside of Laurel, Maryland, to Ral Parr; the property, with its large paddocks and custom-built training track, later became a racetrack itself, the Standardbred track Laurel Raceway. As the 1920s grew to a close, the commander gambled his remaining fortune in the stock market and was able to make some of it back, only to lose it all for good after that. He declared bankruptcy in 1928 and then sued to liquidate a trust he had set up for his wife so that he could pay off his creditors. Divorced from his wife, Ethel, after his bankruptcy, his stable gone, and his fortune spent, Commander Ross moved to Jamaica, where he married Iris de Lisser, daughter of a Jamaican planter, and spent much of his remaining time on the ocean, fishing and sailing until his death in July 1951.[27]

A few months after Commander Ross passed away, H. G. Bedwell died of a heart attack at Yarrow Brae on New Year's Eve 1951.[28] After losing his license and then his job with the Ross Stable because of the Shilling controversy in 1921, "Hard Guy" Bedwell was persona non grata in Maryland for some time, but by 1924 he was once again the country's leading owner and continued to breed horses at Yarrow Brae.[29] The Jockey Club eventually granted him a license once again, and Bedwell returned to form, training for owners such as Ral Parr, who had purchased Ross's farm in Maryland, and cosmetics magnate Elizabeth Arden, who was racing her horses under the name Mrs. Elizabeth G. Lewis.[30] H. G. Bedwell never reached the same heights of success that he saw in 1918–1920, but he did have some success as an owner and trainer in his post–Sir Barton years.[31]

Earl Sande moved on from his bitter ending with the Ross Stable to ride for other prestigious owners such as Samuel Riddle, Harry Sinclair, and William Woodward. In his Hall of Fame career, he won the Kentucky Derby three times and the Belmont Stakes five times; his only win in the Preakness Stakes was in 1930, when he won the second Triple Crown on Gallant Fox. He was the leading jockey in the United States three times during the 1920s and then became a trainer, topping the list of American trainers in 1938.

A rich man from all of his riding exploits, Sande then turned to breeding and owning, but pursuing that rich man's game—which also helped to bankrupt his former employer—was a mistake that left him nearly penniless. After years of refusing jobs promoting racing or working as a steward or racing secretary and determined to work with horses in some way or not at all, Earl Sande, at fifty-five years old, dieted his way to riding weight and rode ten mounts, winning only once before hanging his tack up for good. Broke and ill, Sande moved west to Oregon to be with his ailing father and died in a nursing home in 1968 at age sixty-nine.[32]

Johnny Loftus, the jockey who rode Sir Barton in his Triple Crown campaign in 1919, never regained his jockey's license after losing it in 1920. The Jockey Club did grant him a trainer's license instead; Loftus went on to train Pompoon, a successful handicap horse, among other stakes winners. The man who rode both Sir Barton and Man o' War in his Hall of Fame career retired from training in 1939. He would go on to work as a carpenter, far away from the starting barrier and the spotlight.[33] During his years away from the racing game, he remarried and had a son; he eventually moved to Carlsbad, California, where he lived near his daughter from his first marriage, Eleanor, and her family. One of the greatest jockeys of his time, Johnny Loftus died of a heart attack in 1976, many years and many miles removed from the career that had made him a name forever associated with those golden years of racing.[34]

Cal Shilling also spent the remainder of his career without the jockey license he had sought for so long, floating from track to track, job to job, never regaining the position or prestige that had marked his golden years in the saddle.[35] He all but disappeared, reportedly working on the back-sides of various racetracks, his arrests for vagrancy bringing him once again into the spotlight for only a moment.[36] The brash jockey who had been the best of them all in his day became penniless and homeless in his later years, struggling to remember the highlights of his stellar career. The body of Carroll Shilling, clad in cast-off clothing, was found under a horse van at Belmont Park in January 1950. In the van, the authorities found a stale bread crust; the former jockey had only ninety-eight cents in his pockets.[37] The death of Shilling, divorced, homeless, and far from the spotlight, was a sad end for the jockey who had mentored Earl Sande, had ridden for owners such as Sam Hildreth, and was considered the best rider the latter ever saw.

"At the lonely hour of eleven on Saturday night, October 30, 1937, the still handsome son of Lady Sterling and Star Shoot died," far away from the raucous crowds of horse players and fans, long departed from the dirt ovals that had made him so noteworthy that his obituary ran in papers across the country.[38] Out on a Wyoming mountainside, he had stood stud for his country, a long way from the bluegrass of his birth and the trail that he had blazed from Kentucky to Maryland to New York, his hooves cutting a path that only twelve horses after him (as of 2018) would be able to follow.

Nearly two weeks later, the obituaries shared the news that America's first Triple Crown winner was gone. In these remembrances, the twenty-one-year-old Sir Barton was referred to as the horse who was "outmatched at his peak by only the great Man o' War."[39] Notably, some obituaries got several facts wrong, referring to his spending seventeen years at stud in Wyoming, completely omitting his years at Audley, and implying that the match race with Man o' War was Sir Barton's last start. Most importantly, though, one obituary pointed out that three horses had followed "Sir Barton's all-conquering lead" in winning the three races that were now known as the Triple Crown.[40] By 1937, Gallant Fox and his son Omaha as well as War Admiral, a son of Man o' War, had gone on to duplicate Sir Barton's feat of winning the Kentucky Derby, Preakness Stakes, and Belmont Stakes. Less than twenty years after Sir Barton did it first, not only did his accomplishment in 1919 have a name, but it had also become *a thing*, a pursuit that others sought each year to duplicate. In the intervening years between Sir Barton's three wins and his death, the Kentucky Derby, the Preakness Stakes, and the Belmont Stakes, the jewels of the Triple Crown, secured their spots as the premiere races for three-year-olds in the United States. His record might not have been as stellar as Man o' War's, with thirteen wins, six seconds, and five thirds in thirty-one starts, but his wins in some of his era's most prestigious races, such as the Kentucky Derby, the Saratoga Handicap, and others, put him in the rarefied echelon occupied by Man o' War, Exterminator, and only a few others. Sir Barton's blazing spring season in 1919 created a phenomenon that came to be associated with the pinnacle of his sport, an accomplishment so elite that it would become the yardstick by which horses would be measured from then on.

The questions about hopping that followed H. G. Bedwell, and by extension, Sir Barton, went unmentioned in the first Triple Crown winner's obituaries. Memories of his exploits on the track—the record-breaking performances, the domination of the American classics, and the match race with Man o' War—were the legacy that turf writers and historians shared with the generations that followed. Since his death, the suggestions that Sir Barton was hopped come from rumor and secondhand reports rather than hard evidence. In the end, the first Triple Crown winner's historic accomplishments remain his biggest contribution to the sport of horse racing.

The year 1937 also saw the deaths of A. M. Orpen, the promoter who brought the match race to the masses at Kenilworth, and the race's starter, Harry Morrissey. The glory days of Sir Barton and Man o' War passed away in earnest, leaving only the memories of their moments and the thundering hooves of their progeny to make or break their reputations. As the years wore on and the names and faces of their era passed into memory, Man o' War would be remembered as "the Horse of the Century," but only one horse ever stood next to him as challenger: Sir Barton, the stout son of Star Shoot and Lady Sterling, his chestnut coat shining, white blaze cascading across his beautiful face.

He stood out from birth, one of those horses who made others take notice. He might not have dazzled at first, but once he had the right owner and trainer, he made his mark on his sport forever. With that team behind him, not even a life-threatening illness could keep him from that dirt oval, the bugle's call, and the starting barrier. No one gave him a chance, but he showed what he could do when he truly shone. He took on all challengers and left most in his dust, creating a legacy that grows in stature even in these long years after his death. Another might have come along and burned brighter for a short time, but Sir Barton's mark is still there, his place in history sealed.

Sir Barton, Triple Crown winner, record breaker, history maker.

Epilogue

When Sir Barton crossed the finish line at Belmont Park on June 11, 1919, his win in the Belmont Stakes sealed what came to be known as America's first Triple Crown, but in his day those three wins did not carry the same weight that time has given them. This era would know the Triple Crown as an English triumvirate—the Epsom Derby, the Two-Thousand Guineas, and the St. Leger Stakes—and most references to a Triple Crown in print in the years before and immediately after Sir Barton's triumph would point to this English version. American horse racing still searched for a commensurate accomplishment, something with the same prestige given to those horses that completed the English Triple Crown.

At first, New York led the charge to create that sequence, conceiving races such as the Belmont Stakes, the Withers Stakes, and the Lawrence Realization as a trio of challenges for three-year-olds, borrowing their distances and dates from the British as well.[1] But the state took a hit to its racing industry from the Hart–Agnew Act, and when the purses in New York could not keep pace with those in Kentucky and Maryland, the horses went elsewhere, especially after both the Kentucky Derby and the Preakness Stakes increased their purses.[2] Even after Sir Barton conquered the Kentucky Derby, the Preakness, and the Belmont, these prestigious stakes races for three-year-olds remained separate for a time, but the physical distance between them shrank in proportion with their growing purses as more and more horses made the trek from Louisville to Baltimore to New York each year.

When War Cloud went chasing those burgeoning purses in 1918, he planted a seed that grew, owners and trainers determined to strike gold by following the money. Sir Barton won all three and $57,275, an astronomical sum of money for only three races. By early 1920, the Kentucky Derby and the Preakness double had inspired the Kentucky Jockey Club and the Maryland Jockey Club to coordinate and schedule the two races ten days apart rather than the paltry four days of 1919. In addition, both saw fit to increase their purses again, giving owners and trainers even more incentive to risk shipping their Derby starters from Louisville to Baltimore for the Preakness. From 1920 on, the money that horses won in the three races increased from year to year, but the calendar remained less coordinated. The time between the Derby and the Preakness varied over the next two decades, with both run on the same day in 1922 and a gap of anywhere from five to nine days between races from 1921 to 1930. The Preakness then moved upward on the calendar and for a decade (1923–1932) appeared on the stakes calendar before the Kentucky Derby. Starting in 1932, the Derby slipped into its now familiar slot on the first Saturday of May, but the gap between Churchill Downs and Pimlico remained fairly close, a week in most cases, throughout the 1930s and 1940s.

Once War Cloud in 1918 and then Sir Barton in 1919 showed that the risks were worth the reward, the purses and the schedule evolved to match that nascent pursuit, but this triumvirate of stakes races still remained nameless in the turf media. As late as June 1922, the *Daily Racing Form* mentioned a New York "triple crown," saying that "if a horse can win the Withers and the Belmont his fame is secure, while a victory for these events and the Realization in the Autumn corresponds to the British 'Triple Crown,' which includes the Two Thousand Guineas, Derby and St. Leger."[3] The following year, 1923, the *Daily Racing Form* made its first reference to Sir Barton's Derby–Preakness–Belmont victories as "this American triple crown" in a column discussing these prizes for three-year-olds.[4] W. C. Vreeland, prominent sportswriter for the *Brooklyn Daily Eagle,* lamented the absence of a star three-year-old going into the Belmont Stakes in 1924, and even though other good tests of that age group still remained, he argued that "the triple crown, as our British cousins would say, of the American turf is comprised of the Preakness, the Kentucky Derby, and the Belmont."[5] Through the 1920s, no horse came close to duplicating Sir Barton's feat, so the use of the name "Triple Crown" remained infrequent, although in 1927 a brief newspaper article on the upcoming races for three-year-olds cited Sir Barton as "the only three-year-old that ever won the 'triple crown' in America."[6]

The most often cited origin story for the name "Triple Crown" in connection with the Kentucky Derby, the Preakness Stakes, and the Belmont Stakes generally holds that Charles Hatton, longtime writer first for the *Morning Telegraph* and then for its successor the *Daily Racing Form,* brought the phrase into popular parlance.[7] He needed a shortcut for referring to the three races, ergo "Triple Crown," which he supposedly used as early as Gallant Fox's sweep of the three in 1930. However, the name was sparsely used in the *Form* until Omaha's win in 1935. Sportswriters in other publications instead used the general term *triple crown* starting with Gallant Fox in 1930, increasing that usage as more horses were added to the list of triple winners. The name "Triple Crown" finally shed both its quotation marks and its informal status when it was officially recognized by the Thoroughbred Racing Association in 1950.[8] That year the association awarded its first Triple Crown trophy, a tricornered sterling silver vase created by Cartier, to Commander Ross in recognition of Sir Barton's achievement three decades earlier.[9] Each year thereafter, the Thoroughbred Racing Association presented another Triple Crown trophy to a previous winner, but in 1950 it also created one more, a blank trophy awaiting the next winner.

That trophy would sit ownerless in the association vault for twenty-three years until 1973.

Sir Barton's triple win in 1919 went nameless for almost a decade owing to the unorganized and haphazard nature of the three races' growth. These three races made no sense as a sequence: they were hundreds of miles apart, in three different states, at three different tracks, and, for a long time, on an uncoordinated schedule. Yet Commander Ross and H. G. Bedwell's decision to run their colt in all three and then the rewards they reaped for his dominance ignited a pursuit that would oft be copied and informally renowned for nearly thirty years until the official recognition of the three races as the Triple Crown. William Woodward, contemporary of Commander Ross, followed that same path with his colt Gallant Fox in 1930 and then with Omaha in 1935. Samuel Riddle, who famously shunned the Kentucky Derby in 1920, brought War Admiral, son of Man o' War, to the Derby, finally recognizing that running in all three races held some sort of appeal. He was among the last of the stalwarts who avoided the "western" tracks of Kentucky but finally caved in to the appeal of the ever-increasing purses that awaited horses who were able to score all three races.

The 1940s added four more names to the list of Triple Crown winners, each winning three to four times the amount of money that Sir Barton's wins had brought in 1919. Calumet Farm scored two Triple Crowns in this decade, first with Whirlaway in 1941 and then with Citation in 1948. An injury forced Count Fleet into retirement after his twenty-five-length win in the Belmont Stakes in 1943, but his wins brought close to $140,000, an amount that would be nearly doubled by the time Assault won almost $270,000 in 1946. After winning a little more than $250,000 in his Triple Crown run in 1948, Citation went on to become horse racing's first millionaire. By decade's end, not only was winning the Kentucky Derby a dream of so many horse owners, but winning the Triple Crown also became another of those achievements that drove anyone associated with horse racing. The prolific wins of the 1940s made the Triple Crown look easy, but the next two decades would cast doubt on the viability of the chase.

Within a few years of Citation's win, as horses tried and failed to win even two of the three jewels, grumblings about the Triple Crown crept into the conversation. The races were too close together for horses early in their three-year-old year. Even the shift from one week to two between the Kentucky Derby and the Preakness did not minimize the doubts that the Triple Crown was too difficult to win.[10] As breeding in the United States expanded, the classics became harder to win. As owners pursued the elusive prize, they bred more and more horses to capitalize on the ever-increasing money available in the sport, not just in the classics. In 1945, when Citation was born, 5,819 Thoroughbred foals were registered; in 1950, 9,095 foals were registered; and by the 1960s the number was up to 20,000.[11] As the sport evolved, should the Triple Crown not change as well? Perhaps space the races out more, like the British Triple Crown calendar, which stretched its classics over four months instead of five weeks?[12] Under the current conditions, it was argued, it would take a superhorse to win the Triple Crown again.

Indeed, the 1970s graced the world with one of those superhorses and two worthy successors as well. Secretariat dominated the Triple Crown and the clock in 1973, setting records in all three of the classics. After a twenty-five-year dry spell, he showed America that winning the Triple Crown was possible. Seattle Slew and then Affirmed followed in his wake in 1977 and 1978. Once again, the ease with which these three achieved this ultimate honor made people excited about the Triple Crown, inspiring an uptick in breeding in the 1980s and 1990s in the search of another champion. Those three champions so close together led the sport to expect the next Triple Crown winner to come in short order, but as time went on, the same doubts about whether the triple was even possible began to trickle back into the conversation.

In the century after Sir Barton first won the Derby–Preakness double and then added the Belmont to complete the first Triple Crown, twenty-three horses won the Kentucky Derby and Preakness but were unable to win the Belmont. Each time a horse carried the hopes of adding his name to that elite pantheon, each time fans rested their hopes on the backs of those young horses, the sight of that champion straggling home behind others in that third race broke their hearts and kept them coming back year after year, waiting for the next horse who could dominate the classics. At times, the Triple Crown gained more in status from all of those years in which a horse did *not* win than from the years in which a horse wore the crown. As horses dominated in Louisville and Baltimore and then fell short in New York, those questions about the viability of the Triple Crown grew more frequent with each passing year. Was the five-week schedule, two weeks between the Derby and the Preakness and three between the Preakness and the Belmont, too much for horses early in their three-year-old seasons? When Sir Barton did it in 1919, he ran all three in only thirty-two days, rather than the current thirty-five, and even won the Withers in the interim. With the growth in the number of horses bred each year and the tightening requirements for getting into the Triple Crown races, has the sport basically made it that much harder to win the crown?

In 2015, Bob Baffert, who had trained three horses on that list of Triple Crown near misses, brought American Pharoah to Louisville for the Kentucky Derby, where the bay colt found the toughest test of his career to that point, at first running just off the pace in a crowded field of eighteen. American Pharoah took the lead in the stretch, though, and won by a hard-fought length.[13] Two weeks later, just as the field of eight had their saddles cinched for the Preakness Stakes, a sudden thunderstorm drenched Pimlico in a downpour, but the rain and mud did not faze American Pharoah, who led the entire race and won by seven lengths.[14] In anticipation of a possible Triple Crown, the New York Racing Association limited the number of tickets for June 6, capping the crowd at ninety thousand.[15] Belmont Park was packed for the 147th Belmont Stakes, fans eagerly anticipating American Pharoah's run at history. The colt broke a step late, but jockey Victor Espinoza hustled him to the lead and never looked back. American Pharoah held the lead at every call, and as the field swept out of that final wide turn and into the stretch, the echoes of years of Triple Crown hopefuls who had come up short in those final furlongs of the "Test of the Champion" faded in the cacophony created by the ninety thousand present at Belmont. American Pharoah pulled away from his challengers, sailing into the Triple Crown pantheon with an effortless grace not seen in thirty-seven years. From Belmont Park to television screens across the world, the screams and tears of joy resonated, American Pharoah's visage digging deep into the hearts of racing fans both casual and hard-core. The wonder and the reverence he inspires resound through the consciousness of the sport of horse racing, much like the wonder and reverence inspired by the eleven horses before him, their names sacred in the pantheon of the Thoroughbred. American Pharoah proved that the Triple Crown was still possible; all that was needed was the right horse with the right balance of stamina and speed and heart to conquer these classics.

In 2018, Justify broke still more records in his pursuit of the thirteenth Triple Crown, becoming the first horse who did not race at age two to win the Triple Crown. His first start came in mid-February; by the first Saturday in May, Justify entered the starting gate for the Kentucky Derby as the favorite. On a track deep in standing water, this son of Scat Daddy dominated his competition, reeling off the fastest first quarter-mile time for a Derby winner in the race's history. He held off closers in the waning strides of the Preakness Stakes to take the middle jewel and then led wire to wire in the Belmont Stakes, bringing home America's thirteenth Triple Crown. Only 112 days had elapsed from the colt's maiden win to his crowning triumph in the Belmont Stakes, a stunning illustration of what it takes to win the Triple Crown: a horse so special and so talented that he comes along only thirteen times in a century.

In thirty-two days, Sir Barton brought to these races this same balance of stamina and speed and heart, winning the Kentucky Derby, the Preakness Stakes, and the Belmont Stakes, and in the process igniting a pursuit that commands reverence to this day. His accomplishment might have needed a decade or so to get a name and another two decades for official recognition, but one hundred years later America's Triple Crown and its races occupy an unparalleled place in horse racing. Winning it has become the dream of many an owner, trainer, jockey, breeder, and fan, an accomplishment so rare that only thirteen horses have had their names etched on this roll of elites. At the top of that list stands Sir Barton, the first to sweep all three, the first to inspire this chase for immortality.

Horses come and go; they may shine brightly for a bit, but always another one is right behind them to take their place. A few, though, shine for all of time, their names among the best of them all. Twelve horses on the elite list of Triple Crown winners owe their place among the timeless legends of their sport to the one who started it all: Sir Barton.

Appendix

To find the *Daily Racing Form* charts for each of Sir Barton's thirty-one starts, please consult the *Daily Racing Form*'s archive at drf.uky.edu. The archive is a collaborative project between the Keeneland Racing Association and the University of Kentucky Libraries.

Kentucky Derby, May 10, 1919

CHURCHILL DOWNS FORM CHART

LOUISVILLE, KY., SATURDAY, MAY 10, 1919.—Churchill Downs. First day. Kentucky Jockey Club. Spring Meeting of 19 days. Weather threatening; temperature 68°.

Stewards, Chas. F. Price, S. C. Nuckols, Jr., and S. Goodpaster. Placing Judges, W. H. Shelley, N. H. McClelland and E. Jasper. Starter, A. B. Dade. Racing Secretary, W. H. Shelley.

Racing starts at 2:30 p. m. (Chicago time 2:30 p. m.). W indicates whip, S spurs, B blinkers. Figures in parentheses following the distance of each race indicate date, track record, age of horse and weight carried. *Indicates apprentice allowance.

42301 FIRST RACE—3-4 Mile. (Oct. 16, 1913—1:11—2—105.) Purse $1,000. 3-year-olds and upward. Claiming. Net value to winner $800; second, $125; third, $75.

Index	Horses	A	Wt	PP	St	¼	½	¾	Str	Fin	Jockeys	Owners	Equiv. Odds Str't
42118	GREEN GRASS	w 4	107	3	5	1½	1²	1⁵	1⁵	E Pool	B J Brannon	615-100
(42258)	DR. CARMEN	sb 7	114	5	8	8	5²	2h	2nk	M Garner	R L Baker	815-100
40858²	*PULLUX	wsb 7	109	4	6	7½	7²	3½	3h	H J Burke	W Perkins	1570-100
41751²	TOP COAT	wb 4	111	8	7	3¹	2½	5¹	4h	J Howard	T M Botts	345-100
(42048)	BLUE PARADISE	w 4	109	1	1	4⁴	4½	4⁶	5h	J Hanover	Solomon & Jarmon	625-100
(40526)	*DAVID CRAIG	wb 8	166	7	3	5¹	6½	6²	6h	C Rob'son	J Lowe	685-100
41196³	HIDDEN JEWEL	wb 3	107	6	4	2½	3²	7³	7⁹	O Willis	E Trotter	2410-100
38347	BUT'RSCOTCH II.	wb 5	117	2	2	6½	8	8	8	H Lansf'd	J W Schorr	335-100

Time, 24⅕, 49, 1:16½. Track heavy.

$2 mutuels paid, Green Grass, $14.30 straight, $7.20 place, $5.30 show; Dr. Carmen, $8.20 place, $5.40 show; Pullux, $7.70 show.

Equivalent booking odds—Green Grass, 615 to 100 straight, 260 to 100 place, 165 to 100 show; Dr. Carmen, 310 to 100 place, 170 to 100 show; Pullux, 285 to 100 show.

Winner—Br. g, by Hurst Park—Marsara (trained by B. J. Brannon; bred by Messrs. Stone & Rucker).

Went to post at 2:31. At post 1 minute. Start good and slow. Won easily; second and third driving. GREEN GRASS, favored by the going, raced into the lead with a rush and drew out in the stretch to win as his rider pleased. DR. CARMEN began slowly and had to race wide, but finished well when ridden hard and outstayed PULLUX. The latter lost ground by a wide stretch turn, but finished gamely. TOP COAT showed speed, but tired in the last eighth. BLUE PARADISE had no mishaps. HIDDEN JEWEL quit badly.

Scratched—42266²Harry Burgoyne, 103; 42009²Grey Eagle, 115.

42302 SECOND RACE—1-2 Mile. (May 11, 1909—47—2—110.) $1,000 Added. 2-year-olds. Maidens. Fillies. Allowances. Net value to winner $825; second, $146; third, $89.

Index	Horses	A	Wt	PP	St	¼	½	¾	Str	Fin	Jockeys	Owners	Equiv. Odds Str't
42197	VIOLA GAFFNEY	w	112	7	3			1^{1}	1^{1}	1^{1}	J McIntyre	O A Bianchi	170-100
42197^{3}	GOLDINE	wb	112	1	1			2^{3}	2^{6}	2^{6}	H Thurber	T M Murphy	280-100
41207	ALULA	w	112	4	6			3^{1}	3^{1}	3^{1}	J Groth	A B Spreckels	2755-100
	IRIS	w	112	3	5			$4^{1/2}$	$4^{1/2}$	4^{1}	M Garner	L M Cayce	665-100
	VALLEY P'K MAID	w	112	2	2			6^{1}	$5^{1/2}$	5^{5}	F Murphy	C E Rowe	950-100
	GREAT HAWK	w	112	5	7			$5^{1/2}$	6^{2}	6^{2}	W Crump	J R Allen & Son	1415-100
42197	MONEY MAD	w	112	6	4			7	7	7	J Howard	Williams Bros	925-100

Time, 25, 50⅗. Track heavy.

$2 mutuels paid, Viola Gaffney, $5.40 straight, $3.20 place, $3.10 show; Goldine, $3.40 place, $3.40 show; Alula, $9.30 show.

Equivalent booking odds—Viola Gaffney, 170 to 100 straight, 60 to 100 place, 55 to 100 show; Goldine, 70 to 100 place, 70 to 100 show; Alula, 365 to 100 show.

Winner—B. f, by Jim Gaffney—Viola B. (trained by O. A. Bianchi; bred by Mr. O. A. Bianchi).

Went to post at 3:10. At post 1 minute. Start good and slow. Won handily; second and third driving. VIOLA GAFFNEY ran out and lost much ground on the turn into the stretch, but held on well and outstayed GOLDINE in the final drive. GOLDINE ran well from the start and followed the winner closely throughout, holding on well to the end. ALULA raced forwardly and outstayed IRIS. The latter closed a gap in the last quarter. MONEY MAD was outrun from the start.

42303 THIRD RACE—5 1-2 Furlongs. (Oct. 8, 1913—1:04⅘—2—92.) Purse $1,500. 3-year-olds and upward. Allowances. Net value to winner $1,150; second, $225; third, $125.

Index	Horses	A	Wt	PP	St	¼	½	¾	Str	Fin	Jockeys	Owners	Equiv. Odds Str't
(42254)	HIGH COST	w 4	108	3	3		1^{1}	$1^{1½}$	$1^{1½}$	1^{2}	C Brown	L Erb	535-100
42227	AMERICAN ACE	wb 3	99	5	2		3^{1}	2^{3}	$2^{1½}$	2^{3}	C Rob'son	E Cebrian	60-100
42254^{3}	SEWELL COMBS	wb 4	108	7	4		5^{2}	4^{1}	$3^{1/2}$	$3^{1½}$	F Murphy	Gallaher Bros	810-100
(38676)	BON JOUR	w 3	98	1	5		$4^{1½}$	$3^{1/2}$	$4^{1/2}$	4^{h}	T Murray	E B McLean	1495-100
42241^{3}	HERALD	wsb 4	106	4	7		6^{5}	$5^{1/2}$	5^{6}	5^{10}	H J Burke	H H Hewitt	2185-100
(41540)	COURTSHIP	wb 5	121	2	6		7	7	6^{5}	6^{15}	W Lilley	Marshall Bros	2410-100
(42059)	M. B. THURM'N	wsb 6	106	6	1		$2^{1½}$	6^{2}	7	7	O Willis	W F Cisco	6005-100

Time, 23⅗, 48⅗, 1:01⅘, 1:08⅗. Track heavy.

$2 mutuels paid, High Cost, $12.70 straight, $3.50 place, $2.80 show; American Ace, $2.60 place, $2.30 show; Sewell Combs, $2.70 show.

Equivalent booking odds—High Cost, 535 to 100 straight, 75 to 100 place, 40 to 100 show; American Ace, 30 to 100 place, 15 to 100 show; Sewell Combs, 35 to 100 show.

Winner—B. c, by Von Tromp—Mitten (trained by J. W. Murphy; bred by Mr. Daniel F. Egan).

Went to post at 3:48. At post 2 minutes. Start good and slow. Won easily; second and third driving. HIGH COST, away well and aided by the going, raced into a long lead with a rush and, holding on well in the stretch, outstayed AMERICAN ACE through the last eighth. AMERICAN ACE was saved under restraint for the first three-eighths and finished fast and gamely when called on, but could not overhaul the winner. SEWELL COMBS was well back for the first half and lost ground by coming wide into the stretch, but finished well. BON JOUR ran well and might have been third but for being cut off at the half mile. HERALD finished gamely. The others were well beaten.

Overweights—Bon Jour, 2 pounds.

42304 FOURTH RACE—1 Mile and 70 Yards. (May 27, 1912—1:42⅕—3—97.) Seelbach Hotel Handicap. Purse $1,500. 3-year-olds and upward. Net value to winner $1,150; second, $225; third, $125.

Index	Horses	A	Wt	PP	St	¼	½	¾	Str	Fin	Jockeys	Owners	Equiv. Odds Str't
42074^{2}	DRASTIC	wb 4	109	2	3	3^{1}	2^{h}	2^{2}	2^{2}	$1^{1/2}$	H Lunsf'd	C E Patterson	245-100
(42187)	JIM HEFF'RING	wb 4	105	4	2	$1^{1½}$	$1^{1½}$	1^{2}	$1^{1/2}$	2^{2}	T Murray	M Shields	185-100
(42241)	OMOND	w 3	100	5	5	5^{h}	3^{h}	$3^{1½}$	3^{8}	3^{12}	J McIntyre	M Quinn	1735-100
(42282)	HANOVIA	w 7	107	3	4	4^{h}	6	$5^{1½}$	4^{1}	4^{4}	H Thurber	J Marrone	525-100
42187^{2}	JIFFY	w 4	100	6	6	6	4^{h}	4^{6}	5^{6}	5^{8}	C Rob'son	W Perkins	1220-100
(42240)	BUFORD	w 5	116	1	1	$2^{1/2}$	$5^{1/2}$	6	6	6	C Howard	W F Polson	690-100

Time, 25, 50, 1:16⅗, 1:43⅘, 1:48. Track heavy.

$2 mutuels paid, Drastic, $6.90 straight, $3.40 place, $2.80 show; Jim Heffering, $3.40 place, $3.00 show; Omond, $4.50 show.

Equivalent booking odds—Drastic, 245 to 100 straight, 70 to 100 place, 40 to 100 show; Jim Heffering, 70 to 100 place, 50 to 100 show; Omond, 125 to 100 show.

Winner—B. c, by Hastings—Dragnet (trained by C. E. Patterson; bred by Mr. August Belmont).

Went to post at 4:27. At post 2 minutes. Start good and slow. Won driving; second and third the same. DRASTIC was hard ridden for the entire race and, saving ground when coming into the stretch, outstayed JIM HEFFERING in a game finish. The latter showed high speed from the start and would have won but for swerving out in the last eighth. OMOND ran well and finished gamely. HANOVIA was forced back at the half-mile ground. BUFORD was knocked out of any chance on the last turn.

42305 FIFTH RACE—1 1-4 Miles. (May 9, 1914—2:03⅖—3—114.) Forty-fifth Running KENTUCKY DERBY. $20,000 Added. 3-year-olds. Allowances. Net value to winner $20,825; second, $2,500; third, $1,000; fourth, $275.

Index	Horses	A	Wt	PP	St	¼	½	¾	Str	Fin	Jockeys	Owners	Equiv. Odds Str't
39683^{2}	SIR BARTON	wb	112½	1	1	1^{2}	$1^{1/2}$	1^{2}	$1^{1/2}$	1^{5}	J Loftus	J K L Ross	†260-100
(42081)	BILLY KELLY	w	119	11	8	$3^{1/2}$	3^{4}	2^{3}	2^{4}	2^{1}	E Sande	J K L Ross	†
42227^{2}	UNDER FIRE	w	122	7	11	$9^{1/2}$	$9^{1/2}$	$6^{1/2}$	3^{1}	3^{1}	M Garner	P Dunne	1915-100
42227	VULCANITE	w	110	6	10	$10^{1/2}$	5^{h}	$4^{1/2}$	4^{1}	4^{6}	C Howard	W F Polson	7000-100
42227^{3}	SENNINGS PARK	wb	122	8	9	6^{2}	$4^{1/2}$	$5^{1/2}$	5^{1}	5^{1}	H Lunsf'rd	O A Bianchi	§1410-100
42222^{2}	BE FRANK	w	119	2	6	7^{h}	$7^{1/2}$	$7^{1/2}$	$6^{1/2}$	$6^{1/2}$	J Butwell	C M Garrison	2745-100
(41177)	SAILOR	wb	119	10	12	12	10^{2}	$10^{1/2}$	$8^{1/2}$	7^{8}	J McIntyre	J W McClelland	‡210-100
42227	ST. BERNARD	w	119	4	2	5^{h}	6^{1}	9^{1}	7^{2}	8^{2}	E Pool	B J Brannon	§
(42227)	REGALO	w	117	9	7	8^{2}	$8^{1½}$	8^{1}	9^{2}	9^{4}	F Murphy	Gallaher Bros	605-100
(41798)	ETERNAL	w	122	5	3	$2^{1/2}$	$2^{1/2}$	$3^{1/2}$	10^{5}	10^{10}	A Schu'g'r	J W McClelland	‡
38508	FROGTOWN	w	119	12	4	11^{2}	$11^{1/2}$	11^{2}	11^{10}	11^{20}	J Morys	W S Kilmer	2245-100
(42137)	VINDEX	w	122	3	5	4^{nk}	12	12	12	12	W Knapp	H P Whitney	815-100

†Coupled in betting as J. K. L. Ross entry; ‡J. W. McClelland entry. §Mutuel field.

Time, 24⅕, 48⅗, 1:14, 1:41⅕, 2:09⅘. Track heavy.

$2 mutuels paid, J. K. L. Ross entry, $7.20 straight, $6.70 place, $6.00 show; Under Fire, $10.80 show.

Equivalent booking odds—J. K. L. Ross entry, 260 to 100 straight, 235 to 100 place, 200 to 100 show; Under Fire, 440 to 100 show.

Winner—Ch. c, by Star Shoot—Lady Sterling (trained by H. G. Bedwell; bred by Messrs. Madden & Gooch).

Went to post at 5:10. At post 4 minutes. Start good and slow. Won easily; second and third driving. SIR BARTON raced into the lead at once and, well ridden, led under restraint until reaching the stretch, where he was shaken up and easily held BILLY KELLY safe in the last eighth. BILLY KELLY held to his task well, was under restraint in the early running and finished gamely. UNDER FIRE gained steadily from a slow beginning and finished fast and gamely. VULCANITE ran well and finished close up. ETERNAL was done after going three-quarters. REGALO ran disappointingly. SENNINGS PARK tired in the stretch.

Scratched—(42257)Corson, 122; 42142^{3}Clermont, 122.

Overweights—Sir Barton, 2½ pounds.

42306 SIXTH RACE—1-2 Mile. (May 11, 1909—47—2—110.) Purse $1,200. 2-year-olds. Colts and Geldings. Allowances. Net value to winner $900; second, $200; third, $100.

Index	Horses	A	Wt	PP	St	¼	½	¾	Str	Fin	Jockeys	Owners	Equiv. Odds Str't
42242	LUKE DILLON	wB	110	6	2			2^{h}	1^{1}	1^{2}	H Lunsf'rd	J W Schorr	510-100
41538	ATTA BOY II.	w	109	9	5			3^{3}	2^{h}	2^{3}	J Howard	H Neusteter	675-100
42255	FRIZ	w	118	7	4			1^{h}	3^{3}	3^{n}	R Simpson	H Perkins	500-100
42242^{2}	BLACK PRINCE	w	107	1	1			$5^{\frac{1}{2}}$	4^{1}	$4^{\frac{1}{2}}$	M Garner	W J Young	1720-100
42255	ST. GERMAIN	w	110	3	6			$4^{\frac{1}{2}}$	$5^{\frac{1}{2}}$	5^{2}	A Schu'g'r	J W McClelland	130-100
(42242)	BREAD MAN	wB	110	5	8			$7^{\frac{1}{2}}$	6^{2}	6^{2}	H Thurber	T M Murphy	1965-100
42255	TRAVESTY	w	107	4	7			6^{2}	7^{3}	7^{3}	H J Burke	H H Hewitt	6970-100
	JADDA		109	2	3			8^{10}	8^{10}	8^{15}	W Crump	J Livingston	3385-100
	ANGON	w	108	8	9			9	9	9	J Hanover	R H Anderson	8985-100

Time, 24, 49. Track heavy.

$2 mutuels paid, Luke Dillon, $12.20 straight, $6.60 place, $3.60 show; Atta Boy II., $6.70 place, $3.90 show; Friz, $3.80 show.

Equivalent booking odds—Luke Dillon, 510 to 100 straight, 230 to 100 place, 80 to 100 show; Atta Boy II., 235 to 100 place, 95 to 100 show; Friz, 90 to 100 show.

Winner—Ch. c, by Luke McLuke—Frances Dillon (trained by L. Tauber; bred by Messrs. Keene & Schorr).

Went to post at 5:55. At post 2 minutes. Start good and slow. Won easily; second and third driving. LUKE DILLON, well ridden, was inclined to swerve out on the stretch turn, but came fast in the last eighth and outstayed ATTA BOY II. in the final sixteenth. ATTA BOY II. raced forwardly from the start and held on well in the final drive. FRIZ tired after showing the most speed for three-eighths. BLACK PRINCE was gaining in the last eighth. ST. GERMAIN was always outrun. BREAD MAN had no mishaps.

Scratched—Sams Boy, 110.

Overweights—Jadda, 2 pounds; Angon, 1.

42307 SEVENTH RACE—1 Mile. (Sept. 27, 1911—1:37⅗—3—99.) Purse $1,000. 3-year-olds and upward. Claiming. Net value to winner $800; second, $125; third, $75.

Index	Horses	A	Wt	PP	St	¼	½	¾	Str	Fin	Jockeys	Owners	Equiv. Odds Str't
42226^{3}	*T. COL'N BAWN	w 3	88	4	4	$6^{1\frac{1}{2}}$	3^{h}	$2^{\frac{1}{2}}$	1^{h}	1^{n}	S Boyle	B J Brannon	300-100
42009	MISTR'SS POLLY	wB 4	110	10	8	$9^{1\frac{1}{2}}$	6^{1}	5^{4}	3^{2}	$2^{\frac{1}{2}}$	H Lunsf'd	H Neusteter	1420-100
42266	REDMON	w 4	112	2	1	$1^{1\frac{1}{2}}$	1^{3}	$1^{1\frac{1}{2}}$	2^{h}	3^{6}	M Garner	S K Nichols	1065-100
42182^{4}	*SANS PEUR II.	w 3	98	5	3	$2^{1\frac{1}{2}}$	$2^{1\frac{1}{2}}$	3^{3}	4^{1}	4^{1}	C Rob'son	F J Kelley	900-100
42187^{3}	SEAFARER	wsB 4	110	3	2	3^{h}	$7^{1\frac{1}{2}}$	$6^{\frac{1}{2}}$	$5^{\frac{1}{2}}$	$5^{\frac{1}{2}}$	H J Burke	H Field	555-100
40347	*WHIRLING DUN	w 5	111	11	9	11	11	11	8^{1}	6^{2}	T Murray	J Lowe	3665-100
42184^{3}	GIPSY QUEEN	w 4	108	7	6	5^{h}	4^{2}	4^{h}	6^{1}	7^{3}	J Hanover	Solomon & Jarmon	2155-100
42228	NIGHT OWL	wB 5	109	1	11	8^{2}	5	7^{1}	$7^{\frac{1}{2}}$	8^{2}	C Howard	W F Polson	4530-100
42240	MANOKIN	wB 5	114	8	5	$7^{\frac{1}{2}}$	8^{1}	$8^{1\frac{1}{2}}$	9^{8}	9^{15}	F Murphy	Gallaher Bros	265-100
41587	DIOSCORIDE	wB 4	106	6	7	4^{h}	$9^{1\frac{1}{2}}$	$9^{1\frac{1}{2}}$	10^{8}	10^{15}	O Willis	Marshall Bros	†2665-100
39040	*AMMUNITION	w 4	101½	9	10	10^{2}	10^{2}	10^{1}	11	11	L Jones	G M Hendrie	†

†Mutuel field. Time, 24⅘, 49⅗, 1:16⅖, 1:43⅘. Track heavy.

$2 mutuels paid, The Colleen Bawn, $8.00 straight, $4.30 place, $3.70 show; Mistress Polly, $10.40 place, $6.20 show; Redmon, $5.50 show.

Equivalent booking odds—The Colleen Bawn, 300 to 100 straight, 115 to 100 place, 85 to 100 show; Mistress Polly, 420 to 100 place, 210 to 100 show; Redmon, 175 to 100 show.

Winner—B. f, by Handsel—Bodin (trained by B. J. Brannon; bred by Mr. P. Sheridan).

Went to post at 6:30. At post 3 minutes. Start good and slow. Won driving; second and third the same. THE COLLEEN BAWN gained steadily after going a half mile, but lost much ground by coming wide into the stretch and just lasted long enough to win. MISTRESS POLLY began slowly and had to close an immense gap, but saved much ground on the stretch turn. REDMON tired after setting the pace to the stretch. SANS PEUR II. quit after going three-quarters. NIGHT OWL was given a bad ride. WHIRLING DUN closed a big gap. GIPSY QUEEN quit in the last quarter.

Scratched—38650 James Foster, 107; 42244 Frank Monroe, 109; 42213 Nominee, 105; (42145)Cheer Leader, 106.

Overweights—The Colleen Bawn, 4 pounds; Gipsy Queen, 3; Dioscoride, 1; Ammunition, 1½.

"Churchill Downs Form Chart." *Daily Racing Form*, May 11, 1919.

Preakness Stakes, May 14, 1919

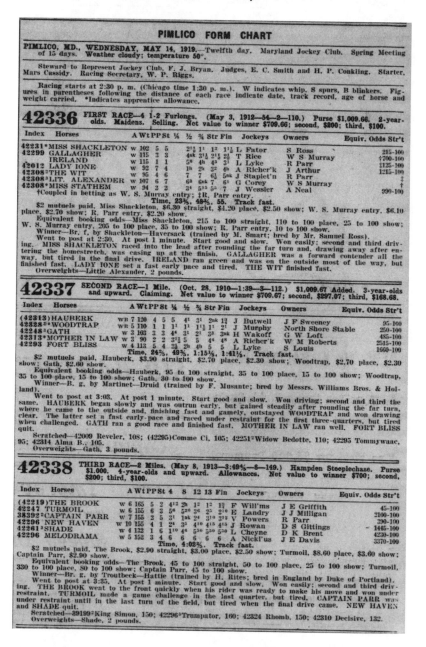

PIMLICO FORM CHART

PIMLICO, MD., WEDNESDAY, MAY 14, 1919.—Twelfth day. Maryland Jockey Club. Spring Meeting of 15 days. **Weather cloudy; temperature 50°.**

Steward to Represent Jockey Club, F. J. Bryan. Judges, E. C. Smith and H. P. Conkling. Starter, Mars Cassidy. Racing Secretary, W. P. Riggs.

Racing starts at 2:30 p. m. (Chicago time 1:30 p. m.). W indicates whip, S spurs, B blinkers. Figures in parentheses following the distance of each race indicate date, track record, age of horse and weight carried. *Indicates apprentice allowance.

42336 **FIRST RACE—4 1-2 Furlongs. (May 3, 1912—54—2—110.) Purse $1,009.66. 2-year-olds. Maidens. Selling. Net value to winner $709.66; second, $200; third, $100.**

Index	Horses	A	Wt	PP	St	¼	½	¾	Str	Fin	Jockeys	Owners	Equiv. Odds Str't
42231*	MISS SHACKLETON	w	102	5	5		$2^{1\frac{1}{2}}$	1^{1}	1^{2}	$1^{1\frac{1}{2}}$	L Fator	S Ross	215-100
42299	GALLAGHER	w	115	3	3		4^{nk}	$3^{1\frac{1}{2}}$	$2^{1\frac{1}{2}}$	$2^{\frac{1}{2}}$	T Rice	W S Murray	†700-100
	IRELAND	w	115	1	1		5^{6}	4^{h}	4^{3}	3^{1}	L Lyke	R Parr	‡125-100
42012	LADY IONE	w	92	7	4		1^{h}	2^{h}	3^{2}	4^{h}	A Richer'k	J Arthur	1215-100
42308^{2}	THE WIT	w	95	4	6		7	7	$6^{\frac{1}{2}}$	5^{nk}	J Stapiet'n	R Parr	‡
42308^{3}	LIT. ALEXANDER	w	107	6	7		6^{3}	6^{nk}	7	6^{1}	G Corey	W S Murray	†
42308*	MISS STATHEM	w	94	2	2		3^{4}	5^{15}	5^{5}	7	J Wessler	A Neal	990-100

†Coupled in betting as W. S. Murray entry; ‡R. Parr entry.

Time, 23⅗, 48⅘, 55. Track fast.

$2 mutuels paid, Miss Shackleton, $6.30 straight, $4.20 place, $2.50 show; W. S. Murray entry, $6.10 place, $2.70 show; R. Parr entry, $2.20 show.

Equivalent booking odds—Miss Shackleton, 215 to 100 straight, 110 to 100 place, 25 to 100 show; W. S. Murray entry, 205 to 100 place, 35 to 100 show; R. Parr entry, 10 to 100 show.

Winner—Br. f. by Shackleton—Haversack (trained by M. Smart; bred by Mr. Samuel Ross).

Went to post at 2:30. At post 1 minute. Start good and slow. Won easily; second and third driving. MISS SHACKLETON raced into the lead after rounding the far turn and, drawing away after entering the homestretch, was easing up at the finish. GALLAGHER was a forward contender all the way, but tired in the final drive. IRELAND ran green and was on the outside most of the way, but finished fast. LADY IONE set a fast early pace and tired. THE WIT finished fast.

Overweights—Little Alexander, 2 pounds.

42337 **SECOND RACE—1 Mile. (Oct. 28, 1910—1:39—3—112.) $1,009.67 Added. 3-year-olds and upward. Claiming. Net value to winner $709.67; second, $297.07; third, $168.68.**

Index	Horses	A	Wt	PP	St	¼	½	¾	Str	Fin	Jockeys	Owners	Equiv. Odds Str't
(42313)	HAUBERK	wB 7	120	4	5	5	4^{1}	3^{1}	2^{nk}	$1^{\frac{3}{4}}$	J Butwell	J F Sweeney	95-100
42328^{2}*	WOODTRAP	wB 5	110	1	1	1^{1}	1^{1}	$1^{1\frac{1}{2}}$	1^{1}	2^{1}	J Murphy	North Shore Stable	250-100
42248^{2}	GATH	w 3	103	3	3	4^{4}	3^{1}	2^{1}	3^{3}	3^{nk}	H Wakoff	G W Loft	485-100
42313*	MOTHER IN LAW	w 3	90	2	2	$3^{1\frac{1}{2}}$	5	5	4^{4}	4^{8}	A Richer'k	W M Roberts	2515-100
42293	FORT BLISS	w 4	113	5	4	$2^{\frac{1}{2}}$	2^{h}	4^{h}	5	5	L Lyke	S Louis	1660-100

Time, 24⅗, 49⅗, 1:15⅕, 1:41⅕. Track fast.

$2 mutuels paid, Hauberk, $3.90 straight, $2.70 place, $2.30 show; Woodtrap, $2.70 place, $2.30 show; Gath, $2.60 show.

Equivalent booking odds—Hauberk, 95 to 100 straight, 35 to 100 place, 15 to 100 show; Woodtrap, 35 to 100 place, 15 to 100 show; Gath, 30 to 100 show.

Winner—B. g. by Martinet—Druid (trained by F. Musante; bred by Messrs. Williams Bros. & Holland).

Went to post at 3:03. At post 1 minute. Start good and slow. Won driving; second and third the same. HAUBERK began slowly and was outrun early, but gained steadily after rounding the far turn, where he came to the outside and, finishing fast and gamely, outstayed WOODTRAP and won drawing clear. The latter set a fast early pace and raced under restraint for the first three-quarters, but tired when challenged. GATH ran a good race and finished fast. MOTHER IN LAW ran well. FORT BLISS quit.

Scratched—42009 Reveler, 108; (42295)Comme Ci, 105; 42251^{2}Widow Bedotte, 110; 42295 Tommywaac, 95; 42314 Alma B., 105.

Overweights—Gath, 3 pounds.

42338 **THIRD RACE—2 Miles. (May 8, 1913—3:49⅘—6—149.) Hampden Steeplechase. Purse $1,000. 4-year-olds and upward. Allowances. Net value to winner $700; second, $200; third, $100.**

Index	Horses	A	Wt	PP	St	4	8	12	13	Fin	Jockeys	Owners	Equiv. Odds Str't
(42219)	THE BROOK	w 6	165	5	2	4^{12}	2^{h}	1^{2}	1^{2}	$1^{\frac{3}{4}}$	F Will'ms	J E Griffith	45-100
42247	TURMOIL	w 6	155	6	3	5^{6}	5^{30}	3^{6}	2^{5}	2^{10}	E Landry	J J Milligan	2100-100
38392^{2}	CAPTAIN PARR	w 7	155	2	5	3^{1}	1^{nk}	2^{4}	3^{10}	3^{12}	V Powers	R Parr	390-100
42296	NEW HAVEN	w 10	155	4	1	2^{4}	3^{5}	4^{10}	4^{15}	4^{15}	J Rowan	D S Gittings	1445-100
42261^{3}	SHADE	w 4	132	1	6	1^{10}	4^{6}	5^{30}	5^{30}	5^{30}	L Cheyne	D K Brent	4230-100
42296	MELODRAMA	w 5	152	3	4	6	6	6	6	6	A Nickl'us	J E Davis	3370-100

Time, 4:02⅘. Track fast.

$2 mutuels paid, The Brook, $2.90 straight, $3.00 place, $2.50 show; Turmoil, $8.60 place, $3.60 show; Captain Parr, $2.90 show.

Equivalent booking odds—The Brook, 45 to 100 straight, 50 to 100 place, 25 to 100 show; Turmoil, 330 to 100 place, 80 to 100 show; Captain Parr, 45 to 100 show.

Winner—Br. g. by Troutbeck—Hattie (trained by H. Rites; bred in England by Duke of Portland).

Went to post at 3:35. At post 1 minute. Start good and slow. Won easily; second and third driving. THE BROOK went to the front quickly when his rider was ready to make his move and won under restraint. TURMOIL made a game challenge in the last quarter, but tired. CAPTAIN PARR was under restraint until in the last turn of the field, but tired when the final drive came. NEW HAVEN and SHADE quit.

Scratched—39199^{2}King Simon, 150; 42296^{3}Trumpator, 160; 42324 Rhomb, 150; 42310 Decisive, 132.

Overweights—Shade, 2 pounds.

42339 FOURTH RACE—1 1-8 Miles. (May 17, 1911—1:51—3—112.) Twelfth Running PREAKNESS STAKES. $25,000 Added. 3-year-olds. Allowances. Net value to winner $24,500; second, $3,000; third, $2,000; fourth, $1,000.

Index	Horses		A	Wt	PP	St	¼	½	¾	Str	Fin	Jockeys	Owners	Equiv. Odds Str't
(42305)	SIR BARTON	wb		126	8	3	1^{1}	1^{1}	1^{2}	1^{6}	1^{4}	J Loftus	J K L Ross	†140-100
42305	ETERNAL	w		126	2	1	$4^{1\frac{1}{2}}$	3^{1}	2^{1}	2^{1}	2^{3}	A Schu'g'r	J W McClelland	920-100
(42250)	SWEEP ON	wsb		126	3	2	3^{2}	$4^{1\frac{1}{2}}$	4^{2}	3^{3}	3^{2}	L McAtee	W R Coe	‡1555-100
42274^{2}	KING PLAUDIT	wb		114	9	4	2^{1}	$2\frac{1}{2}$	3^{2}	4^{3}	$4^{1\frac{1}{2}}$	L Lyke	Brookside Stable	5325-100
(42297)	OVER THERE	w		122	4	10	$8\frac{1}{2}$	8^{3}	7^{3}	7^{6}	5^{nk}	H Myers	W R Coe	‡
42291^{2}	ROUTLEDGE	w		122	12	5	5^{1}	$5\frac{1}{2}$	5^{nk}	$6\frac{1}{2}$	6^{h}	E Ambr'se	W M Jeffords	7080-100
42305	VULCANITE	w		114	1	7	7^{1}	7^{h}	8^{1}	8^{3}	$7^{1\frac{1}{2}}$	R Troxler	W F Polson	3945-100
42121^{3}	MILKMAID	w		109	6	6	6^{nk}	6^{2}	6^{2}	$5\frac{1}{2}$	8^{3}	E Sande	J K L Ross	†
42291	DRUMMOND	wb		114	7	9	$9\frac{1}{2}$	$9\frac{1}{2}$	9^{2}	9^{1}	$9\frac{1}{2}$	A Johnson	M Shea	14500-100
42222	YURUCARI	w		114	11	8	11	$10\frac{1}{2}$	10^{5}	10^{8}	10^{15}	T Rice	Quincy Stable	12540-100
42250	DUNBOYNE	w		126	5	11	10^{2}	11	11	11	11	L Ensor	P A Clark	420-100
42305	VINDEX	wb		115	10	Left at the post.						W Knapp	H P Whitney	365-100

†Coupled in betting as J. K. L. Ross entry; ‡W. R. Coe entry.

Time, 23⅗, 47⅕, 1:13, 1:39⅕, 1:53. Track fast.

$2 mutuels paid, J. K. L. Ross entry, $4.80 straight, $3.20 place, $2.70 show; Eternal, $7.50 place, $6.00 show; W. R. Coe entry, $5.00 show.

Equivalent booking odds—J. K. L. Ross entry, 140 to 100 straight, 60 to 100 place, 35 to 100 show; Eternal, 275 to 100 place, 200 to 100 show; W. R. Coe entry, 150 to 100 show.

Winner—Ch. c, by Star Shoot—Lady Sterling (trained by H. G. Bedwell; bred by Messrs. Madden & Gooch).

Went to post at 4:21. At post 5 minutes. Start good and slow. Won easily; second and third driving. SIR BARTON went to the front while rounding the turn into the backstretch and, setting a terrific pace, drew away into a long lead in the last quarter and was eased up at the finish. ETERNAL was a forward contender from the start, met with no mishaps and ran a game race. SWEEP ON was always prominent in the running, but was tiring at the end. DUNBOYNE began sideways in behind the other horses and had no chance. KING PLAUDIT ran a good race. OVER THERE made a fast finish. ROUTLEDGE and VULCANITE ran well.

Scratched—42221^{2}Terentia, 117; 42291^{3}Natural Bridge, 114; 42273^{3}Pride of India, 114.

Overweights—Vindex, 1 pound.

42340 FIFTH RACE—3-4 Mile. (Nov. 4, 1916—1:11⅗—6—133.) Purse $1,009.67. 3-year-olds and upward. Selling. Net value to winner $709.67; second, $200; third, $100.

Index	Horses		A	Wt	PP	St	¼	½	¾	Str	Fin	Jockeys	Owners	Equiv. Odds Str't
42265^{*}	BELLRINGER		5	115	5	2		4^{6}	3^{h}	2^{nk}	1^{h}	S Wida	E K Bryson	1140-100
42288^{2}	*IRENE	w	4	110	9	6		3^{2}	1^{2}	1^{2}	2^{4}	J Murphy	G W Forman	125-100
42176	BRISK	w	3	105	3	3		1^{h}	2^{1}	$3^{1\frac{1}{2}}$	3^{h}	E Ambr'se	E Trueman	185-100
40876	LE DINOSAURE	w	5	115	7	8		$6^{1\frac{1}{2}}$	5^{1}	5^{2}	4^{3}	W Obert	S Pinkerton	15240-100
42245^{*}	ENCORE	wb	7	115	8	1		2^{h}	4^{4}	4^{2}	5^{1}	J Wessler	B B Rice	4150-100
42164	LITTLE BOY	wb	4	113	6	10		7^{h}	6^{1}	$6^{1\frac{1}{2}}$	6^{h}	T Rice	J Tierney	2255-100
41338^{3}	*SAY	w	8	110	2	4		5^{nk}	$8^{1\frac{1}{2}}$	7^{h}	7^{1}	L Fator	P J Sullivan	4560-100
42181	CLARK M.	wb	9	120	10	9		9^{1}	7^{nk}	8^{3}	8^{5}	J D'minick	G Holmes	2945-100
41978	GARBAGE	w	7	115	1	5		10	10	10	$9\frac{1}{2}$	J Conway	R P Watts	3090-100
42293^{*}	AMERICAN	wb	4	113	4	7		$8\frac{1}{2}$	9^{3}	9^{2}	10	A Richer'k	C R Richards	4375-100

Time, 23⅘, 48⅘, 1:15⅕. Track fast.

$2 mutuels paid, Bellringer, $24.80 straight, $7.00 place, $3.40 show; Irene, $3.10 place, $2.40 show; Brisk, $2.80 show.

Equivalent booking odds—Bellringer, 1140 to 100 straight, 250 to 100 place, 70 to 100 show; Irene, 55 to 100 place, 20 to 100 show; Brisk, 40 to 100 show.

Winner—Ch. g, by Burgomaster—Vespers (trained by W. Cedar; bred by Mr. Harry Payne Whitney).

Went to post at 4:56. At post 2 minutes. Start good and slow. Won driving; second and third the same. BELLRINGER, close up from the start, responded gamely when called on in the stretch and wore IRENE down in the final strides. IRENE showed much the most early speed, but tired in the last sixteenth. BRISK set a fast early pace, but tired and just lasted long enough to outstay LE DINOSAURE. The latter finished with a rush. ENCORE quit after showing speed.

Scratched—42295 Kimpalong, 105.

Overweights—Irene, 2 pounds.

42341 SIXTH RACE—1 Mile. (Oct. 28, 1910—1:39—3—112.) $1,009.67 Added. 3-year-olds and upward. Claiming Handicap. Net value to winner $709.67; second, $230.28; third, $120.20.

Index	Horses		A	Wt	PP	St	¼	½	¾	Str	Fin	Jockeys	Owners	Equiv. Odds Str't
(42003)	*BOLSTER	wb	4	111	3	4	7	7	5^{5}	4^{4}	1^{nk}	A Richer'k	T Francis	245-100
39966	DAMROSCH	w	6	112	2	6	$3^{1\frac{1}{2}}$	3^{2}	2^{4}	3^{1}	$2^{1\frac{1}{2}}$	E Sande	J K L Ross	630-100
(42236)	AMALETTE	w	4	107	4	1	5^{h}	4^{1}	3^{1}	$2\frac{1}{2}$	3^{3}	A Johnson	H S Koppin	†905-100
42209	CURRENCY	wb	4	104	5	3	1^{10}	1^{10}	1^{5}	1^{3}	4^{2}	R Ball	E F Whitney	1685-100
42279^{2}	QUEEN APPLE	wb	6	111	6	7	6^{1}	5^{nk}	4^{h}	5^{10}	5^{12}	L Lyke	H S Koppin	†
42259^{2}	*JOS. P. M'RPHY	wb	4	97	7	5	$2\frac{1}{2}$	$2\frac{1}{2}$	6^{1}	6^{1}	$6\frac{1}{2}$	J Wessler	E McBride	2245-100
42313^{2}	GAME COCK	wsb	4	110	1	2	4^{1}	$6^{1\frac{1}{2}}$	7	7	7	T Rice	H L Pratt	130-100

†Coupled in betting as H. S. Koppin entry.

Time, 24⅘, 49⅘, 1:14⅘, 1:41. Track fast.

$2 mutuels paid, Bolster, $6.90 straight, $4.00 place, $3.20 show; Damrosch, $5.80 place, $4.00 show; H. S. Koppin entry, $3.60 show.

Equivalent booking odds—Bolster, 245 to 100 straight, 100 to 100 place, 60 to 100 show; Damrosch, 190 to 100 place, 100 to 100 show; H. S. Koppin entry, 80 to 100 show.

Winner—Ch. g, by Marco—Permia (trained by J. Arthur; bred in England by Sir John Robinson).

Went to post at 5:37. At post 1 minute. Start good and slow. Won driving; second and third the same. BOLSTER was outpaced in the early running, but worked his way up on the outside and, after coming wide when entering the homestretch, finished with a rush. DAMROSCH ran well and finished gamely, but seemed a trifle high in flesh and the race will probably improve him. AMALETTE ran a good race, but tired right at the end. CURRENCY set a good pace to the last eighth. GAME COCK appeared to sulk and dropped to the rear after going the first quarter.

Scratched—42312 Broom Peddler, 109.

Overweights—Amalette, 1 pound; Queen Apple, 1.

42342 SEVENTH RACE—3-4 Mile. (Nov. 4, 1916—1:11⅗—6—133.) Clubhouse Handicap. Purse $1,009.67. 3-year-olds. Net value to winner $709.67; second, $200; third, $100.

Index	Horses	A Wt	PP	St	¼	½	¾	Str	Fin	Jockeys	Owners	Equiv. Odds Str't
42274^{3}	OPHELIA	wb 109	7	3		1^{1}	1^{3}	$1^{1\frac{1}{2}}$	1^{1}	T Rice	Mrs J E Davis	1810-100
42218	MAHONY	wb 102	9	1		4^{1}	2^{1}	3^{h}	$2^{1\frac{1}{2}}$	L Fator	G W Forman	10960-100
42273^{3}	PRIDE OF INDIA	w 112	3	9		6^{2}	4^{1}	4^{1}	3^{1}	J Butwell	H A Porter	330-100
42043	WAR MARVEL	w 116	5	4		3^{h}	3½	2^{nk}	4^{h}	E Sande	J K L Ross	†185-100
42298	STAR HAMPTON	w 113	8	2		5^{nk}	6^{2}	5^{6}	5^{5}	E Ambr'se	W M Jeffords	560-100
42250^{3}	POLKA DOT	wb 102	1	8		9	$7^{1\frac{1}{2}}$	7^{5}	6^{h}	L Ensor	P A Clark	2515-100
42291	L'EFFARE	wb 109	2	6		$2^{1\frac{1}{2}}$	5^{h}	6½	7^{4}	L McAtee	E M Weld	600-100
42179	WAR PENNANT	wb 126	4	5		7½	8^{3}	8^{1}	8^{8}	J Loftus	J K L Ross	†
42291	ESQUIMAU	wb 112	6	7		8^{nk}	9	9	9	L Lyke	R Parr	1100-100

†Coupled in betting as J. K. L. Ross entry.

Time, 23⅗, 47, 1:13⅘. Track fast.

$2 mutuels paid, Ophelia, $38.20 straight, $17.40 place, $7.50 show; Mahony, $82.00 place, $34.90 show; Pride of India, $5.10 show.

Equivalent booking odds—Ophelia, 1810 to 100 straight, 770 to 100 place, 275 to 100 show; Mahony, 4000 to 100 place, 1645 to 100 show; Pride of India, 155 to 100 show.

Winner—B. f, by Senseless—Ghent Azalea (trained by J. Fitzsimmons; bred in England by Mr. W. P. Purefoy).

Went to post at 6:20. At post 1 minute. Start good and slow. Won handily; second and third driving. OPHELIA dashed into the lead right after the start and raced into a good lead, but was doing her best at the end. MAHONY was a forward contender all the way and made a fast finish. PRIDE OF INDIA began slowly and was bumped in the last eighth when coming fast. WAR MARVEL ran well to the last eighth. STAR HAMPTON finished close up. L'EFFARE quit.

Scratched—42095 Pen Rose, 116; 42339 King Plaudit, 112; 42339 Milkmaid, 120; 40535 Bagheera, 102; 42259 Beaucaire, 95.

Overweights—Pride of India, 2 pounds.

"Pimlico Form Chart." *Daily Racing Form*, May 15, 1919.

Belmont Stakes, June 11, 1919

BELMONT PARK FORM CHART

NEW YORK, N. Y., WEDNESDAY, JUNE 11, 1919.—Belmont Park. Eighteenth and last day. Westchester Racing Association. Spring Meeting of 18 days. **Weather clear; temperature 70°.**

Steward to Represent Jockey Club, F. R. Hitchcock. Placing Judges, E. C. Smith and C. H. Pettingill. Starter, Mars Cassidy. Racing Secretary, A. McL. Earlocker.

Racing starts at 2:30 p. m. (Chicago time 1:30 p. m.). W indicates whip, S spurs, B blinkers. Figures in parentheses following the distance of each race indicate date, track record, age of horse and weight carried. *Indicates apprentice allowance.

42781 FIRST RACE—6 1-2 Furlongs Main Course. (Oct. 14, 1907—1:17⅘—4—124.) Purse $700. 3-year-olds and upward. Selling. Net value to winner $500; second, $125; third, $75.

Index	Horses	A	Wt	PP	St	¼	½	¾	Str	Fin	Jockeys	Owners	O	H	C	P	S
42722	NIGHTSTICK	wb 9	110	5	3		1½	1^{5}	1^{4}	1^{4}	A Schu'g'r	Kentucky Stable	4-5	4-5	3-5	1-4	out
42605	ELECTED II.	w 3	105	1	5		2^{1}	2^{2}	2½	2^{2}	T Nolan	E Sietas	15	25	20	6	2½
42638	*BELLRINGER	w 5	105	7	2		$3^{1\frac{1}{2}}$	3^{3}	3^{1}	$3^{1\frac{1}{2}}$	R McCr'nn	E K Bryson	12	25	20	6	2½
42583^{3}	*HOHOKUS	wb 3	100½	6	7		6^{3}	8^{5}	5½	4^{n}	H Myers	Crown Stable	12	15	15	5	2
42371^{2}	*DOT. VANDIVER	w 3	104	9	4		4^{2}	$4^{1\frac{1}{2}}$	4^{2}	5½	S Wida	W V Casey	6	10	10	3	7-5
42209	JAMES	w 5	116	8	6		7^{3}	6½	8^{5}	6^{1}	H Hanmer	B Barber	20	30	30	10	5
42605^{2}	*ONICO	wb 4	98	3	8		8^{5}	7^{1}	6½	7½	J Wessler	T Francis	3	4½	4	4-5	1-3
42520	ONWA	wb 5	110	2	1		5^{1}	5^{1}	7^{1}	8^{6}	G W Car'l	J J Fitzgerald	20	30	30	10	4
41611	DAHINDA	w 3	95½	4	9		9	9	9	9	H Ericks'n	Tansor & Cline	50	60	60	20	10

Time, 24, 47, 1:12⅘, 1:18⅘. Track fast.

Winner—Ch. g, by Broomstick—Homespun (trained by T. J. Harmon; bred by Mr. Harry Payne Whitney).

Went to post at 2:44. At post 2 minutes. Start good and slow. Won easily; second and third driving. NIGHTSTICK, suddenly improved, set a fast pace and, drawing away easily in the stretch, was cantering at the end. ELECTED II., vigorously ridden, saved ground on the turns and ran a good race. BELLRINGER lost ground when entering the stretch and tired. HOHOKUS was running fast at the end after recovering from early interference. ONICO began slowly, raced wide throughout, lacked speed and was badly ridden. ONWA began fast, but was outpaced.

Scratched—42605^{3}Appleton Wiske, 102; 42524^{3}Orderly, 114; 42722 Scotch Verdict, 110; 42583 Sir William Johnson, 110.

Overweights—Hohokus, 1½ pounds; Dahinda, 2½.

42782 SECOND RACE—About 2 1-4 Miles. (June 9, 1915—4:26—4—130.) Quogue Steeplechase Handicap. $800 Added. 4-year-olds and upward. Net value to winner $685; second, $125; third, $75.

Index	Horses	A	Wt	PP	St	4	8	12	14	Fin	Jockeys	Owners	O	H	C	P	S
(42672)	GOLD BOND	w 5	140	1	1	3^{3}	1½	1^{3}	1^{3}	1^{5}	B Haynes	G C Walsh	8-5	2	17-10	1-2	out
42275	DOUBLET	w 7	150	4	4	4	3	$2^{1\frac{1}{2}}$	2^{5}	2^{10}	F Will'ms	J E Widener	3	6	6	8-5	out
42580	TURMOIL	w 6	138	3	3	2^{4}	2^{1}	3	3	3	N Kenn'dy	M L Schwartz	4	4	3½	4-5	out
42723^{2}	TRUMPATOR	w 6	141	2	2	$1^{1\frac{1}{2}}$	Fell.				W Blake	Dosoris Stable	2	2	9-5	3-5	out

Time, 4:46⅘. Track fast.

Winner—Ch. g, by Dick Welles—Miss Lida (trained by K. K. Karrick; bred by Mr. Jerome B. Respess).

Went to post at 3:10. At post 1 minute. Start good and slow. Won easily; second and third driving. GOLD BOND was saved close up until at the seventh jump, where the pacemaker fell, then took the lead and drew away easily near the end. DOUBLET fenced well and ran a good race, but tired in the final drive. TURMOIL also fenced well, but tired when approaching the thirteenth jump. TRUMPATOR fell after showing the most early speed.

Scratched—42619 Le Marsouin, 148; 42580^{2}Royal Arch, 145; 42659 The Dean, 132.

42783 THIRD RACE—1 Mile. (Sept. 7, 1914—1:36⅗—3—117.) Twentieth Running HARLEM SELLING STAKES. Guaranteed Value $2,000. 3-year-olds and upward. Net value to winner $1,450; second, $300; third, $200.

Index	Horses	A	Wt	PP	St	¼	½	¾	Str	Fin	Jockeys	Owners	O	H	C	P	S
42500^{3}	DAMROSCH	w 6	115	2	2	$3^{1\frac{1}{2}}$	$2^{1\frac{1}{2}}$	2^{1}	1^{nk}	1^{nk}	J Loftus	J K L Ross	3	6	6	7-5	out
(42658)	WAR ZONE	w 3	100½	3	3	$1^{\frac{1}{2}}$	$1^{1\frac{1}{2}}$	$1^{\frac{1}{2}}$	$2^{1\frac{1}{2}}$	2^{3}	H Ham't'n	C W Starr	6	6	4	4-5	out
42749^{4}	JACK STUART	wB 4	101	5	5	5	5	5	5	2^{h}	J Wessler	Marrone Stable	30	30	30	6	2
(42609)	SUNFLASH II.	wB 5	117	4	1	4^{4}	4^{4}	$3^{\frac{1}{2}}$	3^{2}	4^{nk}	E Taplin	S C Hildreth	3-5	3-5	11-20	out	—
42622	MATINEE IDOL	wB 4	112	1	4	2^{h}	3^{nk}	4^{5}	4^{2}	5	L Lyke	Cleveland Stable	8	12	12	3	1

Time, 24, 47, 1:12⅘, 1:37⅘. Track fast.

Winner—Br. h. by Rock Sand—Dissembler (trained by H. G. Bedwell; bred by Mr. August Belmont).

Went to post at 3:41. At post 2 minutes. Start good and slow. Won driving; second and third the same. DAMROSCH followed WAR ZONE to the last turn, where he challenged and outgamed him in a long stretch drive under strong riding. The latter set a great pace and made a game finish. JACK STUART was outpaced in the early racing, but finished gamely and was running fastest at the end. SUNFLASH II., in close quarters in the early running, was pinched back and forced wide at the stretch entrance, then tired and was doing his best to outstay MATINEE IDOL at the end. The latter had no mishaps. SUNFLASH II.'s rider made a general claim of foul against three horses, which was dismissed.

Scratched—(42642)Princeps, 108; (42688)Minto II., 107; 42675^{2}Arrah Go On, 108; 42524^{2}Uncle's Lassie, 90; 42658^{5}Wyndover, 105; 42600 Esquiman, 104.

Overweights—War Zone, 1½ pounds; Matinee Idol, 1.

42784 FOURTH RACE—1 3-8 Miles. (June 16, 1917—2:17⅗—3—126.) Fifty-first Running BELMONT STAKES. Guaranteed Value $10,000. 3-year-olds. Weight-for-Age. Net value to winner $11,950; second, $1,500; third, $750.

Index	Horses	A	Wt	PP	St	¼	½	¾	Str	Fin	Jockeys	Owners	O	H	C	P	S
(42499)	SIR BARTON	wB	126	1	1	2^{2}	2^{3}	2^{5}	1^{3}	1^{5}	J Loftus	J K L Ross	2-5	2-5	7-20	out	—
42725^{2}	SWEEP ON	wB	126	3	2	3	3	3	$2^{\frac{1}{2}}$	2^{8}	C F'b'ther	W R Coe	†2	12-5	12-5	out	—
42751^{2}	NATUR'L BRIDGE	w	126	2	3	1^{2}	1^{8}	1^{1}	3	3	L McAtee	W R Coe	†2	12-5	12-5	out	—

†Coupled in betting; no separate place or show betting.

Time, 2:17⅖ (new American record). Track fast.

Winner—Ch. c, by Star Shoot—Lady Sterling (trained by H. G. Bedwell; bred by Messrs. Madden & Gooch).

Went to post at 4:09. At post 1 minute. Start poor and slow. Won easily; second and third driving. SIR BARTON, after beating the gate, indulged NATURAL BRIDGE with the lead over the Belmont course, then easily took the lead after entering the main course and, drawing away, was easing up at the end. SWEEP ON was saved under early restraint and made a vain challenge at the homestretch entrance, but tired near the end. NATURAL BRIDGE tired badly after pacemaking to the homestretch.

Scratched—42641^{2}Pastoral Swain, 126; 42725 Over There, 126.

42785 FIFTH RACE—1 1-8 Miles. (Sept. 4, 1915—1:51—4—112.) Purse $700. 3-year-olds and upward. Claiming. Net value to winner $500; second, $125; third, $75.

Index	Horses	A	Wt	PP	St	¼	½	¾	Str	Fin	Jockeys	Owners	O	H	C	P	S
42686^{2}*	D'DY'S CHOICE	wB 6	105	3	3	4^{1}	$1^{\frac{1}{2}}$	1^{3}	1^{3}	1^{3}	S Wida	E C Griffith	8-5	2	2	1-2	out
42642^{2}	BENEVOLENT	w 7	110	4	1	$2^{1\frac{1}{2}}$	2^{1}	2^{1}	$2^{\frac{1}{2}}$	$2^{\frac{1}{2}}$	L Stalker	W'dlandS'kF'rm	1	1	4-5	1-5	out
(42686)	POOR BUT'FLY	wB 4	111	2	5	$3^{\frac{1}{2}}$	4^{3}	3^{1}	$3^{1\frac{1}{2}}$	3^{2}	G Walls	H R Schaffer	4	5	5	6-5	out
42713*	HICKORYNUT	wB 5	102	5	2	5	5	4^{5}	4^{10}	4^{15}	H Ham't'n	W Cahill	20	30	30	8	3
42686*	ALMA B.	wB 5	107	1	4	1^{1}	2^{5}	5	5	5	J Wessler	G W Atkinson	20	30	25	7	2

Time, 25, 49, 1:14⅗, 1:40⅗, 1:53⅘. Track fast.

Winner—B. h, by Trap Rock—Earth (trained by G. R. Bryson; bred by Mr. Thomas J. Carson).

Went to post at 4:39. At post 1 minute. Start good and slow. Won easily; second and thrid driving. DADDY'S CHOICE took the lead after going a half and, keeping it, won easing up. BENEVOLENT tired and swerved behind the winner in the final eighth. POOR BUTTERFLY ran well and had no mishaps. ALMA B. tired badly after setting the early pace.

Scratched—42642 Princeps, 116; 42642 N. K. Beal, 114; 42686 Gala Dress, 105; 42662 Millrace, 104; (42752)Caddie, 116.

42786 SIXTH RACE—5-8 Mile Straight. (Sept. 12, 1918—55⅗—2—110.) Purse $700. 2-year-olds. Maidens. Special Weights. Net value to winner $500; second, $125; third, $75.

Index	Horses	A	Wt	PP	St	¼	½	¾	Str	Fin	Jockeys	Owners	O	H	C	P	S
42714^{4}	NEDDAM	w	115	1	1		1^{3}	1^{3}	1^{5}	1^{7}	M Buxton	W Booth	3	4	4	7-10	out
42709^{2}	TATTLE	w	115	4	3		$2^{\frac{1}{2}}$	3^{4}	3^{4}	2^{h}	J P Ryan	T H Wilson	15	15	7	3-2	1-2
	D'M OF THE V'L'Y	wB	115	5	2		3^{1}	2^{3}	$2^{\frac{1}{2}}$	$3^{\frac{1}{2}}$	J Loftus	Glen Riddle F'm	1-2	1-2	9-20	out	—
	BLAZES	w	115	3	4		5	5	5	4^{3}	C Mergler	R Parr	20	30	30	6	2
42353	GONZALO	w	115	2	5		4^{1}	4^{1}	$4^{\frac{1}{2}}$	5	E Ambr'se	M J Daly	15	15	15	4	7-5

Time, 59. Track fast.

Winner—B. c, by Ormondale—Miss Kearney (trained by W. Booth; bred by Mr. John E. Madden).

Went to post at 5:07. At post 2 minutes. Start good and slow. Won easily; second and third driving. NEDDAM began fast, drew away steadily and won pulling up. TATTLE stood a long drive gamely and outstayed DREAM OF THE VALLEY at the end. The latter raced green and, tiring badly, just outfinished BLAZES at the end. GONZALO was always outrun.

Scratched—42750 Hoodwink, 115; 42750 My Laddie, 115.

"Belmont Park Form Chart." *Daily Racing Form,* June 12, 1919.

Kenilworth Park Gold Cup, October 12, 1920

KENILWORTH PARK FORM CHART

WINDSOR, ONT., TUESDAY, OCTOBER 12, 1920.—Kenilworth Park. **Sixth day.** Kenilworth Park Racing Association. Autumn Meeting of 7 days. **Weather clear; temperature 60°.**

Steward to Represent Canadian Racing Associations, Francis Nelson. Stewards, S. McBride and M. N. Macfarlan. Judges, E. W. Cole and S. McBride. Starter, Harry Morrissey. Racing Secretary, W. R. Norvell.

Racing starts at 1:30 p. m. (Chicago time 1:30 p. m.). *Indicates apprentice allowance.

50889 FIRST RACE—3-4 Mile. (July 24, 1917—1:11⅗—4—110.) Purse $1,500. 2-year-olds. Maidens. Allowances. Net value to winner $1,150; second, $250; third, $100.

Index	Horses	A Wt	PP	St	¼	½	¾	Str	Fin	Jockeys	Owners	Equiv. Odds Str't
50539	PETRARCH	w 111	8	3		4^{3}	$4^{1\frac{1}{2}}$	2^{nk}	1^{6}	W Wright	G J Long	250-100
50711	MAB. JOSEPHINE	w 108	4	6		8	$7\frac{1}{2}$	4^{1}	$2^{1\frac{1}{2}}$	I Fletcher	W Alford	1135-100
50510	CAPON	wB 108	3	7		5^{h}	6^{2}	7^{2}	3^{2}	F Chiav'ta	W C Weant	1020-100
50712²	ROMPER	wB 112	6	2		$6^{1\frac{1}{2}}$	5^{nk}	$6^{1\frac{1}{2}}$	4^{1}	H Thurber	W P Johnson	295-100
47198	BROWN BILL	wB 108	5	4		$2^{1\frac{1}{2}}$	$2^{1\frac{1}{2}}$	3^{1}	5^{1}	F Murphy	W M Cain	560-100
50711³	JOSIE GORMAN	w 112	2	5		3^{h}	$3\frac{1}{2}$	1^{1}	$6^{2\frac{1}{2}}$	G Walls	T J Elward	830-100
50712	JOHN ARBOR	w 108	1	8		7^{1}	8	8	7^{3}	H Myers	F St John	2625-100
50237	BERTHA S.	w 108	7	1		1^{1}	1^{nk}	5^{1}	8	J Conway	H Oots	970-100

Time, 24⅘, 49, 1:14⅘. Track fast.

$2 mutuels paid, Petrarch, $7.00 straight, $4.90 place, $3.70 show; Mabel Josephine, $10.70 place, $5.80 show; Capon, $5.50 show.

Equivalent booking odds—Petrarch, 250 to 100 straight, 145 to 100 place, 85 to 100 show; Mabel Josephine, 435 to 100 place, 190 to 100 show; Capon, 175 to 100 show.

Winner—B. c, by Sain or Free Lance—Mytilene, by Falsetto (trained by R. W. Williams; bred by Mr. George J. Long).

Went to post at 1:35. At post 5 minutes. Start good and slow. Won easily; second and third driving. PETRARCH was saved to the stretch turn, from where he moved up swiftly and won pulling up. MABEL JOSEPHINE began slowly and was forced to race wide, but closed a big gap and ran a good race. CAPON finished with a rush. ROMPER also finished fast. BROWN BILL showed speed.

50890 SECOND RACE—3-4 Mile. (July 24, 1917—1:11⅗—4—110.) Purse $1,500. 3-year-olds and upward. Claiming. Net value to winner $1,150; second, $250; third, $100.

Index	Horses	A Wt	PP	St	¼	½	¾	Str	Fin	Jockeys	Owners	Equiv. Odds Str't
50412	SAGAMORE	w 3 106	10	7		6^{1}	$4\frac{1}{2}$	1^{2}	1^{8}	E Hayw'd	P J Jones	570-100
50238	DOUBLE VAN	wB 3 103	3	5		3^{h}	$2\frac{1}{2}$	$3^{1\frac{1}{2}}$	2^{2}	J Dreyer	G S Abbott	3710-100
50513	SENAT'R JAMES	wB 10 108	9	3		2^{1}	$1\frac{1}{2}$	2^{1}	3^{h}	F Murphy	H W Plant	2130-100
50743	FLYING FROG	wB 3 103	8	1		4^{1}	5^{2}	$4\frac{1}{2}$	$4\frac{1}{2}$	L Aron	C Leydecker	2500-100
50796*	CLARK M.	wsB 10 103	1	9		11^{2}	$8\frac{1}{2}$	$7\frac{1}{2}$	5^{h}	E Barnes	G Holmes	590-100
50512	ROCK SILK	w 4 108	7	11		9^{1}	9^{1}	$8\frac{1}{2}$	$6\frac{1}{2}$	W Hinphy	Coronado Stable	575-100
50442	GALOPIN	wB 5 103	5	8		$7\frac{1}{2}$	6^{2}	$5\frac{1}{2}$	7^{2}	J Conway	W G Campbell	†1390-100
50439	MANNCHEN	w 6 112	11	2		$1^{1\frac{1}{2}}$	3^{h}	6^{1}	$8\frac{1}{2}$	J Grune	C Whyte	1265-100
50590²	ELMONT	w 3 107	12	6		8^{1}	7^{1}	9^{2}	$9\frac{1}{2}$	H Thurber	E T Zollicoffer	135-100
50796	TOM LOGAN	wB 3 102	2	10		10^{1}	10^{2}	10^{2}	10^{1}	E Pollard	W M Cain	†
50687	HEMISPHERE	w 4 103	6	4		5^{h}	11^{2}	11^{2}	11^{1}	H Gibson	H Warner	†
50740*	OUR HAZEL	wB 3 98	4	12		12	12	12	12	M Schw'tz	J F Dolan	†

†Mutuel field. Time, 23⅘, 48, 1:13⅘. Track fast.

$2 mutuels paid, Sagamore, $13.40 straight, $7.00 place, $5.10 show; Double Van, $35.60 place, $19.20 show; Senator James, $9.50 show.

Equivalent booking odds—Sagamore, 570 to 100 straight, 250 to 100 place, 155 to 100 show; Double Van, 1680 to 100 place, 860 to 100 show; Senator James, 375 to 100 show.

Winner—Ch. g, by Uncle—Lydia II., by Luke Blackburn (trained by C. Phillips; bred by Mr. Hal Price Headley).

Went to post at 2:16. At post 2 minutes. Start good and slow. Won easily; second and third driving. SAGAMORE moved up on the inside after passing the far turn and, racing into a long lead in the stretch, won pulling up. DOUBLE VAN was a forward contender all the way and finished fast. SENATOR JAMES tired after taking the lead on the last turn. CLARK M. closed a big gap.

Scratched—50823 Susan M., 108; 49733 Cy Merrick, 108; 50411 George Washington, 103.

Overweights—Sagamore, 3 pounds; Rock Silk, 1.

KENILWORTH PARK FORM CHART—Continued from third page.

50891 THIRD RACE—1 Mile and 70 Yards. (July 24, 1917—1:43⅘—6—132.) Purse $1,700. 3-year-olds and upward. Allowances. Foaled in Canada. Net value to winner $1,300; second, $250; third, $150.

Index	Horses	A Wt	PP	St	¼	½	¾	Str	Fin	Jockeys	Owners	Equiv. Odds Str't
50742	ALGONQUIN	wB 3 106	7	6	$1^{1\frac{1}{2}}$	$1^{1\frac{1}{2}}$	1^{2}	1^{2}	1^{2}	E Hayw'rd	J C Fletcher	425-100
(50738)	GALL'NT GROOM	w 3 103	5	5	2^{3}	2^{8}	2^{8}	2^{5}	2^{5}	H Gibson	J Meagher	1205-100
50742²	BUGLE MARCH	w 4 113	4	1	4^{1}	4^{1}	$3\frac{1}{2}$	3^{2}	3^{1}	H Thurber	T Riddle	90-100
50742	WOODBINE	wB 3 107	2	2	5^{2}	5^{6}	5^{6}	5^{10}	4^{4}	F Murphy	Brookdale Stable	630-100
(50685)	MALLOWMOT	w 6 102	6	3	3^{4}	$3\frac{1}{2}$	$4^{1\frac{1}{2}}$	4^{1}	5^{15}	L Aron	F Farrar	510-100
50822	GLENALVA LASS	w 3 100	1	7	7	$6\frac{1}{2}$	6^{4}	6^{3}	6^{5}	W Bog'ski	J O'Neil	8415-100
50325	ADOROCK	w 5 102	3	4	$6^{1\frac{1}{2}}$	7	7	7	7	M Schw'tz	J Anderson	6845-100

Time, 24, 48⅘, 1:13⅘, 1:39⅘, 1:44⅘. Track fast.

$2 mutuels paid, Algonquin, $10.50 straight, $5.10 place, $3.00 show; Gallant Groom, $9.50 place, $3.60 show; Bugle March, $2.50 show.

Equivalent booking odds—Algonquin, 425 to 100 straight, 155 to 100 place, 50 to 100 show; Gallant Groom, 375 to 100 place, 80 to 100 show; Bugle March, 25 to 100 show.

Winner—B. c, by Galatine—Chinka, by Florizel II. (trained by C. Phillips; bred by Mr. Joseph E. Seagram).

Went to post at 2:58. At post 1 minute. Start good and slow. Won easily; second and third driving. ALGONQUIN raced into a quick lead and easily held the race safe all the way. GALLANT GROOM raced in closest pursuit, but could never get to the leader. BUGLE MARCH was sharply cut off by the winner on the first turn and ran well. MALLOWMOT quit.

Overweights—Glenalva Lass, 3 pounds; Gallant Groom, 3; Algonquin, 1.

50892 FOURTH RACE—1 1-4 Miles. (Oct. 18, 1916—2:09⅘—5—102.) KENILWORTH PARK GOLD CUP. $75,000 and $5,000 Gold Cup Added. 3-year-olds and upward. Weight-for-Age. Net value to winner $75,000 and $5,000 Gold Cup.

Index	Horses		A	Wt	PP	St	¼	½	¾	Str	Fin	Jockeys	Owners	Equiv. Odds Str't
(50253)	MAN O' WAR	w	3	120	2	1	1^2	1^3	1^5	1^6	1^7	C Kummer	Glen Riddle Farm	5-100
(49710)	SIR BARTON	wB	4	126	1	2	2	2	2	2	2	F Keogh	J K L Ross	555-100

Time, 23, 46⅘, 59⅕, 1:11⅕, 1:37⅘, 2:03 (new track record). Track fast.

$2 mutuels paid, Man o' War, $2.10 straight; no place or show mutuels sold.

Equivalent booking odds—Man o' War, 5 to 100 straight.

Winner—Ch. c, by Fair Play—Mahubah, by Rock Sand (trained by L. Feustel; bred by Mr. August Belmont).

Went to post at 3:37. At post 1 minute. Start good and slow. Won easily; second driving. MAN O' WAR rushed to the front when the barrier was released and, setting a great pace for this track, won all the way never fully extended. SIR BARTON was under the whip before they had gone a quarter, but was unable to improve his position.

Scratched—50824 Wickford, 126.

50893 FIFTH RACE—1 Mile and 70 Yards. (July 24, 1917—1:43⅗—6—132.) Purse $2,000. 3-year-olds and upward. Handicap. Net value to winner $1,500; second, $300; third, $200.

Index	Horses		A	Wt	PP	St	¼	½	¾	Str	Fin	Jockeys	Owners	Equiv. Odds Str't
50799	MAYOR HOUSE	wB	4	100	5	4	1^1	$1^{1\frac{1}{2}}$	1^1	1^2	$1^{1\frac{1}{2}}$	I Fletcher	C H Gilroy	520-100
50744[2]	NEPPERHAN	wB	5	102	4	5	$2^{\frac{1}{2}}$	2^2	$2^{1\frac{1}{2}}$	$2^{1\frac{1}{2}}$	2^n	J Grune	W Walker	440-100
(50742)	UNCLE JOHN	w	4	122	1	2	3^3	$3^{1\frac{1}{2}}$	4^4	4^4	$3^{1\frac{1}{2}}$	H Thurber	J B Crawford	405-100
50825	ED STONE	w	4	95	3	3	5	$4^{1\frac{1}{2}}$	3^h	3^{nk}	$4^{2\frac{1}{2}}$	E Harb'ne	R A Moore	365-100
(50714)	ESCARPOLETTE	w	3	107	2	1	$4^{\frac{1}{2}}$	5	5	5	5	G Walls	G E Brown	180-100

Time, 23⅗, 48, 1:13⅗, 1:39, 1:43⅗. Track fast.

$2 mutuels paid, Mayor House, $12.40 straight, $5.10 place, $3.60 show; Nepperhan, $4.90 place, $3.20 show; Uncle John, $3.30 show.

Equivalent booking odds—Mayor House, 520 to 100 straight, 155 to 100 place, 80 to 100 show; Nepperhan, 145 to 100 place, 60 to 100 show; Uncle John, 65 to 100 show.

Winner—Br. c, by Hanbridge—Helma S., by Cesarion (trained by G. P. Sherman; bred by Zenaida Stock Farm).

Went to post at 4:22. At post 1 minute. Start good and slow. Won easily; second and third driving. MAYOR HOUSE took the lead soon after the start and, setting a fast pace to the stretch, won easing up. NEPPERHAN raced in closest pursuit, but tired and just lasted long enough to outstay UNCLE JOHN. The latter finished fast and was wearing the leaders down. ED STONE ran fairly well.

50894 SIXTH RACE—1 Mile and 70 Yards. (July 24, 1917—1:43⅗—6—132.) Purse $1,800. 3-year-olds. Claiming. Net value to winner $1,400; second, $250; third, $150.

Index	Horses		A	Wt	PP	St	¼	½	¾	Str	Fin	Jockeys	Owners	Equiv. Odds Str't
50799	TEN CAN	wB		115	2	4	1^1	$1^{1\frac{1}{2}}$	1^{nk}	1^{nk}	1^2	H Thurber	F St John	150-100
50743[2]	*ANZAC	w		106	6	7	$6^{\frac{1}{2}}$	3^{nk}	$3^{\frac{1}{2}}$	3^2	2^2	F Chiav'ta	W C Weant	340-100
(50743)	MURRAY	wB		112	3	1	$2^{\frac{1}{2}}$	$2^{1\frac{1}{2}}$	2^2	2^1	$3^{1\frac{1}{2}}$	E Hayw'rd	R F Coppage	375-100
50743	BALLYBELL	w		100	1	2	7	$6^{1\frac{1}{2}}$	5^2	4^{nk}	$4^{\frac{1}{2}}$	G Walls	Pelican Stable	775-100
50823[2]	*HUSH	w		104	5	5	4^h	5^3	4^{nk}	$5^{1\frac{1}{2}}$	$5^{1\frac{1}{2}}$	E Barnes	G Holmes	1075-100
50743	*WHO CARES	w		105	4	3	5^1	7	6^1	6^4	6^5	L Aron	F Farrar	1630-100
50796	ELEVE	w		104	7	6	$3^{1\frac{1}{2}}$	4^h	7	7	7	F Murphy	G B Cochran	5420-100

Time, 24, 48⅘, 1:13⅘, 1:40⅘, 1:44⅘. Track fast.

$2 mutuels paid, Ten Can, $5.00 straight, $4.00 place, $2.60 show; Anzac, $3.80 place, $2.70 show; Murray, $2.80 show.

Equivalent booking odds—Ten Can, 150 to 100 straight, 100 to 100 place, 30 to 100 show; Anzac, 90 to 100 place, 35 to 100 show; Murray, 40 to 100 show.

Winner—B. c, by Ten Point—Canastota, by Royal Emblem (trained by J. Tigue; bred by Mr. Anthony L. Aste).

Went to post at 5:02. At post 2 minutes. Start good and slow. Won easily; second and third driving. TEN CAN set a fast pace under slight restraint until in the final eighth, where he shook off MURRAY and drew away decisively. ANZAC began slowly and was forced to work his way up on the outside, but finished fast. MURRAY raced in closest pursuit, but tired after running on almost even terms with the winner to the eighth post. BALLYBELL finished well.

Scratched—50743 Keep, 107.

Overweights—Eleve, 2 pounds; Anzac, 1.

50895 SEVENTH RACE—1 1-16 Miles. (July 31, 1917—1:44⅕—5—110.) Purse $1,500. 4-year-olds and upward. Claiming. Net value to winner $1,150; second, $250; third, $100.

Index	Horses		A	Wt	PP	St	¼	½	¾	Str	Fin	Jockeys	Owners	Equiv. Odds Str't
50826	DUKE RUFF	w	4	106	1	2	$1^{\frac{1}{2}}$	1^{nk}	$1^{\frac{1}{2}}$	1^2	1^2	E Hayw'rd	J de Estrampes	780-100
(50797)	FLAME	w	5	98	2	1	$2^{1\frac{1}{2}}$	$2^{\frac{1}{2}}$	2^1	2^2	$2^{1\frac{1}{2}}$	J Grune	P G Christopher	485-100
50796[2]	HONDO	wB	6	103	8	7	$4^{\frac{1}{2}}$	4^h	$4^{\frac{1}{2}}$	$3^{1\frac{1}{2}}$	3^n	H Stearns	W Ritte	570-100
(50569)	DOUGLASS S.	w	6	106	6	8	8	7^1	6^1	5^1	$4^{1\frac{1}{2}}$	F Chiav'ta	T F Bornman	380-100
50744	DOTTA'S BEST	w	4	103	3	3	3^h	3^{nk}	$2^{\frac{1}{2}}$	4^1	$5^{\frac{1}{2}}$	H Thurber	R L Nelson	265-100
50716	CHICK BARKLEY	w	5	103	5	5	6^1	8	8	8	6^1	W Bog'ski	P J Miles	†3370-100
(50796)	DISCORD	w	4	104	7	6	$7^{\frac{1}{2}}$	6^1	6^{nk}	6^3	7^3	F Murphy	S Burnside	335-100
50741	T. F. McMAHON	wB	4	106	4	4	5^{nk}	5^1	7^3	7^1	8	C Duggan	W Walker	†

†Mutuel field. Time, 24, 49⅗, 1:14, 1:40⅗, 1:47⅗. Track fast.

$2 mutuels paid, Duke Ruff, $17.60 straight, $7.90 place, $4.40 show; Flame, $5.90 place, $3.80 show; Hondo, $3.60 show.

Equivalent booking odds—Duke Ruff, 780 to 100 straight, 295 to 100 place, 120 to 100 show; Flame, 195 to 100 place, 90 to 100 show; Hondo, 80 to 100 show.

Winner—Br. g, by Duke Michael—Red Ruff, by Collar (trained by J. Hope; bred by Mr. Thomas F. Ryan).

Went to post at 5:43. At post 1 minute. Start good and slow. Won easily; second and third driving. DUKE RUFF took a quick lead, saved ground on all the turns and drew away in the stretch to win easing up. FLAME ran a game race, but tired in the last eighth and had to be ridden out to outstay HONDO. The latter ran well and was gaining at the end. DOUGLASS S. finished fast. DOTTA'S BEST quit.

Scratched—(50821)Toombeola, 106; 50825 Pierrot, 108; 50741[2]Brookland, 106; 50741 Dandy, 108; 50439 Sky Pilot, 106; 50826 Garbage, 103; 50623 Prunes, 103.

Overweights—Duke Ruff, 3 pounds; Discord, 1.

"Kenilworth Park Form Chart." *Daily Racing Form,* October 13, 1920.

Notes

1. Hello, Harry Hale?

1. Madden's five Kentucky Derby winners include Old Rosebud, Sir Barton, Paul Jones, Zev, and Flying Ebony, and his five Hall of Famers include Grey Lag, Old Rosebud, Zev, Princess Doreen, and Sir Barton. In this book, "Hall of Fame" refers to the National Museum of Racing and Hall of Fame.

2. Edward L. Bowen, *Legacies of the Turf: A Century of Great Thoroughbred Breeders,* vol. 1 (Lexington, KY: Eclipse Press, 2003), 25.

3. Edward L. Bowen, *Masters of the Turf: Ten Trainers Who Dominated Horse Racing's Golden Age* (Lexington, KY: Eclipse Press, 2007), 113.

4. Bowen, *Legacies of the Turf,* 1:25.

5. Ibid., 1:28.

6. The English Triple Crown consists of the Epsom Derby, the Two Thousand Guineas Stakes, and the St. Leger Stakes.

7. Roger Mortimer, *The History of the Derby Stakes* (London: Cassell, 1962), 316. In today's dollars, Isinglass's winnings total more than $8 million.

8. Edward L. Bowen, *Dynasties: Great Thoroughbred Stallions* (Lexington, KY: Eclipse Press, 2000), 22–23.

9. Avalyn Hunter, *American Classic Pedigrees (1914–2002)* (Lexington, KY: Eclipse Press, 2003), 43.

10. Bowen, *Dynasties,* 22–23.

11. Ibid.

12. Bowen, *Legacies of the Turf,* 1:32.

13. Most Horse of the Year and other championship designations came after the fact. In the 1930s, publications such as *Daily Racing Form, Turf and Sport Digest,* and *New York Morning Telegraph* conducted polls to select the best horse of that year. *The Blood-Horse* began retroactively awarding Horse of the Year in the 1960s.

14. Hunter, *American Classic Pedigrees,* 78.

15. "Lady Sterling Is Injured," *Chicago Tribune,* December 12, 1902.

16. Bowen, *Masters of the Turf,* 127.

17. Maurice MacKenzie Leach [Exile, pseud.], "Sir Martin an American Again," *Daily Racing Form,* January 27, 1920.

18. Bowen, *Masters of the Turf,* 128.

19. Bowen, *Legacies of the Turf,* 1:33.

20. Leach, "Sir Martin an American Again."

21. Margaret Phipps Leonard, "A Derby Winner's Odyssey," *The Horse* 19, no. 3 (1938): 11.

22. Bowen, *Legacies of the Turf,* 1:34.

23. The number 187 belonged to Lady Sterling, Sir Barton's dam; the number 16 was the year he was born ("How Far Can Speedy Sir Barton Go," *Daily Racing Form,* June 16, 1919).

24. Leonard, "A Derby Winner's Odyssey," 11–15.

25. Quoted in "Sir Barton Favorite of His Breaker," *Daily Racing Form,* May 16, 1919.

26. J. K. M. Ross, *Boots and Saddles: The Story of the Fabulous Ross Stable in the Golden Days of Racing* (New York: Dutton, 1956), 120.

27. Kent Hollingsworth, *The Wizard of the Turf: John E. Madden of Hamburg Place* (Lexington, KY: self-published, 1965), 96.

28. In the last part of the nineteenth century, a number of African American jockeys, including William Walker, dominated racing in America. Born a slave near Lexington, Kentucky, in 1860, Walker became a jockey at age eleven, rode his first stakes winner at thirteen, and then rode his only Kentucky Derby winner at seventeen. After his riding career was over, he became an owner, a trainer, and a pedigree expert who worked with many owners, including John E. Madden. Walker became Madden's trainer in 1915 (Gerald L. Smith, Karen Cotton McDaniel, and John A. Hardin, *The Kentucky African American Encyclopedia* [Lexington: University Press of Kentucky, 2015], 512–13; Edward Hotaling, *The Great Black Jockeys* [Rocklin, CA: Forum (Prima Publishing), 1999], 230–37, 333–34).

29. Bowen, *Masters of the Turf,* 117–18.

2. The Major Players Emerge

1. "James Ross' Estate Thirteen Millions," *Winnipeg Tribune,* October 23, 1913.

2. J. K. M. Ross, *Boots and Saddles: The Story of the Fabulous Ross Stable in the Golden Days of Racing* (New York: Dutton, 1956), 18, 21.

3. Ibid., 20–21.

4. "J. K. L. Ross Gives $500,000 to Government," *Ottawa Journal,* August 17, 1914.

5. Ross, *Boots and Saddles,* 41.

6. Marc Milner, *Canada's Navy: The First Century* (Toronto: University of Toronto Press, 1999), 47.

7. "Yacht *Winchester* Gone," *Brooklyn Daily Eagle,* May 31, 1915.

8. Milner, *Canada's Navy,* 47.

9. Unknown correspondent to Colonel C. C. Ballantyne, minister of Naval Services, December 4, 1917, Library and Archives Canada, Ottawa.

10. Dorothy Ours, *Man o' War: A Legend Like Lightning* (New York: St. Martin's Press, 2008), 52.

11. Ross, *Boots and Saddles,* 22, 42.

12. "Laurel Entries and Past Performances for Tuesday, October 13," *Daily Racing Form,* October 13, 1914.

13. "Laurel Form Chart," *Daily Racing Form,* October 14, 1914.

14. Ross, *Boots and Saddles,* 42.

15. "Havre de Grace Form Chart," *Daily Racing Form,* April 24, 1915.

16. "Pimlico Form Chart," *Daily Racing Form,* May 18, 1915.

17. Ross, *Boots and Saddles,* 45.

18. Ibid.

19. "Pimlico Form Chart," *Daily Racing Form,* May 16, 1916.

20. "Racing Ends in the East," *Daily Racing Form,* December 1, 1916.

21. Ross, *Boots and Saddles,* 42, 45–46.

22. Ibid., 46–47.

23. Not all of Ross's twelve European acquisitions were brilliant ones. One of his imports, Fitzwilliam, never raced, so he was retired to stud and sired Hallucination, considered the best Canadian racehorse bred during that era.

24. Ross, *Boots and Saddles,* 48.

25. Edward L. Bowen, *Masters of the Turf: Ten Trainers Who Dominated Horse Racing's Golden Age* (Lexington, KY: Eclipse Press, 2003), 84, 94.

26. Ibid., 84.

27. Ross, *Boots and Saddles,* 50. Bedwell got to know Sam Hildreth, Hall of Fame trainer, and Tom Smith, who would eventually become Seabiscuit's trainer, during this period of his life. All three men started their education in horses as cowpunchers living with horses and learning how to train and to care for them, skills that would carry over into their careers in racing.

28. Bowen, *Masters of the Turf,* 84; Ross, *Boots and Saddles,* 51.

29. "Premier Trainer," *Montana Standard,* February 13, 1910.

30. "Free Horse Turned Racer," *Los Angeles Times,* March 26, 1905.

31. "California Horse Gave Famous Trainer Start," *Los Angeles Times,* December 20, 1934.

32. Ibid.

33. John I. Day, "'Lucky's' Loss," *Canandaigua Daily Messenger,* October 20, 1972.

34. Bowen, *Masters of the Turf,* 86.

35. "Helps the Club Pay Expenses," *Daily Racing Form,* December 11, 1908.

36. "Thirty Horses Win $475,000," *New York Sun,* December 5, 1909.

37. "Latonia Form Chart," *Daily Racing Form,* July 4, 1910.

38. "Bedwell Says Horse Was Not Doped, but 'Crazy,'" *Scranton Truth,* July 13, 1910.

39. "Keen Interest in Bedwell Case." *Daily Racing Form,* August 28, 1910.

40. "Latonia Judges Act in Nadzu Case," *Louisville Courier-Journal,* July 6, 1910.

41. "Pinkola Wins Feature at Latonia," *Cincinnati Enquirer,* July 5, 1910.

42. "Latonia Judges Act in Nadzu Case."

43. Quoted in "Gives His Race Horses Arsenic," *Muncie Times,* July 17, 1910.

44. Ours, *Man o' War,* 8.

45. "Bedwell Ruled Off at Latonia," *San Francisco Call,* July 8, 1910. The term *negro* is used in the original source material for the Nadzu incident. I use it here because it is part of the historical record and, as such, must be a part of the narrative for this particular incident.

46. "Pinkertons Engaged by Bedwell," *Mt. Sterling Advocate,* July 27, 1910.

47. "Keen Interest in Bedwell Case." *Daily Racing Form,* August 28, 1910.

48. Ibid.

49. "Not Doped but Crazy," *Scranton Truth,* July 13, 1910.

50. "Turf Gossip," *Oakland Tribune,* August 2, 1910.

51. "Bedwell Decision Is Affirmed by Racing Judges of Kentucky," *Oakland Tribune,* August 25, 1910.

52. "Bedwell to Ship His Stable Here," *San Francisco Call,* August 28, 1910.

53. "H. G. Bedwell and String Barred from Track at Emeryville," *San Francisco Call,* September 7, 1910; "At Last Bedwell Is Reinstated," *Cincinnati Enquirer,* April 30, 1911.

54. "Besom Wins Ladies' Handicap," *Cincinnati Enquirer,* December 14, 1910; "At Last Bedwell Is Reinstated"; "Light Work at Local Tracks," *Louisville Courier-Journal,* May 1, 1911.

55. Ross, *Boots and Saddles,* 48–49.

56. Ibid., 49.

57. Bob Moore, "A Pretty Sharp Guy," *Horseman's Journal,* August 1971, 72.

3. Our Hero Appears

1. "Promising Material Carded for Kentucky's Tracks This Summer," *Reno Gazette-Journal,* March 30, 1918.

2. "Tremont a Wonderful Race," *Daily Racing Form,* July 7, 1918.

3. "Third Race Aqueduct," *Daily Racing Form,* July 6, 1918; "Lord Brighton Shows Rare Courage to Win," *Washington Post,* July 7, 1918; "Hand Grenade, from the Macomber Stable, Wins the Brookdale Handicap," *Cincinnati Enquirer,* July 7, 1918.

4. "Aqueduct Form Chart," *Daily Racing Form,* July 7, 1918.

5. The first organized Thoroughbred races at Saratoga took place on August 3, 1863, with qualifying heats and final races totaling five races on the day. The Travers Stakes, "the Mid-Summer Derby" for three-year-olds, was created in honor of William R. Travers in 1864 (Edward Hotaling, *They're Off: Horse Racing at Saratoga* [Syracuse, NY: Syracuse University Press, 1995], 45, 55).

6. "Forty-Fourth Running of the Popular Two-Year-Old Fixture, the Flash Stakes," *Daily Racing Form,* August 1, 1918.

7. "Omar Khayyam Disabled," *Daily Racing Form,* July 28, 1918.

8. "Spa Meeting Opens To-Morrow with Promise of Fine Fields," *Louisville Courier-Journal,* July 31, 1918.

9. Bert E. Collyer, "Collyer's Comments on the Sport of Kings," *Buffalo Enquirer,* August 1, 1918.

10. "Spa Meeting Opens To-Morrow with Promise of Fine Fields."

11. J. K. M. Ross, *Boots and Saddles: The Story of the Fabulous Ross Stable in the Golden Days of Racing* (New York: Dutton, 1956), 89.

12. "Saratoga Form Chart," *Daily Racing Form,* August 2, 1918.

13. "Roamer Beats Record, Wins Saratoga Handicap," *Binghamton Press and Sun Bulletin,* August 2, 1918.

14. Ross, *Boots and Saddles,* 93.

15. To make the playing field even and fair for every horse, a handicapper would assign a weight to each horse based on its racing record. For a horse such as Billy Kelly, who already had several victories, a larger weight assignment would counterbalance the talent he had shown to that point, whereas a horse such as Sir Barton, who was still a maiden and still lightly raced, would carry lighter weight and have a better chance at keeping up with the gelding. The idea is that each pound is equivalent to a certain number of lengths; if Billy Kelly finished ten lengths in front of Sir Barton in a prior race, for example, then adding ten pounds to Billy Kelly from a set minimum weight (based on the accepted weights for the age group) should make them more even in terms of chances to win.

16. "Crack Eastern Youngsters Are Beaten by Western Whirlwind," *Louisville Courier-Journal,* August 4, 1918.

17. "Billy Kelly Not for Sale," *Daily Racing Form,* August 4, 1918.

18. "Saratoga Form Chart," *Daily Racing Form,* August 3, 1918.

19. J. L. Dempsey, "Billy Kelly Scores Another Impressive Victory at Saratoga in the United States Hotel Stakes," *Daily Racing Form,* August 4, 1918.

20. "Billy Kelly Meets Defeat," *Daily Racing Form,* August 8, 1918.

21. Ross, *Boots and Saddles,* 94.

22. "Billy Kelly Sold for Record Price," *Buffalo Commercial,* August 10, 1918.

23. "Saratoga Form Chart," *Daily Racing Form,* August 15, 1918. Blinkers, or blinders, are a piece of horse tack, a kind of mask fitted over a horse's head that obscures rear and in some cases side vision. These masks have cups that cover the eyes and come in a variety of sizes, depending on the horse's needs. The goal is to keep the horse focused on what is in front of him and to prevent distractions from other horses and other environmental factors. Sir Barton would sport blinkers in each of his races for the rest of his career.

24. "Billy Kelly Proves Right to Two-Year-Old Crown on Muddy Track at Spa," *New York Evening World,* August 15, 1918.

25. "Saratoga Form Chart," *Daily Racing Form,* August 15, 1918.

26. Kent Hollingsworth, *The Wizard of the Turf: John E. Madden of Hamburg Place* (Lexington, KY: self-published, 1962), 27.

27. The exact amount paid for Sir Barton is unknown. Multiple sources report it as $10,000, and J. K. M. Ross says in *Boots and Saddles* that the "price was in the neighborhood of $10,000" (116). Madden was not one to publicize terms whenever he sold a horse, which means that this particular sale lent itself to an ample amount of speculation with little concrete evidence. A press release in 1919, presumably from John E. Madden, listed the amount as $15,000.

28. Dorothy Ours, *Man o' War: A Legend Like Lightning* (New York: St. Martin's Press, 2008), 17, 22–23, 29–30.

29. J. L. Dempsey, "Big Prices for Belmont Yearlings," *Daily Racing Form,* August 17, 1918.

4. Meet the New Boss

1. J. K. M. Ross, *Boots and Saddles: The Story of the Fabulous Ross Stable in the Golden Days of Racing* (New York: Dutton, 1956), 89.

2. Ibid., 123.

3. James Kenneth Matthews Ross was the only son of Commander Ross and his first wife, Ethel. His memoir about this era, *Boots and Saddles,* was published in 1956, and the author credits Van Varner, longtime editor of *Guideposts* magazine and fan of racing, with considerable aid in preparing it for publication. Varner helped not only with the arrangement of the book's subject matter but also with research that supplemented what Ross had in his original manuscript.

4. Ross, *Boots and Saddles,* 22.

5. Margaret Phipps Leonard, "A Derby Winner's Odyssey," *The Horse* 19, no. 3 (1938): 14.

6. Ibid.

7. Ross, *Boots and Saddles*, 119.

8. In *Duel for the Crown: Affirmed, Alydar, and Racing's Greatest Rivalry* (New York: Gallery Books, 2014), Linda Carroll and David Rosner quote John Veitch as saying that Alydar was "all horse" (215)—in other words, a horse whose personality did not tolerate the domestic familiarity that people often want to assign to their animals. This descriptor seems appropriate for the first Triple Crown winner as well.

9. Ross, *Boots and Saddles*, 120.

10. "Sun Briar After Mile Record Today," *Ottawa Journal*, August 29, 1918.

11. "Cudgel Will Be Absentee," *Daily Racing Form*, August 29, 1918.

12. "Billy Kelly Ineligible for Rich Hopeful Stakes," *Buffalo Commercial*, August 5, 1918. W. F. Polson, Billy Kelly's previous owner, did not nominate the gelding for the Hopeful. Entries for the Saratoga races in August 1918 closed the previous December; Polson did not anticipate that Billy Kelly would get the better of Vulcanite when he nominated the latter for the Hopeful. Ross's purchase of the gelding came long after the deadline for Saratoga's entries.

13. "Saratoga Form Chart," *Daily Racing Form*, September 1, 1918.

14. "Eternal Runs a Great Race to Win the Hopeful," *Washington Post*, September 1, 1918.

15. "Roamer No Match for Speedy Johren," *New York Times*, September 1, 1918.

16. "Eternal and Billy Kelly Match Race Would Mean $20,000 for Red Cross," *New York Evening World*, September 3, 1918.

17. "The Famous Futurity Stakes to Be Decided at Belmont Park This Afternoon," *Daily Racing Form*, September 14, 1918.

18. "Dunboyne Wins Futurity," *Daily Racing Form*, September 15, 1918.

19. Neither Billy Kelly's dam (Glena) nor Eternal's dam (Hazel Burke) had been nominated for the Belmont Futurity, so those horses were ineligible for the race. J. K. L. Ross and Eternal's owner, James McClelland, would doubtless have entered their horses had they been eligible.

20. "Dunboyne Looks Best Colt in Futurity Tomorrow," *Brooklyn Daily Eagle*, September 13, 1918.

21. "Dunboyne Wins Futurity Race for Big Purse," *Indianapolis Star*, September 15, 1918.

22. "Dunboyne, Favorite, Wins Belmont Futurity by Two Lengths from Sir Barton," *Pittsburgh Post-Gazette*, September 15, 1918.

23. "Dunboyne Winner of Rich Futurity," *New York Times*, September 15, 1918.

24. Ross, *Boots and Saddles*, 132, 133.

25. "Came Near Losing Sir Barton," *Daily Racing Form,* May 29, 1919.

26. "Current Notes of the Turf," *Daily Racing Form,* October 30, 1918; Ross, *Boots and Saddles,* 134, 135.

27. "Billy Kelly's Owner Insists on Guarantee to Race," *New York Evening World,* September 21, 1918.

28. "Slippery Elm Glides Home in the Oldtown Handicap at Havre de Grace," *Cincinnati Enquirer,* September 20, 1918.

29. "Willing to Race Rain or Shine," *Philadelphia Inquirer,* September 23, 1918.

30. "Two Year Olds to Race at Laurel," *Philadelphia Inquirer,* September 24, 1918.

31. "$30,000 Will Be Donated to the Red Cross," *New York Evening World,* October 2, 1918.

32. "Laurel Curtain Goes Up Tuesday," *Philadelphia Inquirer,* September 29, 1918. Splints occur when a young horse develops swelling in the soft tissues of the interosseous ligament around the splint bones. They can become bony and lead to further problems with lameness as the horse ages.

33. J. V. Fitz Gerald, "The Round-up," *Washington Post,* September 28, 1918.

34. "All Set for Match Race," *Washington Herald,* October 27, 1918.

35. "Date of Special Race Known Soon," *Daily Racing Form,* October 10, 1918.

36. "Laurel Park Form Chart," *Daily Racing Form,* October 13, 1918.

37. "Laurel Racing Suspended," *Daily Racing Form,* October 13, 1918.

38. "Improvement in Maryland," *Daily Racing Form,* October 16, 1918.

39. Ross, *Boots and Saddles,* 137.

40. "All Set for Match Race," *Washington Herald,* October 27, 1918.

41. Ross, *Boots and Saddles,* 135.

42. "Huge Betting at Laurel Track," *Harrisburg Telegraph,* October 30, 1918.

43. Ross, *Boots and Saddles,* 136.

44. C. Edward Sparrow, "Eternal American Ace," *Baltimore Sun,* October 29, 1918.

45. Ross, *Boots and Saddles,* 136.

46. Ibid., 137.

47. Ibid., 137–38.

48. Ibid., 138.

49. Ibid., 139.

50. C. Starr Matthews, "Match Race to Eternal," *Baltimore Sun,* October 29, 1918; "Commander Ross Willing," *Cincinnati Enquirer,* October 30, 1918.

51. "Jockey Schuttinger Receives Record Fee from Eternal's Owner," *New York Evening World,* October 31, 1918.

52. "Commander Ross Willing."

53. "Easily Half Million Changed Hands When Eternal Nosed Out Billy Kelly," *Buffalo Commercial,* October 30, 1918.

54. "Seek Another Race for Billy Kelly," *Daily Racing Form,* October 31, 1918.

55. "Eternal Has Retired for the Season after Victory over Billy Kelly," *Ottawa Journal,* October 31, 1918.

56. "Winter Book on the Next Kentucky Derby," *Pittsburgh Post-Gazette,* March 31, 1919.

5. Long Shot

1. J. K. M. Ross, *Boots and Saddles: The Story of the Fabulous Ross Stable in the Golden Days of Racing* (New York: Dutton, 1956), 19–20.

2. Ibid., 144. Converted into today's dollars, $50,000 in 1919 is the equivalent of nearly $800,000. Arnold Rothstein allegedly was involved in fixing the World Series between the Chicago White Sox and the Cincinnati Reds in 1919. This happened after the bet between Ross and Rothstein was resolved.

3. Several Chicago White Sox players—including pitcher Eddie Cicotte and outfielder "Shoeless" Joe Jackson—were accused of taking bribes from known gamblers in exchange for deliberately losing the World Series to the Cincinnati Reds in 1919. The players allegedly were dissatisfied with their pay and team owner Charles Comiskey. Because players had no union and were subject to a reserve clause governing their employment, they became targets for gamblers. The scandal cast a pall over all sports, including racing.

4. Ross, *Boots and Saddles,* 145.

5. James C. Nicholson, *The Kentucky Derby: How the Run for the Roses Became America's Premier Sporting Event* (Lexington: University Press of Kentucky, 2012), chap. 1.

6. Ibid., chap. 1.

7. "Geldings to Be Barred," *Daily Racing Form,* August 7, 1918.

8. "Kentucky Derby Open to Geldings," *Daily Racing Form,* January 5, 1919.

9. "Oaklawn Draws More Rain," *Daily Racing Form,* March 17, 1919.

10. "Sir Barton and War Marvel May Be Stars among 3-Year-Olds, Bedwell Believes," *Washington Post,* March 6, 1919.

11. J. V. Fitz Gerald, "The Round-Up," *Washington Post,* November 12, 1918.

12. Ross, *Boots and Saddles,* 76.

13. Ibid., 145–46.

14. "Sir Barton Makes a Sensational Derby Trial," *New York Evening World,* April 26, 1919.

15. O'Neil Sevier, "Billy Kelly and Toto Fit for Great Race Classics," *Washington Post,* April 20, 1919.

16. "Derby Cracks Arrive This Week," *Louisville Courier-Journal*, April 29, 1919.

17. "Eternal Has Been Pointed for Derby Classic Saturday," *St. Louis Star and Times*, May 5, 1919.

18. W. C. Vreeland, "Side Bet of $50,000 Adds Class to Kentucky Derby," *Brooklyn Daily Eagle*, May 4, 1919.

19. "Frogtown May Prove to Be Another Exterminator," *St. Louis Post-Dispatch*, May 8, 1919.

20. Sam McMeekin, "Great Field to Strive for Kentucky Derby of 1919," *Louisville Courier-Journal*, May 10, 1919.

21. "Eternal Favorite over Derby Field; Track Very Heavy," *St. Louis Post-Dispatch*, May 10, 1919.

22. Ross, *Boots and Saddles*, 147.

23. Ibid.

24. Johnny Loftus also has the distinction of riding War Cloud in 1918 as War Cloud was the first to traverse what now is known as the Triple Crown trail.

25. Dorothy Ours, *Man o' War: A Legend Like Lightning* (New York: St. Martin's Press, 2008), 53.

26. Ross, *Boots and Saddles*, 146–47.

27. Sam McMeekin, "Leads Field Entire Way; Mate Trails," *Louisville Courier-Journal*, May 11, 1919.

28. Homer Dye, "'They're Off' and Kentucky Sways to Thud of Pounding Hoofs in Great Derby Race," *Louisville Courier-Journal*, May 11, 1919.

29. McMeekin, "Leads Field Entire Way."

30. Ibid.

31. "Churchill Downs Form Chart," *Daily Racing Form*, May 11, 1919.

32. "Obituary: Johnny Loftus," *The Blood-Horse*, March 29, 1976.

33. Ross, *Boots and Saddles*, 148.

34. Billy Kelly was not eligible for the Preakness Stakes because he was a gelding; racing officials were trying to do their part for national defense by making geldings ineligible and thus promoting the breeding of horses suitable for the cavalry. Thoroughbred stallions were considered the best prospects for breeding for the United States Army Remount Service. Some owners would not geld a horse unless they knew that horse was not a good candidate for service as a Remount stallion.

35. McMeekin, "Leads Field Entire Way."

6. Our Hero Heads East

1. Three maidens have won the Kentucky Derby: Buchanan (1884), Sir Barton (1919), and Broker's Tip (1933).

2. J. K. M. Ross, *Boots and Saddles: The Story of the Fabulous Ross Stable in the Golden Days of Racing* (New York: Dutton, 1956), 149.

3. "Eternal Will Get Comeback Chance," *Washington Post,* May 12, 1919.

4. Ross, *Boots and Saddles,* 148.

5. Robert Shoop, *Down to the Wire: The Lives of the Triple Crown Champions* (Everson, WA: Russell Dean, 2004), 6–7, 8. The 1918 Preakness Stakes had so many horses subscribed that the Maryland Jockey Club offered to split the race into two divisions, each with a $15,000 purse. War Cloud won one division; Jack Hare Jr. won the other.

6. The schedule of two weeks between the Kentucky Derby and the Preakness Stakes is a relatively recent phenomenon. The Derby was not always the first Saturday in May, and the Preakness was not always run right after that. In 1917 and 1922, the races were run on the same day. Once it became clear that others would want to duplicate War Cloud's and now Sir Barton's path, racing officials began to schedule the races differently, eventually arriving at our current Triple Crown schedule.

7. From 1875 to 1917, only three horses ran in the Derby and the Preakness. In 1918, War Cloud was the only horse from the 1918 Kentucky Derby (won by Exterminator) to run in the Preakness, no doubt because the Preakness added $15,000 to its purse. The bump in purse money and the seeming fluky nature of Sir Barton's win no doubt lent to the return of four Derby starters in the Preakness.

8. The Preakness was run at a variety of distances from its inception in 1873, but the current distance, 1 3/16 mile, was not put in place until 1925. From 1911 to 1924, the Preakness was 1 1/8 miles.

9. John W. Head, "Fail to Get a Glimpse at Derby Winner," *Indianapolis Star,* May 12, 1919.

10. Ross, *Boots and Saddles,* 149–50.

11. "Derby Horses Arrive from Louisville to Take Part in Preakness Stake," *Cincinnati Enquirer,* May 13, 1919.

12. O'Neil Sevier, "Kentucky Derby Entries Expected to Furnish Class for the Preakness," *Washington Post,* May 11, 1919.

13. "Everything's Fine To-Day for the Preakness Stakes with Dunboyne Favorite," *New York Evening World,* May 14, 1919.

14. Sevier, "Kentucky Derby Entries Expected to Furnish Class for the Preakness."

15. Broncho, "Sir Barton Favored to Win Preakness at Pimlico Today," *Pittsburgh Daily Post,* May 14, 1919.

16. For an example of the effect the start had on a horse in this era, see Man o' War's experience in the Sanford Memorial Stakes in 1919, in which an inauspicious start and short distance spelled defeat for even the best Thoroughbred of the twentieth century.

17. Ross, *Boots and Saddles,* 150–51.

18. C. Edward Sparrow, "Sir Barton Wins Stake," *Baltimore Sun,* May 15, 1919.

19. "Sir Barton Repeats; Wins the Preakness," *Philadelphia Inquirer,* May 15, 1919.

20. Ibid.

21. "Eternal Is Badly Beaten by Ross's Gallant Colt," *New York Tribune,* May 15, 1919.

22. "Sir Barton All the Way from Barrier to Finish," *Washington Herald,* May 15, 1919.

23. "Sir Barton Easily Wins Preakness at Pimlico," *Washington Post,* May 15, 1919.

24. Maryland Jockey Club, "The Preakness," press guide/release, 2015.

25. Ross, *Boots and Saddles,* 152.

26. W. C. Vreeland, "Sir Barton Proves to Turf His Champion 3-Year-Old," *Brooklyn Daily Eagle,* May 15, 1919.

27. "Sir Barton Favorite of His Breaker," *Daily Racing Form,* May 16, 1919.

28. "Sir Barton Is Victor in Big Eastern Event," *Indianapolis Star,* May 15, 1919.

29. "Flags Wins Paumonok," *Daily Racing Form,* May 16, 1919.

30. Quoted in "Sir Barton Better Than Billy Kelly," *Daily Racing Form,* May 18, 1919.

31. "Lady Sterling Now a Famous Dam," *Daily Racing Form,* May 14, 1919.

32. "Commander Ross Buys Maryland Farm and Will Construct Private Race Track," *Cincinnati Enquirer,* May 23, 1919.

33. "J. K. L. Ross to Breed Own Horses," *Daily Racing Form,* May 23, 1919.

34. "Sir Barton to Be Retired at Close of Present Year," *Louisville Courier-Journal,* May 31, 1919.

35. W. C. Vreeland, "Great Horses Swing into Line at Belmont Park," *Brooklyn Daily Eagle,* May 21, 1919.

36. "Sir Barton's Next Engagement," *Daily Racing Form,* May 17, 1919.

37. Vincent Treanor, "Withers Provides Third Meeting of Rivals for Turf Championship," *New York Evening World,* May 24, 1919.

38. Belmont Park switched to running races counterclockwise in the 1920s. The first counterclockwise Belmont Stakes was in 1921 (Kimberly Gatto, *Belmont Park: The Championship Track* [Charleston, SC: History Press, 2013], 61).

39. Ross, *Boots and Saddles,* 156.

40. Ibid., 153.

41. W. C. Vreeland, "Sir Barton Beats Eternal for Rich Withers Stakes," *Brooklyn Daily Eagle,* May 25, 1919.

42. Ross, *Boots and Saddles,* 156–57.

43. Vreeland, "Sir Barton Beats Eternal for Rich Withers Stakes."

44. Ross, *Boots and Saddles,* 153.

45. Ibid., 154.

46. W. J. Macbeth, "Season's Idol Beats Eternal by 2 Lengths," *New York Tribune,* May 25, 1919.

47. Ibid.

48. Vreeland, "Sir Barton Beats Eternal for Rich Withers Stakes."

49. Ross, *Boots and Saddles,* 155.

50. Macbeth, "Season's Idol Beats Eternal by 2 Lengths."

51. Ross, *Boots and Saddles,* 155.

52. Vreeland, "Sir Barton Beats Eternal for Rich Withers Stakes."

53. Macbeth, "Season's Idol Beats Eternal by 2 Lengths."

54. Ross, *Boots and Saddles,* 155.

7. History Made

1. Quoted in "Best of All, He's American Bred," *Louisville Courier-Journal,* May 29, 1919.

2. Colin and Sysonby were colts who dominated the American racing scene in the decade before Sir Barton came along. Sysonby was defeated only once, after his groom admitted to accepting a bribe for drugging the horse to lose. Colin went undefeated in his two-year career, dominating every horse he faced, including Man o' War's sire, Fair Play.

3. Latonia was a racetrack located outside of Covington, Kentucky, south of Cincinnati, Ohio. The original Latonia closed in 1939, reopened in a different location in 1959, and became Turfway Park in 1986.

4. "Sir Barton to Race at Latonia," *Portsmouth Daily Times,* May 27, 1919.

5. W. J. Macbeth, "Salvestra, under Hard Drive, Wins the Ladies' Handicap," *New York Tribune,* June 1, 1919.

6. The price that Commander Ross actually paid for Sir Barton was not recorded for posterity as far as we know. The going wisdom is that Madden's price was $10,000. However, the press release that made it into a number of newspapers in May 1919, one that presumably came from either Ross or Madden, had the $15,000 price tag listed.

7. "How Offer for Sir Barton Was Made," *Daily Racing Form,* May 29, 1919.

8. C. Edward Sparrow, "Ross Not a Seller," *Baltimore Evening Sun,* May 28, 1919.

9. "Military Race to Feature Card at Downs; Cudgel and Royce Rools Arrive for Handicap," *Louisville Courier-Journal,* May 22, 1919.

10. "Great Field to Contest for Kentucky Handicap," *Louisville Courier-Journal,* May 24, 1919.

11. "Sir Barton out of the Latonia Derby," *Buffalo Morning Express,* June 5, 1919.

12. "Weights for the Suburban Handicap," *Daily Racing Form,* June 5, 1919.

13. W. C. Vreeland, "Lanius, with Loftus Up, Suburban Favorite," *Brooklyn Daily Eagle,* June 6, 1919.

14. Bob Saxton, "Be Frank Won Latonia Derby," *Cincinnati Enquirer,* June 8, 1919.

15. Robert Shoop, *Down to the Wire: The Lives of the Triple Crown Champions* (Everson, WA: Russell Dean, 2004), 10.

16. Kimberly Gatto, *Belmont Park: The Championship Track* (Charleston, SC: History Press, 2013), 23–24.

17. Shoop, *Down to the Wire,* 10.

18. "Belmont Park Form Chart," *Daily Racing Form,* June 12, 1919.

19. Shoop, *Down to the Wire,* 11.

20. J. K. M. Ross, *Boots and Saddles: The Story of the Fabulous Ross Stable in the Golden Days of Racing* (New York: Dutton, 1956), 159.

21. "Current Notes of the Turf," *Daily Racing Form,* May 25, 1919; "Off-Day Program at Belmont," *Daily Racing Form,* June 11, 1919.

22. "American Record Lowered by Sir Barton in Belmont," *Louisville Courier-Journal,* June 12, 1919.

23. "Another for Sir Barton," *Daily Racing Form,* June 12, 1919.

24. "American Record Lowered by Sir Barton in Belmont."

25. "Belmont Form Chart," *Daily Racing Form,* June 12, 1919.

26. W. J. Macbeth, "Track Records Topple in Race for Rich Purse," *New York Tribune,* June 12, 1919.

27. "American Record Lowered by Sir Barton in Belmont."

28. "Belmont Form Chart."

29. "American Record Lowered by Sir Barton in Belmont."

30. Broncho, "Sir Barton Proves Turf Sensation with Earnings of More Than $65,000 Resulting from One Month's Racing," *Pittsburgh Daily Post,* June 15, 1919.

31. "Another for Sir Barton."

32. Dorothy Ours, *Man o' War: A Legend Like Lightning* (New York: St. Martin's Press, 2008), 48.

33. "Field of Eleven in the Suburban at Belmont To-Day," *New York Evening World,* June 7, 1919.

34. Ours, *Man o' War,* 62.

35. Ibid.

8. Bumps in the Road

1. Broncho, "Sir Barton Proves Turf Sensation with Earnings of More Than $65,000 Resulting from One Month's Racing," *Pittsburgh Daily Post,* June 15, 1919.

2. "News from the Jamaica Track," *Brooklyn Daily Eagle,* June 18, 1919.

3. Avalyn Hunter, *American Classic Pedigrees (1914–2012)* (Lexington, KY: Eclipse Press, 2003), 43.

4. J. K. M. Ross, *Boots and Saddles: The Story of the Fabulous Ross Stable in the Golden Days of Racing* (New York: Dutton, 1956), 118–19.

5. Ibid., 160.

6. "Ross May Scratch Sir Barton from Dwyer To-Day," *New York Tribune,* July 10, 1919.

7. Ross, *Boots and Saddles,* 160.

8. Most likely, this incident happened on July 5, when Sir Barton worked a mile in 1:40⅖ ("Purchase Works a Mile in 1:37," *Daily Racing Form,* July 6, 1919).

9. "Dwyer Stakes at Aqueduct Today," *Daily Racing Form,* July 10, 1919.

10. "Tosses Hat in Ring," *Baltimore Evening Sun,* September 27, 1918.

11. "Purchase Lame; Injured in Stall," *Louisville Courier-Journal,* April 29, 1919.

12. W. J. Macbeth, "Purchase Wins First Start; Mishap Beats Omar Khayyam," *New York Tribune,* June 7, 1919.

13. "Billy Kelly Goes Down to Defeat," *Philadelphia Inquirer,* June 13, 1919.

14. W. J. Macbeth, "Star's Foul Tactics Cost Ting-A-Ling Second Place," *New York Tribune,* July 8, 1919.

15. Vincent Treanor, "Disciplining of Loftus Cost Ting-A-Ling Backers Lots of Money in Wagers," *New York Evening World,* June 8, 1919.

16. Ibid.

17. Ibid.

18. "Dwyer Stakes at Aqueduct Today."

19. Ibid.

20. Dorothy Ours, *Man o' War: A Legend Like Lightning* (New York: St. Martin's Press, 2008), 78.

21. Broncho, "Has the Great Sir Barton Met His Match in Purchase? Special Race Proposed to Settle Which Is Best 3-Year-Old," *Pittsburgh Daily Post,* July 13, 1919.

22. W. J. Macbeth, "Hildreth Colt Triumphs Easily in $6,000 Stake," *New York Tribune*, July 11, 1919.

23. "Sir Barton Is Beaten," *Baltimore Sun*, July 11, 1919; "Purchase Handily Beats Sir Barton," *Washington Post*, July 11, 1919; Macbeth, "Hildreth Colt Triumphs Easily in $6,000 Stake."

24. "Sir Barton Is Beaten"; Vincent Treanor, "Sir Barton Is No Match for Hildreth's Purchase in $6,000 Dwyer Stakes," *New York Evening World*, July 11, 1919.

25. Frank Graham, "Graham's Corner," *Ottawa Journal*, June 11, 1949.

26. "Kentucky Derby Winner Succumbs to Speedy Rival," *Louisville Courier-Journal*, July 11, 1919.

27. "Sir Barton Lost Shoe in Big Race," *Washington Herald*, July 15, 1919.

28. In *Boots and Saddles*, J. K. M. Ross references Sir Barton's shelly hooves and the fact that he once lost four shoes in a race (118). Frank Hackett, former business agent for Commander Ross, brought up that occurrence in an article published in 1948 (quoted in Dave Lews, "Once Over Lightly," *Long Beach Independent*, November 5, 1948), but no other article written at the time of the Dwyer Stakes in 1919 referred to Sir Barton losing all four shoes. Most articles instead referred to one of the colt's front plates turning around during the first half-mile of the Dwyer.

29. Broncho, "Has the Great Sir Barton Met His Match in Purchase?"

30. "Doubt Felt as to 3-Year-Old Crown," *New York Times*, July 13, 1919.

31. Broncho, "Has the Great Sir Barton Met His Match in Purchase?"

9. Ups and Downs

1. "Great Sir Barton Bows to Purchase," *New York Times*, June 11, 1919.

2. "Hannibal Defeats Fast Field for Travers," *New York Times*, August 17, 1919.

3. W. C. Vreeland, "Purchase Romps Home First in Empire City Derby," *Brooklyn Daily Eagle*, July 20, 1919.

4. W. C. Vreeland, "Vreeland Ranks Purchase with Stars of Former Years," *Brooklyn Daily Eagle*, August 2, 1919.

5. Harry N. Price, "Saranac Handicap Easy for Purchase," *Washington Post*, August 21, 1919.

6. "Hannibal Bows to the Superiority of Purchase," *Buffalo Evening News*, August 27, 1919.

7. W. C. Vreeland, "Purchase Proves His Claim to the Three-Year-Old Title," *Brooklyn Daily Eagle*, August 27, 1919.

8. "Two-Year-Old King Takes Rich Stakes," *New York Times*, August 31, 1919.

9. J. L. Dempsey, "Exterminator Defeats Purchase in the Saratoga Cup," *Cincinnati Enquirer,* August 31, 1919.

10. "Two Firsts for Loftus," *New York Tribune,* June 7, 1919.

11. "Offer of $100,000 for 'Man o' War' Is Declined," *Pittsburgh Press,* August 6, 1919.

12. "Refuses $150,000 for Man o' War," *Baltimore Evening Sun,* August 6, 1919.

13. W. C. Vreeland, "$100,000 Offer for Man-o'-War Refused," *Brooklyn Daily Eagle,* August 6, 1919.

14. Dorothy Ours, *Man o' War: A Legend Like Lightning* (New York: St. Martin's Press, 2008), 92, 109, 100.

15. Ibid., 100.

16. Ibid.

17. Ibid., 101, 102.

18. Ibid., 102.

19. Jack Mahon, "Johnny's Goof on Big Red," *Sports Illustrated,* April 25, 1966.

20. Ours, *Man o' War,* 103, 104.

21. Ibid., 104.

22. Ibid.

23. Ibid., 105.

24. O'Neil Sevier, "Dunboyne and Sir Barton May Battle at Belmont," *Washington Post,* August 31, 1919.

25. "Ross' Great String at Havre de Grace," *Washington Herald,* September 3, 1919.

26. O'Neil Sevier, "Sir Barton, the Chestnut Hope," *Vanity Fair,* September 1919.

27. "Monday Workouts in the East," *Daily Racing Form,* September 9, 1919.

28. Harry N. Price, "Racing Back to Maryland Today," *Washington Post,* September 11, 1919.

29. "The Porter First Home in Harford Handicap," *Wilmington News Journal,* September 12, 1919.

30. "Havre de Grace Form Chart," *Daily Racing Form,* September 12, 1919.

31. Robert W. Maxwell, "Billy Kelly Found among Comebacks of Racing Seasons," *Philadelphia Evening Public Ledger,* September 12, 1919.

32. Harry N. Price, "The Porter and Billy Kelly Take Big Events at Opening of Havre de Grace," *Washington Post,* September 12, 1919.

33. "Harford Handicap Goes to The Porter," *Philadelphia Inquirer,* September 12, 1919.

34. "Current Notes of the Turf," *Daily Racing Form,* September 10, 1919.

35. "At Havre de Grace," *Washington Post,* September 13, 1919.

36. Harry N. Price, "Sir Barton Leads His Stablemates," *Washington Post,* September 14, 1919.

37. "Havre de Grace Entries and Past Performances for Saturday, September 13," *Daily Racing Form,* September 13, 1919.

38. C. Edward Sparrow, "Field Day for Ross," *Baltimore Sun,* September 14, 1919.

39. Price, "Sir Barton Leads His Stablemates."

40. Sparrow, "Field Day for Ross."

41. Ibid.

42. Ibid.

43. "Ross Makes Sweep at Havre de Grace," *New York Times,* September 14, 1919.

44. Price, "Sir Barton Leads His Stablemates."

45. Ibid.

46. W. J. Macbeth, "Juvenile Champion Beats Good Field in $40,000 Race," *New York Tribune,* September 14, 1919.

47. Quoted in ibid.

48. "Mother's Arms for Rider Loftus after Victory in Futurity," *Elmyra Star-Gazette,* September 15, 1919.

49. Macbeth, "Juvenile Champion Beats Good Field in $40,000 Race."

50. "Purchase to Run Here," *Baltimore Sun,* September 22, 1919.

51. "At Havre de Grace," *Washington Post,* September 16, 1919.

52. C. Edward Sparrow, "Ross Colors Fall Again," *Baltimore Sun,* September 25, 1919.

53. "J. F. Schorr's Son of Sweep Shows Way to Sir Barton," *Louisville Courier-Journal,* September 25, 1919.

54. "Turf Chatter," *Ottawa Journal,* September 25, 1919.

55. J. K. M. Ross, *Boots and Saddles: The Story of the Fabulous Ross Stable in the Golden Days of Racing* (New York: Dutton, 1956), 17.

56. "Havre de Grace Form Chart," *Daily Racing Form,* September 28, 1919.

57. A handicapper decides which horses carry which weights. Horses with winning records generally are assigned more weight in an effort to make the contest more egalitarian. Walter Vosburgh was the handicapper for the Jockey Club of New York during Sir Barton's era and generally set the weights that the majority of the racing world would use in assigning weights for their own races.

58. "A Disastrous Day," *Baltimore Evening Sun,* September 16, 1919.

59. "Havre de Grace Form Chart," September 28, 1919.

60. "Cudgel Best in Handicap Run over Fast Track," *Louisville Courier-Journal,* September 28, 1919.

61. "Cudgel's Victory Not Satisfactory," *Louisville Courier-Journal,* September 29, 1919.

62. "Cudgel Is a Winner," *New York Times,* September 28, 1919.

63. "Cudgel Best in Handicap Run over Maryland Track."

64. "Cudgel Runs Fine Race," *Washington Evening Star,* September 28, 1919.

65. Harry N. Price, "Cudgel's Victory Not Satisfactory," *Washington Post,* September 29, 1919.

66. Ibid.

67. "Purchase to Run Here."

10. Break-Up, Shake-Up, Hop

1. "Chicago, Outclassed, Loses First Game 9–1," *Cincinnati Enquirer,* October 2, 1919; "Gameness of My Boys Won, Says Moran; Bad Break Beat Us, Declares Gleason," *Washington Post,* October 2, 1919; Evan Andrews, "The Black Sox Scandal, 95 Years Ago," History.com, n.d., at http://www.history.com/news/the-black-sox-baseball-scandal-95-years-ago, last modified October 9, 2014.

2. "Handicapper Vosburgh's Wisdom," *Daily Racing Form,* October 26, 1919.

3. "Will Retire Sir Barton," *New York Times,* May 30, 1919.

4. Ibid.

5. "Building Track for Own Events," *Washington Times,* November 24, 1919.

6. Mad Hatter was known for having a mind of his own. Jockeys were not allowed to carry a whip when they rode him because he would flinch and bear out or in when hit. He also was inclined to sulk if bumped or would turn in a clunker performance if he did not feel like running that day ("Mad Hatter Temperamental Horse," *Daily Racing Form,* September 1, 1921; "Here and There on the Turf," *Daily Racing Form,* September 27, 1922).

7. "Mad Hatter Shows Form at Jamaica," *New York Times,* September 30, 1919.

8. Harry N. Price, "Last Furlong Rush Beats Mad Hatter Two Lengths," *Washington Post,* October 5, 1919.

9. C. Edward Sparrow, "Barton Is Too Classy," *Baltimore Sun,* October 5, 1919.

10. "Sir Barton Beats Rival, Mad Hatter," *New York Times,* October 5, 1919.

11. Sparrow, "Barton Is Too Classy."

12. "Sir Barton Beats Rival, Mad Hatter."

13. Sparrow, "Barton Is Too Classy."

14. Price, "Last Furlong Rush Beats Mad Hatter Two Lengths."

15. "Sir Barton Beats Rival, Mad Hatter."

16. "Purchase Not in List," *Baltimore Evening Sun*, October 4, 1919.

17. "Heard at Laurel," *Washington Post*, October 9, 1919.

18. "Purchase Goes Lame," *Daily Racing Form*, October 10, 1919.

19. "Autumn Handicap Weights," *Washington Post*, November 1, 1919.

20. Colin [sic], "Ahead of the Hoofbeats," *Washington Post*, November 5, 1919.

21. Dorothy Ours, *Man o' War: A Legend Like Lightning* (New York: St. Martin's Press, 2008), 131.

22. "Pimlico Form Chart," *Daily Racing Form*, November 6, 1919.

23. Ours, *Man o' War*, 131.

24. "Hildreth's Mad Hatter Runs Away from Ross Entry," *Wilmington Morning News*, November 6, 1919; "Pimlico Form Chart," November 6, 1919; Mad Hatter Routs Ross's Sir Barton," *New York Times*, November 6, 1919; Ours, *Man o' War*, 131; "Mad Hatter Wins Maryland Feature Easily Defeating Sir Barton," *Louisville Courier-Journal*, November 6, 1919.

25. Ours, *Man o' War*, 132.

26. "Hildreth's Mad Hatter Runs Away from Ross Entry."

27. Ed Curley, "Is Famous Sir Barton 'Hop' Colt?" *New York American*, March 20, 1920.

28. Bert E. Collyer, "Bedwell Accuses Hildreth of Influencing Loftus," *Collyer's Eye*, November 29, 1919.

29. J. K. M. Ross, *Boots and Saddles: The Story of the Fabulous Ross Stable in the Golden Days of Racing* (New York: Dutton, 1956), 50.

30. Quoted in Curley, "Is Famous Sir Barton 'Hop' Colt?"

31. Ours, *Man o' War*, 138.

32. W. C. Vreeland, "Form Reversals Causing Trouble at Pimlico," *Brooklyn Daily Eagle*, November 8, 1919.

33. Red Smith, "Views of Sport," *Baltimore Sun*, December 4, 1960.

34. Anecdotal evidence from John E. Madden and a veterinarian who treated Sir Barton in 1920 obliquely implies that Lady Sterling, Sir Barton's dam, and Sir Barton may have been hopped. Dr. Frank M. Keller, who worked for the Ross Stable in the early 1920s, suggested that the stable would have been pressured to use such substances in order to keep up with other trainers' methods (Snowden Carter, "Veteran Veterinarian," *Turf and Sport Digest*, February 1962, 12–13, 38). However, this is conjecture only, and no hard evidence about the use of stimulants on either horse exists. Lady Sterling had an inconsistent racing career under several owners, including Madden, who owned her briefly when she was a two-year-old. Keller came on board with the Ross Stable after

Sir Barton's Triple Crown run and could not offer definitive proof about the use of stimulants over the course of the horse's career. Any and all suppositions about Sir Barton's status as a "hopped horse" are just that: conjecture based on rumor.

35. John H. Clark, *Trader Clark: Six Decades of Racing Lore* (Lexington, KY: Thoroughbred Publications, 1991), 214.

36. Vreeland, "Form Reversals Causing Trouble at Pimlico."

37. "Kentucky Derby Winner Annexes Pimlico Serial," *Louisville Courier-Journal*, November 8, 1919.

38. "Scale of Weights for Nov. 1919," *Daily Racing Form*, November 2, 1919.

39. "Pimlico Form Chart," *Daily Racing Form*, November 8, 1919.

40. Vreeland, "Form Reversals Causing Trouble at Pimlico."

41. Harry N. Price, "Sir Barton Runs Improved Race in Winning Serial," *Washington Post*, November 8, 1919; C. Edward Sparrow, "Sir Barton Leads the Way," *Baltimore Sun*, November 8, 1919; "Sir Barton Again in Winning Form," *New York Times*, November 8, 1919.

42. C. Edward Sparrow, "Rounds Out Season Well," *Baltimore Sun*, November 12, 1919.

43. "Pimlico Form Chart," *Daily Racing Form*, November 12, 1919; Sparrow, "Rounds Out Season Well"; "Sir Barton Wins Hollow Victory," *New York Times*, November 12, 1919.

44. Quoted in W. C. Vreeland. "Lucullite Cannot Class with Ross's Sir Barton," *Brooklyn Daily Eagle*, November 12, 1919.

45. Harry N. Price, "Ross Colors to Fore in Serial," *Washington Post*, November 12, 1919.

46. "Another for Sir Barton," *Daily Racing Form*, November 12, 1919.

47. "Ross Colt Is Money Winner on Turf," *Washington Herald*, November 14, 1919.

11. New Year, Same Rivals

1. Star Shoot not only had been the leading sire in the country for five of the previous ten years but had also been in the top twenty continuously since 1905, remaining on that list for almost five years after his death. His progeny won more races and more money than legendary sires of this area, such as Lexington.

2. "John E. Madden to Retire as Breeder of Thoroughbreds," *St. Louis Star and Times*, January 20, 1920.

3. Quoted in "Says Sir Barton King of the Turf," *Ottawa Journal*, November 21, 1919.

4. Quoted in "Racing," *Washington Post,* December 28, 1919.

5. "*Vanity Fair,*" *Encyclopedia Britannica,* n.d., at https://www.britannica.com/topic/Vanity-Fair-American-magazine, last modified March 22, 2018.

6. O'Neil Sevier, "Sir Barton, the Chestnut Hope," *Vanity Fair,* September 1919.

7. "To Get Rich Get Thoroughbreds," *Kingsport Times,* November 28, 1919.

8. Sevier, "Sir Barton, the Chestnut Hope."

9. Both the "three-year-old champion" title and the "Horse of the Year" title for 1919 were retroactively awarded by *Blood-Horse* magazine. During Sir Barton's era, however, they were unofficial designations usually assigned by turf writers and were often dependent on the writers' personal views of the talent that year.

10. "Man O' War Is One of the Greatest Horses Ever Developed in the United States," *Chicago Eagle,* January 31, 1920.

11. Both Woodbine Race Course in Ontario, Canada, and Pimlico Race Course in Maryland currently run a Sir Barton Stakes race. Pimlico's version is run Preakness weekend, and Woodbine runs its in December. Both are 1¹⁄₁₆-mile stakes. In addition, Star Shoot also has a stakes race named in his honor, a six-furlong sprint for fillies, run at Woodbine as well.

12. "Fairgrounds Form Chart," *Daily Racing Form,* January 6, 1920.

13. "Hot Fairground Finishes," *Daily Racing Form,* January 6, 1920.

14. "Four Big Tens in 1919 Racing," *Daily Racing Form,* January 4, 1920.

15. "Ross Stables Equipment of Riders," *Daily Racing Form,* March 20, 1920.

16. W. S. Vosburgh, "Handicap Prospects This Year," *Daily Racing Form,* January 9, 1920.

17. W. C. Vreeland, "Purchase and Sir Barton Rivals for Top Weight Post," *Brooklyn Daily Eagle,* February 1, 1920.

18. "Commander Ross Refuses Huge Sum for Sir Barton," *Nebraska State Journal,* January 4, 1920; J. K. M. Ross, *Boots and Saddles: The Story of the Fabulous Ross Stable in the Golden Days of Racing* (New York: Dutton, 1956), 177.

19. "Kentucky Derby Worth $50,000," *New York Evening World,* January 23, 1920.

20. "Run Preakness to Permit the Derby Starters Entry," *Washington Herald,* March 28, 1920.

21. "Here and There," *New Castle Herald,* April 21, 1920.

22. "No Early Racing for Man O' War," *Daily Racing Form,* February 8, 1920.

23. Dorothy Ours, *Man o' War: A Legend Like Lightning* (New York: St. Martin's Press, 2008), 142.

24. "Public Protected by Jockey Club," *Philadelphia Inquirer,* March 20, 1920.

25. "Johnny Loftus Denied License by Jockey Club," *New York Evening World,* March 18, 1920.

26. Robert L. Ripley, "First under the Wire," *Houston Post,* December 24, 1919; "America's Premier Jockey Has Won Big Stakes," *Harrisburg Telegraph,* January 14, 1920.

27. "Johnny Loftus May Retire," *Wisconsin Rapids Daily Tribune,* February 5, 1920.

28. Ours, *Man o' War,* 133.

29. Henry V. King, "Loftus Is Refused a License to Ride," *New York Herald,* March 18, 1920.

30. Joe Vila, "Maryland Mutuels Placed under Fire," *Philadelphia Inquirer,* March 6, 1920.

31. Lieutenant Colonel Janney is the father of breeder and owner Stuart S. Janney Jr., who bred and owned both the great filly Ruffian and the 1988 Kentucky Derby favorite Private Terms.

32. "Prominent Turfmen," *Cincinnati Enquirer,* March 3, 1920.

33. "Law Makers Face Big Problem over Question of Race Tracks," *Baltimore Sun,* March 6, 1920.

34. "Burke Race Track Bill Is Passed by Maryland Senate," *New York Times,* April 1, 1920.

35. "Ross Horses Are in Shape at Havre de Grace," *Wilmington Morning News,* April 15, 1920.

36. "Current Notes of the Turf," *Daily Racing Form,* March 31, 1920; O'Neil Sevier, "Canadian Holds Whip Hand," *Cincinnati Enquirer,* April 11, 1920.

37. Quoted in "Sir Barton and Billy Kelly Ready," *Daily Racing Form,* April 17, 1920.

38. Speculation about Sir Barton's disposition gives the horse credit for enduring the pain that had to accompany his soft hooves, but no one ever said a champion on the racetrack has to be a placid lover. Dorothy Ours notes similar aggressiveness in Man o' War as a three-year-old (*Man o' War,* 237–38). Perhaps Sir Barton's attitude was more about the need to dominate, a result of his age and instincts.

39. "Sir Barton and Billy Kelly Ready," *Daily Racing Form,* April 17, 1920.

40. "Havre de Grace Form Chart," *Daily Racing Form,* April 20, 1920.

41. "Billy Kelly Romps Home in the Belair Handicap," *New York Herald,* April 20, 1920.

42. Highway, "Billy Kelly Has No Trouble in Capturing Belair Stakes," *Washington Herald,* April 20, 1920.

43. "Billy Kelly Romps Home in the Belair Handicap."

44. "Billy Kelly Wins Sprint," *Louisville Courier-Journal,* April 20, 1920.

45. "Havre de Grace Form Chart," *Daily Racing Form,* April 25, 1920.

46. "Commander Ross Scores a Double," *Brooklyn Daily Eagle,* April 25, 1920; "Sandy Beal Beats Derby Candidates," *New York Herald,* April 25, 1920; "Sandy Beal, a Long Shot, Captures Chesapeake Stakes," *Washington Herald,* April 25, 1920.

47. C. Edward Sparrow, "Careful Lands Stakes," *Baltimore Sun,* April 28, 1920; "Careful Captures Aberdeen Stakes," *New York Times,* April 28, 1920; "Sir Barton Takes Mud from Two Others," *Philadelphia Inquirer,* April 28, 1920.

48. "Oaks Won by Clintonville," *Cincinnati Enquirer,* April 28, 1920.

49. "Sir Barton Takes Mud from Two Others."

50. "Havre de Grace Form Chart," *Daily Racing Form,* May 1, 1920.

51. "Crystal Ford Wins and Pays $214.40," *New York Herald,* May 1, 1920; C. Edward Sparrow, "Pulls a Royce Rools," *Baltimore Sun,* May 1, 1920; "Crystal Ford Pays Backers 106 to 1," *New York Times,* May 1, 1920.

52. "Ruling against A. G. Blakely," *Daily Racing Form,* May 9, 1919.

53. "Crystal Ford at $214 for $2 Captures Philadelphia Stakes," *Washington Herald,* May 1, 1920.

54. "Crystal Ford Wins and Pays $214.40."

55. "Turf Stars Make Way for Outsider in Feature Race," *Washington Post,* May 1, 1920.

56. Bert Collyer, "Collyer's Comment on the Sport of Kings," *Washington Herald,* May 4, 1920.

57. "Saratoga Favorites' Day," *Daily Racing Form,* August 4, 1920.

12. Records and Matches

1. W. C. Vreeland, "Sir Barton Rated Best in Weights for the Suburban," *Brooklyn Daily Eagle,* June 2, 1920.

2. "Weights for the Suburban Handicap," *Daily Racing Form,* June 4, 1920.

3. W. C. Vreeland, "Lucullite Cannot Class with Ross's Sir Barton," *Brooklyn Daily Eagle,* November 12, 1919.

4. A. L. Bronson, "Preakness Stake Tuesday Will Feature Closing Day of Spring Meeting," *Pittsburgh Daily Post,* May 16, 1920.

5. "Rich Preakness Stakes Tuesday," *Daily Racing Form,* May 15, 1920.

6. "King Thrush Easy Winner at Pimlico," *New York Herald,* May 7, 1920.

7. "Boniface Still Winning," *Daily Racing Form,* May 6, 1920.

8. Dorothy Ours, *Man o' War: A Legend Like Lightning* (New York: St. Martin's Press, 2008), 145–46.

9. Harry N. Price, "Man o' War Gallops Off with the Preakness in Close to Track-Record Time," *Washington Post,* May 19, 1920.

10. A. L. Bronson, "Rich Preakness Stakes Features Closing Day at Pimlico Track," *Pittsburgh Daily Post,* May 18, 1920.

11. "Preakness Easy for Man O' War," *Philadelphia Inquirer,* May 19, 1920.

12. Price, "Man o' War Gallops Off with the Preakness."

13. Ours, *Man o' War,* 171.

14. "Only a Gallop for Star Colt," *Louisville Courier-Journal,* May 19, 1920.

15. Ours, *Man o' War,* 161.

16. Quoted in "Noted Sportsmen Stamp Man o' War as World's Greatest Thoroughbred," *New York Herald,* May 30, 1920.

17. Quoted in ibid.

18. Ours, *Man o' War,* 167.

19. W. C. Vreeland, "Riddle's Star Colt Runs 1⅜ Miles in for Mark of 2:14⅕," *Brooklyn Daily Eagle,* June 13, 1920.

20. Ours, *Man o' War,* 177.

21. Daniel [*sic*], "High Lights and Shadows in All Spheres of Sport," *New York Herald,* June 23, 1920.

22. Ours, *Man o' War,* 179.

23. Ibid., 182, 184.

24. Ibid., 185.

25. Ibid., 185, 186.

26. Ibid., 186–87; "Man o' War Again Sets World Mark," *New York Times,* July 11, 1920.

27. W. C. Vreeland, "Man o' War Proves Himself Super Horse of All Times," *Brooklyn Daily Eagle,* July 11, 1920.

28. "Thirty Leading Winning Owners," *Daily Racing Form,* July 11, 1920.

29. "Imposts for Saturday's Rich Race," *Daily Racing Form,* May 19, 1920.

30. "Sir Barton on Way Here to Run in Big Handicap," *Louisville Courier-Journal,* May 20, 1920.

31. "East and West to Clash Again," *Louisville Courier-Journal,* May 22, 1920.

32. "Crack Racer Purchase Breaks Down," *Daily Racing Form,* May 22, 1920.

33. "Warming Up at Saratoga," *Daily Racing Form,* July 30, 1920.

34. "Saratoga Handicap Horses," *Daily Racing Form,* July 28, 1920.

35. W. C. Vreeland, "Saratoga Ready for Sport of Kings, Opens Tomorrow," *Brooklyn Daily Eagle,* August 1, 1920.

36. "Sir Barton Sets New Track Record," *New York Times,* August 3, 1920; "Saratoga Shakes Off Lethargy for Gala Opening; Horses Ready," *Washington Herald,* August 2, 1920.

37. "Saratoga Form Chart," *Daily Racing Form,* August 3, 1920.

38. W. C. Vreeland, "Racing Shift to the Spa May Be Beneficial to All," *Brooklyn Daily Eagle,* August 2, 1920.

39. J. L. Dempsey, "'Comeback' for Sir Barton," *Cincinnati Enquirer,* August 3, 1920.

40. Ibid.

41. "Sir Barton Sets New Track Record."

42. "Belmont Park Entries," *Daily Racing Form,* June 28, 1913.

43. "World Record for Whisk Broom," *New York Times,* June 29, 1913.

44. "Whisk Broom's Record of 2.00 Flat Will Stand," *St. Louis Post-Dispatch,* July 3, 1913.

45. J. K. M. Ross, *Boots and Saddles: The Story of the Fabulous Ross Stable in the Golden Days of Racing* (New York: Dutton, 1956), 192.

46. Quoted in ibid.

47. Ibid., 174.

48. "Sir Barton Sets a New Track Record," *New York Times,* August 3, 1920.

49. Ibid.

50. "Great Showing by Sir Barton at Saratoga," *Pittsburgh Daily Post,* August 2, 1920.

51. "Handicap Event at Saratoga Won by Sir Barton," *Bennington Banner,* August 2, 1920.

52. Henry V. King, "Sir Barton Fast with Weight Up," *Sun and New York Herald,* August 2, 1920.

53. "Sir Barton Sets a New Track Record."

54. Quoted in Vincent Treanor, "Sir Barton's Feat," *New York Evening World,* August 3, 1920.

55. Quoted in Henry V. King, "Saratoga Track Lightning Fast," *New York Herald,* August 4, 1920.

13. Lighting the Match

1. Henry V. King, "Kummer Injured in Spill at Aqueduct," *New York Herald,* July 13, 1920; W. C. Vreeland, "Jockeys Kummer and Barrett Escape Death by a Few Inches," *Brooklyn Daily Eagle,* July 13, 1920.

2. "Crack Jockey Badly Injured," *Louisville Courier-Journal,* July 13, 1920.

3. Dorothy Ours, *Man o' War: A Legend Like Lightning* (New York: St. Martin's Press, 2008), 189.

4. In this era before unions and other employee advocacy organizations, jockeys often would be under contract to a particular stable or owner. Akin to

a baseball or football player's contract, the agreement between a rider and an owner meant that the owner had first call on the rider for any given race and then could outline for whom, where, and when that jockey might ride outside of the contract holder's mounts. Because Ross held Sande's contract, he had first call for Sande's services and thus had to give permission for Sande to ride Man o' War in the Miller.

5. Ours, *Man o' War*, 196.

6. "Man o' War Romps to Easy Victory," *New York Times*, August 8, 1920; Ours, *Man o' War*, 197.

7. Quoted in Ours, *Man o' War*, 198.

8. Quoted in "'Greatest Race Horse,' Says Jockey Sande," *Sun and New York Herald*, August 8, 1920.

9. "Sir Barton Shows Sparkling Race to Fort Erie," *Buffalo Express*, August 12, 1920.

10. "Sir Barton Faces Severe Test Today at Fort Erie," *Buffalo Commercial*, August 12, 1920.

11. "Sir Barton Shows Sparkling Race to Fort Erie."

12. "Ross Stable Wins Dominion Handicap," *Buffalo Enquirer*, August 12, 1920; "Sir Barton in Front," *Cincinnati Enquirer*, August 12, 1920; "Sir Barton Led All the Way in Dominion Handicap," *Buffalo Commercial*, August 12, 1920.

13. "Sir Barton Led All the Way in Dominion Handicap."

14. Quoted in "Sir Barton Shows Sparkling Race to Fort Erie."

15. "New Track Record," *Cincinnati Enquirer*, August 13, 1920.

16. Quoted in Vincent Treanor, "Feustel Calls Bedwell's Bluff on Man O' War–Sir Barton Race," *New York Evening World*, August 17, 1920.

17. Quoted in ibid.

18. Ibid.

19. Quoted in "Man o' War Ready to Meet Sir Barton," *New York Herald*, August 17, 1920.

20. Quoted in ibid.

21. Ours, *Man o' War*, 203.

22. "Man o' War Beats Grier with Ease," *New York Times*, August 22, 1920; Ours, *Man o' War*, 204.

23. "Man o' War Is Invincible," *Daily Racing Form*, August 22, 1920.

24. "Gnome Bred in the Purple," *Daily Racing Form*, August 19, 1920.

25. Ibid. Samuel Ross was not related to Commander Ross.

26. "Gnome Bred in the Purple."

27. "Champion Juvenile Filly," *Daily Racing Form*, August 28, 1920.

28. J. L. Dempsey, "New Mark Set by Sir Barton," *Cincinnati Enquirer*, August 29, 1920.

29. Henry V. King, "Sir Barton Wins in Record Time," *New York Herald*,

August 29, 1920; W. C. Vreeland, "Commodore Ross's Star Runs Smashing Race at Saratoga," *Brooklyn Daily Eagle*, August 29, 1920.

30. "Sir Barton Sets New World Mark," *New York Times*, August 29, 1920.

31. "World's Record Set by Sir Barton at Saratoga," *Pittsburgh Daily Post*, August 29, 1920; Vreeland, "Commodore Ross's Star Runs Smashing Race at Saratoga."

32. King, "Sir Barton Wins in Record Time"; Vreeland, "Commodore Ross's Star Runs Smashing Race at Saratoga"; "World's Record Set by Sir Barton at Saratoga."

33. Henry V. King, "Sir Barton Wins in Record Time," *New York Herald*, August 29, 1920; "Sir Barton Sets New World Mark," *New York Times*, August 29, 1920; "World's Record Set by Sir Barton at Saratoga."

34. Vreeland, "Commodore Ross's Star Runs Smashing Race at Saratoga."

35. Ours, *Man o' War*, 205.

36. Vreeland, "Commodore Ross's Star Runs Smashing Race at Saratoga."

37. Daniel [*sic*], "High Lights and Shadows in All Spheres of Sport," *New York Herald*, August 30, 1920.

38. Ours, *Man o' War*, 205; W. C. Vreeland, "Man o' War Races 1⅝ Miles in 2.40⅘, a World Record," *Brooklyn Daily Eagle*, September 5, 1920.

39. Vreeland, "Man o' War Races 1⅝ Miles in 2.40⅘, a World Record."

40. Ours, *Man o' War*, 213.

41. Ours, *Man o' War*, 209; Henry V. King, "Man o' War Makes a New World Record," *New York Herald*, September 5, 1920; C. J. Fitz Gerald, "Man O' War, Turf Idol and Sire," *The Field Illustrated*, July 1925; "World Mark Again Set by Man o' War," *New York Times*, September 5, 1920.

42. "Lion D'Or Had to Make Fast Time to Win Fall Highweight Handicap," *New York Evening World*, September 7, 1920.

43. Quoted in "Will Not Meet Saturday," *Daily Racing Form*, September 7, 1920.

44. "Seek Test of Champions," *New York Times*, September 5, 1920.

45. Quoted in Henry V. King, "Lion D'Or Defeats High Class Rivals," *New York Herald*, September 7, 1920.

46. W. C. Vreeland, "Sir Barton, Travel Weary, 'Dodges' Man o' War," *Brooklyn Daily Eagle*, September 7, 1920.

47. "Belmont Form Chart, Fourth Race," *Daily Racing Form*, September 12, 1920.

48. "An Outsider's Futurity," *Daily Racing Form*, September 12, 1920.

49. Ours, *Man o' War*, 218.

50. "Ross Agrees to Match Colt against Man O' War," *Louisville Courier-Journal*, September 6, 1920.

51. O'Neil Sevier, "Big Sums Going to Owners," *Cincinnati Enquirer,* September 12, 1920.

52. Ours, *Man o' War,* 219.

53. "Layers Get a Drubbing," *Daily Racing Form*, January 7, 1914.

54. "Triple Victory to Bedwell Stable," *The Gazette* (Montreal, Quebec), September 5, 1916; "Kenilworth Park Form Chart," *Daily Racing Form*, July 27, 1917; "Kenilworth Park Form Chart," *Daily Racing Form*, July 31, 1917.

55. "Offer Purse of $50,000," *Charlotte News,* September 17, 1920; "Havre de Grace Notes," *Washington Post,* September 24, 1920; "Much Interest in Horse Race," *Vancouver Daily World,* September 23, 1920.

56. "Man O' War to Race Sir Barton in Canada," *New York Herald,* September 25, 1920.

57. Ibid.

58. "Winn Makes $75,000 Offer," *Louisville Courier-Journal,* September 24, 1920.

59. "Man O' War and Sir Barton to Race for $75,000," *New York Evening World,* September 25, 1920.

60. "Detroit All Agog over Man o' War Sir Barton Race," *Brooklyn Daily Eagle,* September 29, 1920.

61. "Canada Will Have Great Match Race," *Buffalo Express,* September 26, 1920.

14. Rendezvous with Destiny

1. J. K. M. Ross, *Boots and Saddles: The Story of the Fabulous Ross Stable in the Golden Days of Racing* (New York: Dutton, 1956), 207.

2. W. C. Vreeland, "Man o' War and Sir Barton Should Race in the U.S.A.," *Brooklyn Daily Eagle,* September 27, 1920.

3. "Comment on the Current Events of Sport: Turf," *New York Times,* September 27, 1920.

4. Ross, *Boots and Saddles,* 207.

5. C. Edward Sparrow, "World's Biggest Race to Be Run in Canada," *Baltimore Sun,* September 25, 1920.

6. "Man o' War, Pulled to a Canter, Beats Sir Barton and Drinks from Gold Cup," *New York Herald,* October 13, 1920.

7. Dorothy Ours, *Man o' War: A Legend Like Lightning* (New York: St. Martin's Press, 2008), 232.

8. "Kummer to Get $5000 to Ride Man o' War," *Philadelphia Evening Public Ledger,* September 30, 1920.

9. Ross, *Boots and Saddles,* 212.

10. "Winn Offers $75,000 for Man o' War Race at Latonia Course," *Cincinnati Enquirer,* September 24, 1920.

11. "Great Racing Champions to Meet in Canada," *Bourbon News,* October 1, 1920.

12. Ross, *Boots and Saddles,* 204.

13. "Winn Makes $75,000 Offer," *Louisville Courier-Journal,* September 24, 1920.

14. "Highlights and Shadows in All Spheres of Sport," *Sun and New York Herald,* September 30, 1920.

15. Ross, *Boots and Saddles,* 208–9.

16. Ours, *Man o' War,* 229.

17. "Record Crowd Will See Race," *Detroit Free Press,* October 3, 1920.

18. "Comparison of Champions," *Daily Racing Form,* September 28, 1920.

19. "Dodgers Will Use Left Hand Pitchers," *Philadelphia Inquirer,* September 30, 1920; Ross, *Boots and Saddles,* 217; "Rumor That Sir Barton Has Gone Lame Brings a Denial," *New York Times,* October 4, 1920.

20. Ours, *Man o' War,* 233–34.

21. In the fall of 1920, a grand jury investigated the alleged fixing of the 1919 World Series, known as the "Black Sox scandal." See note 3 in chapter 5.

22. "Match Race to Be Man O' War's Last," *New York Times,* October 3, 1920.

23. "Record Crowd Will See Race," *Detroit Free Press,* October 3, 1920.

24. Ours, *Man o' War,* 234.

25. "Sir Barton in Workout Sets Remarkable Pace," *St. Louis Dispatch,* October 4, 1920.

26. W. C. Vreeland, "Vibrate Shakes Up Dry Moon and Lands Big Bet for Owner," *Brooklyn Daily Eagle,* October 5, 1920.

27. "Spread False Story about Sir Barton," *Buffalo Commercial,* October 5, 1920.

28. Quoted in "Rumor That Sir Barton Has Gone Lame Brings a Denial."

29. Ross, *Boots and Saddles,* 211.

30. The late William Nack, former *Sports Illustrated* writer and author of books such as *Secretariat: The Making of a Champion* (New York: Da Capo, 2002) (formerly titled *Big Red of Meadow Stable* and first published in 1975), knew trainer Hollie Hughes. A Hall of Famer who had trained 1916 Kentucky Derby winner George Smith, Hughes was part of the racing scene during Sir Barton's era. Hughes told Nack that Sir Barton was sore while he was training for the match race and therefore was not the horse he could have been when he met Man o' War at Kenilworth (William Nack, interviewed by the author, Huntsville, AL, April 2015).

31. W. C. Vreeland, "Rumor Says Sir Barton Is Sore; He May Not Race Man o' War," *Brooklyn Daily Eagle,* October 4, 1920.

32. Ours, *Man o' War,* 234.

33. Richard J. Beamish, "Man O' War Ready for $80,000 Match," *Philadelphia Inquirer,* October 6, 1920.

34. Quoted in "Royal Racers May Set a New Record in $80,000 Match," *St. Louis Stars and Times,* October 6, 1920.

35. "Man o' War Left Belmont Park for Windsor to Meet Sir Barton," *Nebraska State Journal,* October 7, 1920.

36. Ross, *Boots and Saddles,* 210.

37. Interestingly, multiple news outlets mentioned everyone who accompanied Sir Barton on his trip to Kenilworth, including this canine mascot "Wolf" (see, for instance, "Keogh's Ride Big Help to Veteran," *Washington Post,* October 7, 1920). But J. K. M. Ross writes in *Boots and Saddles* that Sir Barton eschewed all companionship, including that of stable pets, such as the assorted cats and dogs and other animals that one might see in any barn (119). This is the only time such a pet for the Triple Crown winner was mentioned. Likely, if Ross's account of Sir Barton's personality is to be believed, the dog was more of a companion for the humans than for the horse. Conversely, it is always possible that Sir Barton actually did have at least one stable pet and that Jim Ross's perceptions of his father's champion might be incomplete.

38. "Monarchs of the Turf Are at Kenilworth for Final Workouts," *St. Louis Star and Times,* October 8, 1920.

39. Ours, *Man o' War,* 233.

40. "Man o' War Off in Style with Six Attendants for $75,000 Match Race October 12," *New York Evening World,* October 7, 1920.

41. "40,000 Will See Turf Kings in Big Race Next Week," *St. Louis Star and Times,* October 5, 1920; "Champions to Have Special Guards," *Daily Racing Form,* September 29, 1920.

42. "Man O' War and His Rival Reach Track," *New York Times,* October 8, 1920.

43. "Monarchs of the Turf Are at Kenilworth for Final Workouts."

44. "Great Racers Show Speed in Workouts," *New York Times,* October 9, 1920.

45. Quoted in "Hundreds Entrain for Champion Race," *Philadelphia Inquirer,* October 11, 1920.

46. Quoted in "Man o' War Breezes Easy Quarter in 22⅘ at Kenilworth Track," *St. Louis Star and Times,* October 9, 1920.

47. Quoted in "Man o' War at Windsor for Special Race," *New York Evening World,* October 8, 1920.

48. W. J. Macbeth, "Sir Barton's Time Bettered by Man o' War," *New York Tribune*, October 10, 1920.

49. "All Ready for the Big Race," *Daily Racing Form*, October 10, 1920.

50. W. J. Macbeth, "Man o' War 7–5 Favorite in $75,000 Race Tomorrow," *New York Tribune*, October 11, 1920.

51. "All Ready for the Big Race."

52. Ibid.

53. Quoted in Macbeth, "Sir Barton's Time Bettered by Man o' War."

54. Quoted in ibid.

55. "Man O' War's Great Test Comes Today," *New York Times*, October 12, 1920.

15. Spectacle

1. "Dempsey Defeats Willard," History.com, n.d., at http://www.history.com/this-day-in-history/dempsey-defeats-willard, accessed March 1, 2018.

2. Dorothy Ours, *Man o' War: A Legend Like Lightning* (New York: St. Martin's Press, 2008), 74.

3. Ibid., 239.

4. "7–5 Offered against Sir Barton's Chances in Kenilworth Race," *St. Louis Star and Times*, October 11, 1920.

5. J. K. M. Ross, *Boots and Saddles: The Story of the Fabulous Ross Stable in the Golden Days of Racing* (New York: Dutton, 1956), 207.

6. Ours, *Man o' War*, 241; Ross, *Boots and Saddles*, 207.

7. Ross, *Boots and Saddles*, 213.

8. Ours, *Man o' War*, 242.

9. Ibid.

10. "Man O' War Victor over Sir Barton by Seven Lengths," *New York Times*, October 13, 1920.

11. Ibid.

12. Ibid.

13. "Crowds Gather to See Turf Classic," *New York Times*, October 11, 1920.

14. "Man o' War's Great Test Comes Today," *New York Times*, October 12, 1920.

15. The admission of $5 in 1920 would be equivalent to around $60 today.

16. "7–5 Offered against Sir Barton's Chances in Kenilworth Race."

17. Ellis C. Abrams, "Monarchs of the Track Match Speed Today," *Philadelphia Inquirer*, October 12, 1920; Ours, *Man o' War*, 241; "Man o' War's Great Test Comes Today."

18. Quoted in Vincent Treanor, "Great Horses and Jockeys Are Ready for

Bugle Call in $75,000 Match Race," *New York Evening World*, October 12, 1920.

19. Ours, *Man o' War*, 243.

20. Ross, *Boots and Saddles*, 213.

21. "Man o' War Victor over Sir Barton by Seven Lengths."

22. "Man o' War in Glorious Triumph," *Daily Racing Form*, October 13, 1920.

23. Ours, *Man o' War*, 244.

24. Ross, *Boots and Saddles*, 214.

25. Ibid.

26. Quoted in Charles B. Parmer, *For Gold and Glory: The Story of Thoroughbred Racing in America* (New York: Carrick and Evans, 1939), 191.

27. Henry V. King, "Man o' War, Pulled to a Canter, Beats Sir Barton and Drinks from Gold Cup," *New York Tribune*, October 13, 1920.

28. John Hervey, "The Turf Career of Man o' War," *The Horse*, series published from August 1959 to August 1961.

29. Quoted in Ross, *Boots and Saddles*, 214. J. K. M. Ross says in *Boots and Saddles* that Commander Ross gave his statement at noon (214). Although the statement might have been drafted about that time, according to the *New York Times* it came about an hour before the race, which was the fourth race on the day's card, scheduled for 3:30 p.m. ("Man o' War Victor over Sir Barton by Seven Lengths," *New York Times*, October 13, 1920).

30. Henry V. King, "Sir Barton Wins in Record Time," *New York Herald*, August 29, 1920.

31. "A Big Day Up North," February 1971, clipping, Selima Room, Prince George's County Memorial Library System, Prince George's County, MD.

32. "Man o' War Victor over Sir Barton by Seven Lengths."

33. Ross, *Boots and Saddles*, 214–15.

34. Henry V. King, "Man o' War Romps In," *Washington Post*, October 13, 1920.

35. Ours, *Man o' War*, 246; "Man o' War Victor over Sir Barton by Seven Lengths."

36. "Man o' War's Great Test Comes Today."

37. King, "Man o' War, Pulled to a Canter, Beats Sir Barton and Drinks from Gold Cup."

38. Ibid.

39. Quoted in ibid.

40. King, "Man o' War Romps In."

41. Hervey, "The Turf Career of Man o' War."

42. Man o' War was measured at 16.2 hands, or about five feet six inches, at the withers. Sir Barton was about 15.2 hands, or five feet two inches at the withers.

43. King, "Man o' War, Pulled to a Canter, Beats Sir Barton and Drinks from Gold Cup."

44. King, "Man o' War Romps In."

45. "Man o' War Victor over Sir Barton by Seven Lengths."

46. Hervey, "The Turf Career of Man o' War."

47. King, "Man o' War Romps In."

48. Ross, *Boots and Saddles,* 215.

49. Ibid., 215–16.

50. Hervey, "The Turf Career of Man o' War."

51. Ross, *Boots and Saddles,* 216.

52. Ibid.

53. Hervey, "The Turf Career of Man o' War."

54. Ross, *Boots and Saddles,* 216.

55. King, "Man o' War Romps In."

56. Ross, *Boots and Saddles,* 216–17.

57. King, "Man o' War Romps In."

58. "30,000 Saw Man o' War Capture Race," *Quad City Times,* October 13, 1920.

59. Quoted in King, "Man o' War Romps In."

60. Quoted in ibid.

61. Ross, *Boots and Saddles,* 217.

62. Ibid.

63. "Winn Offers $50,000 Purse," *Louisville Courier-Journal,* October 14, 1920.

64. Ross, *Boots and Saddles,* 217.

65. Quoted in "Sir Barton's Owner Praises Man o' War," *Oregon Daily Journal,* October 13, 1920.

16. Aftermath

1. Dorothy Ours, *Man o' War: A Legend Like Lightning* (New York: St. Martin's Press, 2008), 258–61.

2. "Cheaper Grade of Horses," *Daily Racing Form,* October 16, 1920.

3. "Sir Barton, Canadian Horse, Loser to Man o' War in Winsor [*sic*] Race," *Galveston Daily News,* October 20, 1920.

4. "Jockey Sande Severs Relations with Ross," *Washington Post,* October 14, 1920.

5. "Earl Sande Considering Big Offer to Ride for Hildreth," *New York Times,* October 19, 1920.

6. W. C. Vreeland, "Hilltop Track Patrons Peeved over Lord Herbert," *Brooklyn Daily Eagle,* October 19, 1920.

7. "Earl Sande Considering Big Offer to Ride for Hildreth."

8. "Jockey Sande Will Ride for Sam Hildreth," *Buffalo Commercial,* October 21, 1920.

9. "Best Horses of Older Division," *Daily Racing Form,* November 12, 1920.

10. "Second Stable of This Year," *Daily Racing Form,* December 4, 1920.

11. "Blazes Wins Again," *Cincinnati Enquirer,* October 24, 1920.

12. "Parr's Blazes Lands Second Laurel Stake," *Baltimore Sun,* October 24, 1920.

13. "Blazes Is First in Laurel Stake," *Philadelphia Inquirer,* October 24, 1920.

14. "Blazes Is Winner over Sir Barton at Laurel," *Brooklyn Daily Eagle,* October 24, 1920.

15. "Blazes Wins Big Race," *Washington Evening Star,* October 24, 1920.

16. "Sir Barton Badly Beaten at Laurel by Parr's Blazes," *Wilmington Morning News,* October 25, 1920.

17. "*The Race of the Age,*" *Washington Herald,* October 31, 1920.

18. "Man o' War on the Screen," *Philadelphia Inquirer,* October 31, 1920.

19. "*The Race of the Age.*"

20. "Pimlico Form Chart," *Daily Racing Form,* November 6, 1920.

21. "Buddy Ensor Puts Winner Over in New Track Record," *Washington Post,* November 6, 1920.

22. "Mad Hatter, in Record Victory, Defeats Barton," *New York Tribune,* November 6, 1920.

23. W. C. Vreeland, "Mad Hatter Evens Up the Score against Sir Barton," *Brooklyn Daily Eagle,* November 6, 1920.

24. "Mad Hatter Good Just Now," *New York Evening World,* November 6, 1920.

25. "Pimlico Form Chart," *Daily Racing Form,* November 11, 1920.

26. "Barton Beaten by Kelly in Close Race," *New York Tribune,* November 11, 1920.

27. "Billy Kelly Lowers Sir Barton's Colors," *Philadelphia Inquirer,* November 11, 1920.

28. Ibid.; "Honest Billy Kelly Runs Greatest Race," *Baltimore Sun,* November 11, 1920.

29. "Although Beaten by Man o' War, Sir Barton Is Still the Star of the Older Horses of the Turf," *Winnipeg Tribune,* November 12, 1920.

30. "Best Horses of Older Division."

31. Ibid.

32. J. K. M. Ross, *Boots and Saddles: The Story of the Fabulous Ross Stable in the Golden Days of Racing* (New York: Dutton, 1956), 220.

33. "Second Stable of This Year," *Daily Racing Form*, December 4, 1920.

34. Ibid.

35. Jockey Club, "History of the Jockey Club," JockeyClub.com, n.d., at http://www.jockeyclub.com/Default.asp?section=About&area=0, accessed September 19, 2017.

36. "$12,000 Salary's a Mere Bagatelle to Shilling, Best American Jockey Owns Most of Paris, Texas," *Wichita Beacon,* July 6, 1912.

37. "Stabbed by Jockey Shilling," *New York Sun,* November 1, 1909.

38. "Revoke Shilling's License," *Washington Post,* October 21, 1912.

39. "At the Kentucky Derby Race Track: Watermelon Attracts Attention," *Muncie Star Press,* April 13, 1914.

40. Ross, *Boots and Saddles,* 146.

41. "Monarchs of Track Match Speed Today," *Philadelphia Inquirer,* October 12, 1920.

42. W. C. Vreeland, "Rival Turf Authorities May Clash over Shilling," *Brooklyn Daily Eagle,* November 2, 1920.

43. W. C. Vreeland, "Turf War Is in Sight If Shilling Obtains License," *Brooklyn Daily Eagle,* November 11, 1920.

44. "Stewards Refuse to Allow Shilling to Ride at Pimlico," *Washington Post,* November 11, 1920.

45. W. C. Vreeland, "Armistice Declared between Turf Solons," *Brooklyn Daily Eagle,* November 12, 1920.

46. "J. P. Kennedy Attacked by Pimlico Fans," *Baltimore Sun,* November 12, 1920.

47. Ibid.

48. Vreeland, "Turf War Is in Sight If Shilling Obtains License."

49. C. Edward Sparrow, "Turf War May Follow Ruling over Shilling," *Baltimore Sun,* November 11, 1920.

50. Vreeland, "Armistice Declared between Turf Solons."

51. "Racing Commission Scores Ross," *Baltimore Evening Sun,* November 12, 1920.

52. "Shilling Will Not Ride, Asserts Ross," *Philadelphia Inquirer,* November 13, 1920.

53. "Maryland Racing Commission and Jockey Club to Meet Wednesday," *Baltimore Sun,* October 14, 1920.

54. "Shilling Withdraws Request for License," *Baltimore Sun,* November 19, 1920.

55. "Shilling Is Still on the Ground," *Cincinnati Enquirer,* November 19, 1920.

56. "Jockey Club's Stewards Not Forced to Make a Decision," *Washington Post,* November 19, 1920.

57. Ibid.

58. C. Edward Sparrow, "Shilling and Horsemen Violated Turf Ethics," *Baltimore Sun,* November 22, 1920.

59. "Revoke Shilling's License."

60. "Worth Ruined as a Racer," *Daily Racing Form,* November 7, 1912; C. Edward Sparrow, "Shilling and Horsemen Violated Turf Ethics," *Baltimore Sun,* November 22, 1920.

61. "At the Feedbox," *Baltimore Sun,* March 6, 1920.

62. Ibid.

63. "License Granted to Louis Feustel," *New York Herald,* March 31, 1921.

64. "Feustel Granted Trainer's License," *Philadelphia Inquirer,* March 31, 1921.

65. August Belmont Jr. to William P. Riggs, April 27, 1921, Belmont Family Papers, Rare Book and Manuscript Library, Columbia University, New York.

66. Ours, *Man o' War,* 262.

67. "Fight to Finish Is Now Facing Racing Board," *Baltimore Sun,* April 12, 1921.

68. "Feustel Gets License from Jockey Club," *New York Tribune,* March 31, 1921.

69. "Ross Gets New Trainer," *Washington Evening Star,* April 16, 1921; C. Edward Sparrow, "Ross and Guy Bedwell Sever Turf Relations," *Baltimore Sun,* April 20, 1921.

70. Ross, *Boots and Saddles,* 221.

71. "Work-Outs at Havre de Grace," *Daily Racing Form,* April 16, 1921.

72. "To Retire Sir Barton to Stud," *Daily Racing Form,* April 23, 1921.

73. "Best Pal Scores in Feature," *Cincinnati Enquirer,* April 24, 1921.

74. "Famous Sir Barton Is Sold by Ross," *New York Times,* August 13, 1921. Some sources reported the sum to be up to $150,000, but other sources have the Jones brothers paying $75,000 for the Triple Crown winner.

75. "Sir Barton Now in Virginia," *Baltimore Sun,* September 18, 1921.

17. Good-bye, Sammy

1. J. K. M. Ross, *Boots and Saddles: The Story of the Fabulous Ross Stable in the Golden Days of Racing* (New York: Dutton, 1956), 119.

2. Deena Maloy, *Voices Linger at Old Audley* (Berryville, VA: self-published, 2008), 28.

3. "Hinata Is Won by Furbelow," *Cincinnati Enquirer,* April 27, 1919.

4. "Montfort Jones' Colors Carried to Victory by Thelma E. in Beldame Handicap," *Daily Racing Form,* September 23, 1919.

5. St. Henry was supposed to have been "Sir Henry," following in the

footsteps of both Sir Martin and Sir Barton, other Lady Sterling foals. When this horse was registered, however, he was mistakenly registered as "St." instead of "Sir."

6. Maloy, *Voices Linger,* 28–29.

7. Ibid., 28–29, 30, 31–32.

8. The Jones brothers would go on to buy John E. Madden's share of Sir Barton. The terms of the sale were reported to include Sir Barton splitting his time between Audley and Hamburg Place, but no records survive to indicate whether that plan was followed or not. An article in *The Blood-Horse* in 1949 indicates that Sir Barton possibly stood for a time at Riverview Farm, owned by B. B. Jones's friend Lucien Moseley, in Hopkinsville, Kentucky ("Sir Barton: An Able Performer, First Winner of Triple Crown," *The Blood-Horse,* February 12, 1949). That Sir Barton may have spent some time in Kentucky is supported by a letter to Gordon Turner from Tom Morgan, one of Sir Barton's grooms at Audley (undated, Jim Bolus Collection, Kentucky Derby Museum, Louisville, KY).

9. In his letter to Gordon Turner, Tom Morgan claimed that the price paid was $110,000 (undated, Jim Bolus Collection). An article in the *Kentucky Advocate* quoted the price as being around $150,000 ("Sir Barton Sold," *Kentucky Advocate,* August 18, 1921).

10. Marvin Drager, with Ed McNamara, *The Most Glorious Crown: The Story of America's Triple Crown Thoroughbreds from Sir Barton to American Pharoah* (Chicago: Triumph Books, 2005), 19, quoting Hobson McGehee, former manager of Audley Farm.

11. Margaret Phipps Leonard, "A Derby Winner's Odyssey," *The Horse* 19, no. 3 (1938): 14.

12. Avalyn Hunter, *American Classic Pedigrees (1914–2002)* (Lexington, KY: Eclipse Press, 2003), 43.

13. "Sir Barton," Equineline, n.d., at https://www.equineline.com/, accessed March 5, 2018.

14. J. A. Estes, "The Story of Sir Barton," *The Blood-Horse,* November 20, 1937.

15. Maloy, *Voices Linger,* 36, 37.

16. Ibid., 47.

17. Edward L. Bowen, *Legacies of the Turf: A Century of Great Thoroughbred Breeders,* vol. 1 (Lexington, KY: Eclipse Press, 2003), 35; Edward L. Bowen, *Masters of the Turf: Ten Trainers Who Dominated Horse Racing's Golden Age* (Lexington, KY: Eclipse Press, 2007), 133.

18. Bowen, *Legacies of the Turf,* 1:35.

19. John E. Madden bred five Kentucky Derby winners: Old Rosebud (1914), Sir Barton (1919), Paul Jones (1920), Zev (1923), and Flying Ebony (1925).

20. John. E. Madden, "The Army Remount and Artillery Horse," *Thoroughbred Record,* January 11, 1913.

21. The Quartermaster Corps, among other functions, develops, produces, and acquires supplies for the United States Army, including materials such as gasoline, water, and food. From 1908 to 1951, the Remount Service was part of the Quartermaster Corps, supplying horses and dogs to the army for combat and noncombat functions.

22. Phil Livingston and Ed Roberts, *War Horse: Mounting the Cavalry with America's Finest Horses* (Albany, TX: Bright Sky Press, 2003), 52.

23. Leonard, "A Derby Winner's Odyssey," 15.

24. Antoinette P. Stoddard, "Hylton, Joseph, M.D., and Ara," in *Pages from Converse County's Past* (Douglas: Heritage Book Committee, Wyoming Pioneer Association, 1986), 301–2.

25. Ross, *Boots and Saddles,* 221.

26. Ibid., 224.

27. "Laurel Park Farm Is Sold for $78,700," *Baltimore Sun,* November 10, 1937; "Hutchison, State Harness Racing Pioneer, Dies at 87," *Baltimore Sun,* February 16, 1962; Dorothy Ours, *Man o' War: A Legend Like Lightning* (New York: St. Martin's Press, 2008), 263; "J. K. L. Ross Bankrupt," *Cincinnati Enquirer,* November 3, 1928; "$1,200,000 Trust Fund Declared Void by Court," *Baltimore Sun,* June 22, 1930; "Weds Again," *Brooklyn Daily Eagle,* April 6, 1931.

28. "Guy Bedwell Dies at Age 76," *Baltimore Sun,* January 2, 1952.

29. Bowen, *Masters of the Turf,* 107.

30. Bowen, *Legends of the Turf,* 1:109–10.

31. Despite his status as trainer of the first Triple Crown winner, Bedwell named Ross's champion Cudgel as "the best horse I ever trained" (quoted in Bowen, *Masters of the Turf,* 112).

32. Brien Bouyea, "Remembering Hall of Fame Jockey Earl Sande," *The Saratogian,* August 11, 2015, at http://www.saratogian.com/article/ST/20150811/NEWS/150819905.

33. Jack Mahon, "Johnny's Goof on Big Red," *Sports Illustrated,* April 25, 1966.

34. "Obituary: Johnny Loftus," *The Blood-Horse,* March 29, 1976.

35. Howard Sigmand, "Famous Jockey Cal Shilling Dies Homeless, Penniless," *Munster Times,* January 13, 1950.

36. Paul Bulleit, "Shilling, Famous Derby Winner of 32 Years Ago, Found in Jail," *Louisville Courier-Journal,* March 31, 1944.

37. Sigmand, "Famous Jockey Cal Shilling Dies Homeless, Penniless."

38. Leonard, "A Derby Winner's Odyssey," 15.

39. "Sir Barton Dead on Wyoming Ranch," *New York Times,* November 13, 1937.

40. "Sir Barton, of Turf Fame, Claimed," *San Bernardino County Sun,* November 13, 1937.

Epilogue

1. Marvin Drager, with Ed McNamara, *The Most Glorious Crown: The Story of America's Triple Crown Thoroughbreds from Sir Barton to American Pharoah* (Chicago: Triumph Books, 2016), xix.

2. Dorothy Ours, "Essay: What's in a Name? In This Case, Three Big Wins," in *To the Swift: Classic Triple Crown Horses and Their Race for Glory,* ed. Joe Drape (New York: St. Martin's Press, 2008), 32–34.

3. "Banner Day of the East," *Daily Racing Form,* June 4, 1922.

4. "Here and There on the Turf," *Daily Racing Form,* May 13, 1923.

5. W. C. Vreeland, "Where, Oh, Where Are the Champion Race Horses 4, 3 and 2 Years Old?" *Brooklyn Daily Eagle,* June 2, 1924.

6. "Rich Prizes Loom for Super-Horse at Race Classics," *Indianapolis Star,* May 8, 1927.

7. Robert Shoop, *Down to the Wire: The Lives of the Triple Crown Champions* (Everson, WA: Russell Dean, 2004), 13.

8. "Mythical Triple Crown Made Official by TRA," *Long Beach Independent,* August 18, 1950.

9. "'Triple Crown' Trophy Journeys 20,000 Miles without Any Takers," *Greenville News,* March 13, 1960.

10. John Scheinman, "Five Myths about the Triple Crown," *Washington Post,* May 30, 2014, at https://www.washingtonpost.com/opinions/five-myths-about-the-triple-crown/2014/05/30/9b18f1b2-e69f-11e3-a86b-362fd5443d19_story.html?utm_term=.e72659b25e11.

11. "The Jockey Club Fact Book 2017," JockeyClub.com, n.d., at http://www.jockeyclub.com/factbook/foalcrop-nabd.html, accessed April 19, 2018.

12. Russ Harris, "Should Triple Crown Race Extend to September?" *Palm Beach Post,* June 6, 1969.

13. "Churchill Downs May 2, 2015, Race 11," Equibase.com, n.d., at https://www.equibase.com/yearbook/Chart.cfm?tk=CD&rd=2015-05-02&rn=11&de=D&cy=USA, accessed April 24, 2018.

14. Jennie Rees, "American Pharoah Snags 2nd Leg of Triple Crown," *Louisville Courier-Journal,* May 17, 2015.

15. Mike McAdam, "NYRA to Limit Crowd for Belmont Stakes," *Schenectady Daily Gazette,* May 7, 2015, at https://dailygazette.com/article/2015/05/07/507_BelmontSeats.

Index

Horses in History

Series Editor: James C. Nicholson

For thousands of years, humans have utilized horses for transportation, recreation, war, agriculture, and sport. Arguably, no animal has had a greater influence on human history. Horses in History explores this special human-equine relationship, encompassing a broad range of topics, from ancient Chinese polo to modern Thoroughbred racing. From biographies of influential equestrians to studies of horses in literature, television, and film, this series profiles racehorses, warhorses, sport horses, and plow horses in novel and compelling ways.